T0361124

EVENT MINING
ALGORITHMS
AND APPLICATIONS

Chapman & Hall/CRC
Data Mining and Knowledge Discovery Series

SERIES EDITOR
Vipin Kumar
University of Minnesota
Department of Computer Science and Engineering
Minneapolis, Minnesota, U.S.A.

AIMS AND SCOPE

This series aims to capture new developments and applications in data mining and knowledge discovery, while summarizing the computational tools and techniques useful in data analysis. This series encourages the integration of mathematical, statistical, and computational methods and techniques through the publication of a broad range of textbooks, reference works, and handbooks. The inclusion of concrete examples and applications is highly encouraged. The scope of the series includes, but is not limited to, titles in the areas of data mining and knowledge discovery methods and applications, modeling, algorithms, theory and foundations, data and knowledge visualization, data mining systems and tools, and privacy and security issues.

PUBLISHED TITLES

ACCELERATING DISCOVERY : MINING UNSTRUCTURED INFORMATION FOR HYPOTHESIS GENERATION
Scott Spangler

ADVANCES IN MACHINE LEARNING AND DATA MINING FOR ASTRONOMY
Michael J. Way, Jeffrey D. Scargle, Kamal M. Ali, and Ashok N. Srivastava

BIOLOGICAL DATA MINING
Jake Y. Chen and Stefano Lonardi

COMPUTATIONAL BUSINESS ANALYTICS
Subrata Das

COMPUTATIONAL INTELLIGENT DATA ANALYSIS FOR SUSTAINABLE DEVELOPMENT
Ting Yu, Nitesh V. Chawla, and Simeon Simoff

COMPUTATIONAL METHODS OF FEATURE SELECTION
Huan Liu and Hiroshi Motoda

CONSTRAINED CLUSTERING: ADVANCES IN ALGORITHMS, THEORY, AND APPLICATIONS
Sugato Basu, Ian Davidson, and Kiri L. Wagstaff

CONTRAST DATA MINING: CONCEPTS, ALGORITHMS, AND APPLICATIONS
Guozhu Dong and James Bailey

DATA CLASSIFICATION: ALGORITHMS AND APPLICATIONS
Charu C. Aggarawal

EVENT MINING

ALGORITHMS
AND APPLICATIONS

Edited by

Tao Li

CRC Press
Taylor & Francis Group
Boca Raton London New York

CRC Press is an imprint of the
Taylor & Francis Group, an **informa** business

A CHAPMAN & HALL BOOK

CRC Press
Taylor & Francis Group
6000 Broken Sound Parkway NW, Suite 300
Boca Raton, FL 33487-2742

© 2016 by Taylor & Francis Group, LLC
CRC Press is an imprint of Taylor & Francis Group, an Informa business

No claim to original U.S. Government works

ISBN 13: 978-1-4665-6857-0 (hbk)

Visit the Taylor & Francis Web site at
http://www.taylorandfrancis.com

and the CRC Press Web site at
http://www.crcpress.com

To the School of Computing and Information Sciences (SCIS) at Florida International University (FIU)
and
To the School of Computer Science at Nanjing University of Posts and Telecommunications (NJUPT)

Contents

Preface

Many systems, from computing systems, physical systems, business systems, to social systems, are only observable indirectly from the events they emit. Events can be defined as real-world occurrences and they typically involve changes of system states. Events are naturally temporal and are often stored as logs, e.g., business transaction logs, stock trading logs, sensor logs, computer system logs, HTTP requests, database queries, network traffic data, etc. These events capture system states and activities over time. For effective system management, a system needs to automatically monitor, characterize, and understand its behavior and dynamics, mine events to uncover useful patterns, and acquire the needed knowledge from historical log/event data.

Event mining is a series of techniques for automatically and efficiently extracting valuable knowledge from historical event/log data and plays an important role in system management. The purpose of this book is to present a variety of event mining approaches and applications with a focus on computing system management. It is mainly intended for researchers, practitioners, and graduate students who are interested in learning about the state of the art in event mining. It can also serve as a textbook for advanced courses. Learning about event mining is challenging as it is an inter-disciplinary field that requires familiarity with several research areas and the relevant literature is scattered in a variety of publication venues such as the ACM SIGKDD International Conference on Knowledge Discovery and Data Mining (ACM SIGKDD), IEEE International Conference in Data Mining (IEEE ICDM), IEEE/IFIP Network Operations and Management Symposium (NOMS), International Conference on Network and Service Management (CNSM), and IFIP/IEEE Symposium on Integrated Network and Service Management (IM). We hope that this book will make the field easier to approach by providing a good starting point for readers not familiar with the topic as well as a comprehensive reference for those working in the field.

Although the chapters of the book are mostly self-contained and can be read in any order, they have been grouped and ordered in a way that can provide a structured introduction to the topic. In particular, after Chapter 1 (Introduction), the book is organized as follows:

Part I: Event Generation and System Monitoring

- Chapter 2: Event Generation: From Logs to Events
- Chapter 3: Optimizing System Monitoring Configurations

Part II: Event Pattern Discovery and Summarization

- Chapter 4: Event Pattern Mining
- Chapter 5: Mining Time Lags
- Chapter 6: Log Event Summarization

Part III: Applications

- Chapter 7: Data-Driven Applications in System Management
- Chapter 8: Social Media Event Summarization Using Twitter Streams

I would like to thank Dr. Sheng Ma, Dr. Charles Perng, Dr. Larisa Shwartz, and Dr. Genady Grabarnik for their long-term research collaboration on event mining. The research studies presented in the book are based on the research projects conducted at the Knowledge Discovery Research Group (KDRG) in the School of Computing and Information Sciences (SCIS) at Florida International University (FIU). The research projects have been partially supported by the National Science Foundation (NSF)(NSF CAREER Award IIS-0546280, CCF-0830659, HRD-0833093, DMS-0915110, CNS-1126619, and IIS-1213026), the U.S. Department of Homeland Security under grant award number 2010-ST-062-00039, the Army Research Office under grant number W911NF-10-1-0366 and W911NF-12-1-0431, a 2005 IBM Shared University Research (SUR) Award, and IBM Faculty Research Awards (2005, 2007, and 2008). The research projects have also been supported by Florida International University (FIU), Nanjing University of Posts and Telecommunications (NJUPT), Xiamen University (XMU), Nanjing University of Science and Technology (NJUST), and Xiamen University of Technology (XMUT).

Editing a book takes a lot of effort. I would like to thank the following members of the Knowledge Discovery Research Group (KDRG) in the School of Computing and Information Sciences (SCIS) at Florida International University (FIU) for the contributions of their chapters as well as their help in reviewing and proofreading:

- Dr. Yexi Jiang (now works at Facebook Inc.)

- Dr. Chao Shen (now works at Amazon Inc.)

- Dr. Liang Tang (now works at LinkedIn Inc.)

- Chunqiu Zeng

- Wubai Zhou

I would also like to thank the KDRG group members (Wei Liu, Ming Ni, Bin Xia, Jian Xu, Wei Xue, and Longhui Zhang) for proofreading the book and for their valuable suggestions and comments. I would also like to thank the people at Chapman & Hall/Taylor & Francis for their help and encouragement.

Tao Li

List of Figures

List of Tables

Editor

Dr. Tao Li earned his PhD in computer science from the Department of Computer Science, the University of Rochester in 2004. He is currently a professor and Graduate Program Director in the School of Computing and Information Sciences at Florida International University (FIU). He is also a professor in the School of Computer Science at Nanjing University of Posts and Telecommunications (NJUPT). His research interests are in data mining, information retrieval, and computing system management. He is a recipient of the NSF CAREER Award (2006–2010) and multiple IBM Faculty Research Awards. In 2009, he received the FIU Excellence in Research and Creativities Award, and in 2010, he received an IBM Scalable Data Analytics Innovation Award. He received the inaugural Mentorship Award from the College of Engineering and Computing at FIU in 2011 and the Excellence in Research Award from the College of Engineering and Computing at FIU in 2012. He is currently on the editorial board of *ACM Transactions on Knowledge Discovery from Data (ACM TKDD)*, *IEEE Transactions on Knowledge and Data Engineering (IEEE TKDE)*, and *Knowledge and Information System Journal (KAIS)*. More information about him can be found at http://www.cs.fiu.edu/~taoli.

Contributors

Yexi Jiang
School of Computing and
  Information Sciences, Florida
  International University
Miami, FL, USA

Tao Li
School of Computing and
  Information Sciences, Florida
  International University
Miami, FL, USA

Chao Shen
School of Computing and
  Information Sciences, Florida
  International University
Miami, FL, USA

Liang Tang
School of Computing and
  Information Sciences, Florida
  International University
Miami, FL, USA

Chunqiu Zeng
School of Computing and
  Information Sciences, Florida
  International University
Miami, FL, USA

Wubai Zhou
School of Computing and
  Information Sciences, Florida
  International University
Miami, FL, USA

Chapter 1

Introduction

Tao Li

Florida International University

Nanjing University of Posts and Telecommunications

1.1 Data-Driven System Management

Many systems, from computing systems, physical systems, business systems, to social systems, are only observable indirectly from the events they emit. Events can be defined as real-world occurrences and they typically involve changes of system states. Events are naturally temporal and are often stored as logs, e.g., business transaction logs, stock trading logs, sensor logs, computer system logs, HTTP requests, database queries, network traffic data, etc. These events capture system states and activities over time.

Large and complex systems often have a large number of heterogeneous components and are difficult to monitor, manage, and maintain. For example, modern forms of distributed computing systems (say, cloud) are becoming increasingly more complex, with growing numbers of heterogeneous software and hardware components. The increasing complexity also worsens system dependability, as the failure rate for a system is much higher than before. It is not a trivial task to provide the high performance, dependability, scalability, and manageability that are demanded by enterprise customers. Traditional approaches to system management have been largely based on domain experts through a knowledge acquisition process that translates domain knowledge

1

into operational rules, policies, and dependency models. This has been well known and experienced as a cumbersome, labor intensive, and error prone process. The process is extremely expensive, if not impossible, to keep up with the rapidly changing environment, especially for such complex systems. For instance, it has been estimated that, in medium and large companies, anywhere from 30% to 70% of their information technology resources are used as administrative (maintenance) cost [183]. There is thus a pressing need for automatic and efficient approaches to monitor and manage complex systems.

Significant initiatives, such as the IBM Autonomic Computing (AC) initiative, with the aim of building autonomic systems that are able to manage themselves with minimum human intervention [107, 118], led to awareness of automatic system management in the scientific and industrial communities and helped to introduce more sophisticated and automated procedures, which increase the productivity and guarantee the overall quality of the delivered service. To realize the goal of autonomic systems, the underlying assumption is the ability to define and maintain a knowledge base and to adapt it to the ever-changing environment. To enable self-management capabilities, a system needs to automatically monitor, characterize, and understand its behavior and dynamics, mine events to uncover useful patterns, and acquire the needed knowledge from historical log/event data.

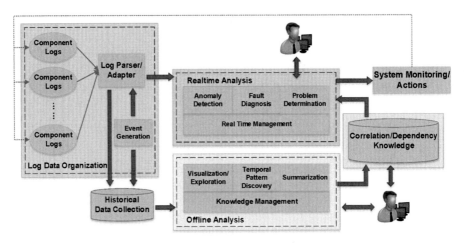

An Integrated Framework on Data-Driven Computing System Management

FIGURE 1.1: The architecture of an integrated data-driven system management framework. (See color insert.)

Figure 1.1 presents an architecture of data-driven system management [137]. The key components of the framework are:

- Log Data Organization: Computing system components and host sensors along with instrumented applications provide the ability to collect log data in the computing system. *Log Parser/Adapter* and *Event Generation* enable generic data collection, integration, and transformation from multiple heterogeneous data sources into the historical data collection.

- Real-time Analysis: Real-time analysis processes incoming data in real time and performs online operations/actions based on knowledge obtained from off-line analysis. Typical real-time analysis techniques include anomaly detection, problem determination, and fault diagnosis.

- Offline Analysis: Offline analysis derives and constructs knowledge bases (e.g., correlation and dependency knowledge) from historical data. Typical offline analysis techniques include temporal pattern discovery and summarization.

Note that the tasks in System Monitoring/Actions include administrator notification, active data collection, sensor/actuator deployment or deactivation, and changing monitoring configurations, etc. Rather than removing the human from the loop, the data-driven integrated framework exploits the synergy of human expertise and automatic intelligent techniques and establishes the pioneering and practical solutions for system management [137].

1.1.1 Examples of System Log Data

The data in the log files indicate the status of each component and record system operational changes, such as the starting and stopping of services, detection of network applications, software configuration modifications, and software execution errors. In this section, we describe some examples of the system log data. The data can be collected from the distributed computing components.

- Application-level log: Application-level log records the application behaviors as well as the generated messages. Examples include Windows system and application log, database activity log, and Linux system log.

- Failure data: Failure data contain the system and application crash dumps as well as the error messages.

- Performance data: Performance data report the performance observations of a component at some time intervals (e.g., CPU utilization of a component every five minutes). Typical performance measures include CPU utilization, memory utilization, swap utilization, average workload, and average response time.

- Reports from operators: These are also known as trouble ticket data and contain the problems and reports described by human operators. In addition, they may also contain possible causes and symptoms for failures.

- Request data: Request data reports the requests (such as time, machine, user id, and application) executed in the system. Examples include Apache and Microsoft IIS logs.

- Other data: Other examples of log data include network traffic data, network-based alert logs, program traces, probes, etc.

1.1.2   Challenges in Data-Driven System Management

Generally system management includes root cause analysis, anomaly detection, and fault diagnosis. There are several challenges for data-driven computing system management:

- The heterogeneous nature of the computing system makes the management task complex and complicated. A typical computing system contains different devices (e.g., routers, processors, and adapters) with different software components (e.g., operating systems, middlewares, and user applications), possibly from different providers (e.g., Cisco, IBM, and Microsoft). The heterogeneity increases the likelihood of poorly understood interactions and unexpected interactions/dependencies [34, 96].

- Large and complex computing systems usually show unexpected behavior during failures, system perturbations, and even normal operations. The scale and complexity of these systems greatly surpass what can be understood by human operators. It is difficult for any system administrator to understand the system at the level of detail necessary for management.

- Current computing systems are dynamic and rapidly changing with a growing number of software and hardware components. The fast rate of change worsens system dependability and exacerbates the difficulty of understanding system behaviors.

- Correctly understanding and interpreting patterns discovered from the log data is a big challenge. In system management applications, many log data are generated and collected in the form of temporal events. Data mining approaches for analyzing temporal events generally focus on discovering frequent or interesting patterns from the data, even if their occurrences may only account for a small fraction of the entire data. It is of critical importance to enable temporal relationships between events for monitoring and managing complex systems.

1.2 Overview of the Book

Event mining is a series of techniques for automatically and efficiently extracting valuable knowledge from historical event/log data and plays an important role in data-driven system management. The purpose of this book is to present a variety of event mining approaches and applications with a focus on computing system management. In particular, these approaches have been proposed and developed to address the aforementioned challenges in Section 1.1.2. In addition, different chapters focus on different components in the data-driven framework. The book is mainly intended for researchers, practitioners, and graduate students who are interested in learning about the state of the art in event mining. It can also serve as a textbook in advanced courses. Learning about event mining is challenging, as it is an inter-disciplinary field that requires familiarity with several research areas and the relevant literature is scattered in a variety of publication venues such as ACM SIGKDD International Conference on Knowledge Discovery and Data Mining (ACM SIGKDD), IEEE International Conference in Data Mining (IEEE ICDM), IEEE/IFIP Network Operations and Management Symposium (NOMS), International Conference on Network and Service Management (CNSM), and IFIP/IEEE Symposium on Integrated Network and Service Management (IM). We hope that this book will make the field easier to approach by providing a good starting point for readers not familiar with the topic as well as a comprehensive reference for those working in the field.

Although the chapters of the book are mostly self-contained and can be read in any order, they have been grouped and ordered in a way that can provide a structured introduction to the topic. In particular, after Chapter 1 (Introduction), the book is organized into three parts as follows:

Part I: Event Generation and System Monitoring

- Chapter 2: Event Generation: From Logs to Events
- Chapter 3: Optimizing System Monitoring Configurations

Part II: Event Pattern Discovery and Summarization

- Chapter 4: Event Pattern Mining
- Chapter 5: Mining Time Lags
- Chapter 6: Log Event Summarization

Part III: Applications

- Chapter 7: Data-Driven Applications in System Management
- Chapter 8: Social Media Event Summarization using Twitter Streams

1.3   Content of the Book

1.3.1   Part I: Event Generation and System Monitoring

When a system alert is detected, performing a detailed analysis for this alert requires a lot of domain knowledge and experience about the particular system. The system administrators usually have to analyze a huge amount of historical system logs. The data in the log files indicate the status of each component and record system operational changes, such as the starting and stopping of services, detection of network applications, software configuration modifications, and software execution errors. System administrators utilize these data to understand the past system behaviors and diagnose the root cause of the alert. Several new aspects of the system log data, including disparate formats/contents and relatively short text messages in data reporting and temporal characteristics in data representation, no repository of semantic information, and large vocabulary size, make the automatic analysis more demanding. Chapter 2 investigates the methods that can transform the log data in disparate formats and contents into a canonical form, which creates consistency across similar fields and improves the ability to correlate across multiple logs. It is necessary that the data organization infrastructure should be capable of accommodating existing heterogeneous data sources as well as data that is supplied with the standard formats and contents. The chapter first reviews three types of approaches (i.e., log parser, classification, and clustering-based methods) that automatically preprocess the raw textual system logs into discrete system events and illustrates their drawbacks. It then presents two new clustering-based approaches for generating the system events from the log data.

Automatic system management and problem detection is typically realized by system monitoring software, such as IBM Tivoli Monitoring [109] and HP OpenView [61]. Many research studies have been reported on developing monitoring conditions (situations) that can identify potentially unsafe functioning of the system. However, it is understandably difficult to recognize and quantify influential factors in the malfunctioning of a complex system. Chapter 3 studies the problem of monitoring optimization: How to define better monitoring configurations. The objective is to eliminate false alerts (false positives) and missing alerts (false negatives) of monitoring by refining the configurations without changing existing deployed monitoring systems. This task requires domain knowledge for particular computing systems. Since acquiring the domain knowledge from experts is difficult, it is necessary to come up with an automatic or semi-automatic approach to extract this knowledge from historical events and tickets to achieve this goal. Moreover, the methodologies should be able to be applied to various IT environments. According to the analysis of large sets of historical monitoring events and tickets, the chapter reveals several main reasons for triggering false positives and false negatives and then proposes the data-driven solutions. The proposed solutions avoid changing the existing deployed monitoring systems and are practical for service providers.

1.3.2 Part II: Pattern Discovery and Summarization

Once the data is transformed into a canonical event form, it is then possible to analyze the historical data across multiple components to discover useful knowledge embedded in the data. Such knowledge, in general, can be used to localize a system-wide failure to a component, identify its root causes, assess its impact, and predict severe failures before they happen. However, the complexity of these systems greatly surpasses what can be understood by human operators, so automated analysis is required. Part II investigates intelligent and efficient approaches that enable us to perform data-driven pattern discovery and problem determination for monitoring and managing complex systems.

Data mining research on temporal data has been mainly focused on the discovery of frequent or interesting patterns from massive datasets, where the problem has been referred to as temporal mining or temporal association [98]. Temporal patterns of interest appear naturally in the system management applications [139, 138]. Specifically, a computer system problem may trigger a series of symptom events/activities. Such a sequence of symptom events provides a natural signature for identifying the root cause. However, in real application domains, diverse requirements often require different types of event patterns for problem solving. For example, in most system management applications, frequent patterns are normal operations while service disruptions are usually infrequent but significant patterns. A lot of work has been done to discover frequent temporal associations in transaction processing, surprising and emerging patterns, periodic patterns, and dependent patterns. Chapter 4 provides a survey of different types of event patterns and presents the corresponding event mining techniques as well as the application scenarios.

Time lag, one of the key features in temporal dependencies, plays an important role in discovering evolving trends of the coming events and predicting the future behavior of its corresponding system. The temporal dependencies among events are characterized by the time lags and time lags provide temporal information for building a fault-error-failure chain, which is useful for root cause analysis. The importance of mining time lags of hidden temporal dependencies from sequential data has also been highlighted in many applications. Thus, the discovery of the time lag is a very important task in event mining. Chapter 5 presents both non-parametric and parametric methods for discovering time lags in temporal data.

In recent years, the scale of modern systems has increased dramatically and each system typically contains tens or hundreds of machines; each machine constantly generates a large number of events. While mining temporal event data to discover interesting patterns has been the object of rapidly increasing research efforts, users of the applications are often overwhelmed by the mining results. The extracted patterns are generally of large volume and hard to interpret. Recently, event summarization techniques have been developed toward the understanding of the seemingly chaotic temporal data. Event summarization aims at providing a concise interpretation of the seemingly chaotic data, so that domain experts may take action upon the summarized models. Chapter 6 first introduces the background of event summarization and discusses its relationships to the relevant event mining techniques. It then provides a summary of different event summarization techniques and also presents an algorithm independent summarization framework that can efficiently support different summarization techniques in real applications.

1.3.3   Part III: Applications

The ability to perform a detailed diagnosis for a system issue (i.e., finding the root cause and resolutions) is crucial for system management. Successful diagnosis offers the promise of enabling system self-configuration and self-management. For example, in a distributed system, identification of a specific node failure can be used to steer a job away from the failing mode. Such diagnosis can help reduce system maintenance costs to avoid unplanned outages. Even if the analysis of an error happens too late to allow proactive action, it can prevent the spread of the error to the entire system and can also be used as a foundation for efficiently identifying root causes. Chapter 7 summarizes several data-driven approaches that can help administrators perform a detailed diagnosis for detecting system issues. In particular, the chapter introduces an algorithm to search sequential textual event segments for problem diagnosis, introduces a Hierarchical Multi-Label classification method based contextual loss to correctly classify incident tickets, and presents a ticket recommendation system for problem resolution.

Part I and Part II are mainly focusing on events in computing system management. However, events are prevalent across different application domains. For example, social media sites (e.g., Twitter, Facebook, and YouTube) have emerged as new information channels for users to receive and to exchange information. As a consequence, large amounts of event data are generated by millions of active users every day. Chapter 8 introduces the application of event summarization with Twitter messages (a.k.a. tweets). Twitter offers an unprecedented advantage on reporting the events happening around the world in real time and the Twitter data streams cover a broad range of events, ranging from unexpected natural disasters to many scheduled events (e.g., sports games, concerts, and conferences). Different from the Log Event Summarization that aims to summarize the temporal patterns from the event log sequence, social media event summarization mainly focuses on presenting the high level overview of the progress of an occurring event in a narrative way. In a typical social media event summarization, multiple aspects of an event will be reported, including the time, the location, the participants, and the progress of the event. Leveraging the summary, people can quickly gain the main idea of the event without reading a large number of posts/tweets. In this chapter, a general framework for social event summarization is discussed. The framework includes three important components: 1) tweet context analysis, which extracts important semantic units (e.g., segments, participants, and topics) about an event from a Twitter stream; 2) sub-event detection, which identifies important moments of an event; and 3) tweet summarization, which generates the text description to describe the progress of the event. The chapter discusses various solutions for each component and also empirical evaluation.

1.4 Conclusion

Modern IT infrastructures are constituted by large scale computing systems including various hardware and software components and often administered by IT service providers. Supporting such complex systems requires a huge amount of domain knowledge and experience. The manpower cost is one of the major costs for all IT service providers. Service providers often seek automatic or semi-automatic methodologies of detecting and resolving system issues to improve their service quality and efficiency. This book provides several data-driven approaches for improving the quality and efficiency of IT service and system management. The improvements focus on several important components of the data-driven framework: event generation, preprocess, system monitoring, offline analysis (temporal pattern discovery and summarization), and online analysis.

Acknowledgment

The research studies presented in the book are based on the research projects conducted at the Knowledge Discovery Research Group (KDRG) in the School of Computing and Information Sciences (SCIS) at Florida International University (FIU). The research projects have been partially supported by the National Science Foundation (NSF)(NSF CAREER Award IIS-0546280, CCF-0830659, HRD-0833093, DMS-0915110, CNS-1126619, and IIS-1213026), the U.S. Department of Homeland Security under grant Award Number 2010-ST-062-00039, the Army Research Office under grant number W911NF-10-1-0366 and W911NF-12-1-0431, a 2005 IBM Shared University Research (SUR) Award, and IBM Faculty Research Awards (2005, 2007, and 2008). The research projects have also been supported by Florida International University (FIU), Nanjing University of Posts and Telecommunications (NJUPT), Xiamen University (XMU), Nanjing University of Science and Technology (NJUST), and Xiamen University of Technology (XMUT).

Part I

Event Generation and System Monitoring

Chapter 2

Event Generation: From Logs to Events

Liang Tang and Tao Li

Florida International University
Nanjing University of Posts and Telecommunications

2.1   Chapter Overview

Modern computing systems are instrumented to generate huge amounts of system log/trace data. The data in the log/trace files indicate the status of each component and are usually collected or reported when some event occurs. Contents of the data may include the running states of the component (e.g., started, interrupted, connected, and stopped), its CPU utilization, and its parameter values. Since most computing systems record the internal operations, status, and errors by logs, it is straightforward to obtain the system events from the system logs. In this chapter we mainly focus on the methodologies of event generation from the system logs. In system management, a lot of studies investigate system event mining and develop many algorithms for discovering the abnormal system behaviors and relationships of events/system components [176, 232, 102, 133, 80, 168, 227, 120]. In those studies, the data is a collection of discrete items or structured events, rather than textual log messages. Discrete or structured events are much easier to be visualized and explored by human experts than raw textual log messages. Many visualization toolkits were developed to provide a quick overview of system behaviors over a large collection of discrete events. However, most of the computing systems only generate textual logs containing detailed information. Therefore, there is a need to convert the textual logs into discrete or structured events. In this chapter, we focus on several data mining based approaches for achieving this goal.

2.1.1   An Example of Converting Textual Logs into Events

Before introducing the details of the approaches, an example is presented to illustrate the benefits of the conversion. Table 2.1 shows an example of the SFTP[1] log collected from FileZilla [2]. In order to analyze the behaviors, the raw log messages need to be translated to several types of events. Figure 2.1 shows the corresponding event timeline created by the log messages. The event timeline provides a convenient platform for people to understand log behaviors and to discover log patterns.

Converting log messages to events provides the capability of canonically describing the semantics of log data and improves the ability of correlating across the logs from multiple components.

Due to the heterogeneous nature of current systems, the log generating mechanisms result in disparate formats and contents focused on individual components. Each component may generate the data using its own format and content. Variability in log languages creates difficulty in deciphering events and errors reported by multiple products and components [220]. For exam-

---

[1]SFTP: Simple File Transfer Protocol.

TABLE 2.1: An example of FileZilla's log

No.	Message
s_1	2010-05-02 00:21:39 Command: put "E:/Tomcat/apps/index.html" "/disk/...
s_2	2010-05-02 00:21:40 Status: File transfer successful, transferred 823 bytes...
s_3	2010-05-02 00:21:41 Command: cd "/disk/storage006/users/lt...
s_4	2010-05-02 00:21:42 Command: cd "/disk/storage006/users/lt...
s_5	2010-05-02 00:21:42 Command: cd "/disk/storage006/users/lt...
s_6	2010-05-02 00:21:42 Command: put "E:/Tomcat/apps/record1.html" "/disk/...
s_7	2010-05-02 00:21:42 Status: Listing directory /disk/storage006/users/lt...
s_8	2010-05-02 00:21:42 Status: File transfer successful, transferred 1,232 bytes...
s_9	2010-05-02 00:21:42 Command: put "E:/Tomcat/apps/record2.html" "/disk/...
s_{10}	2010-05-02 00:21:42 Response: New directory is: "/disk/storage006/users/lt...
s_{11}	2010-05-02 00:21:42 Command: mkdir "libraries"
s_{12}	2010-05-02 00:21:42 Error: Directory /disk/storage006/users/lt...
s_{13}	2010-05-02 00:21:44 Status: Retrieving directory listing...
s_{14}	2010-05-02 00:21:44 Command: ls
s_{15}	2010-05-02 00:21:45 Command: cd "/disk/storage006/users/lt...
...	... ...

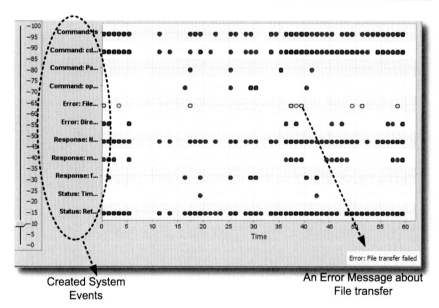

Created System Events

An Error Message about File transfer

FIGURE 2.1: Event timeline for the FileZilla log example.

ple, there are many different ways for the components to report the start up process with the common event format. Some might log "the component has started," while others might say that "the component has changed the state from starting to running." Imagine that we would like to automatically perform the following rule: if any component has started, notify the system operators. Given the inconsistent contents and sometimes subtle differences in the way components report the "started" process, writing a program to automate this simple task is difficult, if not impossible [220]. One would need to know all the messages that reflect the "started" status, for all the components involved in the solution. Every time a new component is installed, the program has to be updated by adding the new component's specific terminology for reporting "started" status. This makes it difficult to perform automated analysis of the historical event data across multiple components when problems occur. Thus to support automated problem determination, it is necessary to encode semantics such as "started" in a log- and system-independent manner.

Converting log messages to events can create consistency across similar fields and improve the ability to correlate across multiple logs. By organizing the messages in the log files into a set of common semantic events (also termed "situations" or "categories"), i.e., adding a semantic situation type to a message [137], the transformed representation provides the ability to canonically describe the semantics of log data as well as the initial connections of syntax to semantics.

2.1.2 Potential Solutions

To convert a collection of textual logs into system events, there are generally three types of solutions: log-parser-based solutions, classification-based solutions, and clustering-based solutions. In this section, we provide an overview for the three types of solutions. The remaining sections of this chapter will further discuss each one of them in detail.

The most straightforward solution is the log-parser-based approach, which is to implement a log parser for a particular system log. Since the log users may be very familiar with the meanings of each log message, they can write a simple text parser and accurately extract all the needed system information from the logs. However, for a large and complex system, implementing the the log parser is not easy. The user may not understand all possible log message generation mechanisms. It is also not efficient to implement different parsers for different types of system logs. Although there are some common formats of logs, how to adapt a log parser to different types of logs is still a challenging issue in reality.

In many event mining applications, people only need to know the type of an event since many mining algorithms are mainly focused on discovering the unknown relationship between different event types. Consequently, in those applications, there is no need to extract the detailed information of a system event, such as system metrics. Therefore, converting a log message into an event is equivalent to finding the type of the log message. As a result, the conversion problem becomes a text classification problem. Many classification algorithms, such as support vector machines (SVMs), can be applied to solve the classification problem. The main disadvantage of these types of method (e.g., classification-based methods) is that the classification algorithms require the users to provide the labeled training data in advance. In other words, a set of labeled log messages has to be prepared. For a complicated large system, this can only be done by domain experts, so it is time consuming and costly.

Clustering-based approaches do not require the user to prepare the labeled training data. They can infer the event type from the log message itself. Although the inferred event types may not be as accurate as those obtained using the classification-based or log-parser-based approaches, they are often acceptable for event mining algorithms or human exploration.

TABLE 2.2: Summary of the three types of approaches

Approach Type	Pros	Cons	Application Scenarios
Log Parser	Very accurate.	Require the user to understand system logs. Hard to adapt to various system logs with different formats. Require human efforts to develop the log parser software.	The application needs accurate generated system events, such as alarm detection systems or monitoring systems.
Classification	Accurate and can be adapted to various system logs.	Require the user to provide the training log data. Labeling the log data by domain experts may be costly and time consuming.	Easy to have labeled training log data.
Clustering	Do not need a lot of human effort and can be adapted to various system logs.	Not very accurate.	Some event mining applications that can be tolerant to some errors or noisy events.

The pros and cons of the three approaches are briefly summarized in Table 2.2. The chapter will mainly focus on clustering-based solutions. The rest of the chapter is organized as follows: Section 2.2 and Section 2.3 introduce the log-parser-based approach and the log-classification-based approach, respectively. Section 2.4 presents an overview of the log-clustering-based approach. Section 2.5 and Section 2.6 present two recent clustering based approaches for event generation: LogTree and LogSig, respectively. Finally, Section 2.7 summarizes the chapter.

2.2 Log Parser

2.2.1 Introduction

Implementing a log parser is a straightforward solution to converting textual logs into structural events for a particular system. However, it requires users to fully understand all kinds of log messages generated from the system. In practice, this is often time consuming, if not impossible, given the complexity of current computing systems. In addition, a specialized log parser is not universal and does not work well for different types of system logs. But for some applications, the implementation can be easily done using simple string regular expression based parsers. As for the previous example shown in Table 2.1, some event mining algorithms may only need the alert types of the log messages: "Command," "Status," "Error," and "Response," which are indicated by the third token of each log message. In such cases, the mining algorithms are mainly used to discover the hidden relations between these alert types. Then, a log parser can be very easy to implement by a simple piece of string splitting code. In software development, there are a lot of log generation library, such as log4j[2] and Apache common logging[3]. The log messages generated by these libraries have some standard formats. Hence, many researchers argue that those logs are structural or semi-structural data, rather than pure textual data. However, log messages generated by many other software packages or systems have no such standard formats. There are two main reasons:

1. Many existing software or system components are legacy systems and were developed many years ago. During the system development, there were very few convenient and reliable log generation libraries, especially for C programming language.

2. Due to the heterogeneous nature of current systems, the log-generating mechanisms result in disparate formats and contents. In addition, the messages generated by the logs are diverse. For example, some systems generate logs for describing the current operations while other systems generate logs for describing their internal status for debugging. It is difficult to unify the formats of various system logs with different purposes of logging.

2.2.2 Build Log Parser Based on Source Code

Many researchers have investigated the approaches to building log parsers based on analysis of the source code [232]. In particular, the Generic Log Adapter (GLA) provided in the IBM Autonomic Computing toolkit allows for generic data collection from multiple heterogeneous data sources by converting individual records and events into the Common Base Event (CBE)

---

[2]http://logging.apache.org/log4j/1.2/
[3]http://commons.apache.org/proper/commons-logging/

format [86]. For those approaches, the input is the source code of the software that generates the log data. The output is a log parser or some information to be embedded into a log parser. Many modern computing systems are open-source, so these approaches can be applied to many software packages, such as Apache Tomcat and Hadoop. Figure 2.2 shows an example of two log messages

```
starting: xact 325 is COMMITTING
starting: xact 346 is ABORTING
```

```
1. CLog.info("starting: " + txn);
2. Class Transaction {
3.   public String toString() {
4.     return "xact "+this.id+ " is "+this.state;
5.   }
6. }
```

FIGURE 2.2: An example of log generation code in [232].

and their generation source code [232]. The log generation code usually has some fixed patterns. For the example in this figure, it often uses the "CLog" class for writing the log messages. From the input parameter of the "info" method, we can infer that "starting" is a constant and "txn" is a variable in the log messages. "txn" is an object of the "Transaction" class. The "info" method will recursively invoke the "toString" method of this class. In the method, the string is also concatenated by constants "xact," "is," variables "id," and "state." As mentioned in [232], the source code can be viewed as the schema of the logs and the structure of the generated logs can be inferred from the schema. Then, the log parser makes use of the schema to determine the event type of each log message. It also can extract the variable values as the attributes of the event.

2.3   Log Message Classification

In many applications, the monitoring and analysis only need to extract the types of events described by the log messages. For instance, a intrusion detection system only needs to know whether the generated log messages are about some security issues or performance issues. If the logs are about some security issues, the intrusion detection system triggers some alerts and sends them to the system administrator. Then, the system administrator checks the recent logs and conducts a further system diagnosis to figure out what happened. The application scenarios are shown in Figure 2.3. In these scenarios, the detailed information, e.g., attribute values of every log message, are not necessary. Moreover, the log messages are allowed to be classified in a hierarchal manner, as illustrated in Figure 2.4.

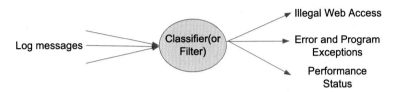

FIGURE 2.3: An example of log message classification.

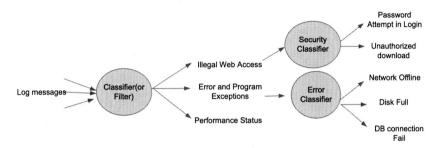

FIGURE 2.4: An example of hierarchal log message classification.

A straightforward approach to identifying the event types of log messages is the classification method, which categorizes a log message into several predefined event types. A simple classification method is to define a regular expression pattern for an event type. Then, when a log message is collected, if it matches a given regular expression, it will then be categorized to the corresponding event type. This type of classification is also called "filter." For example, in syslog-ng[4], the following pattern describes the same message:

```
Accepted password for bazsi from 10.50.0.247 port 42156 ssh2
```

A regular expression matching this message from the logcheck project:

```
Accepted \ (gssapi(-with-mic|-keyex)?|rsa|dsa|password|publickey
|keyboard-interactive/pam) \ for [^[:space:]]+ from [^[:space:]]
+ port [0-9]+( (ssh|ssh2))?
```

A syslog-ng database pattern for this message:

```
Accepted @QSTRING:auth_method: @ for@QSTRING:username: @from\
  @QSTRING:client_addr: @port @NUMBER:port:@ ssh2
```

---

[4]This example is provided by http://www.balabit.com/network-security/syslog-ng/opensource-logging-system/features/pattern-db.

Another approach for log message classification is the learning-based method. Users can provide some labeled log messages, where the event type of each log message is assigned. Then, a learning algorithm builds a classification model using the labeled data to classify incoming log messages. The classification model is built based on the joint distribution of the message terms and the corresponding event type. In text mining, a traditional approach for handling the text information is the *bag-of-words* model [189]. In such a model, each log message is split into a set of terms, where each term represents one feature. For the binary vector space representation, a feature value is 1 or 0 where 1 indicates that the term appears in the log message and 0 indicates that the term does not appear in the log message. Then, any classification algorithms can be applied to train a classification model. However, the learning-based method is not practical in many real-world system management applications. The main reason is that the human cost of labeling log messages may not be less than the cost of implementing a partial log parser or a regular-expression-based filter. The log messages are often short. Given a set of log messages, if you already know how to label them, then it may not be more difficult to define the corresponding parsing logic or write the regular expression.

2.4   Log Message Clustering

Log message clustering is an unsupervised method to categorize the logs to events [135]. Since it does not require preparing a set of labeled training data or regular expressions, this approach is more practical and useful. This section provides a brief introduction to the clustering-based techniques for event generation.

One challenge of performing automated analysis of system logs is transforming the logs into a collection of system events. The number of distinct events observed can be very large and also grow rapidly due to the large vocabulary size as well as various parameters in log generation [21]. In addition, variability in log languages creates difficulty in deciphering events and errors reported by multiple products and components [202, 133]. Once the log data has been transformed into the canonical form, the second challenge is the design of efficient algorithms for analyzing log patterns from the events. Recently, there has been lots of research on using data mining and machine learning techniques for analyzing system logs and most of them address the second challenge [176, 232, 102, 80, 136]. They focus on analyzing log patterns from events for problem determination such as discovering temporal patterns of system events, predicting and characterizing system behaviors, and performing system performance debugging. Most of these works generally assume the log data has been converted into events and ignore the complexities and difficulties in transforming the raw logs into a collection of events.

It has been shown in [202] that log messages are relatively short text messages but could have a large vocabulary size. This characteristic often leads to a poor performance when using the bag-of-words model in text mining on log data. The reason is that each single log message has only a few terms, but the vocabulary size is very large. Hence, the vector space established on sets of terms would be very sparse.

Recent studies [21, 154] apply data clustering techniques to automatically partition log messages into different groups. Each message group represents a particular type of event. Due to the short length and large vocabulary size of log messages [202], traditional data clustering methods based on the *bag-of-words* model cannot perform well when applied to the log message data. Therefore, new clustering methods have been introduced to utilize both the format and the structure information of log data [21, 154]. However, these methods only work well for strictly formatted/structured logs and their performances heavily rely on the format/structure features of the log messages.

2.4.1   Match-Based Similarity Function

In [21], Aharon et al. introduced a similarity function based on the number of matched words between two log messages. As shown in Figure 2.5, if a group

> Failed to connect the mysql server 'm1' at server 192.168.1.110
> Failed to connect the mysql server 'm2' at server 192.168.1.121
> Failed to connect the mysql server 'm3' at server 192.168.1.109

> File server 192.168.1.23 has an unexpected file operation : 'z1.gz'
> File server 192.168.1.21 has an unexpected file operation : 'z2.gz'
> File server 192.168.1.34 has an unexpected file operation : 'z3.gz'

> Java exception throw: Null-Pointer in data packet receiver.
> Java exception throw: Index-Outof-Bound in data packet receiver.

FIGURE 2.5: An example of word simple match based similarity.

of log messages belong to the same event type, they must be generated by the same piece of codes, which is also called "template" in [21]. The only different words in these log messages are the variable terms. In Figure 2.5, the black words are the matched words and other words are the mismatched words. Then, the similarity function between two log messages [21] is defined as

$$sim(L_1, L_2) = \frac{match(L_1, L_2)}{\sqrt{|L_1| \cdot |L_2|}}, \tag{2.1}$$

where L_1, L_2 are two log messages, $match(L_1, L_2)$ is the number of matched words between L_1 and L_2, and $|L_1|$, $|L_2|$ are the lengths of L_1, L_2. Clearly, there is one obvious limitation for this similarity function: if the variable of one template has different numbers of words in different log messages, the *match* function would be totally messed up. A quick solution is to apply the edit-distance to compute the similarity between two log messages. However, the time complexity of edit-distance is high, i.e., $O(|L_1| \cdot |L_2|)$. Another limitation is that this similarity function treats every word as having equal importance. But an intuition is that the non-variable terms should have higher importance than the terms of variables. However, we do not know which terms are non-variable words or variable words if we do not look at other log messages.

2.4.2 An Iterative Clustering Method

In [154], a log message clustering algorithm is presented. The algorithm consists of the following four steps:

1. Partition by the number of words (or tokens);

2. Partition by the word positions;

3. Partition by search for bijection;

4. Discover the descriptive words from each partition.

It should be pointed out that the algorithm tries to identify the template words (non-variable terms) in the clustering algorithm. In the second step, it first discovers some word positions in which the words have a large number of occurrences (say, most frequent words), then partitions the logs using those words' positions. These frequent words actually are very likely to be the template words (non-variable terms). In the third step, the bijection is the relationship between two elements in the most frequent word positions. Once the bijection is found, different token values (or words) of the bijection can be partitioned into different clusters. In other words, the algorithm aims to partition the log messages using the value of those template words. Therefore, the two steps of [154] partition the log messages according to the positions and values of the potential template words. This method can run very fast since the time complexity is linear, so it is applicable for massive log data generated by production systems. However, it still may not work for some types of log data. For example, if the variable terms of one template have a different number of words in different log messages, the first step would fail and the following three steps would not be correct as well. Here the main challenge is the identification of the template words.

2.5   Tree-Structure-Based Clustering

This section presents a tree-structure-based clustering algorithm, `LogTree`, which computes the similarity of log messages based on the established tree representation in the clustering process [208].

2.5.1   Methodology

Formally, a series of system log is a set of messages $S = \{s_1, s_2, \cdots, s_n\}$, where s_i is a log message, $i = 1, 2, \cdots, n$, and n is the number of log messages. The length of S is denoted by $|S|$, i.e., $n = |S|$. The objective of the event creation is to find a representative set of message S^* to express the information of S as much as possible, where $|S^*| = k \leq |S|$, each message of S^* represents one type of event, and k is a user-defined parameter. The intuition is illustrated in the following example.

Example 2.1 *Table 2.1 shows a set of 15 log messages generated by the FileZilla client. It mainly consists of six types of messages, which include four different commands (e.g., "put," "cd," "mkdir," and "ls"), responses, and errors. Therefore, the representative set S^* could be created to be $\{s_1, s_2, s_3, s_7, s_{11}, s_{14}\}$, where every type of the command, response, and error is covered by S^*, and $k = 6$.*

We hope the created events cover the original log as much as possible. The quality of S^* can be measured by the *event coverage*.

Definition 2.1 *Given two sets of log messages S^* and S, $|S^*| \leq |S|$, the event coverage of S^* with respect to S is $J_C(S^*, S)$, which can be computed as follows:*

$$J_C(S^*, S) = \sum_{x \in S} \max_{x^* \in S^*} F_C(x^*, x),$$

where $F_C(x^*, x)$ is the similarity function of the log message x^* and the log message x.

Given a series of system log S with a user-defined parameter $0 \leq k \leq |S|$, the goal is to find a representative set $S^* \subseteq S$ which satisfies

$$\max J_C(S^*, S), \quad \text{subject to} |S^*| = k. \tag{2.2}$$

Clearly, the system event generation can be regarded as a text clustering problem [189] where an event is the centroid or medoid of one cluster. However, those traditional text clustering methods are not appropriate for system logs. We show that those methods, which only extract the information at the word level, cannot produce an acceptable accuracy of the clustering of system logs.

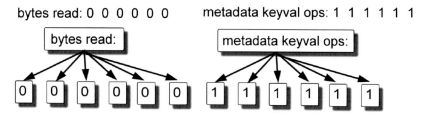

FIGURE 2.6: Two status messages in PVFS2.

It has been shown in [202] that log messages are relatively short text messages but have large vocabulary size. As a result, two messages of the same event type share very few common words. It is possible two messages of the same type have two totally different sets of words. The following is an example of two messages from the PVFS2 log file [12]. The two messages are status messages. Both of them belong to the same event type ***status***, which prints out the current status of the PVFS2 internal engine.

bytes read : 0 0 0 0 0 0

metadata keyval ops : 1 1 1 1 1 1

Note that the two messages have no words in common, and clustering analysis purely based on the word level information would not reveal any similarity between the two messages. The similarity scores between the two messages (the cosine similarity [189], the Jaccard similarity [207], or the word matching similarity [21]) are 0. Although there are no common words between the two messages, the structure and format information implicitly suggest that the two messages could belong to the same category, as shown in Figure 2.6. The intuition is straightforward: two messages are both split by the ':'; the left parts are both English words, and the right parts are six numbers separated by a tab. Actually, people often guess the types of messages from the structure and format information as well.

In real system applications, the structure of log messages often implies critical information. The same type of messages are usually assembled by the same template, so the structure of log messages indicates which internal component generates this log message. Therefore, we should consider the structure information of each log message instead of just treating it as a sentence. Furthermore, two additional pieces of information should be considered as well:

- *symbols* The symbols, such as :,[, are important to identify the templates of the log message. They should be utilized in computing the similarity of two log message segments.

- *word/term categories* If two log messages are generated by the same template, even if they have different sets of words/terms, the categories of words should be similar. In our system, there are six categories

$$T = \{\, word,\ number,\ symbol,\ date,\ IP,\ comment \,\}.$$

Given a term w in a message segment m_1, $t(w)$ denotes the category of the w. $t(w) \in T$.

Based on this intuition, the similarity function of the log messages F_C can be defined as follows:

Definition 2.2 *Given two log messages s_1 and s_2, let $T_1 = \{V_1, E_1, L, r_1, P\}$ and $T_2 = \{V_2, E_2, L, r_2, P\}$ be the corresponding semi-structural log messages of s_1 and s_2, respectively, the coverage function $F_C(s_1, s_2)$ is computed as follows:*

$$F_C(s_1, s_2) \quad = \quad \frac{F'_C(r_1, r_2, \lambda) + F'_C(r_2, r_1, \lambda)}{2},$$

where

$$F'_C(v_1, v_2, w) = w \cdot d(L(v_1), L(v_2)) + \sum_{(v,u) \in M^*_C(v_1, v_2)} F'_C(v, u, w \cdot \lambda),$$

$M^*_C(v_1, v_2)$ *is the best match between v_1's children and v_2's children, and λ is a parameter, $0 \leq \lambda \leq 1$.*

Note that the function F_C is obtained by another recursive function F'_C. F'_C computes the similarity of two subtrees rooted at two given nodes v_1 and v_2, respectively. To compare the two subtrees, besides the root nodes v_1 and v_2, F'_C needs to consider the similarity of their children as well. Then, there is a problem of which child of v_1 should be compared with which child of v_2. In other words, we have to find the best match $M^*_C(v_1, v_2)$ in computing F'_C. Finding the best match is actually a maximal weighted bipartite matching problem. In the implementation, we can use a simple greedy strategy to find the match. For each child of v_1, we assign it to the maximal matched node in unassigned children of v_2. This time complexity of the greedy approach is $O(n_1 n_2)$ where n_1 and n_2 are the numbers of children of v_1 and v_2, respectively. F'_C requires another parameter w, which is a decay factor. In order to improve the importance of higher level nodes, this decay factor is used to decrease the contribution of similarities at a lower level. Since $\lambda \leq 1$, the decay factor w decreases along with the recursion depth.

2.5.2 Evaluation

This section presents two evaluations for the tree-structure-based clustering method on several real datasets.

2.5.2.1 Experimental Platforms

The comparison is conducted in Java 1.5 Platform. Table 2.3 shows the summary of two machines where we run our experiments. All experiments except for the scalability test are conducted in Machine1, which is a 32-bit machine. As for the scalability experiment, the program needs over 2G main memory, so the scalability experiment is conducted in Machine2, which is a 64-bit machine. All the experimental programs are single threaded.

TABLE 2.3: Experimental machines

Machine	OS	CPU	Memory	JVM Heap Size
Machine1	Windows 7	Intel Core i5 @2.53GHz	4G	1.5G
Machine2	Linux 2.6.18	Intel Xeon(R) X5460@3.16GHz	32G	3G

2.5.2.2 Data Collection

In order to evaluate our work, we collect the log data from four different and popular real systems. Table 2.4 shows the summary of our collected log data. The log data is collected from the server machines/systems in the computer lab of a research center. Those systems are very common system services installed in the many data centers.

- FileZilla client 3.3 [2] log, which records the client's operations and responses from the FTP/SFTP server.

- MySQL 5.1.31 [11] error log. The MySQL database is hosted in a developer machine, which consists of the error messages from the MySQL database engine.

- PVFS2 server 2.8.2 [12] log. It contains errors, internal operations, and status information of one virtual file sever.

- Apache HTTP Server 2.x [1] error log. It is obtained from the hosts for the center website. The error log mainly records various bad HTTP requests with corresponding client information.

TABLE 2.4: Log data summary

System	System Type	#Messages	#Words per message	#Types
FileZilla	SFTP/FTP Client	22,421	7 to 15	4
MySQL	Database Engine	270	8 to 35	4
PVFS2	Parallel File System	95,496	2 to 20	4
Apache	Web Server	236,055	10 to 20	5

2.5.2.3   Comparative Methods

In order to evaluate the effectiveness of different methods, we use four other related and traditional methods in the experiments. Table 2.5 shows all the comparative methods used in the experiments. For "Tree Kernel", the tree structure is the same as that used in the our method *LogTree*. Since the tree node of the log message is not labeled, we can only choose a sparse tree kernel for "Tree Kernel" [62]. The experiments of the event generation are conducted using two clustering algorithms, K-Medoids [98] and Single-Linkage [207]. The reason that we choose the two algorithms is that K-Medoids is the basic and classical algorithm for data clustering, and Single-Linkage is a typical hierarchical clustering which is actually used in our system. It should be pointed out that our comparisons focus on similarity measurements which are independent from a specific clustering algorithm. We expect that the insights gained from our experiment comparisons can be generalized to other clustering algorithms as well.

TABLE 2.5: Summary of comparative methods

Method	Description
TF-IDF	The classical text-clustering method using the vector space model with tf-idf transformation.
Tree Kernel	The tree kernel similarity introduced in [62].
Matching	The method using word matching similarity in [21].
LogTree	Logtree.
Jaccard	Jaccard Index similarity of two log messages.

2.5.2.4   The Quality of Events Generation

The entire log is split into different time frames. Each time frame is composed of 2000 log messages and labeled with the frame number. For example, Apache2 denotes the second frame of the Apache log. The quality of the results is evaluated by the F-measure (F1-score) [189]. First, the log messages are manually classified into several types. Then, the cluster label for each log message is obtained by the clustering algorithm. The F-measure score is then computed from message types and clustered labels. Table 2.6 and Table 2.7 show the F-measure scores of K-Medoids and Single-Linkage clusterings with different similarity approaches, respectively. Since the result of the K-Medoids algorithm varies by initial choice of seeds, we run five times for each K-Medoids clustering and the entries in Table 2.6 are computed by averaging the five runs.

TABLE 2.6: F-Measures of K-Medoids

Logs	TF-IDF	Tree Kernel	Matching	LogTree	Jaccard
FileZilla1	0.8461	**1.0**	0.6065	**1.0**	0.6550
FileZilla2	0.8068	**1.0**	0.5831	**1.0**	0.5936
FileZilla3	0.6180	**1.0**	0.8994	**1.0**	0.5289
FileZilla4	0.6838	0.9327	**0.9545**	0.9353	0.7580
PVFS1	0.6304	0.7346	0.7473	**0.8628**	0.6434
PVFS2	0.5909	0.6753	**0.7495**	0.6753	0.6667
PVFS3	0.5927	0.5255	0.5938	**0.7973**	0.5145
PVFS4	0.4527	0.5272	0.5680	**0.8508**	0.5386
MySQL	0.4927	0.8197	**0.8222**	**0.8222**	0.5138
Apache1	0.7305	0.7393	0.9706	**0.9956**	0.7478
Apache2	0.6435	0.7735	0.9401	**0.9743**	0.7529
Apache3	0.9042	0.7652	0.7006	**0.9980**	0.8490
Apache4	0.4564	0.8348	0.7292	**0.9950**	0.6460
Apache5	0.4451	0.7051	0.5757	**0.9828**	0.6997

TABLE 2.7: F-Measures of Single-Linkage

Logs	TF-IDF	Tree Kernel	Matching	LogTree	Jaccard
FileZilla1	0.6842	**0.9994**	0.8848	0.9271	0.6707
FileZilla2	0.5059	0.8423	0.7911	**0.9951**	0.5173
FileZilla3	0.5613	**0.9972**	0.4720	0.9832	0.5514
FileZilla4	0.8670	**0.9966**	0.9913	0.9943	0.6996
PVFS1	0.7336	0.9652	0.6764	**0.9867**	0.4883
PVFS2	0.8180	**0.8190**	0.7644	0.8184	0.6667
PVFS3	0.7149	0.7891	0.7140	**0.9188**	0.5157
PVFS4	0.7198	0.7522	0.6827	**0.8136**	0.6345
MySQL	0.4859	0.6189	**0.8705**	0.8450	0.5138
Apache1	0.7501	0.9148	0.7628	**0.9248**	0.7473
Apache2	0.7515	**0.9503**	0.8178	0.9414	0.7529
Apache3	0.8475	0.8644	0.9294	**0.9594**	0.8485
Apache4	0.9552	0.9152	0.9501	**0.9613**	0.6460
Apache5	0.7882	0.9419	0.8534	**0.9568**	0.6997

Only Tree Kernel and LogTree need to set parameters. Tree Kernel has only one parameter, λ_s, to penalize matching subsequences of nodes [62]. We run it under different parameter settings, and select the best result for comparison. Another parameter k is the number of clusters for the clustering algorithm, which is equal to the number of log message types. Table 2.8 shows the parameters used for Tree Kernel and LogTree.

FileZilla log consists of four types of log messages. One observation is that the root node of the semi-structural log is sufficient to discriminate the message type. Meanwhile, the root node produces the largest contribution in

TABLE 2.8: Parameter settings

Log Type	k	λ_s	λ	α
FileZilla	4	0.8	0.7	0.1
MySQL	4	0.8	0.3	0.1
PVFS2	4	0.8	0.7	0.1
Apache	5	0.8	0.01	0.1

the similarity in Tree Kernel and LogTree. So the two methods benefit from the structural information to achieve a high clustering performance.

PVFS2 log records various kinds of status messages, errors, and internal operations. None of the methods can perform perfectly. The reason is that, in some cases, two log messages composed of distinct sets of words could belong to one type. Thus, it is difficult to cluster these kinds of messages into one cluster.

MySQL error log is small, but some messages are very long. These messages are all assembled by fixed templates. The parameter part is very short compared with the total length of the template, so the similarity of [21] based on the templates wouldn't be interfered with by the parameter parts very much. Therefore, "Matching" always achieves the highest performance.

Apache error log is very similar to FillZilla log. But it contains more useless components to identify the types of the error message, such as the client information. In our semi-structural log, these useless components are located at low level nodes. Therefore, when the parameter λ becomes small, their contributions to the similarity are reduced, and the overall performance is better.

To sum up, the Tree Kernel and LogTree methods outperform other methods. The main reason is that the two methods capture both the word level information and the structural and format information of the log messages. In the next subsection, we show that our LogTree is more efficient than Tree Kernel.

2.5.2.5   A Case Study

We have developed a log analysis toolkit using *Logtree* for events generation from system log data. Figure 2.7 shows a case study using our developed toolkit for detecting configuration errors in Apache Web Server. The configuration error is usually cased by humans, which is quite different from random TCP transmission failures or disk read errors. As a result, configuration errors typically lead to certain patterns. However, the Apache error log file has over 200K log messages. It is difficult to discover those patterns directly from the raw log messages. Figure 2.7 shows the event timeline window of our toolkit, where the user can easily identify the configuration error in the time frame. This error is related to the permission setting of the HTML file. It causes continuous permission denied errors in a short time. In addition, by using the hierarchical clustering method, *LogTree* provides multi-level views of the events. The user could use the slider to choose a deeper view of events to check detail information about this error.

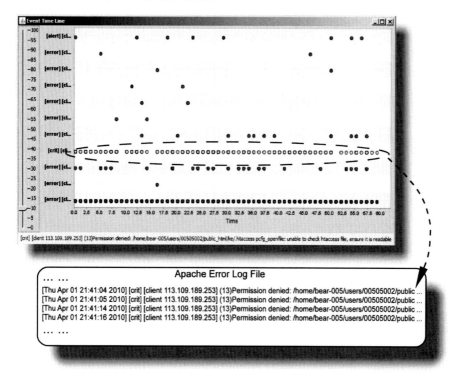

FIGURE 2.7: A case study of the Apache HTTP server log. (See color insert.)

2.6   Message-Signature-Based Event Generation

Message-signature-based clustering is another approach for converting textual logs into system events [210]. Since this algorithm is based on the captured message signature, it is called `LogSig`. Each log message consists of a sequence of terms. Some of the terms are variables or parameters for a system event, such as the host name, the user name, IP address, and so on. Other terms are plain text words describing semantic information of the event. For example, three sample log messages of the Hadoop system [3] describing one type of event about the IPC (Inter-Process Communication) subsystem are listed below:

```
1. 2011-01-26 13:02:28,335 INFO org.apache.hadoop.ipc.
Server: IPC Server Responder: starting;

2. 2011-01-27 09:24:17,057 INFO org.apache.hadoop.ipc.
Server: IPC Server listener on 9000: starting;

3. 2011-01-27 23:46:21,883 INFO org.apache.hadoop.ipc.
Server: IPC Server handler 1 on 9000: starting.
```

The three messages contain many different words (or terms), such as the date, the hour, the handler name, and the port number. People can identify them as the same event type because they share a common subsequence: "*INFO: org.apache.hadoop.ipc .Server: IPC Server:starting*".

Let's consider how the three log messages are generated by the system. The Java source code for generating them is described below:

```
logger = Logger.getLogger("org.apache.hadoop.ipc.Server");
logger.info("IPC Server "+handlerName+": starting");
```

where `logger` is the log producer for the IPC subsystem. Using different parameters, such as `handlerName`, the code can output different log messages. But the subsequence "*INFO: org.apache.hadoop.ipc.Server: IPC Server : starting*" is fixed in the source code. It will never change unless the source code is modified.

Therefore, the fixed subsequence can be viewed as a **signature** for an event type. In other words, we can check the signatures to identify the event type of a log message. Other parameter terms in the log message should be ignored, since messages of the same event type can have different parameter terms. Note that some parameters, such as the `handlerName` in this example, consist of different numbers of terms. Consequently, the position of a message signature may vary in different log messages. Hence, the string matching similarity proposed in [21] would mismatch some terms. Another method, IPLoM proposed in [154], also fails to partition log messages using the term count since the length of `handlerName` is not fixed and three log messages have different numbers of terms. Given an arbitrary log message, we do not know in advance which item is of its signature, or which term is its parameter. That is the key challenge to address.

The goal is to identify the event type of each log message according to a set of message signatures. Given a log message and a set of signatures, we need a metric to determine which signature best matches this log message. Therefore, we propose the *Match Score* metric first.

Let $\mathcal{D}$ be a set of log messages, $\mathcal{D} = \{X_1, ..., X_N\}$, where X_i is the ith log message, $i = 1, 2, ..., N$. Each X_i is a sequence of terms, i.e.,

$X_i = w_{i_1} w_{i_2} .... w_{i_{n_i}}$. A message signature S is also a sequence of terms $S = w_{j_1} w_{j_2} .... w_{j_n}$.

Given a sequence $X = w_1 w_2 ... w_n$ and a term w_i, $w_i \in X$ indicates w_i is a term in X. $X - \{w_i\}$ denotes a subsequence $w_1 ... w_{i-1} w_{i+1} ... w_n$. $|X|$ denotes the length of the sequence X. $LCS(X, S)$ denotes the *Longest Common Subsequence* between two sequences X and S.

Definition 2.3 (Match Score) *Given a log message X_i and a message signature S, the* match score *is computed by the function below:*

$$match(X_i, S) = |LCS(X_i, S)| - (|S| - |LCS(X_i, S)|)$$
$$= 2|LCS(X_i, S)| - |S|.$$

Intuitively, $|LCS(X_i, S)|$ is the number of terms in X_i matched with S. $|S| - |LCS(X_i, S)|$ is the number of terms in X_i not matched with S. $match(X_i, S)$ is the number of matched terms minus the number of not-matched terms. We illustrate this by a simple example below:

Example 2.2 *A log message $X = abcdef$ and a message signature $S = axcey$. The longest common subsequence $LCS(X, S) = ace$. The matched*

TABLE 2.9: Example of match score

X	a	b	c	d	e	f
S	<u>a</u>	*x*	<u>c</u>		<u>e</u>	*y*

terms are a, c, and e, shown by underlining in Table 2.9. x and y in S are not matched with any term in X. Hence, $match(X, S) = |ace| - |xy| = 1$.

Note that this score can be negative. $match(X_i, S)$ is used to measure the degree of the log message X_i owning the signature S. If two log messages X_i and X_j have the same signature S, then we regard X_i and X_j as of the same event type. The longest common subsequence matching is a widely used similarity metric in biological data analysis [33] [166], such as RNA sequences.

If all message signatures $S_1, S_2,...,S_k$ are known, identifying the event type of each log message in $\mathcal{D}$ is straightforward. But we don't know any message signature at the beginning. Therefore, we should partition log messages and find their message signatures simultaneously. The optimal result is that, within each partition, every log message matches its signature as much as possible. This problem is formulated below.

Problem 2.1 *Given a set of log messages $\mathcal{D}$ and an integer k, find k message signatures $\mathcal{S} = \{S_1, ..., S_k\}$ and a k-partition $C_1,...,C_k$ of $\mathcal{D}$ to maximize*

$$J(\mathcal{S}, \mathcal{D}) = \sum_{i=1}^{k} \sum_{X_j \in C_i} match(X_j, S_i).$$

The objective function $J(\mathcal{S}, \mathcal{D})$ is the summation of all match scores. It is similar to the k-means clustering problem. The choice of k depends on the user's domain knowledge of the system logs. If there is no domain knowledge, we can borrow the idea from the method finding k for k-means [97], which plots clustering results with k. We can also display generated message signatures for $k = 2, 3, ..$ until the results can be approved by experts.

2.6.1 Comparing with K-Means Clustering Problem

Problem 2.1 is similar to the classic K-means clustering problem, since a message signature can be regarded as the representative of a cluster. We may ask the following questions:

- Why do we propose the *match* function to find the optimal partition?

- Why not use the *LCS* as the similarity function to do k-means clustering?

The answer to the two questions is that our goal is not to find good clusters of log messages, but to find the message signatures of all types of log messages. K-means can ensure every two messages in one cluster share a subsequence. However, it cannot guarantee that there exists a common subsequence shared by all (or most) messages in one cluster. We illustrate this by the following example.

Example 2.3 *There are three log messages X_1: "abcdef," X_2: "abghij," and X_3: "xyghef." Clearly, $LCS(X_1, X_2) = 2$, $LCS(X_2, X_3) = 2$, and $LCS(X_1, X_3) = 2$. However, there is no common subsequence that exists among all X_1, X_2, and X_3. In our case, it means there is no message signature to describe all three log messages. Hence, it is hard to believe that they are generated by the same log message template.*

Problem 2.1 is an NP-hard problem, even if $k = 1$. When $k = 1$, we can reduce the *Multiple Longest Common Subsequence* problem to Problem 2.1. The *Multiple Longest Common Subsequence* problem is a known NP-hard problem [153].

Lemma 2.1 *Problem 2.1 is an NP-hard problem when $k = 1$.*

Proof: Let $\mathcal{D} = \{X_1, ..., X_N\}$. When $k = 1$, $\mathcal{S} = \{S_1\}$. Construct another set of N sequences $\mathcal{Y} = \{Y_1, ..., Y_N\}$, in which each term is unique in both $\mathcal{D}$ and $\mathcal{Y}$. Let $\mathcal{D}' = \mathcal{D} \cup \mathcal{Y}$,

$$J(\mathcal{S}, \mathcal{D}') = \sum_{X_j \in \mathcal{D}} match(X_j, S_1) + \sum_{Y_l \in \mathcal{Y}} match(Y_l, S_1).$$

Let S_1^* be the optimal message signature for $\mathcal{D}'$, i.e.,

$$S_1^* = \arg\max_{S_1} J(\{S_1\}, \mathcal{D}').$$

Then, the longest common subsequence of $X_1,...,X_N$ must be an optimal solution S_1^*. This can be proved by contradiction as follows. Let S_{lcs} be the longest common subsequence of $X_1,...,X_N$. Note that S_{lcs} may be an empty sequence if there is no common subsequence among all messages.

Case 1: If there exists a term $w_i \in S_1^*$, but $w_i \notin S_{lcs}$. Since $w_i \notin S_{lcs}$, w_i is not matched with at least one message in $X_1,...,X_N$. Moreover, $Y_1,...,Y_N$ are composed of unique terms, so w_i cannot be matched with any of them. In $\mathcal{D}'$, the number of messages not matching w_i is at least $N+1$, which is greater than the number of messages matching w_i. Therefore,

$$J(\{S_1^* - \{w_i\}\}, \mathcal{D}') > J(\{S_1^*\}, \mathcal{D}'),$$

which contradicts $S_1^* = \arg\max_{S_1} J(\{S_1\}, \mathcal{D}')$.

Case 2: If there exists a term $w_i \in S_{lcs}$, but $w_i \notin S_1^*$. Since $w_i \in S_{lcs}$, $X_1,...,X_N$ all match w_i. The total number of messages that match w_i in $\mathcal{D}'$ is N. Then, there are N remaining messages not matching w_i: $Y_1,...,Y_N$. Therefore,

$$J(\{S_{lcs}\}, \mathcal{D}') = J(\{S_1^*\}, \mathcal{D}'),$$

which indicates S_{lcs} is also an optimal solution to maximize objective function J on $\mathcal{D}'$.

To sum up the two cases above, if there is a polynomial time-complexity solution to find the optimal solution S_1^* in $\mathcal{D}'$, the *Multiple Longest Common Subsequence problem* for $X_1,...,X_N$ can be solved in polynomial time as well. However, the *multiple Longest Common Subsequence problem* is an NP-hard problem [153].

Lemma 2.2 *If, when $k = n$, Problem 2.1 is NP-hard, then, when $k = n+1$, Problem 2.1 is NP-hard, where n is a positive integer.*

Proof-Sketch: This can be proved by contradiction. We can construct a message Y whose term set has no overlap to the term set of messages in $\mathcal{D}$ in a linear time. Suppose the optimal solution for $k = n$ and $\mathcal{D}$ is $\mathcal{C} = \{C_1, ..., C_k\}$, then the optimal solution for $k = n+1$ and $\mathcal{D} \cup \{Y\}$ should be $\mathcal{C}' = \{C_1, ..., C_k, \{Y\}\}$. If there is a polynomial time solution for Problem 2.1 when $k = n+1$, we could solve Problem 2.1 when $k = n$ in polynomial time.

Since the original problem is NP-hard, we can solve an approximated version of Problem 2.1 that is easy to come up with an efficient algorithm. The first step is to separate every log message into several pairs of terms. The second step is to find k groups of log messages using *local search* strategy such that each group share as many common pairs as possible. The last step is to construct message signatures based on identified common pairs for each message group.

2.6.2 An Approximated Version of the Problem

Notations: Let X be a log message, $R(X)$ denotes the set of term pairs converted from X, and $|R(X)|$ denotes the number of term pairs in $R(X)$.

Problem 2.2 *Given a set of log messages $\mathcal{D}$ and an integer k, find a k-partition $\mathcal{C} = \{C_1, ..., C_k\}$ of $\mathcal{D}$ to maximize objective function $F(\mathcal{C}, \mathcal{D})$:*

$$F(\mathcal{C}, \mathcal{D}) = \sum_{i=1}^{k} | \bigcap_{X_j \in C_i} R(X_j)|.$$

Object function $F(\mathcal{C}, \mathcal{D})$ is the total number of common pairs over all groups. Intuitively, if a group has more common pairs, it is more likely to have a longer common subsequence. Then, the match score of that group would be higher. Therefore, maximizing function F is approximately maximizing J in Problem 2.1. Lemma 2.4 shows the average lower bound for this approximation.

Lemma 2.3 *Given a message group C, it has n common term pairs; then the length of the longest common subsequence of messages in C is at least $\lceil \sqrt{2n} \rceil$.*

Proof-sketch: Let l be the length of a longest common subsequence of messages in C. Let $T(l)$ be the number of term pairs generated by that longest common subsequence. Since each term pair has two terms, this sequence can generate at most $\binom{l}{2}$ pairs. Hence, $T(l) \leq \binom{l}{2} = l(l-1)/2$. Note that each term pair of the longest common subsequence is a common term pair in C. Now, we already know $T(l) = n$, so $T(l) = n \leq l(l-1)/2$. Then, we have $l \geq \lceil \sqrt{2n} \rceil$.

Lemma 2.4 *Given a set of log messages $\mathcal{D}$ and a k-partition $\mathcal{C} = \{C_1, ..., C_k\}$ of $\mathcal{D}$, if $F(\mathcal{C}, \mathcal{D}) \geq y$, y is a constant, we can find a set of message signatures $\mathcal{S}$ such that on average:*

$$J(\mathcal{S}, \mathcal{D}) \geq |\mathcal{D}| \cdot \lceil \sqrt{\frac{2y}{k}} \rceil.$$

Proof-sketch: Since $F(\mathcal{C}, \mathcal{D}) \geq y$, on average, each group has at least y/k common pairs. Then for each group, by Lemma 2.3, the length of the longest common subsequence must be at least $\lceil \sqrt{\frac{2y}{k}} \rceil$. If we choose this longest common subsequence as the message signature, each log message can match at least $\lceil \sqrt{\frac{2y}{k}} \rceil$ terms of the signature. As a result, the match score of each log message is at least $\lceil \sqrt{\frac{2y}{k}} \rceil$. $\mathcal{D}$ has $|\mathcal{D}|$ messages. Then, we have the total match score $J(\mathcal{S}, \mathcal{D}) \geq |\mathcal{D}| \cdot \lceil \sqrt{\frac{2y}{k}} \rceil$ on average.

Lemma 2.4 shows that maximizing $F(\mathcal{C}, \mathcal{D})$ is approximately maximizing the original objective function $J(\mathcal{S}, \mathcal{D})$. But $F(\mathcal{C}, \mathcal{D})$ is easier to optimize because it deals with discrete pairs.

2.6.3 Local Search

The `LogSig` algorithm applies the *local search* strategy to solve Problem 2.2. It iteratively moves one message to another message group to increase the objective function as much as possible. However, unlike the classic *local search* optimization method, the movement is not explicitly determined by objective function $F(\cdot)$. The reason is that the value of $F(\cdot)$ may only be updated after a bunch of movements, not just after every single movement. We illustrate this by the following example.

Example 2.4 *Message set $\mathcal{D}$ is composed of 100 "ab" and 100 "cd." Now we have 2-partition $\mathcal{C} = \{C_1, C_2\}$. Each message group has 50% of each message type, as shown in Table 2.10. The optimal 2-partition in C_1 has 100 "ab" and*

TABLE 2.10: Example of two message groups

group term pair	C_1	C_2
"ab"	50	50
"cd"	50	50

C_2 has 100 "cd," or in the reverse way. However, beginning with current C_1 and C_2, $F(\mathcal{C}, \mathcal{D})$ is always 0 until we move 50 "ab" from C_2 to C_1, or move 50 "cd" from C_1 to C_2. Hence, for the first 50 movements, $F(\mathcal{C}, \mathcal{D})$ cannot guide the local search because no matter what movement you choose, it is always 0.

Therefore, $F(\cdot)$ is not proper to guide the movement in the local search. The decision of every movement should consider the *potential* value of the objective function, rather than the immediate value. So we develop the *potential function* to guide the local search instead.

Notations: Given a message group C, $R(C)$ denotes the union set of term pairs from messages of C. For a term pair $r \in R(C)$, $N(r, C)$ denotes the number of messages in C which contains r. $p(r, C) = N(r, C)/|C|$ is the portion of messages in C having r.

Definition 2.4 *Given a message group C, the potential of C is defined as $\phi(C)$,*

$$\phi(C) = \sum_{r \in R(C)} N(r, C)[p(r, C)]^2.$$

The potential value indicates the overall "purity" of term pairs in C. $\phi(C)$ is maximized when every term pair is contained by every message in the group. In that case, for each r, $N(r, C) = |C|$, $\phi(C) = |C| \cdot |R(C)|$. It also means all term pairs are common pairs shared by every log message. $\phi(C)$ is minimized when each term pair in $R(C)$ is only contained by one message in C. In that case, for each r, $N(r, C) = 1$, $|R(C)| = |C|$, $\phi(C) = 1/|C|$.

Definition 2.5 *Given a k-partition $\mathcal{C} = \{C_1, ..., C_k\}$ of a message set $\mathcal{D}$, the* *overall potential of $\mathcal{D}$ is defined as $\Phi(\mathcal{D})$,*

$$\Phi(\mathcal{D}) = \sum_{i=1}^{k} \phi(C_i),$$

where $\phi(C_i)$ is the potential of C_i, $i = 1, ..., k$.

2.6.4 Connection between Φ and F

Objective function F computes the total number of common term pairs in each group. Both Φ and F are maximized when each term pair is a common term in its corresponding message group. Let's consider the average case.

Lemma 2.5 *Given a set of log messages $\mathcal{D}$ and a k-partition $\mathcal{C} = \{C_1, ..., C_k\}$ of $\mathcal{D}$, if $F(\mathcal{C}, \mathcal{D}) \geq y$, y is a constant, then in the average case, $\Phi(\mathcal{D}) \geq y \cdot |\mathcal{D}|/k$.*

Proof-sketch: Since $F(\mathcal{C}, \mathcal{D}) \geq y$, there are at least y common term pairs distributed in message groups. For each common term pair r_i, let C_i be its corresponding group. On average, $|C_i| = |\mathcal{D}|/k$. Note that the common pair r_i appears in every message of C_i, so $N(r_i, C_i) = |C_i| = |\mathcal{D}|/k$ and $p(r_i, C_i) = 1$. There are at least y common term pairs; by Definition 2.4, we have $\Phi(\mathcal{D}) \geq y \cdot |\mathcal{D}|/k$.

Lemma 2.5 implies, in the average case, if we try to increase the value of F to at least y, we have to increase the overall potential Φ to at least $y \cdot |\mathcal{D}|/k$. As for the local search algorithm, we mentioned that Φ is easier to optimize than F.

Let $\Delta_{iXj}\Phi(\mathcal{D})$ denote the increase of $\Phi(\mathcal{D})$ by moving $X \in \mathcal{D}$ from group C_i into group C_j, $i, j = 1, ..., k$, $i \neq j$. Then, by Definition 2.5,

$$\Delta_{iXj}\Phi(\mathcal{D}) = [\phi(C_j \cup \{X\}) - \phi(C_j)]$$
$$-[\phi(C_i) - \phi(C_i - \{X\})],$$

where $\phi(C_j \cup \{X\}) - \phi(C_j)$ is the potential increase brought about by inserting X to C_j, and $\phi(C_i) - \phi(C_i - \{X\})$ is the potential loss brought about by removing X from C_i. Algorithm 1 is the pseudocode of the local search algorithm in LogSig. Basically, it iteratively updates every log message's group according to $\Delta_{iXj}\Phi(\mathcal{D})$ to increase $\Phi(\mathcal{D})$ until no more update operations can be done.

2.6.5 Why Choose This Potential Function?

Given a message group C, let $g(r) = N(r, C)[p(r, C)]^2$, then $\phi(C) = \sum_{r \in R(C)} g(r)$. Since we have to consider all term pairs in C, we define $\phi(C)$ as the sum of all $g(r)$. As for $g(r)$, it should be a convex function. Figure

---

Algorithm 1 LogSig_localsearch $(\mathcal{D}, k)$

Parameter: $\mathcal{D}$: log messages set; k: the number of groups to partition;
Result: $\mathcal{C}$: log message partition;

1: $\mathcal{C} \leftarrow RandomSeeds(k)$
2: $\mathcal{C}' \leftarrow \emptyset$ // Last iteration's partition
3: Create a map G to store message's group index
4: **for** $C_i \in \mathcal{C}$ **do**
5:    **for** $X_j \in C_i$ **do**
6:       $G[X_j] \leftarrow i$
7:    **end for**
8: **end for**
9: **while** $\mathcal{C} \neq \mathcal{C}'$ **do**
10:    $\mathcal{C}' \leftarrow \mathcal{C}$
11:    **for** $X_j \in D$ **do**
12:       $i \leftarrow G[X_j]$
13:       $j^* = \underset{j=1,..,k}{\arg\max} \, \Delta_{i \underset{\rightarrow}{X} j} \Phi(\mathcal{D})$
14:       **if** $i \neq j^*$ **then**
15:          $C_i \leftarrow C_i - \{X_j\}$
16:          $C_{j^*} \leftarrow C_{j^*} \cup \{X_j\}$
17:          $G[X_j] \leftarrow j^*$
18:       **end if**
19:    **end for**
20: **end while**
21: **return** $\mathcal{C}$

2.8 shows a curve of $g(r)$ by varying the number of messages having r, i.e., $N(r, C)$.

The reason $g(r)$ is convex is that we hope to give larger awards to r when r is about to become a common term pair. That is because, if $N(r, C)$ is large, then r is more likely to be a common term pair. Only when r becomes a common term pair can it increase $F(\cdot)$. In other words, r has more potential to increase the value of objective function $F(\cdot)$, so the algorithm should pay more attention to r first.

2.6.6 An Empirical Study

This section provides an empirical evaluation for comparing the event generation methods mentioned previously. All the algorithms are implemented in the Java 1.6 platform. Table 2.11 summarizes the experimental environment.

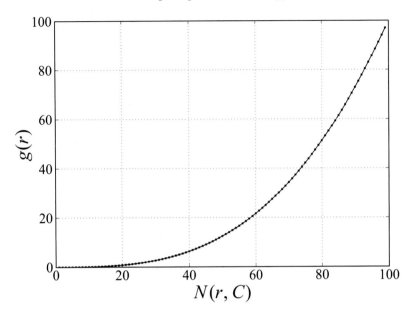

FIGURE 2.8: Function $g(r)$, $|C| = 100$.

TABLE 2.11: Experimental machine

OS	CPU	Bits	Memory	JVM Size	Heap
Linux 2.6.18	Intel Xeon(R) @ 2.5GHz, 8 core	64	16G	12G	

2.6.6.1 Data Collection

The log data is collected from five different real systems, which are summarized in Table 2.12. Logs of FileZilla [2], PVFS2 [12] Apache [1], and Hadoop [3] are described in Section 2.5.2.2. Log data of ThunderBird [14] is collected from a supercomputer in Sandia National Lab. The true categories of log messages are obtained by specialized log parsers. For instance, FillZilla's log messages are categorized into four types: *"Command," "Status," "Response," "Error."* Apache error log messages are categorized by the error types: *"Permission denied," "File not exist,"* and so on.

The vocabulary size is an important characteristic of log data. Figure 2.9 exhibits the vocabulary sizes of the five different logs along with the data size. It can be seen that some vocabulary sizes could become very large if the data size is large.

TABLE 2.12: Summary of collected system logs

System	Description	#Messages	#Terms Per Message	#Category
FileZilla	SFTP/FTP Client	22,421	7 to 15	4
ThunderBird	Supercomputer	3,248,239	15 to 30	12
PVFS2	Parallel File System	95,496	2 to 20	11
Apache Error	Web Server	236,055	10 to 20	6
Hadoop	Parallel Computing Platform	2,479	15 to 30	11

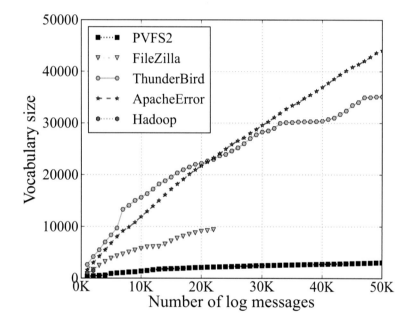

FIGURE 2.9: Vocabulary size.

The comparative algorithms are described in Table 2.13. Six of them are unsupervised algorithms which only look at the terms of log messages. Three of them are semi-supervised algorithms which are able to incorporate the domain knowledge. IPLoM [154] and StringMatch [21] are two methods proposed in recent related work. VectorModel [189], Jaccard [207], and StringKernel [148] are traditional methods for text clustering. VectorModel and semi-StringKernel are implemented by the K-means clustering algorithm [207]. Jaccard and StringMatch are implemented by the K-medoid algorithm [98], since they cannot compute the centroid point of a cluster. As for Jaccard, the Jaccard similarity is obtained by a hash table to accelerate the computation. VectorModel and StringKernel use *Sparse Vector* [189] to reduce the computation and space costs.

Note that semi-LogSig, semi-StringKernel, and semi-Jaccard are

TABLE 2.13: Summary of comparative algorithms

Algorithm	Description
VectorModel	Vector space model proposed in information retrieval
Jaccard	Jaccard similarity based k-medoid algorithm
StringKernel	String kernel based k-means algorithm
IPLoM	Iterative partition method proposed in [154]
StringMatch	String matching method proposed in [21]
LogSig	Message signature based method
semi-LogSig	LogSig incorporating domain knowledge
semi-StringKernel	Weighted string kernel based k-means
semi-Jaccard	Weighted Jaccard similarity based k-medoid

semi-supervised versions of LogSig, StringKernel, and Jaccard respectively. To make a fair comparison, all these semi-supervised algorithms incorporate the **same** domain knowledge offered by users. Specifically, the three algorithms run on the same transformed feature layer, and the same sensitive phrases $\mathcal{P}_S$ and trivial phrases $\mathcal{P}_T$. Obviously, the choices of features $\mathcal{P}_S$ and $\mathcal{P}_T$ have a huge impact on the performances of semi-supervised algorithms. But we only compare a semi-supervised algorithm with other semi-supervised algorithms. Hence, they are compared under the same choice of features $\mathcal{P}_S$ and $\mathcal{P}_T$. The approaches for these three algorithms to incorporate with features $\mathcal{P}_S$ and $\mathcal{P}_T$ are described as follows:

Feature Layer: Replacing every log message by the transformed sequence of terms with features.

$\mathcal{P}_S$ **and** $\mathcal{P}_T$**:** As for semi-StringKernel, replacing Euclidean distance by Mahalanobis distance [38]:

$$D_M(x, y) = \sqrt{(x - y)^T M (x - y)},$$

where matrix M is constructed according to term pairs $\mathcal{P}_S$, $\mathcal{P}_T$, and λ'. As for semi-Jaccard, for each term, multiply a weight λ' (or $1/\lambda'$) if this term appears in $\mathcal{P}_S$ (or $\mathcal{P}_T$).

Jaccard, StringMatch, and semi-Jaccard algorithms apply the classic K-medoid algorithm for message clustering. The time complexity of the K-medoid algorithm is very high: $O(tn^2)$ [218], where t is the number of iterations, n is the number of log messages. As a result, these three algorithms are not capable of handling large log data. Therefore, for the accuracy comparison, we split our log files into smaller files by time frame, and conduct the experiments on the small log data. The amounts of log messages, features, and term pairs in $\mathcal{P}_S$ and $\mathcal{P}_T$ are summarized in Table 2.14.

TABLE 2.14: Summary of small log data

Measure	#Message	#Feature	$|R(\mathcal{P})_S|$	$|R(\mathcal{P})_T|$
FileZilla	8555	10	4	4
ThunderBird	5000	10	11	9
PVFS2	12570	10	10	1
Apache Error	5000	2	4	2
Hadoop	2479	2	7	3

TABLE 2.15: Average F-measure comparison

Log Data / Algorithm	FileZilla	PVFS2	ThunderBird	Apache Error	Hadoop
Jaccard	0.3794	0.4072	0.6503	0.7866	0.5088
VectorModel	0.4443	0.5243	0.4963	0.7575	0.3506
IPLoM	0.2415	0.2993	**0.8881**	0.7409	0.2015
StringMatch	0.5639	0.4774	0.6663	0.7932	0.4840
StringKernel$_{0.8}$	0.4462	0.3894	0.6416	0.8810	0.3103
StringKernel$_{0.5}$	0.4716	0.4345	0.7361	**0.9616**	0.3963
StringKernel$_{0.3}$	0.4139	0.6189	0.8321	0.9291	0.4256
LogSig	**0.6949**	**0.7179**	0.7882	0.9521	**0.7658**
semi−Jaccard	0.8283	0.4017	0.7222	0.7415	0.4997
semi-StringKernel$_{0.8}$	0.8951	0.6471	0.7657	0.8645	0.7162
semi-StringKernel$_{0.5}$	0.7920	0.4245	0.7466	**0.8991**	0.7461
semi-StringKernel$_{0.3}$	0.8325	0.7925	0.7113	0.8537	0.6259
semi-LogSig	**1.0000**	**0.8009**	**0.8547**	0.7707	**0.9531**

2.6.6.2 Quality of Generated Events

Table 2.15 shows the accuracy comparison of generated system events by different algorithms. The accuracy is evaluated by F-measure (F1 score) [189], which is a traditional metric combining *precision* and *recall*. Since the results of K-medoid, K-means, and LogSig depend on the initial random seeds, we run each algorithm **10 times**, and put the average F-measures into Table 2.15. From this table, it can be seen that StringKernel and LogSig outperform other algorithms in terms of overall performance.

Jaccard and VectorModel apply the *bag-of-words* model, which ignores the order information about terms. Log messages are usually short, so the information from the bag-of-words model is very limited. In addition, different log messages have many identical terms, such as *date* and *username*. That is the reason the two methods cannot achieve high F-measures. IPLoM performs well in ThunderBird log data, but poorly in other log data. The reason is that the first step of IPLoM is to partition a log message by the term count. One type of log message may have different numbers of terms. For instance, in FileZilla logs, the length of *Command* messages depends on the type of SFTP/FTP command in the message. But for ThunderBird, most event types are strictly associated with one message format. Therefore, IPLoM could easily achieve the highest score.

Due to the *curse of dimensionality* [207], K-means based StringKernel is

TABLE 2.16: Discovered message signatures

System Log	Message Signature	Associated Category
FileZilla	*Date Hours Number Number* Status: ...	Status
	Date Hours Number Number Response: *Number*	Response
	Date Hours Number Number Command:	Command
	Date Hours Number Number Error: File transfer failed	Error
Apache Error	*Timestamp* (13) Permission denied: /home/bear-005/users/xxx/public_html/ke/.htaccess pcfg_openfile: unable to check htaccess file ensure it is readable	Permission denied
	Timestamp Error [client] File does not exist: /opt/website/sites/users.cs.fiu.edu/ data/favicon.ico	File does not exist
	Timestamp Error [client 66.249.65.4] suexec *policy* violation: see suexec log for more details	Policy violation
	Timestamp /home/hpdrc-demo/sdbtools/public_html/ hpdrc2/.htaccess: AuthName takes one argument The *Authentication* realm (e.g. "Members Only")	Authentication
	Timestamp Error [client] 2010-04-01 using	N/A
	Timestamp Error [client]	N/A

not easy to converge in a high dimensional space. Figure 2.9 shows that 50K ThunderBird log messages contain over 30K distinct terms. As a result, the transformed space has over $(30K)^2 = 900M$ dimensions. It is quite sparse for 50K data points.

It is worth noting that in Thunderbird and Apache Error logs the vocabulary size increases almost infinitely (see Figure 2.9); then LogSig does not achieve the best performance. The main reason is that, when the vocabulary size is large, the number of possible choices of the signature terms is also large. Then the performance of LogSig may suffer from the large solution space for the local search algorithm.

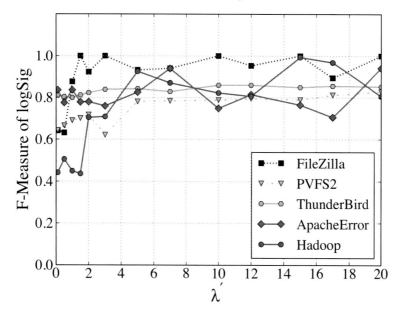

FIGURE 2.10: Varying parameter λ'.

Generated message signatures are used as descriptors for system events, so that users can understand the meanings of those events. Due to the space limit, we cannot list all message signatures. Table 2.16 shows generated signatures of FileZilla and Apache Error by `semi-LogSig`, in which features are indicated by *italic words*.

As for the FileZilla log, each message signature corresponds to a message category, so that the F-measure of FileZilla could achieve 1.0. But for the Apache Error log, Only four message signatures are associated with corresponding categories. The other two signatures are generated by two ill-partitioned message groups. They cannot be associated with any category of Apache Error logs. As a result, their "Associated Category" in Table 2.16 is "N/A." Therefore, the overall F-measure on the Apache Error log in Table 2.15 is only 0.7707.

All those algorithms have the parameter k, which is the number of events to create. We let k be the actual number of message categories. The string kernel method has an additional parameter λ, which is the decay factor of a pair of terms. We use `StringKernel`$_\lambda$ to denote the string kernel method using decay factor λ. In our experiments, we set up string kernel algorithms using three different decay factors: `StringKernel`$_{0.8}$, `StringKernel`$_{0.5}$, and `StringKernel`$_{0.3}$.

As for the parameter λ' of our algorithm `LogSig`, we set $\lambda' = 10$ based on the experimental result shown by Figure 2.10. For each value of λ', we run the algorithm for **10 times**, and plot the average F-measure in this figure. It can be seen that the performance becomes stable when λ' is greater than 4.

2.7 Summary

This chapter investigates several approaches for generating the system events from the log data. In most computing systems, log data is the only channel to inspect the internal status and operations; thus it is worth studying the event generation methods from the log data. Basically, three types of approaches are introduced in this chapter (i.e., log-parser-, classification-, and clustering-based methods) and they are briefly summarized in Table 2.2. Log parser is a straightforward solution but its implementation is time consuming or not applicable for some complex systems. The classification-based method is widely used in natural language processing; however, it requires a lot of annotated training log messages. In this chapter, we focus on the clustering-based methods because we think these approaches are convenient to archive our goal in practice. Recent studies apply clustering algorithms on the log messages to generate the events; however, the accuracy of their work heavily relies on the format/structure of the targeting logs. We present two novel clustering-based approaches: `LogTree` and `LogSig`. The `LogTree` algorithm is a novel and algorithm-independent framework for event generation from raw textual log messages. `LogTree` utilizes the format and structural information of log messages in the clustering process and increases the clustering accuracy. The `LogSig` algorithm is a message-signature-based clustering algorithm. By searching the most representative message signatures, `LogSig` categorizes the textual log messages into several event types. `LogSig` can handle various types of log data and is able to incorporate the domain knowledge provided by experts to achieve a high clustering accuracy. We conduct experiments on real system logs. The experimental results show that the two algorithms outperform alternative clustering algorithms in terms of the accuracy of event generation.

2.8 Glossary

Log Classification: A process to classify each log message into a category or type, in which a classification model is used. The classification model is trained by a collection of labeled training data.

Log Clustering: A process to dispatch the entire log data into several clusters (or subsets), in which there is no labeled training data needed to be prepared in advance.

Log Parser: A software program that is able to parse the log messages and extract useful information from the raw textual logs.

Message Signature: Unique sequential characters that can identify the type or category of a message.

Message Term: A character of a message or string.

Potential Function: A mathematical function that indicates the state of the current solution and where and how it is able to potentially change.

String Kernel: A function measuring the similarity of a pair of strings. Usually it is based on a mapping function that maps a string into a vector and then computes the cosine similarity of two vectors as the string similarity.

Structured Event: A relational data representation of a system event, where each event is represented by a database record and the fields of this record represent the attribute values of this event.

System Event: Discrete time-stamped data records about the system operation. System event can be seen as an abstract level of information from the raw system logs.

System Log: The data generated by the system to describe the internal operations, status, errors, or some other information about the system.

Unstructured Event: A textual data representation of a system event, where each event is represented by a textual message.

Chapter 3

Optimizing System Monitoring Configurations

Liang Tang and Tao Li

Florida International University
Nanjing University of Posts and Telecommunications

3.1 Chapter Overview

The previous chapter discussed generating system events from logs, which is a passive approach, where the events can only be obtained after the computing systems output their logs. This passive approach is only applied to offline system analysis and is limited by the information described by the logs. Modern system management often seeks an active approach that can capture system events on its own initiative. This active approach is also known as *monitoring*.

In modern Information Technology (IT) services, system monitoring, as part of the automated service management, has become a significant research area of the IT industry in the past few years. For example, commercial products such as IBM Tivoli [5], HP OpenView [4], and Splunk [13] provide system monitoring.

System monitoring is an automated reactive system that provides an effective and reliable means of problem diagnosis and determination. In particular, system monitoring ensures that degradation of the vital signs, defined by acceptable thresholds or monitoring conditions (situations), is flagged as a problem candidate (monitoring event) and sent to the service delivery teams as an incident ticket. Defining appropriate monitoring situations requires the knowledge of a particular system and its relationships with other hardware and software systems. It is a known practice to define conservative conditions in nature, thus erring on the side of caution. This practice leads to a large number of tickets that require no action (false positives). Continuous updating of modern IT infrastructures also leads to a number of system faults that are not captured by system monitoring (false negatives).

In this chapter, we shall discuss several related practical issues in event generation via monitoring. We provide a brief introduction to several monitoring techniques and then investigate two important problems in monitoring: eliminating false positives and false negatives.

3.2 Automatic Monitoring

Monitoring techniques have been studied for decades. The commercial monitoring software and products have been used in various IT infrastructures. Here we only briefly introduce these techniques so that the motivation of the rest part of this chapter will be more clear. Figure 3.1 shows the relation-

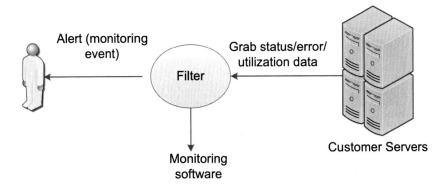

FIGURE 3.1: Relationship of monitoring software, administrators, and customer servers.

ship among the administrator, monitoring software tools, and the customer servers. The primary goal of monitoring is to actively collect the information from the customer servers and decide whether or not they have some malfunctions or emergent situations. The monitoring targets include the components or subsystems of IT infrastructures, such as the hardware components of the system (CPU, hard disk) or the software components (a database engine, a web server). Clearly, the main purpose of using a monitoring tool is to reduce the human cost for maintaining the systems. Once certain system alarms are captured, the system monitoring tool will generate the event tickets into the ticketing system. Figure 3.1 provides a simple example of system monitoring. Modern IT service management has a much more complicated infrastructure of monitoring that consists of multiple machines and software packages; therefore, in the rest of this chapter we often say "monitoring system" rather than "monitoring tool."

3.2.1 Monitoring Situation

A monitoring situation is a typical system status that should be captured by monitoring. Different monitoring situations indicate different system statuses. For instance, a high CPU situation is defined as the status that the CPU utilization is greater than 90%. A disk situation is defined as the status that the free space of a disk is less than 5%. Since a modern computing system consists of various devices and components, real-world systems often have thousands of monitoring situations. Even for the same component or device, people can define multiple situations with different thresholds, e.g., the CPU utilization with 90% can be a warning situation and with 95% can be a fatal situation. Figure 3.2 is a screenshot of the portal (user control interface) of IBM Tivoli monitoring [6]. In this portal, the system administrator can create, modify, remove, or deploy various monitoring situations. These monitoring situations are regarded as a core component of the monitoring configurations. It is known that the monitoring configuration heavily determines the quality and efficiency of monitoring. Therefore, defining appropriate monitoring situations for a particular IT infrastructure requires a lot of IT domain knowledge and experience. In IT service, this work is handled by a number of senior and dedicated system administrators, who are also often called the monitoring team. However, modern IT infrastructures become more complex and dynamic. It is not practical to set up appropriate monitoring configurations purely by humans. Thus, in this chapter, we shall discuss several event mining techniques that are able to assist the monitoring team in accomplishing this task.

3.2.2 False Negative and False Positive

The enterprise IT environments can be very different due to different infrastructures and requirements. They are also likely to change over time. This causes the automatic monitoring to produce inaccurate monitoring events,

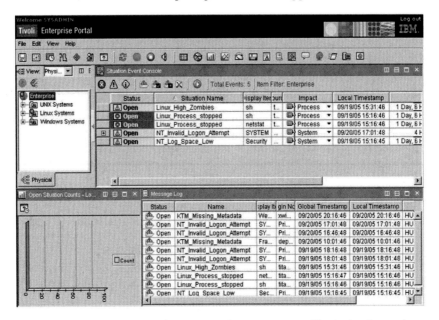

FIGURE 3.2: Portal of IBM Tivoli monitoring. (See color insert.)

such as false positives and false negatives. For the monitoring system, the false positives are incorrectly identified alerts. False positives do not need any action from the human, so they are also called non-actionable alerts. The false negatives are the alerts that are missed by the monitoring system. In modern IT monitoring, the detected alert (or event) usually triggers the incident ticket creation in a ticketing system. False positive alerts and false negative alerts associate with false positive tickets and false negative tickets, respectively. Table 3.1 summarizes the definitions we mentioned here. Transient alerts are a type of false positive alert that will automatically disappear in a short time.

Whether a ticket is real or false is determined by the resolution message entered by the system administrator in the ticket tracking database. It is not rare to observe entire categories of alerts, such as CPU or paging utilization alerts, that are almost exclusively false positives. When reading the resolution messages one by one, it can be simple to find an explanation: Anti-virus processes cause prolonged CPU spikes at regular intervals; databases may reserve a large amount of disk space in advance, making the monitors believe the system is running out of storage. With only slightly more effort, one can also fine-tune the thresholds of certain numerical monitored metrics, such as the metrics involved in paging utilization measurement. There are rarely enough human resources, however, to correct the monitoring situations one system at a time, and we need an algorithm that is capable of discovering these usage-specific rules. Many efforts have been made to develop the monitoring conditions (situations) that can identify potentially unsafe functioning

TABLE 3.1: Definitions for alert, event, and ticket

False Positive Alert	An alert for which the system administrator does not need to take any action.
False Negative Alert	A missed alert that is not captured due to inappropriate monitoring configuration.
False Alert	False positive alert
Real Alert	An alert that requires the system administrator to fix the corresponding problem on the server.
Alert Duration	The length of time from an alert creation to its clearing.
Transient Alert	An alert that is automatically cleared before the technician opens its corresponding ticket.
Event	The notification of an alert to the Enterprise Console.
False Positive Ticket	A ticket created from a false positive alert.
False Negative Ticket	A ticket created manually identifying a condition that should have been capture by automatic monitoring.
False Ticket	A ticket created from a false alert.
Real Ticket	A ticket created from a real alert.

of the system [105, 182]. It is understandably difficult, however, to recognize and quantify influential factors in the malfunctioning of a complex system. Therefore, classical monitoring tends to rely on periodical probing of a system for conditions that could potentially contribute to the system's misbehavior. Upon detection of the predefined conditions, the monitoring systems trigger events that automatically generate incident tickets.

3.2.3 Network Monitoring and System Monitoring

Many studies have been reported on monitoring distributed networks [117, 20, 161, 229, 76, 180]. Generally, network monitoring is used to check the "health" of communications by inspecting data transmission flow, sniffing data packets, analyzing bandwidth, etc. [117, 20, 161, 229, 76, 180]. It is able to detect node failures, network intrusions, or other abnormal situations in the distributed system. The main difference between network monitoring and system monitoring is the monitored targets, as they can be any components or subsystems, hardware components (such as CPU or hard disk) or software components (such as a database engine or web server) in system monitoring. Only the system administrators, who are working with the monitored servers, can determine whether an alert is real or false.

3.3   Eliminating False Positives

The objective of eliminating false positives is to eliminate as many false alerts as possible while retaining all real alerts. A naive solution is to build a predictive classifier and adjust the monitoring situations according to the classifier. Unfortunately, no prediction approach can guarantee 100% success for real alerts, but a single missed one may cause serious problems, such as system crashes or data loss. The vast majority of the false positive alerts are transient, such as temporary spikes in CPU and paging utilization, service restarts, and server reboots. These transient alerts automatically disappear after a while, but their tickets are created in the ticketing system. When system administrators open the tickets and log into the server, they cannot find the problem described by those tickets. Figure 3.3 shows the duration histogram of false positive alerts raised by one monitoring situation. This particular situation checks the status of a service and generates an alert without delay if the service is stopped or shut down. These false positive alerts are collected from one server of a customer account for 3 months. As shown by this figure, more than 75% of the alerts can be cleared automatically by waiting 20 minutes. It is

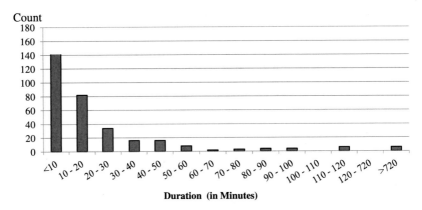

FIGURE 3.3: False positive alert duration.

possible for a transient alert to be caused by a real system problem. From the perspective of the system administrators, however, if the problem cannot be found when logging on the server, there is nothing they can do with the alert, no matter what happened before. Some transient alerts may be indications of future real alerts and may be useful. But if those real alerts arise later on, the monitoring system will detect them even if the transient alerts were ignored. Therefore, all transient alerts are considered as false positives.

Although we cannot have 100% confidence in removing all false positive alerts, we can have 100% confidence in eliminating all transient alerts. These transient alerts contribute to a large number of false positives. Therefore, eliminating transient alerts can significantly reduce the number of false positives in most monitoring systems. In this chapter, we introduce a simple solution to achieve this goal. This solution first predicts whether an alert is real or false. If it is predicted as real, a ticket will be created. Otherwise, the ticket creation will be postponed. Even if a real alert is incorrectly classified as false, its ticket will eventually be created before violating the Service Level Agreement(SLA). Figure 3.4 shows a flowchart of an incoming event. It reveals two key problems

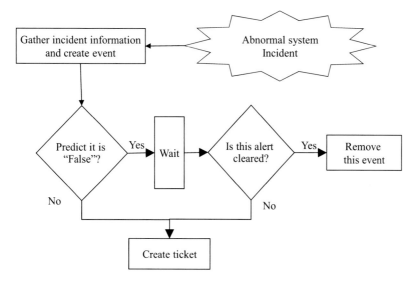

FIGURE 3.4: Flowchart for ticket creation.

for this approach: (1) How to predict whether an alert is false or real. (2) If an alert is identified as false, how long should the system wait before creating a ticket?

3.3.1 Predict Whether an Alert Is False or Real

In this approach, the predictor is implemented by a rule-based classifier based on the historical tickets and events. The ground truth of the events is obtained from the associated tickets. Each historical ticket has one column that suggests the ticket is real or false. This column is manually filled by the system administrators and stored in the ticketing system. There are two reasons for choosing a rule-based predictor. First, each monitoring situation is equivalent to a quantitative rule. The predictor can be directly implemented in the existing monitoring system. Other sophisticated classification algorithms, such as *support vector machine* and *neural network*, may have a higher precision in predicting. Their classifiers, however, are very difficult to implement as monitoring situations in real systems. Second, a rule-based predictor is easily verifiable by the end users. Other complicated classification models represented by linear/non-linear equations or neural networks are quite difficult for end users to interpret and verify. If the analyzed results could not be verified by the system administrators, they would not be utilized in real production servers.

The alert predictor roughly assigns a label to each alert, "false" or "real." It is built on a set of predictive rules that are automatically generated by a rule-based learning algorithm [199] based on historical events and alert tickets. Example 3.1 shows a predictive rule, where "*PROC_CPU_TIME*" is the CPU usage of a process. Here "*PROC_NAME*" is the name of the process.

Example 3.1 if PROC_CPU_TIME > 50% **and** PROC_NAME = 'Rtvscan', **then** this alert is false.

A predictive rule consists of a rule condition and an alert label. A rule condition is a conjunction of *literals*, where each *literal* is composed of an event attribute, a relational operator, and a constant value. In Example 3.1, "*PROC_CPU_TIME > 50%*" and "*PROC_NAME = 'Rtvscan'*" are two *literals*, where "*PROC_CPU_TIME*" and "*PROC_NAME*" are event attributes, ">" and "=" are relational operators, and "50%" and "*Rtvscan*" are constant values. If an alert event satisfies a rule condition, we say this alert is covered by this rule.

Predictive Rule Generation

The rule-based learning algorithm [199] first creates all *literals* by scanning historical events. Then, it applies a breadth-first search for enumerating all *literals* in finding predictive rules, i.e., those rules having predictive power. This algorithm has two criteria to quantify the minimum predictive power: the minimum confidence *minconf* and the minimum support *minsup* [199]. In our case, *minconf* is the minimum ratio of the numbers of the covered false alerts and all alerts covered by the rule, and *minsup* is the minimum ratio of the number of alerts covered by the rule and the total number of alerts. The two criteria govern the performance of our method, defined as the total number of false alerts removed. To achieve the best performance, we loop through the values of *minconf* and *minsup* and compute their performances.

Predictive Rule Selection

Although the predictive rule learning algorithm can learn many rules from the historical events with tickets, we only select those with strong predictive power. In our solution, Laplace accuracy [236, 171, 132] is used for estimating the predictive power of a rule. According to the SLA, real tickets must be acknowledged and resolved within a certain time. The maximum allowed delay time is specified by a user-oriented parameter $delay_{max}$ for each rule. In the calculation of Laplace accuracy, those false alerts are treated as real alerts if their durations are greater than $delay_{max}$. $delay_{max}$ is given by the system administrators according to the severity of system incidents and the SLA.

Another issue is rule redundancy. For example, let us consider the two predictive rules:

X. $PROC\_CPU\_TIME > 50\%$ **and** $PROC\_NAME =$ 'Rtvscan'

Y. $PROC\_CPU\_TIME > 60\%$ **and** $PROC\_NAME =$ 'Rtvscan'

Clearly, if an alert satisfies Rule Y, then it must satisfy Rule X as well. In other words, Rule Y is more specific than Rule X. If Rule Y has a lower accuracy than Rule X, then Rule Y is redundant given Rule X (but Rule X is not redundant given Rule Y). Redundant rule pruning can be used to discard the more specific rules with lower accuracies [211].

3.3.2 Waiting Time before Ticket Creation

Waiting time is the duration by which tickets should be postponed if their corresponding alerts are classified as false. It is not unique for all monitoring situations. Since an alert can be covered by multiple predictive rules, we set up different waiting times for each of them. The waiting time can be transformed into two parameters in monitoring systems, the length of the polling interval with the minimum polling count [6]. For example, the situation described in Example 3.1 predicts false alerts about CPU utilization of 'Rtvscan.' We can also find another predictive rule as follows:

if $PROC\_CPU\_TIME > 50\%$ **and** $PROC\_NAME = perl\ logqueue.pl$, **then** *this alert is false.*

The job of perl, however, is different from that of Rtvscan. Their durations are not the same, and the waiting time will differ accordingly. In order to remove as many false alerts as possible, we set the waiting time of a selected rule as the longest duration of the transient alerts covered by it. For a selected predictive rule p, its waiting time is

$$wait_p = \max_{e \in \mathcal{F}_p} e.duration,$$

where $\mathcal{F}_p = \{e | e \in \mathcal{F}, isCovered(p, e) =' true'\}$, and $\mathcal{F}$ is the set of transient events. Clearly, for any rule $p \in \mathcal{P}$, $wait_p$ has an upper bound $wait_p \leq delay_{max}$. Therefore, no ticket can be postponed for more than $delay_{max}$.

3.4 Eliminating False Negatives

False negative alerts are the missing alerts that are not captured by the monitoring system due to some misconfiguration. Real-world IT infrastructures are often over-monitored. False negative alerts are much fewer than false positive alerts. Since the number of false negative alerts is quite small, we only focus on the methodologies for discovering them with their corresponding monitoring situations. The system administrators can easily correct the misconfiguration by referring the results. The false negative tickets are recorded by the system administrators in the manual tickets. Each manual ticket consists of several textual messages that describe the detailed problem.

In addition to system fault issues, manual tickets also track many other customer requests such as asking for resetting database passwords and installing a new web server. The customer request is the majority of the manual tickets. In our system the work for false negative alerts is to find out those monitoring related tickets among all manual tickets. This problem is formed as a binary text classification problem. Given an incident ticket, our method classifies it into "1" or "0," where "1" indicates the ticket is a false negative ticket, otherwise it is not. For each monitoring situation, a possible solution is to build a binary text classification model.

There are two challenges for building the classification model. First, the manual ticket data is highly imbalanced since most of the manual tickets are customer requests and only very few are false negative tickets. Figure 3.5 shows various system situation issues in two manual ticket sets. This manual ticket set is collected from a large customer account in IBM IT service centers. There are 9854 manual tickets in the first month, and 10109 manual tickets in the second month. As shown in this figure, only about 1% of the manual tickets are false negatives. Second, labeled data is very limited. Most system

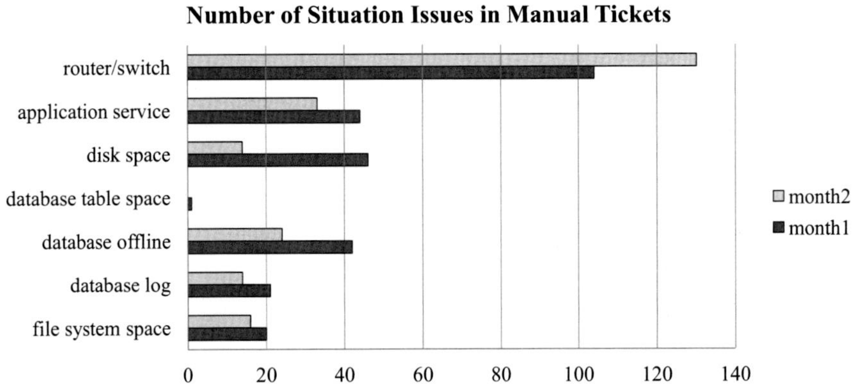

Number of Situation Issues in Manual Tickets

FIGURE 3.5: Number of situation issues in two months of manual tickets.

administrators are only working on some parts of incident tickets. Only a few experts can label all tickets. For the first challenge, in machine learning and data mining, over-sampling and reweighing data instances are two typical approaches to dealing with the imbalance issue. For the second challenge, active learning or semi-supervised learning techniques are potential approaches that can help to reduce some human labeling cost. In this chapter, we present a selective labeling approach to address the challenges [213, 215].

3.4.1 Selective Ticket Labeling

It is time consuming for human experts to scan all manual tickets and label their classes for training. In our approach, we only select a small proportion of tickets for labeling. A naive method is randomly selecting a subset of the manual tickets as the training data. However, the selection is crucial to the highly imbalanced data. Since the monitoring related tickets are very rare, the randomly selected training data would probably not contain any monitoring related ticket. As a result, the classification model cannot be trained well. On the other hand, we do not know which ticket is related to monitoring or not before we obtain the tickets' class labels. To solve this problem, we utilize domain words in system management for the training ticket selection. The domain words are some proper nouns or verbs that indicate the scope of the system issues. For example, everyone uses "DB2" to indicate the concept of IBM DB2 database. If a ticket is about the DB2 issue, it must contain the word "DB2." Note that "DB2" is a domain word. There are not many variabilities for the concepts described by the domain words. Therefore, these domain words are very helpful in reducing the ticket candidates for labeling. Table 3.2 lists examples of the domain words with their corresponding situations. The domain words can be obtained from the experts or related documents.

TABLE 3.2: Domain word examples

Situation Issue	Words
DB2 Tablespace Utilization	DB2, tablespace
File System Space Utilization	space, file
Disk Space Capacity	space, drive
Service Not Available	service, down
Router/Switch Down	router

In the training ticket selection, we first compute the relevance score of each manual ticket and rank all the tickets based on the score, and then select the top k tickets in the ranked list, where k is a predefined parameter. Given a ticket T, the relevance score is computed as follows:

$$score(T) = \max\{|w(T) \cap M_1|, ..., |w(T) \cap M_l|\},$$

where $w(T)$ is the word set of ticket T, l is the number of predefined situations, M_i is the given domain word set for the ith situation, $i = 1, ..., l$. Intuitively, the score is the largest number of the common words between the ticket and the domain words.

In dual supervision learning [196], the domain words are seen as the labeled features , which can also be used in active learning for selecting unlabeled data instances. In this application, only the positive features are presented, and the data is highly imbalanced. Therefore, the uncertainty-based approach and the density-based approach in active learning are not appropriate here.

Classification Model Building

The situation ticket is identified by applying a Support Vector Machine (SVM) classification model [207] on the ticket texts. For training this model, we have two types of input data: 1) the selectively labeled tickets, and 2) the domain words. To utilize the domain words, we treat each domain word as a *pseudo-ticket* and put all *pseudo-tickets* into the training ticket set. To deal with the imbalanced data, the minority class tickets are over-sampled until the number of positive tickets is equal to the number of the negative tickets [60]. Figure 3.6 shows the flow chart for building the SVM classification model.

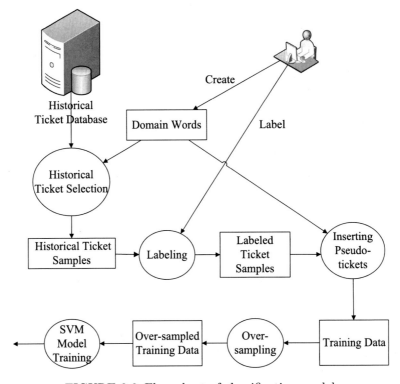

FIGURE 3.6: Flow chart of classification model.

3.5   Evaluation

This section presents empirical studies on the collected historical data to validate the performance of the algorithms.

3.5.1 Experimental Setup

Our system is developed by Java 1.6. The testing machine is Windows XP with Intel Core 2 Duo CPU 2.4GHz and 3GB of RAM. Experimental

TABLE 3.3: Data summary

dataset	$|\mathcal{D}|$	N_{non}	# Attributes	# Situations	# Nodes
Account1	50,377	39,971	1082	320	1212

monitoring events and tickets are collected from production servers of the IBM Tivoli Monitoring system [5], summarized in Table 3.3. The dataset of each account covers a period of 3 months. $|\mathcal{D}|$ is the number of events that generated tickets in the ticketing systems. N_{non} is the number of false events in all ticketed events. # Attributes is the total number of attributes of all events. # Situations is the number of monitoring situations. # Nodes is the number of monitored servers. In addition to the auto-generated tickets, we also collect manual tickets for two months. The first month has 9584 manual tickets. The second month has 10109 manual tickets.

3.5.1.1 Evaluation for False Positives

There are two performance measures:

- FP: The number of false tickets eliminated.

- FD: The number of real tickets postponed.

To achieve a better performance, a system should have a larger FP with a smaller FD. We split each dataset into the training part and the testing part. "Testing Data Ratio" is the fraction of the testing part in the dataset, and the rest is the training part. For example, "Testing Data Ratio=0.9" means that 90% of the data is used for testing and 10% is used for training. All FP and FD are only evaluated for the testing part.

Based on the experience of the system administrators, we set $delay_{max} = 360$ minutes for all monitoring situations. Figures 3.7, 3.8, and 3.9 present the experimental results. Our method eliminates more than 75% of the false alerts and only postpones less than 3% of the real tickets.

Since most alert detection methods cannot guarantee no false negatives, we only compare our method with the idea mentioned in [52], *Revalidate*, which revalidates the status of events and postpones all tickets. *Revalidate* has only one parameter, the postponement time, which is the maximum allowed delay time $delay_{max}$. Figure 3.9 compares the respective performances of our method and *Revalidate*, where each point corresponds to a different test data ratio. While *Revalidate* is clearly better in terms of elimination of false alerts, it postpones all real tickets, and the postponement volume is about 1000 to 10,000 times larger than our method.

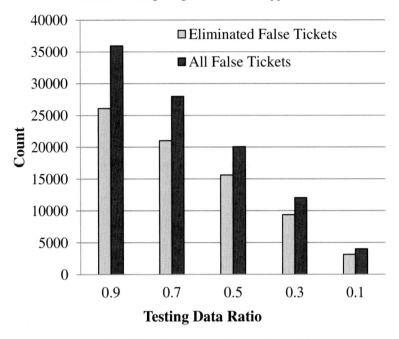

FIGURE 3.7: Eliminated false positive tickets.

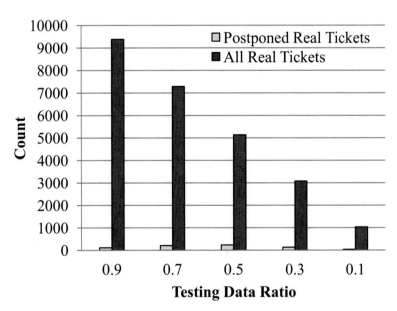

FIGURE 3.8: Postponed real tickets.

Tables 3.4 lists several discovered predictive rules for false alerts, where $wait_p$ is the delay time for a rule, FP_p is the number of false alerts eliminated

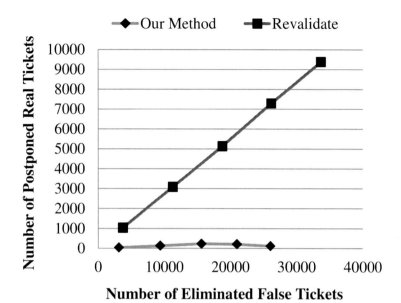

FIGURE 3.9: Comparison with revalidate method.

by a rule in the testing data, and FD_p is the number of real tickets postponed by a rule in the testing data.

TABLE 3.4: Sampled rules for Account2 with testing data ratio = 0.3

Situation	Rule Condition	$wait_p$	FP_p	FD_p
cpu_xuxw_std	N/A	355 min	7093	5
monlog_3ntw_std	current_size_64 >= 0 **and** record_count >= 737161	80 min	23	0
svc_3ntw_vsa_std	binary_path = R:\IBMTEMP\VSA\VSASvc_Cli.exs	30 min	27	0
fss_xuxw_std	inodes_used <= 1616 **and** mount_point_u = /logs	285 min	12	2
fss_xuxw_std	inodes_used <= 1616 **and** sub_origin = /logs	285 min	12	2

3.5.1.2 Evaluation for False Negatives

The effectiveness is evaluated by the accuracy of the situation discovery. The accuracy is measured by precision, recall, and F1 score, which are the standard accuracy metrics in classification problems [189]. We use one month's tickets as the training data, and the other month's tickets as the testing data. We first test the accuracy of the word-match method. The words are defined in Table 3.5.

Figures 3.10 to 3.13 show the tested F1 scores [207] of four monitoring situations about file system space issues, disk space issues, service availabil-

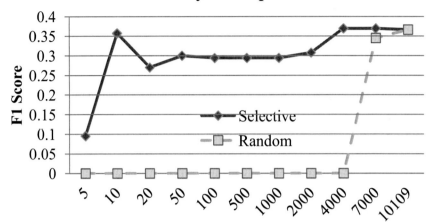

FIGURE 3.10: Accuracy of situation discovery for file system space alert.

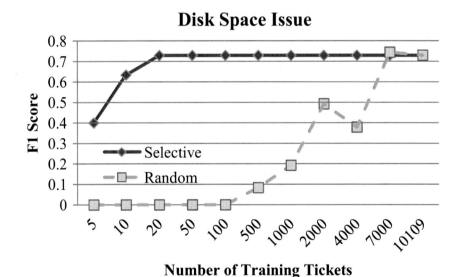

FIGURE 3.11: Accuracy of situation discovery for disk space alert.

ity, and router/switch issues. Our method is denoted as "Selective," and the second baseline method is denoted as "Random." The "Random" method randomly selects a subset of manual tickets as the training data for building the SVM model. The domain words for our "Selective" method are shown in Table 3.5. As shown by those figures, the "Random" method can only achieve

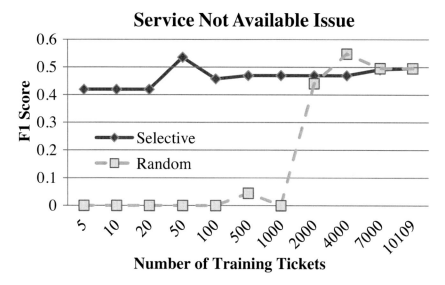

FIGURE 3.12: Accuracy of situation discovery for service not available.

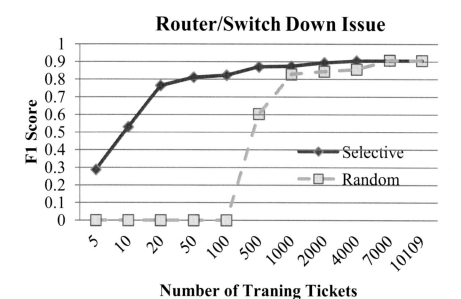

FIGURE 3.13: Accuracy of situation discovery for router/switch down.

the same accuracy as our method when the number of training tickets is large (above 5000). This is because the real situation tickets are in the minority of

TABLE 3.5: Accuracy of the word-match method

Situation	Words	Precision	Recall	F1 Score
File System Space	space, file	0.0341	0.8	0.0654
Disk Space	space, drive	0.1477	0.9565	0.2558
Service Not Available	service, down	0.1941	0.75	0.3084
Router/Switch Down	router	0.6581	0.7404	0.6968

the training dataset. The training tickets in "Random" cannot capture real situation tickets unless the training data is large. If the training data is large, however, labeling would be time consuming for humans.

3.6 Summary

Monitoring is an important and widely used approach for collecting system events from enterprise IT infrastructures. Unlike event generation from raw logs, monitoring provides an active way to capture the internal system status, errors, and alarms. It can directly generate structured event information. However, there are still many open issues in various monitoring technologies, such as false positives and false negatives, where false positives are the false alerts (or false alarms) and false negatives are the missing alerts. As a result, the quality of generated events also suffers from these issues that arise from monitoring. This chapter presents two simple and practical data-driven solutions for eliminating the false positives and false negatives in IT system monitoring. By combining the system event data and ticket data collected from IT service centers, the solutions reduce the number of false positive (non-actionable) alerts and the number of false negative (missing) alerts for the automatic monitoring system. It minimizes the cost of providing effective and reliable means for problem detection. However, as modern IT infrastructures become more complex, diverse, and dynamic, the quality control of monitoring events still requires a lot of human effort to achieve in reality.

3.7 Glossary

False Positive: An alert for which the system administrator does not need to take any action.

False Negative: A missed alert that is not captured due to inappropriate monitoring configuration.

False Positive Alert: False positive.

False Negative Alert: False negative.

False Alert: False positive alert.

Real Alert: An alert that requires the system administrator to fix the corresponding problem on the server.

Alert Duration: The length of time from an alert creation to its clearing.

Transient Alert: An alert that is automatically cleared before the technician opens its corresponding ticket.

False Positive Ticket: A ticket created from a false positive alert.

False Negative Ticket: A ticket created manually identifying a condition that should have been captured by automatic monitoring.

False Ticket: A ticket created from a false alert.

Real Ticket: A ticket created from a real alert.

Part II

Pattern Discovery and Summarization

Chapter 4

Event Pattern Mining

Chunqiu Zeng and Tao Li

Florida International University
Nanjing University of Posts and Telecommunications

4.1   Introduction

With the rapid advance in data collection and storage technologies, the discovery of hidden information from temporal data, where temporal information is explicitly considered during data analysis, has gained great interest during the last two decades. Basically, temporal data is often referred to as a collection of data items associated with timestamps, describing the state changes or evolving trends over time.

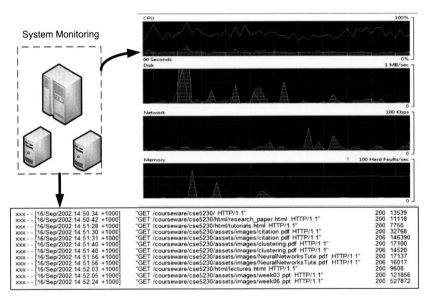

FIGURE 4.1: Temporal data in system management. (See color insert.)

Temporal data is prevalent across different application domains. A typical example for temporal data in system management is illustrated in Figure 4.1. System monitoring, one important component in system management, tracks the states of a system by collecting system information such as the CPU utilization, the memory usage, the number of data bytes written and read on disk, the amount of data received and sent through the network, the sequence of requests and responses processed on an application server, etc. All the system information is collected with a fixed frequency and each data item is recorded with its timestamp. The boom in social network applications such as Twitter, Facebook, and Linkedin also leads to a large scale of temporal data produced by millions of active users every day. As shown in Figure 4.2, the temporal data herein is represented as a sequence of posts describing some breaking news, local events, social activities, etc. More concrete examples are also shown in Figure 4.2, such as car accidents, earthquakes, national election

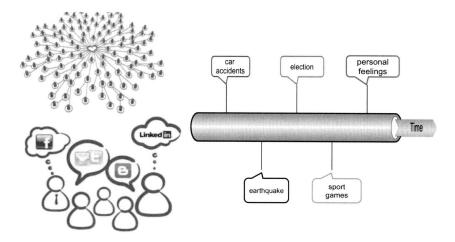

FIGURE 4.2: Social events in social media. (See color insert.)

campaign, sport games, and personal feelings. These posts are associated with timestamps and temporally organized. Besides the examples in the aforementioned two application domains, temporal data can be found as well in many other application domains such as health care, stock market, environment, and climate.

In light of the different types of data items, temporal data are generally divided into two categories: time series and event data. Time series are used to describe the temporal data where the value of the data item is continuous. Event data denotes the temporal data with discrete data item values. For example, in the system management shown in Figure 4.1, the CPU utilization, the memory usage, and the number of data bytes written and read on disk, the amount of data received and sent through the network are represented as time series. The requests and responses processed by an application server in system management and the posts occurring in social media are referred to as event data since their values are categorical. Although mining both types of temporal data has attracted increasing attention in recent years, our main focus in this chapter is on the event data.

Event mining utilizes the combination of techniques from data mining, machine learning, statistics, and database areas to discover the hidden patterns, unexpected trends, or other subtle relationships among events. The event patterns discovered can be used by analysts to make decisions for the behaviors of future events. Diverse requirements in various application domains dictate different types of event patterns for problem solving. In this chapter, we provide a survey of different types of event patterns and present the corresponding event mining techniques as well as the application scenarios.

In the following parts of this chapter, many typical temporal patterns are discussed in Section 4.2 to Section 4.10. A case study of mining sequential patterns from web query logs is presented in Section 4.11. At the end of this chapter, a brief summary of temporal patterns is presented.

4.2   Sequential Pattern

The sequential pattern mining problem was first introduced by Agrawal and Srikant in [19], with the purpose of discovering frequent subsequences as patterns from a sequence database. One example to illustrate the sequential patterns is from massive amounts of sales data, where each transaction consists of the purchased items along with the purchasing time stamps. Such patterns are able to describe that customers usually buy a fitted sheet, a flat sheet, and pillow cases in one transaction first, followed by another transaction containing a comforter, and they finally purchase drapes and ruffles in a new transaction after a number of days have passed (as shown in Figure 4.3). In comparison with frequent pattern mining [18], which is to find frequent item sets within each transaction, sequential pattern mining mainly focuses on the patterns across different transactions by considering their sequential order. Besides sales data, similar examples of such sequential patterns can be found in other data, such as web usage data describing the browsing activities of web visitors and genome sequence data encoding the elements of the DNA sequence.

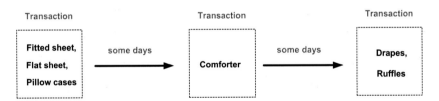

FIGURE 4.3: A sequential pattern example.

4.2.1   Problem Definition

The problem of mining sequential patterns can be formally described as follows. A sequence database D is defined as a set of sequences $D = \{S_0, S_1, ..., S_i, ..., S_n\}$. Each sequence $S_i \in D$ is a sequence of itemsets, denoted as $S_i =< T_1, ..., T_j, ..., T_m >$ where T_j is a non-empty set of items and all the itemsets in the sequence are organized in temporal order. For a sequence, if itemset T_i happens before itemset T_j, we denote it as $T_i \prec T_j$. A sequence containing k itemsets is also referred to as a k-sequence. A non-empty itemset T_j can be further represented as $T_j = \{I_1, I_2, ..., I_k, ..., I_l\}$, where I_k is an item.

In sequential pattern mining, the non-empty itemset T_j is also referred to as an event, so these two concepts are interchangeable in this chapter.

A sequence $R =< T_{R1}, T_{R2}..., T_{Rm} >$ is a subsequence of $S =< T_{S1}, T_{S2}, ..., T_{Sn} >$ if existing m itemsets $T_{Si1} \prec T_{Si2} \prec ... \prec T_{Sim}$ in S satisfy $T_{R1} \subseteq T_{Si1}$, $T_{R2} \subseteq T_{Si2}$, ..., $T_{Rm} \subseteq T_{Sim}$. It is also said that S contains R.

For example, there are six items $\{I_1 = Fitted\ sheet, I_2 = Flat\ sheet, I_3 = Pillow\ cases, I_4 = Comforter, I_5 = Drapes, I_6 = Ruffles\}$ in Figure 4.3. Each transaction contains one itemset. Thus, there are three itemsets $T_1 = \{I_1, I_2, I_3\}$, $T_2 = \{I_4\}$, and $T_3 = \{I_5, I_6\}$. The sequence is presented as $S =< T_1, T_2, T_3 >$ satisfying $T_1 \prec T_2$, $T_1 \prec T_3$ and $T_2 \prec T_3$. Let $T_4 = \{I_1, I_2\}$, $T_5 = \{I_6\}$, and $R =< T_4, T_5 >$. It is easy to verify that R is a subsequence of S since $T_4 \subseteq T_1$ and $T_5 \subseteq T_3$.

Given a sequence database D, we define the support of a sequence S as the fraction of all data sequences that contains S. Sequential patterns are those sequences whose supports are not less than a predefined threshold with respect to the sequence database D.

TABLE 4.1: An example of a sequence database

sequence ID	sequence
S_1	$< \{a, b, d\}, \{b, c\}, \{e\} >$
S_2	$< \{a, b\}, \{b, c, d\} >$
S_3	$< \{a, b\}, \{b, c, d\}, \{b, d, e\} >$
S_4	$< \{b\}, \{c, d\}, \{d, e\} >$
S_5	$< \{a, c\}, \{b, d, e\} >$

An example of a sequence database is given in Table 4.1. There are five sequences in the sequence database, each of which is labeled with a unique sequence ID. To specify the sequential patterns with respect to the given sequence database, we predefine the support threshold $\tau = 60\%$. If $R =< \{b\}, \{c\}, \{e\} >$, then R is the subsequence of S_1, S_3, and S_4. Accordingly, the support of R as to the sequence database is 60%. R is a sequential pattern since its support is not less than the threshold τ.

4.2.2 Mining Sequential Pattern

Sequential pattern mining is a computationally challenging task because there are exponentially many sequences contained in a given data sequence [207]. Take the sequence $S =< \{a, b\}, \{c\}, \{d, e\} >$ as an instance. There are $2^5 - 1 = 31$ possible subsequences of S since each item either appears or does not appear in a subsequence and a subsequence should contain one itemset at least. Since the sequential pattern mining problem was introduced in [19], various studies and strategies with respect to this problem have been presented. Typically, the related algorithms in the literature for sequential pattern discovery are classified broadly into two groups: Apriori-based and pattern-growth-based methods.

4.2.2.1 Apriori-Based Algorithms

The main characteristics of Apriori-based algorithms involve three aspects [111]. First, Apriori-based algorithms are described as level-wise search algorithms since all the k-sequences are constructed in the kth iteration of the algorithms when traversing the search space. Second, after the candidates are generated, pruning techniques are used for removing those candidates which cannot be sequential patterns. Third, Apriori-based algorithms often require multiple scans of the sequence database with a high I/O cost.

Accompanying the definition of sequential pattern mining in [19], the AprioriAll algorithm is first proposed to address the sequential pattern discovery problem utilizing the Apriori property (which is also referred to as the anti-monotone property). The Apriori property is that, if a sequence is not a sequential pattern, then all of its supersequences cannot be sequential patterns either. On the basis of Apriori and AprioriAll algorithms, a set of improved algorithms utilizing the Apriori property are proposed.

The GSP (i.e., **G**eneralized **S**equential **P**attern) algorithm proposed in [200] requires multiple scans of the sequence database. In comparison with AprioriAll, the GSP algorithm defines the length of a sequence as the number of items instead of the number of itemsets. During each level-wise search, the candidates with the same number of items are generated. The candidate generation involves two steps: join phase and prune phase. In the join phase, it generates each candidate sequence with k items by joining two sequential patterns with $k - 1$ items. In the prune phase, those candidates with k items are removed if any of their subsequences with $k - 1$ items are not sequential patterns. For example, given the sequential patterns with three items in the left column of Table 4.2, two candidate sequences with four items are generated during the join phase. Because $< \{a, b\}, \{e\} >$ containing three items is not a sequential pattern, it is removed during the prune phase. As a consequence, only one candidate sequence is produced in the right column. With the generated candidate sequences, the GSP algorithm scans the sequence database to count the support for every candidate sequence. All the candidate sequences with support not less than the predefined threshold τ are sequential patterns.

An algorithm named SPIRIT (i.e., **S**equential **P**attern m**I**ning with **R**egular express**I**on cons**T**raints) is proposed in [81] for sequential pattern mining. This algorithm is capable of discovering sequential patterns with flexible constraints represented in regular expression. Because of the sufficient expressive power of regular expressions, a wide range of interesting, non-trivial pattern constraints can be specified and the SPIRIT algorithm takes advantage of such constraints to prune the search space of sequential patterns during computation.

SPADE (i.e., **S**equential **PA**ttern **D**iscovery using **E**quivalence classes), a

TABLE 4.2: Candidate generation in GSP

Sequential Pattern with 3 items	Join Phase with 4 items	Prune Phase with 4 items
$< \{a, b\}, \{c\} >$	$< \{a, b\}, \{c, d\} >$	$< \{a, b\}, \{c, d\} >$
$< \{a, b\}, \{d\} >$	$< \{a, b\}, \{c\}, \{e\} >$	
$< \{a\}, \{c, d\} >$		
$< \{a, c\}, \{e\} >$		
$< \{b\}, \{c, d\} >$		
$< \{b\}, \{c\}, \{e\} >$		

TABLE 4.3: Example for SPADE

Sequence ID	Timestamp	Event	Sequence ID	Timestamp	Event
	1	(a, e, g)		1	(b)
	2	(b)	2	2	(d, f)
	3	(h)		3	(e)
1	4	(f)		1	(f)
	5	(c)	4	2	(a, g)
	6	(b, f)		3	(b, f, h)
3	1	(b, f, g)		4	(b, f)

new algorithm for fast mining of sequential patterns in a large database, is presented in [237]. The SPADE algorithm transforms the sequential dataset into a vertical ID-List database format, where each sequence is associated with a list of objects occurring in the sequence and along with the timestamps. All the sequential patterns can be enumerated via simple temporal joins on ID-Lists. The SPADE algorithm requires three passes of database scanning to complete the sequential pattern mining. For example, there are four sequences in the sequence database(shown in Table 4.3). Since item a occurs in both sequence 1 and sequence 4, the ID-List for $< (a) >$ is $< (1, 1), (4, 2) >$, where $(1, 1)$ and $(4, 2)$ mean that $< (a) >$ happens at timestamp 1 of sequence 1 and at time stamp 2 of sequence 4. To illustrate the temporal joins, it can be found that the ID-Lists of $< (a, g), (f) >$ and $< (a, g), (h) >$ are $< (1, 4), (1, 6), (4, 4) >$ and $< (1, 3), (4, 3) >$, respectively. By joining the two 3-sequences, we get a 4-sequence $< (a, g), (h), (f) >$ with its ID-List $< (1, 4), (1, 6), (4, 4) >$. Since $(1, 4)$ and $(1, 6)$ are in the same sequence, $< (a, g), (h), (f) >$ happens only in two distinct sequences. Thus, the support of $< (a, g), (h), (f) >$ is 2. However, given a large number of candidate sequences, the SPADE algorithm has a high cost to repeatedly merge the ID-Lists of sequential patterns.

To reduce the cost of merging, SPAM (i.e., **S**equential **PA**ttern **M**ining) is proposed in [27]. The SPAM algorithm represents each ID-List as a vertical bitmap data structure. As a consequence, the space for storing ID-Lists is reduced so that the ID-Lists can be completely stored in the main memory during sequential pattern mining.

4.2.2.2 Pattern-Growth-Based Algorithms

Pattern-growth-based algorithms utilize efficient data structures to prune candidate sequences early in the sequential pattern mining process. The search space of sequential patterns is typically represented as a tree data structure. The Apriori property can be used when the tree is traversed for searching sequential patterns in either breadth-first or depth-first order. Based on the tree data structure representation of the search space, it allows partitioning of the generated search space of large candidate sequences for efficient memory management [111]. Once the search space is partitioned, each smaller partition can be mined in parallel. Several pattern-growth-based algorithms have been proposed in the literature.

FreeSpan (i.e., **Fre**quent pattern-projected **S**equential **Pa**ttern) is one of the initial pattern-growth-based algorithms for sequential pattern mining [99]. The novel idea of this method is to integrate the mining of sequential patterns with the mining of frequent patterns. It also uses projected sequence databases to confine the search and the growth of subsequence fragments. Given a sequence $S = < T_1, ..., T_k, ..., T_m >$, the itemset $T = \cup_{k=1}^{m} T_k$ is the projected itemset of S. A useful property is that, if an itemset T is infrequent, any sequence whose projected itemset is a superset of T cannot be a sequential pattern. Based on the property, the efforts of candidate subsequence generations are greatly reduced during the process of sequential pattern mining. FreeSpan finds the sequential patterns by partitioning the search space based on the projected itemsets. For example, a list of frequent items $FL = (I_1, ..., I_i, ..., I_n)$ is given. The space of all the sequential patterns can be divided into n disjoint subspaces: a subspace of the sequential patterns containing only item I_1, a subspace of sequential patterns containing only item I_2, and so on. The partitioning can be done recursively and the complete set of sequential patterns can be found from different partitions without duplication. As a result, FreeSpan examines a substantially smaller number of combinations of subsequences and outperforms the GSP algorithm in terms of time cost.

TABLE 4.4: An example of the FreeSpan algorithm

sequence ID	sequence
S_1	$< \{a\}, \{a, b, c\}, \{a, c\}, \{d\}, \{c, f\} >$
S_2	$< \{a, d\}, \{c\}, \{b, c\}, \{a, e\} >$
S_3	$< \{e, f\}, \{a, b\}, \{d, f\}, \{c\}, \{b\} >$
S_4	$< \{e\}, \{g\}, \{a, f\}, \{c\}, \{b\}, \{c\} >$
frequent item list (*item : support*)	
$(a : 4), (b : 4), (c : 4), (d : 3), (e : 3), (f : 3)$	
sequential patterns with length 1 ($< seq >$: *support*)	
$(< a >: 4), (< b >: 4), (< c >: 4), (< d >: 3), (< e >: 3), (< f >: 3)$	

To illustrate the FreeSpan algorithm, a sequence database containing four sequences is given in Table 4.4. The support threshold is set to 2. The FreeSpan algorithm collects the support for each item and finds the set of frequent items by scanning the sequence database in one pass. The frequent item list is given in support descending order and the sequential patterns with length 1 are shown in the table. According to the frequent item list, the space of sequential patterns can be divided into six disjoint subspaces. All the sequential patterns can be acquired by combining sequential patterns from six projected databases.

The WAP-Mine (i.e., **W**eb **A**ccess **P**attern **Mine**) algorithm is proposed to mine access patterns from web logs in [174]. This algorithm takes advantage of a novel data structure named WAP-tree (**W**eb **A**ccess **P**attern **tree**) for efficient mining of access patterns from pieces of logs. This algorithm takes two passes of scanning the sequence database to build the WAP-tree. An additional header table is built to maintain the first occurrence of each item of a frequent itemset in the tree. This data structure is helpful for mining frequent sequences built upon their suffix. Although this algorithm is able to avoid the issue of generating a huge number of candidates like Apriori-based approach, WAP-Mine suffers from the huge memory consumption problem because of recursive reconstruction of numerous intermediate WAP-trees during sequential pattern mining.

PrefixSpan (i.e., **Prefix**-projected **S**equential **pattern** mining), a novel sequential pattern mining method, is proposed in [173]. The PrefixSpan algorithm takes advantage of prefix projection techniques to substantially reduce the size of projected databases and leads to efficient processing for sequential pattern mining. PrefixSpan projects the sequences into overlapping groups such that all the sequences in each group share the same prefix which corresponds to a sequential pattern. For instance, our task is to mine the sequential patterns from the sequence database in Table 4.3. Assuming the support threshold is 2, the PrefixSpan algorithm scans the sequence database and acquires the sequential pattern with length 1, i.e., $< a >, < b >, < e >, < f >, < g >, < h >$. Then PrefixSpan generates the projected database for each sequential pattern. The projected database with the sequential pattern $< a >$ as prefix is shown in Table 4.5 where the original sequence database is shown Table 4.3 and the support threshold is set to 2. PrefixSpan continues the discovery of the sequential pattern containing one item from the projected database and forms the sequential patterns with length 2 by combining the prefix $< a >$. In this way, PrefixSpan can recursively generate the projected database for each sequential pattern containing k items to find the sequential patterns with $k + 1$ items. The performance study shows that PrefixSpan algorithm outperforms both the Apriori-based GSP algorithm and the pattern-growth-based FreeSpan algorithm in mining large sequence databases.

TABLE 4.5: Projected database of $< a >$ in PrefixSpan

sequence ID	sequence
1	$< (\_, e, g), (b), (h), (f), (c), (b, f) >$
4	$< (\_, g), (b, f, h), (b, f) >$

4.3   Fully Dependent Pattern

In system management, the system administrators typically have much more interest in the patterns that are capable of predicting undesirable situations such as service disruptions and security intrusions. As matter of fact, however, such patterns do not happen frequently but have statistically significant dependency, especially in a well-managed systems. Therefore, traditional frequent pattern mining methods are no longer suitable/feasible in the application scenarios of system management.

Several issues cause the pattern discovery to be a challenging task. First, the patterns to be found are typically infrequent but can be statistically dependent events which can provide insights into the system. For example, in a computer network, the knowledge acquired from the dependent temporal event sequences enables the prediction of incoming events. In particular, if the events are related to malfunctions or service disruptions, such knowledge can be used for problem detection and root cause determination. Unfortunately, in order to discover the infrequent patterns, the support thresholds should be set very low. Consequently, this would raise a new issue that a large number of unimportant patterns are mixed in with a few patterns of interest. Second, the event data are collected in a noisy environment. For the applications depending on networks, data may be lost because of the traffic-overloaded communication lines or the overflowing router buffer. In addition, the data may be corrupted because of human errors during data processing. As a result, some valid patterns may be missed due to the presence of noise. Third, the distribution of events is often skewed in the whole data collection. As a consequence, a fixed minimum support threshold is not applicable for mining patterns from such event data.

In [141], to address the aforementioned issues, the concept of a fully dependent pattern, known as a d-pattern, is proposed to discover the infrequent, but dependent event patterns. To avoid the issue brought about by the fixed minimum support threshold, the hypothesis test is applied for a dependency test.

Let Ω be the item space and assume that there are k distinct items (i.e., $|\Omega| = k$) in the item space. An event is an itemset $E = \{I_1, ..., I_i, ..., I_m\}$ where I_i is an item from the item space. An event is considered to be a random variable taking values of all possible subsets of the item space. Assume that there exists an unknown distribution P on the 2^k possible states of E. Given an event database D, all events $E \in D$ are assumed to independently and identically follow the distribution P. Obviously, if all the items in an event E are independent, the probability of event E occurring can be derived as follows.

$$p_E = P(I_1, ..., I_i, ...I_m) = \prod_{i=1}^{m} P(I_i) = \prod_{i=1}^{m} p_i, \tag{4.1}$$

where p_i is the probability of occurrence of item I_i. On the other hand, the probability of their occurrence should be higher than the one under the independent assumption. Let $p^* = \prod_{i=1}^{m} p_i$; then the hypothesis test for dependency is given as below.

$$\begin{aligned} H_0 \ (null \ hypothesis) &: p_E = p^* \\ H_1 \ (alternative \ hypothesis) &: p_E > p^* \end{aligned} \tag{4.2}$$

Since the real values of p_is are not available, in order to calculate p^*, all p_is are replaced by their estimators $\hat{p}_i = \frac{support(I_i)}{|D|}$, where $support(I_i)$ is the number of events containing item I_i and $|D|$ is the number of events in the event database D. If the *null hypothesis* in Eq. (4.2) is true, then the random variable $C_E = support(E)$ follows a binomial distribution $B(p^*, n)$, where $support(E)$ is the occurring number of event E in event database D. The *null hypothesis* should be rejected if C_E is bigger than some threshold. The threshold can be determined by a pre-specified significance level α, where α is known as the upper bound for the probability of a false positive.

Accordingly, a new random variable can be derived as follows:

$$Z = \frac{C_E - np^*}{\sqrt{np^*(1-p^*)}}. \tag{4.3}$$

Typically, the number of events in D is very large, so Z is assumed to follow the standard normal distribution $N(0,1)$ according to the central limiting theorem [75]. With Eq. (4.3), the dependency test is equivalent to test whether C_E is greater than $minsup(E)$, which is given in

$$minsup(E) = np^* + z_\alpha \sqrt{np^*(1-p^*)}, \tag{4.4}$$

where z_α is the corresponding $1 - \alpha$ normal quantile which can be easily found in any normal table or calculated. Different events Es should have different $minsup(E)$s since their p^*s have different values.

However, the dependency test is neither upward nor downward closed. Therefore, it is computationally infeasible to discover all events that are dependent. In order to discover all such dependent events efficiently, a stronger dependency condition is given to define such patterns, which are referred to as d-patterns.

Definition 4.1 *Given a significant level α, an event $E = \{I_1, ..., I_i, ..., I_m\}$* *($m \geq 2$) is a qualified d-pattern if the two conditions below are satisfied.*
   (1) $support(E) \geq minsup(E)$.
   (2) If $E_S \subseteq E$ and $|E_S| > 1$, then $support(E_S) \geq minsup(E_S)$.

With condition (2) in Definition 4.1, the d-pattern can be proved to be downward closed. It can also be shown that the minimum support $minsup(E)$ increases as the frequency of items increases, when the product $p^* \leq 0.5$. With the help of the downward property, the d-patterns can be efficiently discovered by a level-wise search algorithm similar to the Apriori algorithm.

With the definition of d-pattern, three fundamental issues of traditional association mining are addressed so that it is capable of discovering the patterns which are infrequent from noise and unevenly distributed data. Although the strong dependency test requires not only an event but also all its subsets satisfying the dependency test, a level-wise algorithm can be constructed to discover all d-patterns regardless of their supports.

4.4   Partially Periodic Dependent Pattern

4.4.1   Problem Description

Periodicity is one of the most common phenomena in the real world. People tend to go to work at almost the same time of each day. The installation policies of IT departments require rebooting the printers every morning. Animal migration happens at the same season of every year. Students usually follow weekly schedules for classes. The seasonal sale of notebooks increases at the beginning of each semester. With the advanced technology for data collection, such periodic patterns can be identified from the collected applications data such as web logs, stock data, alarms of telecommunications, and event logs of computer networks.

The characteristics of periodic patterns help analysts gain great insights into the data. First, periodic patterns indicate the persistent occurrence of events. With the help of this characteristic, periodic patterns can be applied for the anomaly detection and problem diagnosis. Second, periodic patterns provide evidence for the predictability of events. It is helpful for analysts to predict the behavior of coming events and study the evolving trends in the future.

However, the limitations of data collection methods and the inherent complexity of periodic behaviors pose a great challenge for periodic pattern detection. In real practice, several issues need to be considered [152].

- First, the periodic behaviors are not persistent. Take complex networks as an example. Periodic problem reports are initialized when there occurs an exception such as disconnection of the network and stops once the problem is fixed.

- Second, imprecise time information is recorded due to lack of clock synchronization, rounding, and network delays.

- Third, periods are not known in advance. It is computationally infeasible to discover the true period by exhaustively searching for all possible periods.

- Furthermore, a fixed support level has difficulty in capturing the periods for all the patterns, since the numbers of occurrences of periodic patterns vary drastically. For example, a daily periodic pattern results in at most seven occurrences in a week, while an hourly pattern results in 168 occurrences for one week.

- Finally, events may be missing from a periodic pattern, or random events may be introduced into a periodic pattern. As a result, the periodicity may be disrupted due to noise.

To discover periodic patterns considering the above five issues, partial patterns (i.e., p-patterns) are discussed in this section.

4.4.2 Definition

As defined in previous sections, an event corresponds to an itemset with its occurring timestamp. To simplify the definition, the corresponding itemset of an event is defined as the type of the event, where the type can be further mapped to an integer or a letter. Therefore, an event is defined as a tuple $(type, time)$, where $type$ is the event type and $time$ is the occurring timestamp of the event. For example, in Figure 4.4, there are four types of events, i.e., A, B, C, D. In this figure, the x-axis represents the evolving time and the y-axis denotes different types of events. With an occurrence of any type of event, a filled circle is plotted in the figure corresponding to both its type and timestamp. The leftmost black circle a_1 of this figure depicts an event of type A happening at timestamp 1. This event can be represented as a tuple $a_1 = (A, 1)$ where $type(a_1) = A$ and $time(a_1) = 1$.

Definition 4.2 *An **event sequence** is defined as a collection of events ordered by the occurring timestamps, i.e., $S =< e_1, ..., e_i..., e_n >$, where $e_i = (type_i, time_i)$. A **point sequence** is an ordered collection of timestamps with respect to a given event type A, $P_A =< t_1, t_2, ..., t_i, ..., t_n >$, where t_i is a timestamp.*

For instance, in Figure 4.4, $S =< d_1, a_1, b_1, ... >$ is an event sequence. A point sequence of event type A can be represented as $P_A =< 1, 5, 9, 13, 17 >$.

Let $P_A =< t_1, ..., t_i, ..., t_n >$ represent the point sequence of a given event type A. Assume p is the period and δ is the time tolerance. Then, a periodic

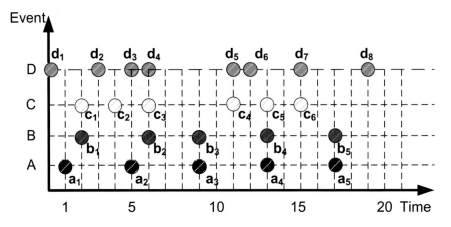

FIGURE 4.4: Event sequences are illustrated with timestamps.

pattern satisfying $t_{i+1} - t_i = p \pm \delta$, where $1 \leq i \leq n$. In Figure 4.4, $P_A =<$ $1, 5, 9, 13, 17 >$ is a periodic pattern with period $p = 4$ and time tolerance $\delta = 0$, while $P_B =< 2, 6, 9, 13, 17 >$ is also a periodic pattern with period $p = 4$ and time tolerance $\delta = 1$. Unfortunately, P_C and P_D cannot be represented simply with periodic patterns since there exists a big gap from timestamp 6 and timestamp 11. Take P_C as an example. If the time is split into 3 segments, $s_1 = [0, 6]$, $s_2 = [6, 11]$, and $s_3 = [11, 15]$, it is straightforward to acquire that a periodic pattern of C with period $p = 2$ and tolerance $\delta = 0$ occurs on both s_1 and s_3. This is a common phenomena in system management where an exception, which causes a periodic event C, happens during s_1 and s_3, while no exception occurs during s_2. In [152], the two different situations as to the event C are defined as on-segment and off-segment, respectively. Herein, both s_1 and s_3 are the on-segments, and s_2 is an off-segment.

Definition 4.3 *A **partially periodic point process** of a given event type A is a point sequence $P_A =< t_1, ..., t_i, ..., t_n >$. Assume p is the period and δ is the time tolerance. If t_i and t_{i+1} are on the same on-segment, then $t_{i+1} - t_i = p \pm \delta$, where $1 \leq i \leq n$.*

Based on the definition of a **partially periodic point process**, the concept of a partially periodic temporal association is given as follows.

Definition 4.4 *Given an event sequence S, let T_S be the set of all the event types occurring in S, δ be the time tolerance of period length, ω be the length of time window, minsup be the minimum support threshold, and p be the period length. A set of event types $T \subseteq T_S$ is a **partially periodic temporal association**, referred to as a **p-pattern**, if the number of qualified instances of T in S exceeds the minimum support threshold minsup. A qualified instance S_1 satisfies the following conditions.*
(1) All types of events in T happen in S_1, where there exists a timestamp t

such that for all $e_i \in S_1$, $t \leq time(e_i) \leq t + \omega$.

(2) The point sequence for each event type in S_1 is a partially periodic point process with parameters p and δ.

Given the example in Figure 4.4, assume $\omega = 1$, $\delta = 1$, and $minsup = 2$. Then $\{A, B\}$ is a p-pattern with a period of 4 since there are four pairs of event instances of A and B satisfying the conditions in the definition of a p-pattern.

4.4.3 Solution

According to the definition of the p-pattern, it can be verified that p-patterns satisfy the downward closure property. For example, in Figure 4.4, all non-empty subsets of $\{A, B\}$ such as $\{A\}$ and $\{B\}$ are p-patterns with length 1. Because of this property, a level-wise search algorithm can be proposed for computational efficiencies. To discover p-patterns, δ, ω, and $minsup$ are supposed to be given. Therefore, the task for p-pattern discovery includes two steps: finding possible periods p and discovering p-patterns with parameters ω, δ, and $minsup$. The two steps are illustrated in Figure 4.5.

4.4.3.1 Period Determination

One existing method to find the periods of a point process is to use the **F**ast **F**ourier **T**ransform (i.e., FFT). However, some issues of p-pattern discovery make an FFT algorithm infeasible. The random on-segments and off-segments are introduced in the p-pattern discovery; as a result, an FFT algorithm cannot cope with such a situation well. Moreover, the computational efficiency of FFT is $O(NlogN)$ where N is the number of time units and the number of time units is typically large. In [152], an approach based on chi-squared tests is proposed to find periods.

Let $P = < t_1, ..., t_i, ...t_N >$ be a point process over time window $[0, T]$, where $0 \leq t_i \leq T$. The ith inter-arrival time is defined as $\tau_i = t_{i+1} - t_i$, where $1 \leq i < N$. The intuitive idea is that the distribution of inter-arrival time τs in a partially periodic sequence should be quite different from the one in a random process. In an ideal partially periodic sequence, points occur periodically during the on-segments and no point happens during the off-segments. In Figure 4.4, event C happens periodically in segments $[0, 6]$ and $[11, 15]$, while no point occurs during segment $[6, 11]$. In a random point sequence, the points take place randomly and uniformly in the time window $[0, T]$.

Let $\rho_i = 1$ if both t_i and t_{i+1} are in the same on-segment, otherwise $\rho_i = 0$. If $\rho_i = 1$, the inter-arrival time $\tau_i = p + \epsilon_i$, where $-\delta \leq \epsilon_i \leq \delta$. On the other hand, if $\rho = 0$, then $\tau_i = \gamma_i$, where γ_i is a random variable describing the length of the ith off-segment. Therefore, the inter-arrival time can be formulated as below.

$$\tau_i = \rho_i(p + \epsilon_i) + (1 - \rho_i)\gamma_i. \tag{4.5}$$

τ is an arbitrary inter-arrival time and δ is predefined. Let C_τ be the total number of inter-arrival time values falling in $[\tau - \delta, \tau + \delta]$. If τ is not equal to p, C_τ is supposed to be small; otherwise, C_τ should be large. However, it is difficult to come up with a fixed threshold to determine whether C_τ is sufficiently large, since the C_τ also depends on the period p. If p is large, the number of observations happening in $[0, T]$ should be small, otherwise, it should be large. Therefore, the method based on the chi-squared test is applied to address this problem.

Let p_r be the probability of an inter-arrival falling in $[\tau - \delta, \tau + \delta]$ for a random sequence. If there are N inter-arrival times, the expected number of inter-arrivals in $[\tau - \delta, \tau + \delta]$ for a random sequence should be Np_r. Accordingly, the chi-squared statistic is defined as

$$\chi^2 = \frac{(C_\tau - Np_r)^2}{Np_r(1 - p_r)}. \tag{4.6}$$

With the help of the confidence level, χ^2 can be computed. For example, a 95% confidence level leads to $\chi^2 = 3.84$. Then the threshold of C_τ is acquired by the following equation.

$$C_\chi = \sqrt{3.84Np_r(1 - p_r)} + Np_r. \tag{4.7}$$

If

$$C_\tau > C_\chi, \tag{4.8}$$

then it is said that τ is a possible period with confidence level 95%.

To compute C_χ, p_r can be estimated with the assumption that the random sequence approaches a Poisson arrival sequence when the number of points gets larger.

$$p_r = \int_{\tau - \delta}^{\tau + \delta} \lambda e^{-\lambda x} dx \approx 2\delta \lambda e^{-\lambda \tau}, \tag{4.9}$$

where $\lambda = N/T$ is the mean inter-arrival time.

In order to obtain possible periods, all the inter-arrival time values would be tested with Eq.(4.8). The period determination is shown in step 1 of Figure 4.5. There are $N - 1$ inter-arrival time values, so the time complexity is $O(n)$.

4.4.3.2 P-Pattern Discovery

When all the possible periods for each event type are discovered, the subsequent task is to find the p-patterns.

- As shown in step 2 of Figure 4.5, each possible period p is given. First, a set A_p of event types is built, where the period p is one possible period for each event type in A_p.

- Second, with the confidence level, similar to Eq.(4.8), the minimum support threshold C_χ can be computed.

- Based on the parameter *minsup*, ω, the p-patterns can be found with a level-wise search algorithm similar to Apriori algorithm.

Then, all the p-patterns can be discovered by combining all the p-patterns produced in each iteration of step 2. This method is also called period-first algorithm [152]. After the periods are found, the p-patterns are generated from A_p, which is supposed to be small subset of all the event types. Thus, this algorithm can discover p-patterns more efficiently.

Step 1: Find all possible periods

(1) Get the point sequence
for each event type.

(2) Find possible periods for
each event type.

Step 2: Find P-Patterns

For each period p {

    (1) Get the set A_p of all the related
event types with period p.

    (2) Get the minsup = C_x with p.

    (3) With parameter minsup and
w. Find all the p-patterns which
are a subset of A_p.

}

FIGURE 4.5: Steps of p-pattern discovery.

In [152], according to different orders for period determination and p-pattern discovery, two other algorithms (i.e., association-first and hybrid algorithms) are proposed as well. The Association-first algorithm starts with temporal association mining and then selects only those associations whose event types occur in a periodic point process with the same period p and tolerance δ. The association-first algorithm suffers a computational complexity comparable to that of temporal mining, where a substantial amount of cost would be caused in the case of large patterns and low support levels. However, the association-first algorithm is more robust to noise [152]. The hybrid algorithm is a trade-off between the period-first and association-first algorithms. The former provides efficiency while the latter provides robustness to noise.

4.5   Mutually Dependent Pattern

In some application domains, including problem detection in computer networks, intrusion detection in computer systems, and fraud detection in financial systems, normal behaviors dominate compared with rare abnormal behaviors such as failures and intrusions [151]. Therefore, in these applications, it is more interesting to discover such patterns that comprise infrequent, but highly correlated items than the frequent patterns whose occurring frequencies exceed a predefined minimum support threshold. An example from network management is considered. Three events, i.e., network interface card failure, unreachable destination, and cold start trap, are commonly generated from a router. Typically, the occurrence of cold start trap indicates the router has failed and restarted. Thus, informed of the occurrences of the first two events, the monitoring system can provide an advance warning that the third event will happen.

It is difficult to mine such infrequent but strongly correlated patterns. One intuitive way is to apply the traditional frequent pattern mining method with a very low minimum support threshold to get the initial pattern set. Then, significantly correlated patterns can be identified from these initial pattern set. However, it is impractical since a large number of irrelevant patterns dominate the whole initial pattern set. In order to address the issue, mutually dependent patterns are proposed, which are also known as m-patterns.

Assume that an event is a non-empty set of items associated with its timestamp. Let S be a sequence of events, and E_1 and E_2 be two events. Given S, the dependency of E_1 on E_2 is quantified by the empirical conditional probability denoted by $P_S(E_1|E_2)$.

$$P_S(E_1|E_2) = \frac{support(E_1 \cup E_2)}{support(E_2)}, \tag{4.10}$$

where $E_1 \cup E_2$ represents a new event containing all the items from E_1 and E_2, and $support(E)$ is the number of occurrences of E in sequence S.

Definition 4.5 *Given the minimum dependence threshold $0 \leq minp \leq 1$, two events E_1 and E_2 are **significantly mutually dependent** with respect to the sequence S iff $P_S(E_1|E_2) \geq minp$ and $P_S(E_2|E_1) \geq minp$.*

Definition 4.6 *Given a sequence S and the minimum dependence threshold minp, let E be an event from S. If any two events $E_1 \subseteq E$ and $E_2 \subseteq E$ are significantly mutually dependent with respect to S, then E is referred to as an* **m-pattern**.

According to the definition, an m-pattern can be discovered regardless of the frequency of its occurrence. M-patterns are different from the frequent association rules and correlated patterns.

1. An m-pattern E requires mutual dependence, which is a two-way dependence. An association rule $E_1 \rightarrow E_2$ only requires one-way dependence (i.e., E_2 depends on E_1). A correlated pattern refers to an itemset whose items are not independent according to a statistical test.

2. An m-pattern does not require minimum support. This property makes it possible to find all infrequent m-patterns. In contrast, association rule mining is not applicable for infrequent pattern discovery since low minimum support often leads to a large number of irrelevant patterns.

3. E is an m-pattern if any two sub-events of E are dependent on each other. This requirement makes the correlations in m-patterns more significant than those in both association rules and correlated patterns.

TABLE 4.6: An example to illustrate m-patterns

ID	Transaction
T_1	$\{a, b, c, d, e, f, g\}$
T_2	$\{d, f, g\}$
T_3	$\{a, b, d, g\}$
T_4	$\{a, d, g\}$
T_5	$\{f, g\}$
T_6	$\{e, f, g\}$
T_7	$\{e, g\}$

To highlight the unique characteristic of m-patterns, a transaction database is given in Table 4.6 [151]. There are seven transactions in total. To mine the frequent patterns, set $minsup = 3$. Accordingly, both $\{a, d\}$ and $\{a, g\}$ are frequent patterns since their supports are 3. In contrast, m-patterns are defined by mutual dependence using the threshold $minp$. Let $minp = 0.5$. As a consequence, $\{a, b\}$ is an m-pattern, while $\{a, g\}$ is not an m-pattern. This is because g happens in every transaction, $P_S(a|g) = \frac{3}{7} \leq minp = 0.5$. Therefore, it cannot be inferred that $g \rightarrow a$, although $\{a, g\}$ is a frequent itemset.

The definition of m-patterns offers several nice properties, which can be used to develop efficient algorithms for m-pattern discovery.

Lemma 4.1 *An event E is an m-pattern iff $P_S(E - \{I\}|\{I\}) \geq minp$, for every item $I \in E$.*

Proof: Since this is an IFF statement, the proof includes two parts for both necessity and sufficiency, respectively.

Necessity Let $E_1 = E - \{I\}$ and $E_2 = \{I\}$. Therefore, $E_1 \subset E$ and $E_2 \subset E$. According to the definition of m-pattern, $P_S(E_1|E_2) \geq minp$. After replacing E_1 and E_2, it can be inferred that $P_S(E - \{I\}|\{I\}) \geq minp$.

Sufficiency In this part, we show that if $P_S(E - \{I\}|\{I\}) \geq minp$ for every item $I \in E$, then E is an m-pattern. Let E_1 and E_2 be any two non-empty subsets of E. Without loss of generality, we assume $I \in E_2$. Then, $support(\{I\}) \geq support(E_2)$. Similarly, $E_1 \cup E_2$ is subset of E, $support(E_1 \cup E_2) \geq support(E)$. Therefore, $P_S(E_1|E_2) = \frac{support(E_1 \cup E_2)}{support(E_2)} \geq \frac{support(E)}{support(\{I\})} = P_S(E - \{I\}|\{I\}) \geq minp$. Since E_1 and E_2 are any two subsets of E, we have proven that E is an m-pattern according to the definition of m-pattern.

With the help of Lemma 4.1, to show that E is an m-pattern, we only need to check that $P_S(E - \{I\}|\{I\}) \geq minp$ for each item $I \in E$ in linear time $O(|E|)$.

Similar to frequent itemset discovery, the number of all potential m-patterns is huge. An efficient algorithm is required to search for all m-patterns.

Lemma 4.2 *Let E' and E be two events satisfying $E' \subseteq E$. If E is an m-pattern, then E' is an m-pattern as well.*

Proof: Let E_1 and E_2 be any two subsets of E'. Accordingly, E_1 and E_2 are two subsets of E as well, since $E' \subseteq E$. Because E is an m-pattern, $P_S(E_1|E_2) \geq minp$ and $P_S(E_2|E_1) \geq minp$. Therefore, E' is an m-pattern.

The property given in Lemma 4.2 is the downward closure property of an m-pattern. Similar to the Apriori algorithm, a level-wise search algorithm is proposed for efficient m-pattern discovery.

Lemma 4.3 *If E is an m-pattern with minp, then*

$$\frac{support(E - \{I\})}{support(\{I\})} \geq minp$$

for any item $I \in E$.

Proof: Since E is an m-pattern, according to the definition of an m-pattern, we have

$$\frac{support(E)}{support(\{I\})} \geq minp.$$

Due to the fact that $(E - \{I\}) \subset E$, we have $support(E - \{I\}) \geq support(E)$. Therefore,

$$\frac{support(E - \{I\})}{support(\{I\})} \geq minp.$$

Provided along with Lemma 4.3, the supports of patterns found at level 1 and $k - 1$ can be used to prune the impossible m-pattern at level k. Clearly, the smaller the candidate set is, the faster the m-pattern searching algorithm can perform.

The m-pattern discovery algorithm [151] is similar to the Apriori algorithm [18]. The only difference is that more pruning techniques can be incorporated according to Lemma 4.2 and Lemma 4.3.

4.6   T-Pattern

In system management, the analysis of historical event data helps to discover some interesting patterns, which can provide great insights into system behavior. Specifically, a computer system problem may trigger a series of symptom events, which indicates a natural signature for identifying the root cause of system problems. As summarized in [101, 108], a problem manifests itself as a sequence of events propagating from origin and low layer to high software layer through the dependency tree. Thus knowing the temporal patterns can help us pinpoint the root cause and take proper actions.

The pairwise temporal dependency among events has been given much attention for several reasons. First, the pairwise temporal dependency can be well visualized and easily interpreted by domain experts. Moreover, complex temporal dependencies can be constructed on the basis of pairwise temporal dependencies. Therefore, the t-pattern is proposed in [133] as a pairwise temporal dependent pattern.

With respect to a given event sequence S, a **t-pattern** describes a statistical dependency between events, where the temporal dependency is characterized by the timing information indicating that one event is followed by another event within a time lag interval.

Mining frequent episodes from an event sequence typically can be done by predefining a fixed time window size [157]. With the help of window size, items in the same sliding window are viewed as items in a single transaction. Then the idea of mining frequent itemsets from transaction data is applied for discovering frequent episodes. However, this method causes two issues which must be addressed in applications. First, the fixed time window scheme cannot explore precise temporal information within a window, and misses the opportunity to mine temporal relationships longer than the window size. For example, in real system management applications, the temporal relationships discovered have time distances ranging from one second to one day. Second, as is well known for transaction data, frequent pattern framework misses significant, but infrequent patterns. Taking an example in most system management applications, frequent patterns are normal operations and service disruptions are usually infrequent but significant patterns.

To address the aforementioned two issues, in [133, 134], a novel algorithm is proposed for discovering temporal patterns without predefined time windows. The task of discovering temporal patterns is divided into two sub-tasks. First, statistic techniques are used for dependence testing and candidate removal. Second, the temporal relationships between dependent event types are identified. The idea is that the dependence problem is formulated as the problem of comparing two probability distributions and is solved using a technique reminiscent of the distance methods used in the spatial point process, while the latter problem is solved using an approach based on chi-squared tests. The statistical properties provide meaningful characterizations for the patterns and are usually robust against noise.

Herein, both **event sequence** and **point sequence** are described in Definition 4.2. Let $S = < e_1, ..., e_i, ..., e_n >$, where $e_i = (type_i, time_i)$. A point sequence as to event type A is denoted as $P_A = < a_1, a_2, ..., a_j, ..., a_m >$, where a_j is a timestamp and $a_i < a_{i+1}$. Assume the time range for a point sequence P_A is $[0, T]$. Given a point z, we define the distance from z to the point sequence P_A as

$$d(z, P_A) = \inf_{x \in P_A \wedge x \geq z} ||x - z||. \qquad (4.11)$$

Intuitively, the distance is defined to be the shortest distance from the point z to its closest neighbor in P_A.

Definition 4.7 *Given two point sequences $P_A = < a_1, a_2, ..., a_j, ..., a_m >$ and $P_B = < b_1, b_2, ..., b_i, ..., b_n >$ for event A and event B, respectively, a **t-pattern** defined over P_A and P_B is denoted as $A \rightarrow_{[\tau - \delta, \tau + \delta]} B$, where τ is B's waiting period after the occurrence of A and δ is the time tolerance. It indicates that B is statistically dependent on A, and that most B's waiting periods after the occurrences of A fall into the interval $[\tau - \delta, \tau + \delta]$.*

To qualify a t-pattern, a two-stage method is proposed in [133]. At the first stage, the dependency between events is tested statistically. The task of the second stage is to identify the waiting periods between two possible dependent events. In order to test the dependency in t-pattern $A \rightarrow_{[\tau - \delta, \tau + \delta]} B$, two distributions are defined as follows.

Definition 4.8 *The unconditional distribution of the waiting time of event B is defined as*
$$F_B(r) = P(d(x, P_B) \leq r),$$

where x and r are any real numbers. $F_B(r)$ describes the probability of having event B occurring within time r.

In Figure 4.6, an example to illustrate the unconditional distribution $F_B(r)$ is shown in (a). B is an event type occurring in the time interval $[0, 90]$. Let X be an event type which can happen at any point $x \in [0, 90]$ uniformly. $F_B(r)$ can also be interpreted as the probability that X is followed by an event B

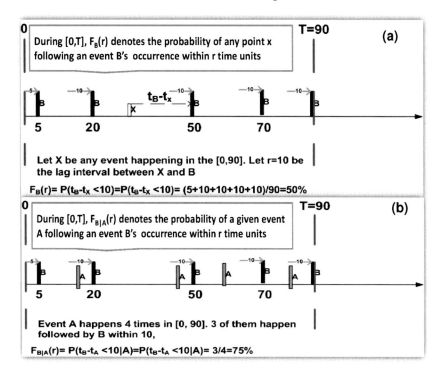

FIGURE 4.6: T-patterns are qualified by a statistical hypothesis test. (See color insert.)

within r time units. Assuming $r = 10$, any point $x \in ([0, 5] \cup [10, 20] \cup [40, 50] \cup [60, 70] \cup [80, 90])$ has an event B happening within 10 time units. $F_B(10)$ can be computed as the ratio between the length of $([0, 5] \cup [10, 20] \cup [40, 50] \cup [60, 70] \cup [80, 90])$ and the one of $[0, 90]$. Therefore, $F_B(10) = (5 + 10 + 10 + 10 + 10)/90 = 50\%$. Motivated by the example, $F_B(r)$ can be computed as below.

Let $t_i = b_i - b_{i-1}$ denote the inter-arrival time for

$$P_B =< b_1, b_2, ..., b_i, ..., b_n >, 1 \le i \le n, b_0 = 0.$$

Let $D_B = (t_1, ..., t_i, ..., t_n)$. Note that $(t_{(1)}, t_{(2)}, ..., t_{(n)})$ denotes the ordered permutation of D_B and $t_{(i)} \le t_{(i+1)}$. The estimate of $F_B(r)$ is the observed proportion of distance values satisfying

$d(x, T_B) \leq r.$

$$F_B(r) = \frac{length(\{x \in [0,T] : d(x, P_B) \leq r\})}{length([0,T])}$$

$$= \begin{cases} \frac{nr}{T}, & 0 \leq r \leq t_{(1)}; \\ \frac{t_{(1)} + (n-1)r}{T}, & t_{(1)} \leq r \leq t_{(2)}; \\ \cdots, & \cdots; \\ \frac{\sum_{i=1}^{n-1} t_{(i)} + r}{T}, & t_{(n-1)} \leq r \leq t_{(n)}. \end{cases} \qquad (4.12)$$

Eq.(4.12) can be illustrated with the example in Figure 4.6(a). The ordered list of the inter-arrival times for P_B is $(5, 15, 20, 20, 30)$. Since $r = 10$, $F_B(10) = \frac{5+(5-1)\times 10}{90} = 50\%$, which is the same result as the one shown in Figure 4.6(a).

Definition 4.9 *The conditional distribution of the waiting time of event type B with respect to event type A is defined as*

$$F_{B|A}(r) = P(d(x, P_B) \leq r : x \in P_A),$$

where r is a real number and x is any point in the point sequence P_A. $F_{B|A}(r)$ describes the conditional probability distribution given there is an event A at time x.

In Figure 4.6, an example to illustrate the conditional distribution $F_{B|A}(r)$ is shown in (b). A and B are two types of events. $F_{B|A}(r)$ can be computed as the proportion between the number of event A followed by B within r time units and the total number of event A. Assuming $r = 10$, since event A happens 4 times in $[0, 90]$, and 3 of them happen followed by B within 10 time units, $F_{B|A}(10) = 3/4 = 75\%$. In general, the computation is formally described as follows.

Let m be the number of points in sequence P_A and $d_j = d(a_j, P_B)$ where $1 \leq j \leq m$. Let $D_{B|A} = (d_1, ..., d_j, ..., d_m)$. Let $(d_{(1)}, d_{(2)}, ..., d_{(j)}, ..., d_{(m)})$ denote the ordered permutation of $D_{B|A}$ where $d_{(j)} \leq d_{(j+1)}$. The estimate of $F_{B|A}(r)$ is the observed proportion of distance values satisfying $d(a_j, T_B) \leq r$.

$$F_{B|A}(r) = \frac{|\{a_j : d(a_j, P_B) \leq r \wedge a_j \in P_A\}|}{m}$$

$$= \begin{cases} 0, & 0 \leq r \leq d_{(1)}; \\ \frac{1}{m}, & d_{(1)} \leq r \leq d_{(2)}; \\ \cdots, & \cdots; \\ \frac{m-1}{m}, & d_{(m-1)} \leq r \leq d_{(m)}; \\ 1, & d_{(m)} \leq r. \end{cases} \qquad (4.13)$$

Eq.(4.13) can be illustrated by the example in Figure 4.6(b). Assuming $r = 10$, event A has $m = 4$ occurrences in total, while $m - 1 = 3$ occurrences of

A followed by B within r time units. Moreover, it satisfies $d_{(m-1)} \leq r \leq d_{(m)}$. Thus $F_{B|A}(10) = \frac{m-1}{m} = \frac{3}{4} = 75\%$, which is the same result as the one shown in the figure.

With the help of the two distributions $F_B(r)$ and $F_{B|A}(r)$, the dependency between event A and event B is given in the following definition.

Definition 4.10 *Given two point sequences P_A and P_B corresponding to two event types A and B, respectively, $A \rightarrow B$, indicating that B is directly dependent on A, can be statistically true if $F_B(r)$ is significantly different from $F_{B|A}(r)$.*

The dependency test between A and B is based on the comparison between the first moments of $F_B(r)$ and $F_{B|A}(r)$. Let M_B and $M_{B|A}$ denote the first moments of $F_B(r)$ and $F_{B|A}(r)$, respectively. M_B and $M_{B|A}$ can be computed as below.

$$M_B = \sum_{i=1}^{n} \int_{t_{(i-1)}}^{t_{(i)}} \frac{n-i+1}{T} r \, dr = \frac{1}{2T} \sum_{i=1}^{n} t_i^2, \qquad (4.14)$$

where $t_{(0)} = 0$, t_i and $t_{(i)}$ are defined in Eq.(4.12). Similarly,

$$M_{B|A} = \frac{1}{m} \sum_{j=1}^{m} d_j, \qquad (4.15)$$

where d_j is defined in Eq.(4.13).

Under the hypothesis that A and B are independent, all the d_is are independently distributed as $F_B(r)$. Then, according to the central limiting theorem,

$$Z = \frac{|M_B - M_{B|A}|}{\sqrt{var(F_B(r))/m}} \sim N(0, 1), \qquad (4.16)$$

where $var(F_B(r))$ denotes the variance of distribution $F_B(r)$ and can be computed by

$$var(F_B(r)) = \frac{1}{3T} \sum_{i=1}^{n} t_i^3 - (\frac{1}{2T} \sum_{i=1}^{n} t_i^2)^2.$$

Given a confidence level α, we could compute the corresponding confidence interval $[-z_\alpha/\sqrt{k}, z_\alpha/\sqrt{k}]$, where z_α is the corresponding $1 - \alpha$ quantile and k is the sample size. If the value of Z falls outside the interval, then it is considered that the two distributions are different and hence B is independent of A. However, counterexamples can be constructed in which A and B are dependent but the first moments of two distribution functions are the same. So testing based on the first moment difference is conservative and will generate false positives. However, the conservative property does not affect the two-stage approach since stage one only serves as a preprocessing step to reduce the candidate space.

After stage one, the next task in stage two is to identify the dependence between the candidate pairs and finding the waiting period between two dependent events. Let δ be the time tolerance accounting for factors such as phase shifts and lack of clock synchronization.

Definition 4.11 *Given B depending on A, the waiting period of B after A is τ if the distance sequence $D_{B|A}$ has a period τ with time tolerance δ.*

The discovery of the waiting periods is carried out using the chi-squared test-based approach introduced in [152]. Given an arbitrary element τ in $D_{B|A}$ and a fixed δ, let C_τ be the total number of elements of $D_{B|A}$ that fall into the interval $[\tau - \delta, \tau + \delta]$. Intuitively, if τ is not a period, C_τ should be small; otherwise it should be large. The idea here is to compare C_τ with the number of elements in $[\tau - \delta, \tau + \delta]$ that would be expected from a random sequence. The procedure for identifying the relationship is essentially a one-dimensional clustering process.

4.7 Frequent Episode

In event sequences, an episode is a collection of events that occur relatively close to each other with respect to a given partial order in terms of timestamps [158]. Typically, a window size is given to describe that all the events within one episode are close to each other. For example, as shown in Figure 4.7, there are six types of events (i.e., A, B, C, D, E, F). The episode with window size 2 happens several times, where event E is followed by event F (e.g., $< e_1, f_1 >, < e_2, f_2 >, < e_3, f_3 >, < e_5, f_4 >$). The episodes occurring

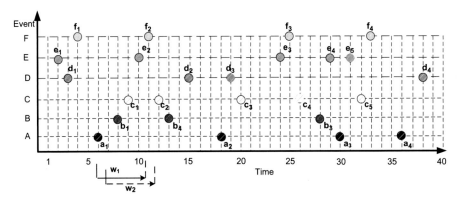

FIGURE 4.7: Episodes of event sequences.

with high frequencies (i.e., greater than a given threshold) are referred to as frequent episodes. One of the basic problems in event mining is to discover recurrent episodes from event sequences.

According to Definition 4.2, the event sequence in Figure 4.7 can be represented as $S =< e_1, d_1, f_1, a_1, b_1, c_1, ..., c_5, f_4, a_4, d_4 >$, where each element is characterized with its event type and timestamp (e.g., $e_1 = (E, 2)$). Let T_S and T_E denote the starting and the ending time of event sequence S. Accordingly, $T_S = 0$ and $T_E = 40$, as shown in the figure.

In order to describe the episodes of event sequence S, a window w is defined as a slice of the event sequence S. In particular, w can be denoted as $w = (S_w, w_s, w_e)$, where S_w is the subsequence of S whose timestamps fall into $[w_s, w_e)$, and $w_s \geq T_s$ and $w_e \leq T_e$ are the starting time and the ending time of the window w, respectively. Let W be the set of all possible windows on event sequence S. For instance, two time windows w_1 and w_2 are marked in Figure 4.7, where $w_1 = (< a_1, b_1, c_1, e_2 >, 6, 11)$ and $w_2 = (< b_1, c_1, e_2, f_2 >, 7, 12)$.

With the help of the definition of window, episodes can be described as directed acyclic graphs. According to the directed acyclic graphs, episodes are divided into three categories, shown in Figure 4.8.

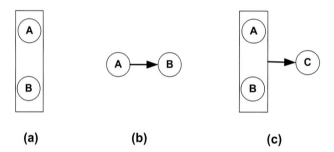

(a)   (b)   (c)

FIGURE 4.8: There are three types of episodes: (a) parallel episode; (b) serial episode; (c) composite episode. The vertical box indicates that all the event types in the box happen in a single episode, but the order of events does not matter. The arrow means the order of events.

- A parallel episode is defined by a set of event types and a given window, where all the event types happen within the time window, without considering the order of them. For example, in Figure 4.8(a), A and B are two types of events. In a single episode, A and B can happen in any order.

- A serial episode is defined by a set of event types and a given window as well. The window contains occurrences of all the event types, and the occurrences of them should keep in a consistent order. For example, in Figure 4.8(b), A must be followed by B.

- A is built recursively from events by serial and parallel composition. That is, a composite episode is either an event or the serial composition of two or more events or the parallel composition of two or more events. For example, in Figure 4.8(c), the composite episode is serially composed of two events. One is an parallel composition of A and B, and the other is an event C. This composite episode indicates that A and B happen before C, while the order of occurrence of A and B does not matter.

Definition 4.12 *Given the window size, let W be the set of all possible episodes on event sequence S. The frequency of an episode α is defined as follows:*

$$freq(\alpha) = \frac{|\{w \in W : \alpha \ occurs \ in \ w\}|}{|W|}.$$

If $freq(\alpha)$ is no less than the predefined minimum frequency threshold min_freq, then α is referred to as a frequent episode.

For example, in Figure 4.8, if the window size is 3, the number of all possible windows $|W| = T_e - T_s + 3 - 1 = 40 + 3 - 1 = 42$. If α is a serial episode, then $freq(\alpha) = 4/42 = 2/21$.

Based on the definition of frequent episode [158], a useful lemma is described as follows.

Lemma 4.4 *If an episode α is frequent in an event sequence S, then all subepisodes β of α are frequent as well.*

According to Lemma 4.4, similar to the Apriori algorithm, a level-wise searching algorithm can be applied to discover all the frequent episodes with respect to the event sequence S [158]. Extended work on the frequent episode discovery in different scenarios can be found in [127] and [128] as well.

4.8   Event Burst

The boom in social network applications, such as Facebook, Twitter, Weibo, LinkedIn, and Google Plus, leads to a large scale of temporal data produced by millions of active users every day. The temporal data is represented as a sequence of posts to describe some breaking news, local events, and social activities. More concrete examples include car accidents, earthquakes, national election campaign, sport games, personal feelings, and so forth. The underlying intuitive idea is that when a social activity happens, the appearance of the related topics in the posts sequence is signaled by a burst, with certain features rising sharply in frequency and, as time evolves, the particular topics may fade away again. The appearance of an event burst indicates the occurrence of a social activity. In this section, we focus on how to detect the event burst in an event sequence.

As a matter of fact, the arrival of a single focused topic in a sequence is characterized by the rate at which the relevant events happen. Generally, an event burst is identified based on the high occurrence rate of the events.

One of intuitive ways to model the random arrival time of events is based on the exponential distribution [121]. Let x be the inter-arrival time between event e_i and event e_j. Then x follows the exponential distribution with the following density function.

$$f(x) = \alpha e^{-\alpha x}, \tag{4.17}$$

where α^{-1} is the expected gap and α is referred to as the rate of event arrivals. Accordingly, the event burst can be modeled by a relatively larger α.

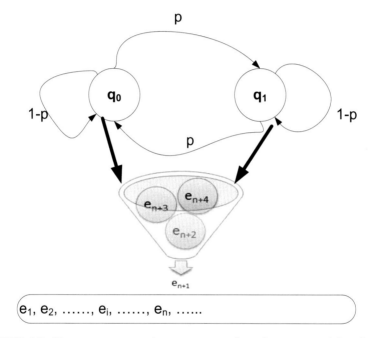

FIGURE 4.9: Two states q_0 and q_1 correspond to the states with a low rate and a high rate, respectively. p denotes the probability of state change. The events generated in both states q_0 and q_1 are mixed into an event sequence.

To make the model clear, only two states q_0 and q_1 are given in Figure 4.9, which correspond to the states with a low rate α_0 and a high rate α_1 (i.e., $\alpha_0 \leq \alpha_1$), respectively. Intuitively, periods with a low rate are usually interleaved with periods with a high rate. Thus, let p denote the probability of a state changing from one to the other. $1 - p$ is the probability of staying in the same state. The events happen in both states q_0 and q_1 are organized into an event sequence with respect to temporal information.

This model is also referred to as a two-state model in [121]. The two-state model can be used to generate the sequence of events in the natural way. The beginning state is q_0, where events are emitted at a low rate and the inter-arrival gaps follow an exponential distribution according to the density function $f_0(x) = \alpha_0 e^{-\alpha_0 x}$. A state may change to another state with the probability p or stay put with the probability $1 - p$. If the current state is q_1, then the inter-arrival gaps between events follow the distribution according to $f_1(x) = \alpha_1 e^{-\alpha_1 x}$.

Suppose that there is a given sequence of $n + 1$ events, each of which is associated with its timestamp. A sequence of inter-arrivals $x = (x_1, x_2, ..., , x_n)$ can be determined by the given event sequence. According to the Bayes theory, the possible state sequence $q = (q_{i_1}, q_{i_2}, ..., q_{i_n})$ can be inferred by maximizing the condition probability of the state sequence given the inter-arrival sequence. The conditional probability is shown as follows:

$$P(q|x) = \frac{P(q)P(x|q)}{Z}, \tag{4.18}$$

where $Z = \sum_q P(q)P(x|q)$ is the normalizing constant. $P(x|q)$ can be computed as,

$$P(x|q) = \prod_{t=1}^{n} f_{i_t}(x_t). \tag{4.19}$$

Let b denote the number of state transitions in sequence q. Then $P(q)$ is

$$P(q) = \left(\prod_{i_t \neq i_{t+1}} p \right)\left(\prod_{i_t \neq i_{t+1}} (1 - p) \right) = \left(\frac{p}{1 - p}\right)^b (1 - p)^n. \tag{4.20}$$

Therefore, $P(q|x)$ is equal to

$$P(q|x) = \frac{1}{Z}\left(\frac{p}{1 - p}\right)^b (1 - p)^n \prod_{t=1}^{n} f_{i_t}(x_t). \tag{4.21}$$

Applying ln on both sides to maximize the likelihood above is equivalent to minimizing the cost function $c(q|x)$ in

$$c(q|x) = bln(\frac{1 - p}{p}) + \left(\sum_{t=1}^{n} -ln(f_{i_t}(x_t))\right). \tag{4.22}$$

In order to minimize the cost described in the Eq.(4.22), the intuitive idea is motivated by its two terms. The first term on the right of Eq.(4.22) indicates that the sequences with a small number of state changes are preferred, while the second term shows that the sequences should conform well to the inter-arrival sequence. In [121], the two-state model is extended to an infinite-state model where there are infinite states and each state has different occurrence rates for events. Based on the infinite-state model, a hierarchical structure from the pattern of bursts can be extracted.

4.9 Rare Event

In some applications, it is important to predict infrequent but highly correlated events, such as an attack on a computer network and a fraudulent transaction in a financial institution. However, there are several challenges in the prediction task. First, since the prediction targets are rare events, only a few subsequences of events are able to contribute to the prediction problem. Second, because of the categorical features of events, the uneven inter-arrival times are considered to be another difficulty. Moreover, because of noise the time recordings can only approximate the true arrival times.

Most prediction methods assume that the data has balanced class distributions. As a consequence, it is difficult to adopt traditional discriminative analysis methods to differentiate the target rare events from other frequent events. In [222], a new strategy is proposed to improve the efficiency, accuracy and interpretability of rare event prediction. The main idea is to transform the rare event prediction problem into a search for all frequent event sets preceding target rare events. The unbalanced distribution problem is overcome by searching for patterns on the rare events exclusively. The patterns discovered are then combined into a rule-based model for prediction.

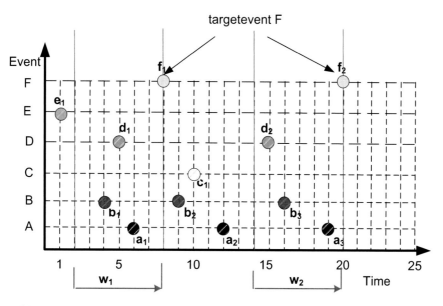

FIGURE 4.10: A fixed window size 6 is given. Predicting rare event F is transformed to searching for the frequent patterns preceding event F. (See color insert.)

The idea of rare event prediction is illustrated in Figure 4.10. There are six event types. An event sequence $S = < e_1, b_1, d_1, a_1, f_1, ..., b_3, a_3, f_2 >$ is presented in the figure. Let D_{target} be the subset of event types to be predicted, e.g., $D_{target} = \{F\}$.

Definition 4.13 *Given a set of event types Z and a window size w, if each event type in Z can be found in a window, then the window is matched by Z. The support of Z is $s\%$ if $s\%$ of windows with size w preceding target events are matched by Z. Z is frequent if s is above a predefined minimum threshold τ.*

For example, in Figure 4.10, $D_{target} = \{F\}$ and $Z = \{A, B, D\}$ matches the sets of events within the two time windows w_1 and w_2 preceding the target event F. Because there are two windows preceding F in total and both windows are matched by Z, the support of Z is 100%. If the threshold is $\tau = 50\%$, then Z is frequent.

Definition 4.14 *The subset of event types Z has confidence $c\%$ if $c\%$ of all windows of size w matched by Z preceding the target event. If the confidence of Z is greater than a predefined threshold, then Z is accurate.*

For example, the confidence of $\{A, B, D\}$ is 100% with respect to the target event F. However, the support and confidence of $\{A, B\}$ are 100% and 67%, respectively.

It is very straightforward to mine the frequent Z. The general idea is to maintain in memory all events with a window of size w. All the events in a single window are considered to be a transaction. Thus the original problem is transformed to mining frequent patterns from a transaction database, where the *Apriori* [18] algorithm is applicable.

In order to mine the accurate Z, the basic idea is to count the number of times each of the frequent event sets occurs outside the time windows preceding target events, denoted by x_2. If the support number of Z is x_1, then the confidence is $\frac{x_1}{x_1+x_2}$. With the help of confidence, the accurate Z can be found.

The rule-based model is built based on frequent and accurate event type sets. All the sets are ranked properly and the rule set is chosen from the event type sets [222].

4.10 Correlated Pattern between Time Series and Event

Despite the importance of correlation analysis in various real applications such as system management and advertisement, limited research efforts have been reported in mining the correlations between two different types of temporal data, that is, the correlation between continuous time series data and temporal event data. Such types of correlation analysis are common, especially in system management. A typical example of system management is given in [150] to illustrate the importance of correlation between time series and events in real applications (as shown in Figure 4.11). There are two types of temporal data in the example. CPU Usage is continuous time series data describing the burden on the CPU. CPU Intensive Program and Disk Intensive Program are temporal events describing the running status of different programs. Every time a CPU intensive program starts, the usage of CPU will increase significantly. However, the CPU usage does not suffer a significant burden due to the starting of the disk intensive program. Therefore, it is considered that the CPU intensive program is highly correlated with CPU Usage, while there is no obvious correlation between the disk intensive program and CPU usage.

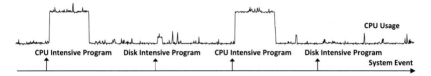

FIGURE 4.11: The CPU usage is continuous time series data, while the system events are identified when starting different types of tasks such as disk intensive task and CPU intensive task.

In [150], a novel approach is proposed to identify the correlation between two types of temporal data in three aspects: (a) determining the existence of correlation between the time series and events, (b) finding the time delay of the correlation, (c) identifying the monotonic effect describing whether the correlation is positive or negative. In order to clearly demonstrate the method to identify the correlation between two types of temporal data, three terms are defined, as shown in Figure 4.12. Given a time window size, the front sub-series is a snippet of time series just before the occurrence of an event and the length of the snippet is fixed with the time window size. Similarly, the rear sub-series is a snippet of time series after the occurrence of the event with the same length as the front sub-series. And a random sub-series is constructed by randomly sampling a snippet of time series with the same window size length. As a consequence, three sets of sub-series can be obtained, including front sub-series set F, rear sub-series set R, and random sub-series set Λ.

The intuitive idea is that, if an event type E and a time series S have a correlation, every time an event E happens, there is a corresponding change of the time series S. Therefore, in [150] a hypothesis test is applied to verify the correlation statistically.

Given an event sequence E and a time series S, let F be the collection of front sub-series, R be the collection of rear sub-series, and Λ be the set of random sub-series. Several cases with respect to the correlation are listed as follows:

1. E and S are correlated and E often occurs after the changes of S,

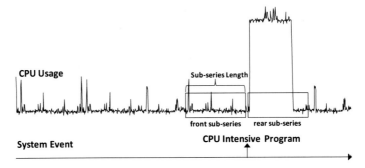

FIGURE 4.12: The front sub-series is a snippet of time series with a fixed time window size before the occurrence of an event, while the rear sub-series is a snippet of time series with the same fixed time window size after the occurrence of the event.

denoted as $S \rightarrow E$, if and only if the distribution of sub-series in F is statistically different from the one in Λ.

2. E and S are correlated and E often occurs before the changes of S, denoted as $E \rightarrow S$, if and only if the distribution of sub-series in R is statistically different from the one in Λ.

3. E and S are correlated if $S \rightarrow E$ or $E \rightarrow S$.

As described above, the correlation analysis can be transformed to a multivariate two-sample hypothesis test problem. A nearest-neighbor-based method is proposed in [150] to analyze the correlation between events and time series.

4.10.1 Pattern Summary

All the event patterns discussed in this chapter are summarized in Table 4.7. Admittedly, there are some other patterns we do not cover, such as spatial-temporal co-location patterns [53, 24, 165].

4.11 A Case Study

In this section, a case study is presented to illustrate the sequential query patterns which are mined from the user query logs of GIS applications. The patterns discovered are then applied to help users with online spatial data analysis.

TABLE 4.7: Summary of mining event patterns

Pattern	Data	Output	Description
Sequential Pattern ([19],[181],[200],[111],[207], [81],[237],[27],[99],[174], [173] [162],[59])	Event sequences	Frequent event subsequences, e.g., $< \{A\}, \{B, C\} >$.	All the subsequences with occurrence frequency not less than a given threshold are discovered. Two categories of algorithms are presented, i.e., Apriori-based and pattern-growth-based algorithms.
Fully Dependent Pattern([141])	An event database	All the items in a pattern are correlated with each other, e.g., {A,B,C} is a fully dependent pattern iff any of its subsets is a fully dependent pattern.	Hypothesis test is applied for identifying the correlation of items in a pattern.
Partially Periodic Dependent Pattern ([152])	An event sequence	Periodic pattern with period p and tolerance δ, e.g., $A \rightarrow_{[p-\delta, p+\delta]} A$.	Periodic patterns are discovered from a given event sequence, where the periodic patterns happen on some segments of the sequence, rather than on the whole sequence. The partially periodic dependent pattern is identified by chi-squared hypothesis test.
Mutually Dependent Pattern([151])	An event sequence	Events in a mutually dependent pattern $\{A, B\}$ depend on each other, i.e., $A \rightarrow B$ and $B \rightarrow A$.	Mutually dependent patterns are identified if the conditional probabilities in both directions are greater than a predefined minimum dependence threshold.
T-Pattern([133, 134])	An event sequence	Patterns like $A \rightarrow_{[\tau-\delta, \tau+\delta]} B$ are discovered, where τ is the time interval and δ is the tolerance.	T-Pattern is defined on two events, indicating that an event implies the other one within a time interval.
Frequent Episode ([157, 158, 16, 15, 170])	An event sequence	Given window size p, an episode containing event pattern is frequent if its frequency is not less than a predefined threshold.	Three types of frequent episodes include the serial episode, the parallel episode, and the composite episode.
Event Burst([121, 201, 235, 164])	An event sequence	Event burst is defined over a period $[t_1, t_2]$ if the occurrence frequency of a given event is high.	The event burst detection can be used for monitoring the occurrence of a significant event automatically.
Rare Event([222])	An event sequence	Given a rare event T, a prediction rule is produced like $\{A, B\} \rightarrow E$.	An anomaly is typically a rare event. The prediction rule can be used to predict the anomaly according to historical events.
Correlation between Time Series and Event ([150])	An event sequence and a time series	Given an event E and a time series S, patterns like $S \rightarrow E$ or $E \rightarrow S$ are produced.	Such patterns are useful in practice, for example, the correlation between CPU usage and running a computing job.

4.11.1 Optimizing Online Spatial Data Analysis

4.11.1.1 Background

TerraFly GeoCloud is designed and developed to support spatial data analysis and visualization [149]. Point and polygon spatial data can be accurately visualized and manipulated in TerraFly GeoClould. It allows users to visualize and share spatial data related to different domains such as real property, crime, and water resources. Online analysis of spatial data is supported by the spatial data analysis engine of TerraFly GeoCloud as well. In order to efficiently support complex spatial data analysis and flexible visualization of the analysis results, MapQL, an SQL-like language, is implemented to represent the analysis queries in TerraFly GeoClould. A MapQL statement is capable of defining an analysis task and customizing the visualization of analysis results. According to the queries, the spatial data analysis engine completes the analysis task and renders the customized visualization of analysis results. For instance, given the real property data, a user may want to explore the house prices near Florida International University. The corresponding MapQL statement for such an exploration is shown in Figure 4.13.

```
SELECT
        '/var/www/cgi-bin/house.png' AS T_ICON_PATH,
        r.price AS T_LABEL,
        '15' AS T_LABEL_SIZE,
        r.geo AS GEO
FROM
        realtor_20121116 r
WHERE
        ST_Distance(r.geo, GeoFromText('POINT(-80.27, 25.757228)')) < 0.3;
```

FIGURE 4.13: A MapQL query on real property data is given, where POINT (-80.27,25.757228) is the location of Florida International University.

A MapQL statement extends the semantics of traditional SQL statements by introducing new reserved key words. As shown in Figure 4.13, *T_ICON_PATH*, *T_LABEL*, *T_LABEL_SIZE*, and *GEO* are four additional reserved words in a MapQL statement. These four reserved key words are used in the *"expression AS < reserved word >"* clause, which provides the expression with additional semantics. In particular, *GEO* describes the spatial search geometry; *T_ICON_PATH* customizes the icon resource for the spatial search geometry; *T_LABEL* provides the icon label to be shown on the map; and *T_LABEL_SIZE* gives the size of the label in pixels. The corresponding spatial query results for the MapQL statement in Figure 4.13 are presented in Figure 4.14.

Compared with using a GIS application programming interface (API), MapQL provides a better interface to facilitate the use of TerraFly map for

FIGURE 4.14: The MapQL query result on real property data is displayed on the map.

both developers and end users without any functionality limitation. Similar to GIS API, MapQL enables users to flexibly create their own maps. However, our further study of TerraFly GeoCloud reveals three interesting and crucial issues which present similar challenges in other online spatial analysis systems.

The first issue is the difficulty in authoring MapQL queries. Though most developers who are familiar with SQL can pick up MapQL quickly, the learning curve for end users who had no idea about SQL before is very steep. Authoring MapQL queries remains a challenge for the vast majority of users. As a result, it is difficult for these end users to utilize MapQL to complete a spatial analysis task from scratch.

The second issue is the complexity of a spatial analysis task. A typical spatial analysis task tends to involve a few sub-tasks. Moreover, those sub-tasks are not completely independent of each other, where the outputs of some sub-tasks are used as the inputs for other sub-tasks. According to the dependencies, a spatial data analysis task can be naturally presented as a workflow. The complexity of building such a workflow turns out to be a great obstacle for users in the online spatial data analysis.

The third issue is the inefficiency of sequentially executing the workflow of a spatial analysis task. Even though the sub-tasks in a workflow are not linearly dependent on each other, the sub-tasks can only be sequentially executed by end users one by one. As a consequence, it fails to take advantage of the distributed environment to optimize the execution of independent sub-tasks in parallel.

The above three issues pose big challenges for users to freely and flexibly explore spatial data using an online spatial analysis system. In this case study, we employ sequential pattern mining algorithms to discover the sequential query patterns from the MapQL query logs of TerraFly GeoCloud. With the help of the sequential query patterns discovered, the workflows of spatial data analysis tasks are first constructed. FIU-Miner [238] is then employed to optimize the execution of the spatial data analysis tasks by maximizing the parallelization of sub-tasks in the corresponding workflow.

System Overview

To address the highlighted issues of TerraFly GeoCloud in Section 4.11.1.1, the online spatial analysis system is optimized by integrating the FIU-Miner framework [238], which is capable of assembling sub-tasks into a workflow in accordance with the dependencies of sub-tasks and scheduling each sub-task for execution in a distributed environment. The overview of the integrated system is given in Figure 4.15.

The system consists of four tiers: User Interface, Geo-Spatial Web Service, Computing Service, and Storage.

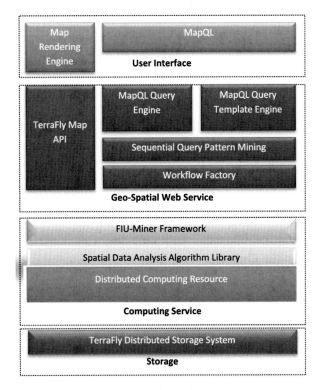

FIGURE 4.15: System overview.

In the layer of User Interface, the Map Rendering Engine is responsible for rendering the geo-objects on the map nicely based on the visualization customized by users. The component of MapQL accepts MapQL statements that describe the spatial analysis task and the required elements for map rendering.

The second layer is Geo-Spatial Web Service. In this layer, TerraFly Map

API provides the interface to access the spatial data for other components in the same layer and the Map Rendering Engine in the User Interface layer. MapQL Query Engine is responsible for analyzing the MapQL statements and guarantees their syntactic and semantic correctness. Sequential Query Pattern Mining is utilized to discover the sequential query pattern from the MapQL query log data. The sequential query patterns discovered can be used to generate the query templates by the MapQL Query Template Engine. Users are able to rewrite the MapQL query template to construct new MapQL statements in the User Interface layer. A sequential query pattern contains a sequence of MapQL queries and is used to form a workflow by the Workflow Factory. Each query in a sequential pattern corresponds to a sub-task in the corresponding workflow.

The third layer is Computing Service. FIU-Miner Framework takes a workflow from the second layer as an input. FIU-Miner takes the load balance of distributed environment into account to schedule the sub-tasks of a workflow for execution. The spatial data analysis library is deployed in the distributed environment. The library can be extended by developers. The computing resource is used to support the spatial data analysis tasks.

The last layer is mainly responsible for storing and managing the spatial data. All the spatial data in TerraFly is stored in the distributed file system, where a replica of the data guarantees the safety and reliability of the system.

Sequential Query Pattern
In our system, users mainly use MapQL statements to accomplish their online spatial data analysis tasks. Although MapQL is powerful and flexible enough to satisfy the analysis requirement of the users, it requires end users to compose the statements, typically from scratch. Based on the user query logs, the sequential MapQL query pattern is proposed to partially address the problem.

Sequential MapQL Query Pattern
Let D be a collection of sequences of queries, denoted as $D = \{S_1, S_2, ..., S_n\}$, where S_i is a sequence of queries occurring within a session, ordered according to their timestamps. Therefore, $S_i =< q_1, q_2, ..., q_i, ..., q_m >$ is a sequence including m queries in temporal order. If q_i is a compound query composed of two sub-queries q_{i0} and q_{i1}, then $S_i =< q_1, q_2, ..., (q_{i0}, q_{i1}), ..., q_m >$. Sub-queries in parentheses are from a compound query occurring at the same timestamp.

A k-subsequence of S_i is a sequence of queries with length k denoted as $T =< t_1, t_2, ..., t_k >$, where each $t \in T$ corresponds to only one query $q \in S_i$, and all the queries in T are kept in temporal order. $T \sqsubseteq S_i$ is used to indicate that T is a subsequence of S_i.

Given the query sequence data collection D, a sequential query pattern is a query sequence whose occurrence frequency in the query log D is no less than a user-specified threshold $min\_support$. Formally, the support of sequence T

is defined as

$$support(T) = |\{S_i | S_i \in D \wedge T \sqsubseteq S_i\}|.$$

A sequence T is a sequential query pattern only if $support(T) \geq min\_support$.

The process of discovering all the sequential query patterns from the MapQL logs generally consists of two stages. The first stage is to generalize the representation of MapQL statements by parsing the MapQL text into syntax units. Based on the syntax representation of MapQL statements, the second stage is to mine the sequential query patterns from the sequences of MapQL statements.

Representation of MapQL

As shown in Figure 4.15, the MapQL Query Engine collects the MapQL statements and records them in the log files. A snippet of MapQL logs is given in Table 4.8. Each MapQL statement is associated with a user session ID and a timestamp. All the statements are organized in temporal order. Those MapQL statements sharing the same session ID are those issued by a user within a session. Our goal is to discover interesting patterns from the query logs. For example, according to the log data in the Table 4.8, an interesting pattern is that users who viewed a particular street are more likely to look for the hotels along that street.

In order to discover patterns from the query logs, intuitively, existing sequential pattern mining algorithms can be directly applied to the raw logs of MapQL statements, where different texts of MapQL statements are treated as different items. However, representing a query item by the text of the MapQL statement is often too specific. As a consequence, it is difficult to discover the meaningful sequential patterns with such representations. For instance, the first and third records in Table 4.8 are identified as different query items during sequential query pattern mining, although both MapQL statements share the same semantics (i.e., locating a street given its partial name).

To address the aforementioned problem, the representation of a query in our system is generalized by parsing a MapQL statement into a collection of syntax units. The syntax units are organized as a syntax tree. For instance, the syntax tree for the first record of Table 4.8 is presented in Figure 4.16. There are two types of labels in the node of the syntax tree. One is the type of syntax unit, such as "Select Clause." The other label in the parenthesis is the content of a syntax unit, for example, "sw 8th." Provided with the syntax tree, the MapQL query can be generalized by representing any nodes with their types instead of their actual contents. For instance, assuming the node with 'Value' type in the syntax tree is represented as "#Value#" rather than using its text content, the original MapQL statements in both the first and third row of Table 4.8 are rewritten as "SELECT geo FROM street WHERE name LIKE #Value#;". Therefore, the two MapQL statements with the same semantics share the same query item. In addition, to simplify the extraction of patterns, each query item is identified with a unique integer number.

TABLE 4.8: A snippet of MapQL logs

Session ID	Timestamp	MapQL statement
1	20140301 13:26:33	SELECT geo FROM street WHERE name LIKE 'sw 8th';
1	20140301 13:28:26	SELECT h.name FROM street s LEFT JOIN hotel h ON $ST\_Distance(s.geo, h.geo) < 0.05$ WHERE s.name = 'sw8 th' AND h.star $>=$ 4;
2	20140315 14:21:03	select geo from street where name like 'turnpike';
2	20140315 14:25:21	SELECT h.name FROM street s LEFT JOIN hotel h ON $ST\_Distance(s.geo, h.geo) < 0.05$ WHERE s.name = 'turnpike' AND h.star $>=$ 4;
3	20140316 10:23:08	SELECT zip FROM us_zip;
4	20140319 11:19:21	SELECT count(*) FROM hotel;
...	...	...

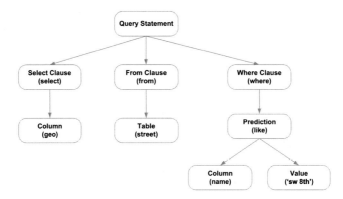

FIGURE 4.16: The syntax tree for a MapQL statement "SELECT geo FROM street WHERE name LIKE 'sw 8th';".

4.11.1.2 Pattern Mining

Mining Sequential Query Patterns

Based on the properly generalized representation of a MapQL query, the PrefixSpan algorithm [173] is applied to efficiently discover all the sequential query patterns from the MapQL query log data.

The main idea of the PrefixSpan algorithm is to recursively partition the whole dataset into some sub-datasets, where the query sequences in a sub-dataset share the same prefix subsequence. The number of query sequences in each sub-dataset indicates the *support* of its corresponding prefix subsequence. If a prefix subsequence T whose *support* is no less than the user specified threshold $min\_support$, T is a sequential query pattern. Given two sequences T and R, $T \sqsubseteq R$ if T is a subsequence of R. An important property (i.e., downward closure property) is that R cannot be a sequential query pattern if T is not a sequential query pattern. According to the property, the recursive partition to search for a super-pattern is not terminated until the size of current the sub-dataset is smaller than $min\_support$.

The PrefixSpan algorithm is illustrated in Figure 4.17. The top table presents the original collection of query sequences which contains two sequences of queries $S_1 = < (q_0, q_1) >$ and $S_2 = < (q_0), (q_2) >$. Sequence S_1 has only one compound query composed of q_0 and q_1. The other sequence S_2 has two queries named q_0 and q_2. Let $min\_support = 2$. The procedure of mining sequential query patterns is described as follows.

1. Find the frequent subsequences with a single query: $< q_0 >$, $< q_1 >$, $< q_2 >$.

2. Take the subsequences found in step 1 as the prefixes. Based on the prefixes, the original dataset is partitioned into three sub-datasets, where each of them is specified by a prefix subsequence. The support of the

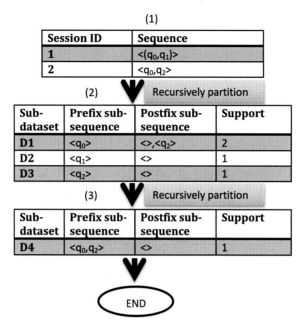

FIGURE 4.17: An example illustrating the PrefixSpan algorithm.

prefix subsequence is the number of postfix sequences in its corresponding sub-dataset. The prefix patterns are extracted if their supports are larger than $min\_support$. Only the prefix subsequence in $D1$ is a sequential query pattern.

3. Recursively partition $D1$. As a result, only one sub-dataset is generated and its support is 1.

4. Terminate the partition since no new prefix patterns can be further derived.

In the end, PrefixSpan discovers one sequential query pattern $< q_0 >$.

Query Template
Query template is generated by the MapQL Query Template Engine in the system. This function alleviates the burden of users since MapQL queries can be composed by rewriting query templates. Based on the sequential query patterns discovered, a query template is generated by Algorithm templateGen [239]. This algorithm scans the syntax trees in the sequential query pattern and replaces the specific table, column, and constant value with template parameters. The algorithm guarantees that the same table, column, or constant value appearing at multiple places, even multiple queries of a sequence, ac-

quires the same template parameter. Users can easily convert the template to executable queries by assigning the template parameters with specific values.

```
Template(#arg1#, #arg2#, #arg3#):

    SELECT      geo
    FROM        street
    WHERE
                name LIKE #arg1#;

    SELECT      h.name
    FROM        street s
    LEFT JOIN   hotel h
    ON          ST_Distance(s.geo,h.geo) < #arg2#
    WHERE       s.name LIKE #arg1#
    AND         h.star >= #arg3#;
```

FIGURE 4.18: Example of a generated template.

Given a sequential query pattern that contains the two queries with session ID 1 in Table 4.8, we can apply Algorithm templateGen [239] to generate the template for the sequential query pattern. The generated template is shown in Figure 4.18. This template has three parameters (i.e., #arg1#, #arg2#, #arg3#). Provided with the values of these parameters, the executable sequence of queries can be easily derived from the template.

Spatial Data Analysis Workflow

All the MapQL queries in a sequential pattern are organized in a workflow, where the template parameters indicate the data transmission between queries. A sequence of queries constitutes a spatial data analysis task and a typical spatial data analysis task often involves a few sub-tasks. The dependencies among those sub-tasks make spatial data analysis very complicated. The complexity of spatial data analysis dictates the support of workflow. In our system, The Workflow Factory is designed and implemented in support of executing a complex spatial data analysis task in a workflow. A workflow is represented as a directed and connected graph consisting of nodes (denoting the sub-tasks) and edges (describing the dependencies among the sub-tasks). Data transmission between dependent sub-tasks is supported in our system.

In order to facilitate the spatial data analysis, we design seven types of nodes, as shown in Figure 4.19.

1. **Start Node** This type of node indicates the start of the workflow. There is only one such node in a valid workflow. This start node must link to one other node.

2. **Parallel Node** This type of node has one input link and more than one output link. After the work is completed in the parent node, the parallel

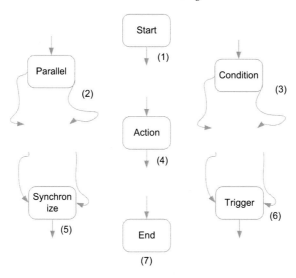

FIGURE 4.19: Node types in a workflow.

node triggers the sub-tasks in its children nodes. All the sub-tasks of its children are executed in parallel.

3. **Condition Node** One input link and more than one output link are associated with this type of node. When the control flow reaches a condition node, it will check the input data and then move along one of its output links.

4. **Action Node** One input link and one output link are associated with this type of node. It often accommodates the sub-tasks for spatial data analysis. The data from the input link is fed into the sub-task and the resulting data of this sub-task is forwarded along its output link.

5. **Synchronize Node** This type of node has more than one input link and one output link. This node does not direct the control flow to its output link until all the sub-tasks in its parent nodes are completed.

6. **Trigger Node** More than one input link and one output link are associated with this type of node. The node starts the sub-tasks in its output link once one of the sub-tasks in its parent nodes is finished.

7. **End Node** Any valid workflow should have one and only one end node. It indicates the end of the workflow.

Based on the template generated in Figure 4.18, two simple workflows are constructed in Figure 4.20. These two workflows accomplish the same spatial data analysis task described in Figure 4.18. In (1) of Figure 4.20, the two

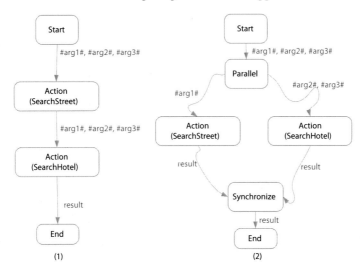

FIGURE 4.20: Workflow examples.

sub-tasks (i.e., SearchStreet and SearchHotel) are executed sequentially. However, SearchStreet needs the template parameter #arg1# as its input, while SearchHotel needs all three parameters. Provided with the three parameters, both sub-tasks can be executed independently. Thus, in (2) of Figure 4.20, a parallel workflow is introduced to complete the spatial data analysis task. Since our data analysis tasks are scheduled by FIU-Miner, which takes full advantage of the distributed environment, the parallel workflow is preferable to our system in terms of efficiency.

4.11.1.3   System Demonstration

Besides providing the powerful API to support GIS applications, the TerraFly platform has a rich collection of GIS datasets. TerraFly has US and Canada road data, US Census demographic and socioeconomic data, the property lines and ownership data of 110 million parcels, 15 million records of businesses with company stats and management roles and contacts, 2 million physicians with expertise detail, various public place datasets, Wikipedia, extensive global environmental data, etc. Users can explore these datasets by issuing MapQL queries in our system.

House Property Exploration

The proposed system provides an optimized solution to spatial data analysis problems by explicitly constructing a workflow. It supports many different applications by analyzing the corresponding datasets. One typical application scenario is to locate a house property with a good appreciation potential for

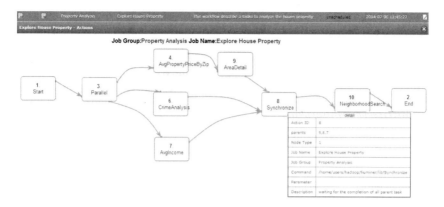

FIGURE 4.21: The workflow of searching for house properties with a good appreciation potential. All the sub-tasks in the workflow are scheduled by FIU-Miner and are executed in the distributed environment.

investment. Intuitively, it is believed that a property is deserving of investment if the price of the property is lower than the ones of surrounding properties. Our system is capable of helping users (e.g., investors) easily and conveniently identify such properties. According to the historical query logs collected in our system, the sequential query patterns are extracted. Based on the sequential query patterns discovered, the query templates are then generated automatically. The templates related to the house property case study are assembled to build a workflow for house property data analysis. The workflow is presented in Figure 4.21.

In the workflow, there are nine sub-tasks, denoted as rectangles, in the complete house property analysis. A user can view the detailed information of each sub-task from a pop-up layer as long as the mouse hovers on the corresponding node. The workflow begins with a start node, which is used to prepare the required setting and parameters. The start node links to the parallel node with three out links. The parallel node indicates that the three sub-tasks along its out links can be executed simultaneously.

The AvgPropertyPriceByZip node in the workflow calculates the average property price. An overview of analysis results is presented in Figure 4.22. Note that the property prices of red regions are higher than those of blue regions. From the overview, users are often interested in the regions marked with a green circle since the average property price of the region is lower than the ones of its surroundings.

In the next step, users check more detailed information on the region in the green circle by conducting data analysis in the AreaDetail node. The spatial auto-correlation analysis on the average property prices by zip code data in Miami is conducted in this node and the analysis results are shown in Figure 4.23. Each point in the scatter plot corresponds to one zip code. Moran's I

FIGURE 4.22: Average property prices by zip code in Miami. (See color insert.)

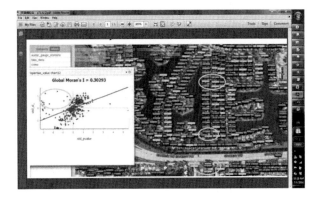

FIGURE 4.23: Detailed properties in Miami.

measure is applied during the auto-correlation analysis [25, 131]. The points in the first and third quadrants show positive associations with their surroundings, while the points in the second and fourth quadrants indicate negative associations. Herein, users are generally interested in the points of the second quadrant, having lower property prices than the ones of their surrounding regions. The interesting points are marked with yellow circles. The analysis leads to the result that most of the cheap properties with good appreciation potential are along the Gratigny Pkwy.

In order to make sure that the areas with cheap properties have good appreciation potential, spatial data analysis to investigate the crime rate and average income of these areas is conducted. The two data analysis sub-tasks are described in CrimeAnalysis and AvgIncome nodes, respectively. These two sub-tasks are executed in parallel with the properties analysis. The Synchronize node waits for the completion of all three sub-tasks along the in links. Parallel execution accelerates the whole spatial data analysis and reduces the time cost.

```
SELECT
  CASE
    WHEN    h.pvalue >= 400000
      THEN    '/var/www/cgi-bin/redhouse.png'
    WHEN    h.pvalue BETWEEN 200000 AND 400000
      THEN    '/var/www/cgi-bin/bluehouse.png'
    WHEN    h.pvalue BETWEEN 100000 AND 200000
      THEN    '/var/www/cgi-bin/bluehouse.png'
    ELSE    '/var/www/cgi-bin/darkhouse.png'
  END AS T_ICON_PATH,
  h.geo AS GEO
FROM
    osm_fl o
  LEFT JOIN
    south_florida_house_price h
  ON
    ST_Distance(o.geo, h.geo) < 0.05
WHERE
    o.name = #arg1# AND
    h.std_pvalue < 0 AND
    h.std_sl_pvalue > 0;
```

FIGURE 4.24: A template for searching the neighborhood, given the partial name of the street.

Without discovering any abnormalities in the crime rate and average income, users proceed to acquire more detailed property information along the Gratigny Pkwy by executing the sub-task in the NeighborhoodSearch node. The MapQL query given in Figure 4.24 is executed in the NeighborhoodSearch node by passing the 'Gratigny Pkwy' as the input parameter. The MapQL statement employs different colors to mark the regions with various property prices. The final analysis results are presented in Figure 4.25. The dark regions have the cheapest property prices and good appreciation potential.

FIGURE 4.25: Final analysis results. (See color insert.)

With the completion of the sub-task in the NeighborhoodSearch node, the control flow reaches the end node of the workflow. Compared to the analysis procedure without workflow, where sub-tasks can only be executed sequentially, our system takes full advantage of FIU-Miner to schedule multiple tasks simultaneously in the distributed environments. It greatly reduces the time consumed by a complex spatial data analysis task and increases the throughput of our system.

4.12 Conclusion

In this chapter, we provide a review of different types of event patterns and present the corresponding event mining techniques as well as application scenarios. All the event patterns discussed in this chapter are summarized in Table 4.7.

Although many patterns have been proposed in different application domains, there are still some challenges to be addressed for temporal pattern discovery in the future.

1. Facing various patterns, the analysts demand for a general and principle framework which can help to determine the most appropriate temporal patterns to address the specific problems for a given application.

2. Most event mining methods mentioned in this chapter require hypothesis tests to identify the temporal patterns. As a consequence, most of these methods are time consuming. A big challenge is how to efficiently discover temporal patterns, especially when large amounts of event data are available.

3. It is very common that temporal data contain both categorical events and numerical time series. An interesting challenge is how to best analyze all possible temporal data in a uniform framework. Although some methods are presented in the literature for correlation analysis between time series and event data, their accuracy of pattern discovery is sensitive to the predefined time window size.

4.13 Glossary

Composite Episode: An episode containing both parallel events and serial events.

Dependent Pattern: Event pattern containing correlated events.

Episode: A time window containing several events.

Event: Temporal data with discrete data item values.

Event Burst: Event with a high frequency of occurrence during a time period.

Event Pattern: Unexpected trends or other subtle relationships among events.

Parallel Episode: An episode containing events occurring in a parallel model.

Rare Event: Event with a relatively low occurrence frequency compared with other frequent events.

Sequential Pattern: Frequent subsequences from a sequence database.

Serial Episode: An episode containing events in a serial order.

Time Lag: The time interval between events, describing the temporal order of events.

Time Series: Temporal data with continuous data item values.

Chapter 5

Mining Time Lags

Chunqiu Zeng, Liang Tang, and Tao Li

Florida International University
Nanjing University of Posts and Telecommunications

5.1 Introduction

The importance of mining time lags of hidden temporal dependencies from sequential data is highlighted in many domains, including system management, stock market analysis, climate monitoring, and more [241].

Time lag, one of the key features in various temporal patterns (shown in Table 5.1), plays an important role in discovering evolving trends of coming events and predicting the future behavior of its corresponding system. For instance, a network adapter problem typically leads to disconnecting an instant messaging tool running on that machine after several failed retries for communication. In this scenario, the event of *network interface down* leads to a *disconnect event* of the instant messaging tool after several failed re-tries with

123

TABLE 5.1: Temporal patterns with time lag

Temporal Pattern	An Example	Temporal Dependency with Lag Interval
Mutually dependent pattern [151]	$\{A, B\}$	$A \rightarrow_{[0,\delta]} B$, $B \rightarrow_{[0,\delta]} A$
Partially periodic pattern [152]	A with periodic p and a given time tolerance δ	$A \rightarrow_{[p-\delta, p+\delta]} A$
Frequent episode pattern [158]	$A \rightarrow B \rightarrow C$ with a given time window p	$A \rightarrow_{[0,p]} B$, $B \rightarrow_{[0,p]} C$
Loose temporal pattern [134]	B follows by A before time t	$A \rightarrow_{[0,t]} B$
Stringent temporal pattern [134]	B follows by A about time t with a given time tolerance δ	$A \rightarrow_{[t-\delta, t+\delta]} B$

a given time lag. The temporal dependencies among events are characterized by time lags. Time lags provide temporal information for building a fault-error-failure chain [26], which is useful for root cause analysis. In addition, events triggered by a single issue can be correlated given the appropriate time lags. Merging those correlated events in one ticket saves effort of an administrator for problem diagnosis and incident resolution. Thus, the discovery of the time lag is a very important task during temporal dependency mining.

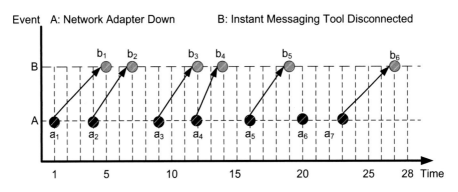

FIGURE 5.1: The temporal dependencies between A and B are denoted as direct edges.

The situation in real-world systems becomes complicated due to the limitation of sequential data collecting methods and the inherent complexity of the systems. However, events detected by monitoring systems are typically studied with the following assumption: the time lag between correlated events is constant and fluctuations are limited and can be ignored [212]. Although such an approach is undoubtedly applicable to a wide range of systems, fluctuations can render the deterministic classical picture qualitatively incorrect, especially when correlating events are limited. Taking the randomness of the time lag into account makes the detection of the hidden time lags between interleaved events a challenging task.

First, the fluctuating interleaved temporal dependencies pose a challenging problem when attempting to discover the correct hidden time lag between two events. For example, two events A and B, corresponding to the events *network interface down* and *disconnect event* of an instant messaging tool, respectively, are shown in Figure 5.1. Both A and B occur with multiple instances in the sequential dataset. The ith instance of A and the jth instance of B are associated with their timestamps a_i and b_j. Because the true temporal dependencies are interleaved with each other, it is difficult to determine which b_j is implied by a given a_i. The different mapping relationships between a_i and b_j lead to varying time lags. In this example, a_1 can be mapped to any b_j. Therefore, the time lag ranges from $b_1 - a_1$ to $b_6 - a_1$ time units. It is not feasible to find the time lag with an exhaustive search from large scale sequential event data.

Second, due to the clocks out of sync and the limitations of the data collecting method, the time lags presented in the sequential data may oscillate with noise. In Figure 5.1, a_6 does not correspond to any instance of event B for several possible reasons: (1) its corresponding instance of B is missing from the sequential dataset; (2) the network adapter returns to normality in such a short time that there is no need to eject an instance of B since the instant messaging tool successfully continues to work after only one try; and (3) even though the correct instance mapping between A and B is provided, time lags are still observed with different values due to recording errors brought about by system monitoring.

In summary, the above difficulties pose a big challenge for time lag mining. In this chapter, both non-parametric methods and parametric methods are presented for discovering the time lag of temporal dependencies.

5.2 Non-Parametric Method

Previous work for discovering temporal dependencies does not consider interleaved dependencies [133, 44, 158]. For $A \rightarrow B$ where A and B are events, they assume that an item A can only have a dependency with its first following B. However, it is possible that an item A has a dependency with any following B. For example, in Figure 5.2, the time lag for two dependent A and B is from 5 to 6 minutes, but the time lag for two adjacent A's is only 4 minutes. All A's have a dependency with the second following B, not the first following B. Hence, the dependencies among these dependent A and B are interleave. For two item types, the numbers of timestamps are both $O(n)$. The number of possible time lags is $O(n^2)$. Thus, the number of lag intervals is $O(n^4)$. The challenge of our work is how to efficiently find appropriate lag intervals over the $O(n^4)$ candidates.

Let N be the number of event types and n be the number of distinct timestamps. An efficient algorithm with time complexity $O(n^2 log n)$ and space complexity $O(N)$ is proposed in [212].

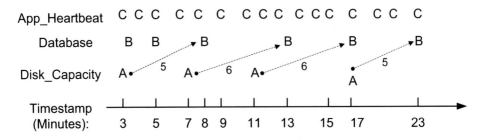

FIGURE 5.2: Lag interval for temporal dependency.

5.2.1 Qualified Lag Interval

Given an item sequence $S = x_1 x_2 ... x_N$, x_i denotes the type of the ith item, and $t(x_i)$ denotes the timestamp of x_i, $i = 1, 2, ..., N$. Intuitively, if there is a temporal dependency $A \rightarrow_{[t_1, t_2]} B$ in S, there must be a lot of A's that are followed by some B with a time lag in $[t_1, t_2]$. Let $n_{[t_1, t_2]}$ denote the observed number of A's in this situation. For instance, in Figure 5.2, every A is followed by a B with a time lag of 5 or 6 minutes, so $n_{[5,6]} = 4$. Only the second A is followed by a B with a time lag of 0 or 1 minute, so $n_{[0,1]} = 1$. Let $r = [t_1, t_2]$ be a lag interval. One question is what is the minimum required n_r that we can utilize to identify the dependency of A and B with r. In this example, the minimum required n_r cannot be greater than 4 since the sequence has at most 4 A's. However, if we let $r = [0, +\infty]$, we can easily have $n_r = 4$. Ma and Hellerstein [152] proposed a chi-square test approach to determine the minimum required n_r, where the chi-square statistic measures the degree of independence by comparing the observed n_r with the expected n_r under the independent assumption. The null distribution of the statistic is approximated by the chi-squared distribution with 1 degree of freedom. Let χ_r^2 denote the chi-square statistic for n_r. A high χ_r^2 indicates the observed n_r in the given sequence cannot be explained by randomness. The chi-square statistic is defined as follows:

$$\chi_r^2 = \frac{(n_r - n_A P_r)^2}{n_A P_r (1 - P_r)}, \tag{5.1}$$

where n_A is the number of A's in the data sequence, and P_r is the probability of a B appearing in r from a random sequence. Hence, $n_A P_r$ is the expected number of A's that are followed by some B with a time lag in r. $n_A P_r (1 - P_r)$ is the variance. Note that the random sequence should have the same sampling rate for B as the given sequence S. The randomness is only for the positions of B items. It is known that a random sequence usually follows the Poisson process, which assumes the probability of an item appearing in an interval is proportional to the length of the interval [186]. Therefore,

$$P_r = |r| \cdot \frac{n_B}{T}, \tag{5.2}$$

where $|r|$ is the length of r, $|r| = t_2 - t_1 + w_B$, w_B is the minimum time lag of two adjacent B's, $w_B > 0$, and n_B is the number of B's in S. For lag interval r, the absolute length is $t_2 - t_1$. w_B is added to $|r|$ because without w_B when $t_1 = t_2$, $|r| = 0$, P_r is always 0 no matter how large the n_B is. As a result, χ_r^2 would be overestimated. In reality, the timestamps of items are discrete samples, and w_B is the observed sampling period for B items. Hence, the probability of a B appearing in $t_2 - t_1$ time units is equal to the probability of a B appearing in $t_2 - t_1 + w_B$ time units.

The value of χ_r^2 is defined in terms of a confidence level. For example, a 95% confidence level corresponds to $\chi_r^2 = 3.84$. Based on Eq.(5.1), the observed n_r should be greater than $\sqrt{3.84 n_A P_r (1 - P_r)} + n_A P_r$. Note that we only care about positive dependencies, so

$$n_r - n_A P_r > 0. \tag{5.3}$$

To ensure a discovered temporal dependency fits the entire data sequence, *support* [18, 200, 152] is used in our work. For $A \rightarrow_r B$, the support $supp_A(r)$ (or $supp_B(r)$) is the number of A's (or B's) that satisfies $A \rightarrow_r B$ divided by the total number of items N. *minsup* is the minimum threshold for both $supp_A(r)$ and $supp_B(r)$ specified by the user [200, 152]. Based on the two minimum thresholds χ_c^2 and *minsup*, Definition 5.1 defines the qualified lag interval that we try to find.

Definition 5.1 *Given an item sequence S with two item types A and B, a lag interval $r = [t_1, t_2]$ is qualified if and only if $\chi_r^2 > \chi_c^2$, $supp_A(r) > minsup$, and $supp_B(r) > minsup$, where χ_c^2 and minsup are two minimum thresholds specified by the user.*

A straightforward algorithm (i.e., a *brute-force* algorithm) is developed for finding all qualified lag intervals first. Then, *STScan* and *STScan** algorithms, which are much more efficient, are proposed in [212].

5.2.2 Brute-Force Algorithm

To find all qualified lag intervals, a straightforward algorithm is to enumerate all possible lag intervals, compute their χ_r^2 and supports, and then check whether they are qualified or not. This algorithm is called *brute-force*. Clearly, its time cost is very large. Let n be the number of distinct timestamps of S and r be an interval $r = [t_1, t_2]$. The numbers of possible t_1 and t_2 are $O(n^2)$, and then the number of possible r is $O(n^4)$. For each lag interval, there is at least $O(n)$ cost to scan the entire sequence S to compute the χ_r^2 and the supports. Therefore, the overall time cost of the *brute-force* algorithm is $O(n^5)$, which is not affordable for large data sequences.

5.2.3   STScan Algorithm

To avoid re-scanning the data sequence, we develop an algorithm based on a sorted table. A sorted table is a sorted linked list with a collection of sorted integer arrays. Each entry of the linked list is attached to two sorted integer arrays. Figure 5.3 shows an example of the sorted array. In our algorithm,

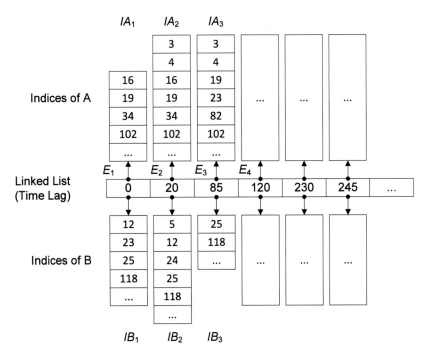

FIGURE 5.3: A sorted table.

we store every time lag $t(x_j) - t(x_i)$ into each entry of the linked list, where $x_i = A$, $x_j = B$, and i, j are integers from 1 to N. Two arrays attached to the entry $t(x_j) - t(x_i)$ are the collections of i and j. In other words, the two arrays are the indices of A's and B's. Let E_i denote the ith entry of the linked list and $v(E_i)$ denote the time lag stored at E_i. IA_i and IB_i denote the indices of A's and B's that are attached to E_i. For example, in Figure 5.3, $x_3 = A$, $x_5 = B$, $t(x_5) - t(x_3) = 20$. Since $v(E_2) = 20$, IA_2 contains 3 and IB_2 contains 5. Any feasible lag interval can be represented as a subsegment of the linked list. For example, in Figure 5.3, $E_2 E_3 E_4$ represents the lag interval $[20, 120]$.

To create the sorted table for a sequence S, each time lag between an A and a B is first inserted into a red-black tree. The key of the red-black tree node is the time lag, and the value is the pair of indices of A and B. Once the tree is built, we traverse the tree in ascending order to create the linked list of the sorted table. In the sequence S, the numbers of A and B are both $O(N)$, so the number of $t(x_j) - t(x_i)$ is $O(N^2)$. The time cost of creating the red-black tree is $O(N^2 \log N^2) = O(N^2 \log N)$. Traversing the tree costs $O(N^2)$. Hence, the overall time cost of creating a sorted table is $O(N^2 \log N)$, which is the known lower bound of sorting $X + Y$ where X and Y are two variables [103]. The linked list has $O(N^2)$ entries, and each attached integer array has $O(N)$ elements, so it seems that the space cost of a sorted table is $O(N^2 \cdot N) = O(N^3)$. However, Lemma 5.1 shows that the actual space cost of a sorted table is $O(N^2)$, which is same as the red-black tree.

Lemma 5.1 *Given an item sequence S having N items, the space cost of its sorted table is $O(N^2)$.*

Proof: Since the numbers of A's and B's are both $O(N)$, the number of pairs (x_i, x_j) is $O(N^2)$, where $x_i = A$, $x_j = B$, $x_i, x_j \in S$. Every pair is associated with three entries in the sorted table: the timestamp distance, the index of an A, and the index of a B. Therefore, each pair (x_i, x_j) introduces 3 space cost. The total space cost of the sorted table is $O(3N^2) = O(N^2)$.

Once the sorted table is created, finding all qualified lag intervals is scanning the subsegments of the linked list. However, the number of entries in the linked list is $O(N^2)$, so there are $O(N^4)$ distinct subsegments. Scanning all subsegments is still time consuming. Fortunately, based on the minimum thresholds on the chi-square statistic and the support, the length of a qualified lag interval cannot be large.

Lemma 5.2 *Given two minimum thresholds χ_c^2 and minsup, the length of any qualified lag interval is less than $\frac{T}{N} \cdot \frac{1}{minsup}$.*

Proof: Let r be a qualified lag interval. Based on Eq.(5.1) and Inequality.(5.3), χ_r^2 increases along with n_r. Since $n_r \leq n_A$,

$$\frac{(n_A - n_A P_r)^2}{n_A P_r(1 - P_r)} \geq \chi_r^2 > \chi_c^2 \implies P_r < \frac{n_A}{\chi_c^2 + n_A}.$$

By substituting Eq.(5.2) in the previous inequality,

$$|r| < \frac{n_A}{\chi_c^2 + n_A} \cdot \frac{T}{n_B}.$$

Since $n_B > N \cdot minsup$, $\chi_c^2 > 0$, we have

$$|r| < \frac{T}{N} \cdot \frac{1}{minsup} = |r|_{max}.$$

$\frac{T}{N}$ is exactly the average period of items, which is determined by the sampling rate of this sequence. For example, in system event sequences, the monitoring system checks the system status every 30 seconds and records system events into the sequence. The average period of items is 30 seconds. Therefore, we consider $\frac{T}{N}$ as a constant. Since $minsup$ is also a constant, $|r|_{max}$ is also a constant.

Algorithm 2 *STScan* $(S, A, B, ST, \chi_c^2, minsup)$

Input: S: input sequence; A, B: two item types; ST: sorted table; χ_c^2: minimum chi-square statistic threshold; $minsup$: minimum support.

Output: a set of qualified lag intervals;

1: $R \leftarrow \emptyset$
2: Scan S to find w_B
3: **for** $i = 1$ to $len(ST)$ **do**
4:     $IA_r \leftarrow \emptyset$, $IB_r \leftarrow \emptyset$
5:     $t_1 \leftarrow v(E_i)$
6:     $j \leftarrow 0$
7:     **while** $i + j \leq len(ST)$ **do**
8:         $t_2 \leftarrow v(E_{i+j})$
9:         $r \leftarrow [t_1, t_2]$
10:        $|r| \leftarrow t_2 - t_1 + w_B$
11:        **if** $|r| \geq |r|_{max}$ **then**
12:            **break**
13:        **end if**
14:        $IA_r \leftarrow IA_r \cup IA_{i+j}$
15:        $IB_r \leftarrow IB_r \cup IB_{i+j}$
16:        $j \leftarrow j + 1$
17:        **if** $|IA_r|/N \leq minsup$ **or** $|IB_r|/N \leq minsup$ **then**
18:            **continue**
19:        **end if**
20:        Calculate χ_r^2 from $|IA_r|$ and $|r|$
21:        **if** $\chi_r^2 > \chi_c^2$ **then**
22:            $R \leftarrow R \cup r$
23:        **end if**
24:     **end while**
25: **end for**
26: **return** R

Algorithm *STScan* states the pseudocode for finding all qualified lag intervals. $len(ST)$ denotes the number of entries of the linked list in sorted table ST. This algorithm sequentially scans all subsegments starting with E_1, E_2,..., $E_{len(ST)}$. Based on Lemma 5.2, it only scans the subsegment with $|r| < |r|_{max}$. To calculate the χ_r^2 and the supports, for each subsegment, it cumulatively stores the aggregate indices of A's and B's and the corresponding lag interval r. For each subsegment, $n_r = |IA_r|$, $supp_A(r) = |IA_r|/N$, and $supp_B(r) = |IB_r|/N$.

Lemma 5.3 *The time cost of* STScan *is* $O(N^2)$, *where* N *is the number of items in the data sequence.*

Proof: For each entry E_{i+j} in the linked list, the time cost of merging IA_{i+j} and IB_{i+j} to IA_r and IB_r is $|IA_{i+j}| + |IB_{i+j}|$ by using a hash table. Let l_i be the largest length of the scanned subsegments starting at E_i. Let l_{max} be the maximum l_i, $i = 1, ..., len(ST)$. The total time cost is

$$
\begin{aligned}
T(N) &= \sum_{i=1}^{len(ST)} \sum_{j=0}^{l_i-1} (|IA_{i+j}| + |IB_{i+j}|) \\
&\leq \sum_{i=1}^{len(ST)} \sum_{j=0}^{l_{max}-1} (|IA_{i+j}| + |IB_{i+j}|) \\
&\leq l_{max} \cdot \sum_{i=1}^{len(ST)} (|IA_i| + |IB_i|)
\end{aligned}
$$

$\sum_{i=1}^{len(ST)} (|IA_i| + |IB_i|)$ is exactly the total number of integers in all integer arrays. Based on Lemma 5.1, $\sum_{i=1}^{len(ST)} (|IA_i| + |IB_i|) = O(N^2)$. Then $T(N) = O(l_{max} \cdot N^2)$. Let $E_k...E_{k+l}$ be the subsegment for a qualified lag interval, $v(E_{k+i}) \geq 0$, $i = 0, ..., l$. Note that the length of this lag interval is $|r| = v(E_{k+l_{max}}) - v(E_k) < |r|_{max}$. Then $l_{max} < |r|_{max}$ and l_{max} does not depend on N. Assuming Δ_E is the average $v(E_{k+1}) - v(E_k)$, $k = 1, ..., len(ST) - 1$, we obtain a tighter bound of l_{max}, i.e., $l_{max} \leq |r|_{max}/\Delta_E \leq \frac{T}{N \cdot \Delta_E} \cdot \frac{1}{minsup}$. Therefore, the overall time cost is $T(N) = O(N^2)$.

5.2.4   STScan* Algorithm

To reduce the space cost of the *STScan* algorithm, we develop an improved algorithm *STScan** which utilizes an incremental sorted table and sequence compression.

A. Incremental Sorted Table

Lemma 5.1 shows the space cost of a complete sorted table is $O(N^2)$. Algorithm *STScan* sequentially scans the subsegments starting from E_1 to $E_{len(ST)}$, so it does not need to access every entry at every time. Based on this observation, we develop an incremental sorted table based algorithm with an $O(N)$ space cost. This algorithm incrementally creates the entries of the sorted table along with the subsegment scanning process.

The linked list of a sorted table can be created by merging all time lag lists of A's (Figure 5.4), where A_i and B_j denote the i-th A and the j-th B, $i, j = 1, 2, ...$ The j-th entry in the list of A_i stores $t(B_j) - t(A_i)$. The time lag lists of all A's are not necessary to be created in the memory because we only need to know $t(B_j)$ and $t(A_j)$. This can be done just with indices arrays of all A's and all B's, respectively. By using an N-way merging algorithm, each entry of the linked list would be created sequentially. The indices of A's and B's attached to each entry are also recorded during the merging process. Based on Lemma 5.2, the length of a qualified lag interval is at most $|r|_{max}$. Therefore, we only keep track of the recent l_{max} entries. The space cost for storing l_{max} entries is at most $O(l_{max} \cdot N) = O(N)$. A heap used by the merging process

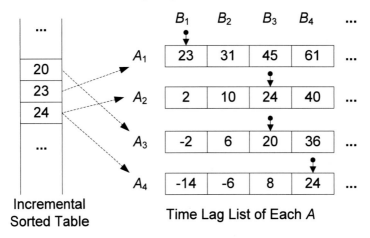

FIGURE 5.4: Incremental sorted table.

costs $O(N)$ space. Then, the overall space cost of the incremental sorted table is $O(N)$. The time cost of merging $O(N)$ lists with a total of $O(N^2)$ elements is still $O(N^2 \log N)$.

B. Sequence Compression

In many real-world applications, some items may share the same time stamp since they are sampled within the same sampling cycle. To save the time cost, we compress the original S to another compact sequence S'. At each timestamp t in S, if there are k items of type I, we create a triple (I, t, k) into S', where k is the cardinality of this triple. To handle S', the only needed change of our algorithm is that the $|IA_r|$ and $|IB_r|$ become the total cardinalities of triples in IA_r and IB_r, respectively. Clearly, S' is more compact than S. S' has $O(n)$ triples, where n is the number of distinct timestamps of S, $n \leq N$. Creating S' costs an $O(N)$ time complexity. By using S', the time cost of $STScan^*$ becomes $O(N + n^2 \log n)$ and the space cost of the incremental sorted table becomes $O(n)$.

5.3 Parametric Method

In this subsection, a parametric model is applied to formulate the randomness of time lags for temporal dependencies between events [241]. Next, an EM-based approach is proposed to discover the maximal likelihood model of time lags for the temporal dependencies. Finally, an efficient approximation method is arrived at, which allows the discovery of time lags from massive events without much loss of accuracy.

5.3.1 Problem Formulation

A. Problem Description

In temporal pattern mining, the input data is a sequence of events. Given the event space Ω of all possible events, an event sequence $\mathbf{S}$ is defined as ordered finite sequence $\mathbf{S} =< e_1, e_2, ..., e_i, ..., e_k >$, where e_i is an instance of an event. We consider temporal events, i.e., each e_i is a tuple $e_i = (E_i, t_i)$ of event $E_i \in \Omega$ and a timestamp t_i of event occurrence.

Let A and B be two types of events from the event space Ω. Focusing on a specific event A, we define $\mathbf{S_A} =< (A, a_1), ..., (A, a_m) >$ to be a subsequence from $\mathbf{S}$, where only the instances of A are kept and a_i is the timestamp of ith event A. Since all the instances happening in the sequence $\mathbf{S_A}$ belong to the same type of event A, $\mathbf{S_A}$ can be simply denoted as a sequence of timestamps, i.e., $\mathbf{S_A} =< a_1, ..., a_m >$. Similarly, $\mathbf{S_B}$ is denoted as $\mathbf{S_B} =< b_1, ..., b_n >$. Discovering the temporal dependency between A and B is equivalent to finding the temporal relation between $\mathbf{S_A}$ and $\mathbf{S_B}$.

Specifically, if the jth instance of event B is associated with the ith instance of event A after a time lag $(\mu + \epsilon)$, it indicates

$$b_j = a_i + \mu + \epsilon, \tag{5.4}$$

where b_j and a_i are the timestamps of two instances of B and A, respectively, μ is the true time lag to describe the temporal relationship between A and B, and ϵ is a random variable used to represent the noise during data collection. Because of the noise, the observed time lag between a_i and b_j is not constant. Since μ is a constant, the lag $L = \mu + \epsilon$ is a random variable.

Definition 5.2 *The temporal dependency between A and B is defined as $A \rightarrow_L B$, which means that the occurrence of A is followed by the occurrence of B with a time lag L. Here L is a random variable.*

In order to discover the temporal dependency rule $A \rightarrow_L B$, we need to learn the distribution of random variable L.

We assume that the distribution of L is determined by the parameter Θ, which is independent of the occurrence of A. The occurrence of an event B is defined by the time lag L and the occurrence of A. Thus, the problem is equivalent to learning the parameter Θ for the distribution of L. The intuitive idea to solve this problem is to find the maximal likelihood parameter Θ given both sequences S_A and S_B. It is expressed formally by

$$\hat{\Theta} = \underset{\Theta}{\operatorname{argmax}} P(\Theta | \mathbf{S_A}, \mathbf{S_B}). \tag{5.5}$$

The value of $P(\Theta | \mathbf{S_A}, \mathbf{S_B})$ in Eq.(5.6) is found using the Bayes Theorem.

$$P(\boldsymbol{\Theta}|\mathbf{S_A}, \mathbf{S_B}) = \frac{P(\mathbf{S_B}|\mathbf{S_A}, \boldsymbol{\Theta}) \times P(\boldsymbol{\Theta}) \times P(\mathbf{S_A})}{P(\mathbf{S_A}, \mathbf{S_B})}. \qquad (5.6)$$

Applying ln to both sides of Eq.(5.6), we get

$$\ln P(\boldsymbol{\Theta}|\mathbf{S_A}, \mathbf{S_B}) = \ln P(\mathbf{S_B}|\mathbf{S_A}, \boldsymbol{\Theta}) + \ln P(\boldsymbol{\Theta}) \\ + \ln P(\mathbf{S_A}) - \ln P(\mathbf{S_A}, \mathbf{S_B}). \qquad (5.7)$$

In Eq.(5.7), only $\ln P(\mathbf{S_B}|\mathbf{S_A}, \boldsymbol{\Theta})$ and $\ln P(\boldsymbol{\Theta})$ are related to $\boldsymbol{\Theta}$. We assume that a large number of small factors contribute to the distribution of L, i.e., it is uniformly distributed. As a result, the problem is reduced to maximizing the likelihood defined by

$$\hat{\boldsymbol{\Theta}} = \underset{\boldsymbol{\Theta}}{\operatorname{argmax}} \ln P(\mathbf{S_B}|\mathbf{S_A}, \boldsymbol{\Theta}). \qquad (5.8)$$

Therefore, the temporal dependency $A \rightarrow_L B$ can be found by solving Eq.(5.8).

B. Computing Log-Likelihood

To solve Eq.(5.8) we need to compute the log-likelihood $\ln P(\mathbf{S_B}|\mathbf{S_A}, \boldsymbol{\Theta})$.

We assume that timestamps b_j in $\mathbf{S_B}$ are mutually independent given the sequence $\mathbf{S_A}$ and value of parameters $\boldsymbol{\Theta}$ if event B is caused by A. Therefore,

$$P(\mathbf{S_B}|\mathbf{S_A}, \boldsymbol{\Theta}) = \prod_{j=1}^{n} P(b_j|\mathbf{S_A}, \boldsymbol{\Theta}). \qquad (5.9)$$

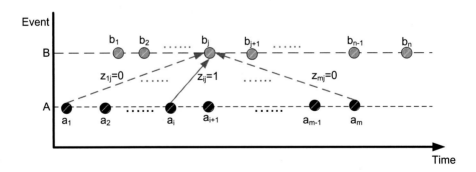

FIGURE 5.5: The jth event B occurring at b_j can be implied by any event A. Variable $z_{ij} = 1$ if the jth event B is associated with i^{th} event A, and 0 otherwise.

Given the sequence of timestamps $\mathbf{S_A}$ of event A, the instance of event B occurring at b_j is identified by possible instances of A happening at a specific timestamp a_i in the sequence $\mathbf{S_A}$, as shown in Figure 5.5. In order to model the relation between a_i and b_j, we introduce a latent variable z_{ij} defined as follows.

$$z_{ij} = \begin{cases} 1, & \text{the } i^{th} \text{ event } A \text{ implies the } j^{th} \text{ event } B; \\ 0, & \text{otherwise.} \end{cases} \quad (5.10)$$

Thus, given the sequence $\mathbf{S_A}$, each b_j is associated with a binary vector $\mathbf{z_{\bullet j}}$, where each component is either 1 or 0 and only one component of $\mathbf{z_{\bullet j}}$ is 1. For instance, in Figure 5.5, only the ith component z_{ij} is 1 since a_i implies b_j, and the remaining components are 0s. We apply the latent matrix $\mathbf{Z} = \{z_{ij}\}_{n \times m}$ to denote the relation mapping between two sequences $\mathbf{S_A}$ and $\mathbf{S_B}$.

Using $\mathbf{Z}$, we obtain the following equations:

$$P(b_j | \mathbf{z_{\bullet j}}, \mathbf{S_A}, \Theta) = \prod_{i=1}^{m} P(b_j | a_i, \Theta)^{z_{ij}}. \quad (5.11)$$

$$P(\mathbf{z_{\bullet j}}) = \prod_{i=1}^{m} P(z_{ij} = 1)^{z_{ij}}. \quad (5.12)$$

Combining Eq.(5.11) and Eq.(5.12), we rewrite $P(b_j | \mathbf{S_A}, \Theta)$ as follows:

$$P(b_j, \mathbf{z_{\bullet j}} | \mathbf{S_A}, \Theta) = \prod_{i=1}^{m} (P(b_j | a_i, \Theta) \times P(z_{ij} = 1))^{z_{ij}}. \quad (5.13)$$

Furthermore, the joint probability $P(b_j | \mathbf{S_A}, \Theta)$ in Eq.(5.13), is described by Lemma 5.4.

Lemma 5.4 (marginal probability) *Given $\mathbf{S_A}$ and Θ, the marginal probability of b_j is as follows.*

$$P(b_j | \mathbf{S_A}, \Theta) = \sum_{i=1}^{m} P(z_{ij} = 1) \times P(b_j | a_i, \Theta). \quad (5.14)$$

Proof: The marginal probability is acquired by summing up the joint probability over all the $\mathbf{z_{\bullet j}}$, i.e.,

$$P(b_j | \mathbf{S_A}, \Theta) = \sum_{\mathbf{z_{\bullet j}}} \prod_{i=1}^{m} (P(b_j | a_i, \Theta) \times P(z_{ij} = 1))^{z_{ij}}.$$

Among all m components in vector $\mathbf{z_{\bullet j}}$, there is only one component with value 1. Without any loss of generality, let $z_{ij} = 1$ given $\mathbf{z_{\bullet j}}$. Thus,

$$\prod_{i=1}^{m} (P(b_j | a_i, \Theta) \times P(z_{ij} = 1))^{z_{ij}} = P(b_j | a_i, \Theta) \times P(z_{ij} = 1).$$

Then, $P(b_j|\mathbf{S_A}, \mathbf{\Theta}) = \sum_{\mathbf{z}_{\bullet j}} P(b_j|a_i, \mathbf{\Theta}) \times P(z_{ij} = 1)$. There are m different $\mathbf{z}_{\bullet j}$ with $z_{ij} = 1$ where i ranges from 1 to m. Thus,

$$P(b_j|\mathbf{S_A}, \mathbf{\Theta}) = \sum_{i=1}^{m} P(z_{ij} = 1) \times P(b_j|a_i, \mathbf{\Theta}).$$

Based on Eq.(5.8), Eq.(5.9), and Eq.(5.14), the log-likelihood is:

$$\ln P(\mathbf{S_B}|\mathbf{S_A}, \mathbf{\Theta}) = \sum_{j=1}^{n} \ln \sum_{i=1}^{m} P(z_{ij} = 1) \times P(b_j|a_i, \mathbf{\Theta}). \qquad (5.15)$$

According to Eq.(5.15), the evaluation of the log-likelihood relies on the description of $P(b_j|a_i, \mathbf{\Theta})$. The explicit form of $P(b_j|a_i, \mathbf{\Theta})$ expressed in terms of the time lag model is presented in the following section.

C. Modeling Time Lag

According to the discussion regarding Eq.(5.4), the time lag L is a random variable that is the sum of the true time lag μ and the noise ϵ. The noise contributed to the true lag can be viewed as a result of diverse factors, such as missing records, incorrect values, and recording delay, that happened during log collection. In light of the central limit theorem, we assume that the noise ϵ follows the normal distribution with zero-mean value, since we can always move the mean of the distribution to the constant μ. Let σ^2 be the variance of the lags distribution. Then,

$$\epsilon \sim \mathcal{N}(0, \sigma^2). \qquad (5.16)$$

Since $L = \mu + \epsilon$ where μ is a constant, the distribution of L can be expressed as

$$L \sim \mathcal{N}(\mu, \sigma^2). \qquad (5.17)$$

Parameter $\mathbf{\Theta}$ determines the distribution of L. Based on the model of L described in Eq.(5.17), apparently $\mathbf{\Theta} = (\mu, \sigma^2)$. Thus, the discovery of time lag L is reduced to learning the parameters μ and σ^2.

Assume that the event A is followed by the event B with a time lag L, where $L \sim \mathcal{N}(\mu, \sigma^2)$. Specifically, as shown in Figure 5.6, the ith event A is associated to the jth event B where the time lag $(b_j - a_i)$ between the two events is a random variable L distributed as $\mathcal{N}(b_j - a_i|\mu, \sigma^2)$. Thus,

$$\begin{aligned} P(b_j|a_i, \mathbf{\Theta}) &= P(b_j|a_i, \mu, \sigma^2) \\ &= \mathcal{N}(b_j - a_i|\mu, \sigma^2). \end{aligned} \qquad (5.18)$$

Hence, by replacing $P(b_j|a_i, \mathbf{\Theta})$ based on Eq.(5.18), the log-likelihood in Eq.(5.15) is expressed as

$$\ln P(\mathbf{S_B}|\mathbf{S_A}, \mathbf{\Theta}) = \sum_{j=1}^{n} \ln \sum_{i=1}^{m} P(z_{ij} = 1) \times N(b_j - a_i|\mu, \sigma^2). \qquad (5.19)$$

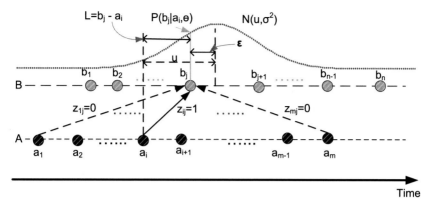

FIGURE 5.6: $A \to_L B$, where $L \sim \mathcal{N}(\mu, \sigma^2)$. An event A that occurred at time a_i is associated with an event B that occurred at b_j with probability $\mathcal{N}(b_j - a_i | \mu, \sigma^2)$. Here μ is the expected time lag of an occurrence of B after a_i. (see color insert.)

Here $P(z_{ij} = 1)$ denotes the probability that the jth event B is implied by the ith event A. Assume that there are m events A, so we assume that $\sum_{i=1}^{m} P(z_{ij} = 1) = 1$. To simplify the description, let $\pi_{ij} = P(z_{ij} = 1)$.

Based on the expression of the log-likelihood in Eq.(5.19), Eq.(5.8) is equivalent to the following

$$(\hat{\mu}, \hat{\sigma}^2) = \underset{\mu, \sigma^2}{\operatorname{argmax}} \sum_{j=1}^{n} \ln \sum_{i=1}^{m} \pi_{ij} \times \mathcal{N}(b_j - a_i | \mu, \sigma^2).$$

$$\text{s.t.} \sum_{i=1}^{m} \pi_{ij} = 1.$$

(5.20)

5.3.2 Algorithm and Solution

The algorithms to maximize the log-likelihood of parameters μ and σ^2 are given in the following.

Eq.(5.20) is an optimization problem. The gradient ascent method is supposed to be used to solve it. However, this method is not applicable here since we cannot directly derive the closed-form partial derivatives with respect to the unknown parameters μ and σ^2. The problem described in Eq.(5.20) is a typical mixture model. It can be solved by using iterative expectation maximization (i.e., EM-based method) [39].

Given $\mathbf{S_A}$ and $\mathbf{\Theta}$, Eq.(5.13), the expectation of $\ln P(\mathbf{S_B}, \mathbf{Z} | \mathbf{S_A}, \mathbf{\Theta})$ with respect to $P(z_{ij}|\mathbf{S_B}, \mathbf{S_A}, \mathbf{\Theta'})$ is

$$E(\ln P(\mathbf{S_B}, \mathbf{Z}|\mathbf{S_A}, \mathbf{\Theta})) =$$
$$\sum_{j=1}^{n}\sum_{i=1}^{m} E(z_{ij}|\mathbf{S_B}, \mathbf{S_A}, \mathbf{\Theta'}) \times (\ln \pi_{ij} + \ln \mathcal{N}(b_j - a_i|\mu, \sigma^2)), \qquad (5.21)$$

where $\mathbf{\Theta'}$ is the parameter estimated on the previous iteration.

Since z_{ij} is an indicator variable, $E(z_{ij}|\mathbf{S_B}, \mathbf{S_A}, \mathbf{\Theta'}) = P(z_{ij} = 1|\mathbf{S_B}, \mathbf{S_A}, \mathbf{\Theta'})$. Let $r_{ij} = E(z_{ij}|\mathbf{S_B}, \mathbf{S_A}, \mathbf{\Theta'})$. Then,

$$r_{ij} = \frac{\pi'_{ij} \times \mathcal{N}(b_j - a_i|\mu', \sigma'^2)}{\sum_{i}^{m} \pi'_{ij} \times \mathcal{N}(b_j - a_i|\mu', \sigma'^2)}. \qquad (5.22)$$

The new parameters π_{ij}, as well as μ and σ^2, can be learned by maximizing $E(\ln P(\mathbf{S_B}, \mathbf{Z}|\mathbf{S_A}, \mathbf{\Theta}))$.

$$\mu = \frac{1}{n}\sum_{j=1}^{n}\sum_{i=1}^{m} r_{ij}(b_j - a_i), \qquad (5.23)$$

$$\sigma^2 = \frac{1}{n}\sum_{j=1}^{n}\sum_{i=1}^{m} r_{ij}(b_j - a_i - \mu)^2. \qquad (5.24)$$

$$\pi_{ij} = r_{ij}. \qquad (5.25)$$

Based on Eq.(5.25), Eq.(5.22) is equivalent to

$$r_{ij} = \frac{r'_{ij} \times \mathcal{N}(b_j - a_i|\mu', \sigma'^2)}{\sum_{i}^{m} r'_{ij} \times \mathcal{N}(b_j - a_i|\mu', \sigma'^2)}. \qquad (5.26)$$

To find maximum likelihood estimates of parameters, we use an EM-based algorithm, *lagEM* [241]. The time cost of the *lagEM* algorithm is $O(rmn)$, where m and n are the number of events A and B, respectively, and r is the number of iterations needed for parameters to stabilize. As the time span of the event sequence grows, more events will be collected. Since m and n are the counts of two types of events, it is reasonable to assume that m and n have the same order of magnitude. Therefore, the time cost of *lagEM* is a quadratic function of events counts.

Observation 1 *During each iteration of lagEM, the probability r_{ij} describing the likelihood that the jth event B is implied by the ith event A, becomes smaller when the deviation of $b_j - a_i$ from the estimated time lag μ increases.*

Thus, as $|b_j - a_i - \mu|$ becomes larger, r_{ij} approaches 0. Further, if r_{ij} is small enough, the contribution by b_j and a_i to estimate the new parameters μ and σ^2 according to Eq.(5.23) and Eq.(5.24) is negligible. As a matter of fact, the time span of the sequence of events is very long. Hence, most of r_{ij} are small. Therefore, we can estimate new parameters μ and σ^2 without significant loss of accuracy by ignoring those $r_{ij}(b_j - a_i)$ and $r_{ij}(b_j - a_i - \mu)$ with small r_{ij} in both Eq.(5.23) and Eq.(5.24). During each iteration of *lagEM*, given b_j, we can boost the algorithm by not summing up all the m components for parameter estimation.

Given b_j, let ϵ_j be the sum of the probabilities r_{ij} whose component is neglected during the iteration. That is, $\epsilon_j = \sum_{\{i|a_i \ is \ neglected\}} r_{ij}$. Let ϵ be the largest one among all the ϵ_j, i.e., $\epsilon = \max_{1 \leq j \leq n} \{\epsilon_j\}$. Let μ_δ and σ_δ^2 be neglected parts in the estimates of μ and σ^2 during each iteration. Formally, we get

$$\mu_\delta = \frac{1}{n} \sum_{j=1}^{n} \sum_{\{i|a_i \ is \ neglected\}} r_{ij}(b_j - a_i),$$

$$\sigma_\delta^2 = \frac{1}{n} \sum_{j=1}^{n} \sum_{\{i|a_i \ is \ neglected\}} r_{ij}(b_j - a_i)^2.$$

The following lemma provides the bounds of the neglected part μ_δ and σ_δ^2.

Lemma 5.5 *Let $\bar{b}$ be the mean of all the timestamps of event B, i.e., $\bar{b} = \frac{1}{n} \sum_{j=1}^{n} b_j$. Let $\bar{b^2}$ be the second moment of the timestamps of event B, i.e., $\bar{b^2} = \frac{1}{n} \sum_{j=1}^{n} b_j^2$. Then we get*

$$\mu_\delta \in [\epsilon(\bar{b} - a_m), \epsilon(\bar{b} - a_1)]. \tag{5.27}$$

Let $\phi = \max\{\bar{b^2} - 2\bar{b}a_1 + a_1^2, \bar{b^2} - 2\bar{b}a_1 + a_m^2\}$, then

$$\sigma_\delta^2 \in [0, \epsilon\phi]. \tag{5.28}$$

Proof: Since $< a_1, a_2, ..., a_m >$ is a time sequence, we can assume that $a_1 \leq a_2 \leq ... \leq a_m$. Thus, $b_j - a_i \in [b_j - a_m, b_j - a_1]$. Moreover, $\epsilon_j = \sum_{i|a_i \ is \ neglected} r_{ij}$, where $\epsilon_j \leq \epsilon$. Therefore,

$$\frac{1}{n} \sum_{j=1}^{n} \epsilon(b_j - a_m) \leq \mu_\delta \leq \frac{1}{n} \sum_{j=1}^{n} \epsilon(b_j - a_1).$$

Then, we get $\mu_\delta \in [\epsilon(\bar{b} - a_m), \epsilon(\bar{b} - a_1)]$.

In addition, $(b_j - a_i)^2 \leq \max\{(b_j - a_1)^2, (b_j - a_m)^2\}$. Thus,

$$\sigma_\delta^2 \leq \frac{1}{n} \epsilon \sum_{j=1}^{n} \max\{(b_j^2 - 2b_j a_1 + a_1^2, b_j^2 - 2b_j a_m + a_m^2)\}.$$

Then, we get

$$\sigma_\delta^2 \leq \epsilon \max\{\bar{b^2} - 2\bar{b}a_1 + a_1^2, \bar{b^2} - 2\bar{b}a_1 + a_m^2\}.$$

So, $\sigma_\delta^2 \in [0, \epsilon\phi]$.

Based on Lemma 5.5, if ϵ is small enough, $|\mu_\delta|$ and σ_δ^2 approach 0 and the parameters μ and σ^2 are close to the ones without ignoring components.

Given a timestamp b_j, there are m possible corresponding timestamps of event A. Our problem is how to choose a subset C_j of timestamps of event A to estimate the parameters during each iteration. To guarantee that the probability of the neglected part is less than ϵ, the probability for the subset C_j should be greater than $1 - \epsilon$. In order to optimize the time complexity, our goal is to minimize the size of C_j. It can be solved efficiently by applying a greedy algorithm, which adds a_i to C_j with its r_{ij} in decreasing order until the summation of r_{ij} is greater than $1 - \epsilon$.

Based on Observation 1 and the fact that all the timestamps of event A are in increasing order, the index i for timestamps of event A in C_j should be consecutive. Given b_j, the minimum and maximum indexes of a_i in C_j can be found by algorithm *greedyBound* [241]. The time cost of *greedyBound* is $O(\log m + K)$ where $K = |C_j|$ and m is the number of events A.

Based on Lemma 5.5 and algorithm *greedyBound*, we propose an approximation algorithm *appLagEM* [241].

The total time cost of algorithm *appLagEM* is $O(rn(\log m + K))$ where r is the number of iterations, and K is the average size of all C_j. Typically, in the event sequence, $K << n$ and $\log m << n$. Therefore, the time cost of algorithm *appLagEM* is close to a linear function of n in each iteration.

5.4 Empirical Studies

In this section, experimental results on synthetic and real datasets are presented on mining the temporal lag from fluctuating events for correlation and root cause analysis.

5.4.1 Mining Temporal Lag from Fluctuating Events

As mentioned in Section 5.1, there are two approaches for mining temporal lag from events, i.e., non-parametric models and parametric models. Herein, the parametric model is applied for temporal lag discovery from fluctuating events. Algorithm *lagEM*, an EM-based algorithm, is used for temporal lag discovery. In order to improve the performance of *lagEM*, an approximation algorithm *appLagEM* is proposed. Both synthetic and real data are used for demonstrating the efficiency and effectiveness of the two algorithms.

All algorithms are implemented using Java 1.7. All experiments are conducted on the experimental environment running Linux 2.6.32. The computer is equipped with an Intel(R) Xeon(R) CPU with 24 cores running at a speed of 2.50GHZ. The total volume of memory is 158G.

5.4.1.1 Synthetic Data

In this part we describe experiments conducted on six synthetic datasets. The synthetic data generation is defined by the parameters shown in Table 5.2.

TABLE 5.2: Parameters for synthetic data generation

Name	Description
β_{min}	Describes the minimum value for choosing the average inter-arrival time β.
β_{max}	Describes the maximum value for choosing the average inter-arrival time β.
N	The number of events in the synthetic event sequence.
μ_{min}	Describes the minimum value for the true time lag μ.
μ_{max}	Describes the maximum value for the true time lag μ.
σ^2_{min}	Describes the minimum value for the variance of time lag.
σ^2_{max}	Describes the maximum value for the variance of time lag.

We employ exponential distribution to simulate the inter-arrival time between two adjacent events [133]. The average inter-arrival time β is randomly generated in the range $[\beta_{min}, \beta_{max}]$. The true lag μ is randomly generated in the range $[\mu_{min}, \mu_{max}]$. And the variance of time lag σ^2 is generated between σ^2_{mix} and σ^2_{max} randomly.

With chosen parameters β, μ, and σ^2, the procedure of generating synthetic data for the temporal dependency $A \rightarrow_\mu B$ is given below.

- Generate N timestamps for event A, where the inter-arrival time between two adjacent events follows the exponential distribution with parameter β.

- For each timestamp a_i of event A, the time lag is randomly generated according to a normal distribution with parameters μ and σ^2.

- Combine all the timestamps associated with their types to build a synthetic dataset.

We set $\beta_{min} = 5$, $\beta_{max} = 50$, $\mu_{min} = 25$, $\mu_{max} = 100$, $\sigma^2_{min} = 5$, and $\sigma^2_{max} = 400$ to synthesize the six datasets with different parameters N. The numbers of events for the synthetic datasets are 200, 1k, 2k, 10k, 20k, and 40k, respectively. Recall that here the number of events only describes the number of events of two types we are interested in. In practice, a real dataset typically gets more than hundreds of events types in addition to the two types of events considered. Thus 40k events of two types compare with a real dataset containing 2 million events of 100 types.

TABLE 5.3: Experimental results on synthetic datasets.

	Ground Truth		lagEM			appLagEM $\epsilon = 0.001$			appLagEM $\epsilon = 0.05$			appLagEM $\epsilon = 0.1$		
N	μ	σ^2	$\bar\mu$	$\bar\sigma^2$	LL_{opt}	$\bar\mu$	$\bar\sigma^2$	LL_{opt}	$\bar\mu$	$\bar\sigma^2$	LL_{opt}	$\bar\mu$	$\bar\sigma^2$	LL_{opt}
200	77.01	44.41	77.41 [73.46, 81.36]	20.74 [18.75, 22.73]	-292.47	77.85 [73.52, 82.18]	24.68 [20.64, 28.72]	-290.99	78.21 [74.38, 82.03]	24.79 [20.62, 28.96]	-299.89	78.135 [74.16, 82.11]	25.02 [21.24, 28.80]	-300.05
1k	25.35	12.51	25.5 [25.0, 25.98]	8.66 [8.52, 8.80]	-1275.5	25.45 [25.12, 25.78]	8.62 [8.52, 8.72]	-1247.01	25.94 [24.39, 27.49]	9.296 [5.83, 12.77]	-1248.34	25.97 [25.59, 27.59]	9.36 [5.71, 13.0]	-1248.35
2k	38.54	30.88	38.68 [38.19, 39.17]	16.57 [16.38, 16.75]	-2847.0	38.81 [38.42, 39.40]	16.51 [16.45, 16.57]	-2820.6	39.78 [37.76, 41.78]	17.82 [14.17, 21.47]	-2822.60	39.32 [37.49, 41.14]	17.26 [14.36, 20.16]	-2822.57
10k	54.92	13.51	55.07 [54.60, 55.54]	8.84 [8.68, 9.0]	-12525.0	55.82 [53.97, 57.66]	10.92 [5.24, 16.60]	-12523.68	55.29 [54.23, 56.34]	9.40 [7.28, 11.52]	-12526.0	55.80 [53.99, 57.60]	10.85 [5.17, 16.53]	-12526.04
20k	59.35	17.22	59.42 [59.27, 59.57]	11.35 [11.32, 11.40]	-26554.2	59.67 [58.86, 60.50]	11.7 [10.35, 13.05]	-26332.68	59.38 [59.1, 59.70]	11.38 [11.30, 11.5]	-26332.06	59.34 [58.96, 59.72]	11.42 [11.2, 11.63]	-26336.39
40k	80.18	8.48	N/A	N/A	N/A	82.51 [77.76, 87.25]	5.26 [0.3, 10.3]	-40024.01	81.7 [78.15, 85.25]	4.45 [0.86, 8.04]	-40187.73	81.59 [77.9, 85.3]	4.4 [0.85, 7.94]	-40185.64

Synthetic Data Evaluation

Since the EM-based approach cannot guarantee the global optimum [39], we define a batch as running the experiments 20 rounds with different initial parameters chosen at random, where we empirically find out 20 rounds is reasonable for our problem. We choose the one with the maximum likelihood among 20 rounds as the solution of a batch. Ten such batches are conducted over each dataset. With 10 pairs of parameters μ and σ^2 learned from 10 batches, $\bar\mu$ and $\bar\sigma^2$ are calculated as average values of μ and σ^2, respectively. Furthermore, 95% confidence intervals of μ and σ^2 are provided by assuming both μ and σ^2 follow the normal distribution as the prior [39]. Additionally, LL_{opt} denotes the maximum log-likelihood value learned by our proposed algorithms. , The results of experiments running $lagEM$ and $appLagEM$ are presented in Table 5.3. In the table, the size of data ranges from 200 to 40k and LL_{opt} is the maximum log-likelihood. Assuming μ and σ^2 follow the normal distribution, $\bar\mu$ and $\bar\sigma^2$ are provided with their 95% confidence interval for each algorithm over every dataset. Entries with "N/A" are not available since it takes more than 1 day to obtain corresponding parameters.

Each algorithm stops searching as it converges or the number of iterations exceeds 500. Algorithm $appLagEM$ takes one more parameter ϵ as its input, where ϵ determines the proportion of the neglected components during the parameter estimation of each iteration. Herein, ϵ has been set to 0.001, 0.05, and 0.1. For all datasets listed in Table 5.3, time lags μ's learned by $lagEM$ and $appLagEM$ are quite close to the ground truth. In addition, the smaller ϵ is, the more probable that algorithm $appLagEM$ will get a larger log likelihood.

Further, we employ the Kullback-Leibler (KL) divergence as the metric to measure the difference between the distribution of time lag given by the ground truth and the results discovered [125]. Since each algorithm with a different initial setting of parameters runs for 10 batches over a given dataset, we take the average KL divergence of 10 batches to evaluate the experimental result. As shown in Figure 5.7, the KL divergence caused by *appLagEM* is almost as small as the one produced by *lagEM*. Besides, as ϵ increases, the KL divergence of *appLagEM* becomes larger.

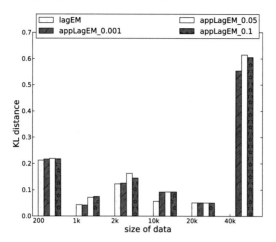

FIGURE 5.7: The KL distance between the ground truth and the one learned by each algorithm.

Figure 5.8 presents the comparison of time cost over the synthetic datasets. It shows that the approximation algorithm *appLagEM* is much more efficient than *lagEM*. It also shows that the larger ϵ is, the less time *appLagEM* takes to find the optimal distribution of time lags. Algorithm *appLagEM*, even with $\epsilon = 0.001$, is about two orders of magnitude faster than algorithm *lagEM*.

In conclusion, based on the comparative discussion of both *lagEM* and *appLagEM*, it is possible to achieve a good balance in terms of accuracy and efficiency.

5.4.1.2 Real Data

TABLE 5.4: Snippet of discovered time lags

	Dependency	μ	σ^2	Signal-to-noise ratio
	$TEC\_Error \rightarrow_L Ticket\_Retry$	0.34059	0.107178	1.04
dataset1	$AIX\_HW\_ERROR \rightarrow_L AIX\_HW\_ERROR$	10.92	0.98	11.03
	$AIX\_HW\_ERROR \rightarrow_L NV390MSG\_MVS$	33.89	1.95	24.27
	$AIX\_HW\_ERROR \rightarrow_L Nvserverd\_Event$	64.75	2.99	37.45
	$AIX\_HW\_ERROR \rightarrow_L generic\_postemsg$	137.17	18.81	31.63
	$generic\_postemsg \rightarrow_L TSM\_SERVER\_EVENT$	205.301	39.36	32.72
	$generic\_postemsg \rightarrow_L Sentry2\_0\_diskusedpct$	134.51	71.61	15.90
	$MQ\_CONN\_NOT\_AUTHORIZED \rightarrow_L TSM\_SERVER\_EVENT$	1167.06	142.54	97.75
dataset2	$MSG\_Plat\_APP \rightarrow_L Linux\_Process$	18.53	2053.46	**0.408**
	$SVC\_TEC\_HEARTBEAT \rightarrow_L SVC\_TEC\_HEARTBEAT$	587.6	7238.5	6.90

We perform the experiment over two real event datasets collected from several IT outsourcing centers by the IBM Tivoli monitoring system [6]. These events are generated by the automatic monitoring system with software agents

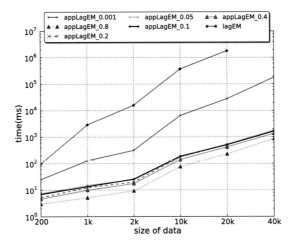

FIGURE 5.8: Time cost comparison. ϵ of *appLagEM* is set to 0.001, 0.05, 0.1, 0.2, 0.4, and 0.8. The sizes of the datasets range from 200 to 40k.

running on the servers of an enterprise customer, which computes metrics for the hardware and software performance at regular intervals. The metrics are then compared to acceptable thresholds, known as monitoring situations, and any violation results in an alert. If the alert persists beyond a certain delay specified in the situation, the monitor emits an event. Therefore, a monitoring event corresponds to one type of system alert and one monitoring situation configured in the IBM Tivoli monitoring system. In this experiment, discovering temporal dependencies with time lags on monitoring events has several practical usages:

Monitoring Redundancy Removal: Many temporally dependent monitoring events are caused by correlated monitoring situations. For example, two situations monitoring CPU utilizations with similar thresholds are correlated. If the CPU has a high utilization, the two situations will generate one CPU event almost simultaneously. Then two CPU events are temporally dependent. Therefore, the temporal dependencies discovered can reveal the correlation of monitoring situations, in parallel monitoring. Removing this redundancy can reduce the running cost of monitoring agents on customer servers.

Event Correlation: Dependent monitoring events are usually triggered by the same system issue. The event correlation can merge dependent events into one ticket and help system administrators diagnose the system issue.

Root Cause Determination: Some temporal dependencies of system alerts can be regarded as a fault-error-failure chain, indicating the origin of the system issue. This chain can help the system administrator find the root cause of the related system issue and carry out an effective system diagnosis.

Each real event set is collected from one IT environment of an enterprise customer. The number of events and types are listed in Table 5.5. The *dataset*1 consists of a sequence of events including 104 distinct event types, which are collected within the time span of 32 days. There are 136 types of events in *dataset*2 where $1000k$ events happen within 54 days. In both datasets, hundreds of types of events result in tens of thousands of pairs of event types. Since our algorithm takes a pair of events as the input, it would be time consuming to consider all the pairs. In order to efficiently find the time lag of most possible dependent events, we filter out the types of events that appear fewer than 100 times in a corresponding dataset.

TABLE 5.5: Real event dataset

Name	# of events	# of types	Time span
dataset1	$100k$	104	32 days
dataset2	$1000k$	136	54 days

We employ the *appLagEM* with $\epsilon = 0.001$ to mine the time lag of temporal dependency between two events. To increase the probability of getting the global optimal value, we run the algorithm in a batch of 50 rounds by feeding in random initial parameters every round. A snippet of some interesting time lags discovered is shown in Table 5.4. The metric signal-to-noise ratio [192], a concept in signal processing, is used to measure the impact of noise relative to the expected time lag. Signal-to-noise ratio (SNR) is given as

$$SNR = \frac{\mu}{\sigma}.$$

The larger the SNR, the less the relative impact of noise on the expected time lags.

$TEC\_Error \rightarrow_L Ticket\_Retry$ is a temporal dependency discovered from *dataset*1, where time lag L follows the normal distribution with $\mu = 0.34$ and the variance $\sigma^2 = 0.107178$. The small expected time lag, μ less than 0.1 second, indicates that the two events appear almost at the same time. The small variance shows that most time lags between the two event types are around the expected time lag μ. In fact, TEC_Error is caused whenever the monitoring system fails to generate an incident ticket to the ticket system. Note that $Ticket\_Retry$ is raised when the monitoring system tries to generate the ticket again.

$AIX\_HW\_Error \rightarrow_L AIX\_HW\_Error$ in *dataset*1 describes a pattern related to the event AIX_HW_Error. With the discovered values of μ and σ^2, the event AIX_HW_Error happens with an expected period of about 10 seconds with small variance less than 1 second. In a real production environment, the event AIX_HW_Error is raised when the monitoring system polls an AIX server which is down. The failure to respond to the monitoring system leads to an event AIX_HW_Error almost every 10 seconds.

In *dataset*2, the expected time lag between MSG_Plat_APP and $Linux\_Process$ is 18.53 seconds. However, the variance of the time lags is quite large in comparison with the expected time lag with $SNR = 0.4$. This leads to a weak confidence in temporal dependency between these two events because the discovered time lags get involved in too much noise. In practice, MSG_Plat_APP is a periodic event which is the heartbeat signal sent by the applications. However, the event $Linux\_Process$ is related to the different processes running on Linux. So it is reasonable to assume a weak dependency between them.

The event $SVC\_TEC\_HEARTBEAT$ is used to record the heartbeat signal for reporting the status of service instantly. The temporal dependency discovered from $dataset2$ shows that $SVC\_TEC\_HEARTBEAT$ is a periodic event with an expected period of 10 minutes. Although the variance seems large, the standard deviation is relatively small compared with the expected period μ. Therefore, it still strongly indicates periodic temporal dependency.

The inter-arrival pattern can also be employed to find the time lag between events such as $TEC\_Error \rightarrow_{[t-\delta,t+\delta]} Ticket\_Retry$ where t and δ are very small. However, it fails to find the temporal pattern such as $MQ\_CONN\_NOT\_AUTHORIZED \rightarrow_L TSM\_SERVER\_EVENT$ with a large expected time lag of about 20 minutes. The reason is that the inter-arrival pattern is discovered by only considering the inter-arrival time lag, and the inter-arrival time lags are exactly the small time lags.

In [212], the $STScan$ algorithm based on the support and the χ^2 test is proposed to find the interleaved time lags between events. $STScan$ can find the temporal pattern such as $AIX\_HW\_Error \rightarrow_{[25,25]} AIX\_HW\_Error$ and $AIX\_HW\_Error \rightarrow_{[8,9]} AIX\_HW\_Error$ by setting the support threshold and the confidence level of the χ^2 test. In our algorithm, we describe temporal patterns through the expected time lag and its variance. The temporal dependencies are demonstrated in Section 5.4.3.

5.4.2   System Overview

In order to facilitate concurrent interactions for multiple users to mine temporal dependencies with time lags from large scale event data, a temporal dependency mining system named TDMS is proposed based on a distributed environment. There are two external components shown in the left part of Fig.5.9, working with TDMS. Users as one external component interact with TDMS by issuing HTTP requests for both event queries and temporal dependencies discovery. The other external component is composed of a large number of monitored customer servers, where all the alerts and events generated by hosted applications are collected and stored in TDMS.

TDMS has three layers, displayed in the right part of Figure 5.9. The bottom layer depicts the storage for event data. To leverage the computing power of the distributed environment for temporal dependency discovery, all event data are available to all the computing nodes by placing them on a distributed file system such as HDFS (Hadoop Distributed File System).

The middle layer is the distributed computing layer containing three components: Job Cache, Distributed Job Scheduler, and Mining Algorithm Library. The Job Cache component is used to alleviate the computing burden of

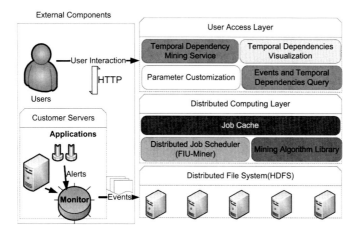

FIGURE 5.9: The overview of the temporal dependency mining system (TDMS). (See color insert.)

the system. The mining results are indexed by their parameters and dataset names, and stored in the cache. As a result, the mining result of the requested job can be retrieved directly from the cache without redundant computation if the same job has been computed before. The Distributed Job Scheduler is responsible for scheduling the requested jobs in the distributed environment by considering the resource balance. The Distributed Job Scheduler is implemented by FIU-Miner, a fast, integrated, and user-Friendly system for data mining in distributed environment [238]. The third component in this layer is the algorithm library. The detailed algorithms for temporal dependency mining are given in subsequent sections.

The top layer is the User Access Layer serving as the user interaction with TDMS. Users are able to access all the stored events and query the temporal dependencies discovered, in two ways, including Temporal Dependency Service and Web-Based Temporal Dependencies Visualization. Moreover, users can customize the parameters of the mining algorithms and specify the event dataset to discover the temporal dependencies for the interests of users.

5.4.3 System Demonstration

Several user interfaces for TDMS are presented in Figure 5.11 and Figure 5.10, which are generated by running the appLagEM algorithm over two real datasets from some IT outsourcing centers by the IBM Tivoli monitoring system. In Figure 5.11, the temporal dependencies discovered are displayed in a table, where each row corresponds to a temporal dependency rule. From each row, we can tell both the expected value and variance of the time lag between two dependent events. In the top part of Figure 5.11, the threshold

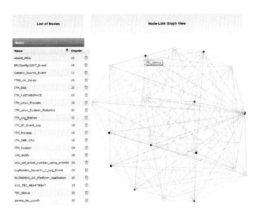

FIGURE 5.10: Temporal dependencies are shown in a graph where each node denotes an event, and an edge between two nodes indicates the corresponding two events are dependent. (See color insert.)

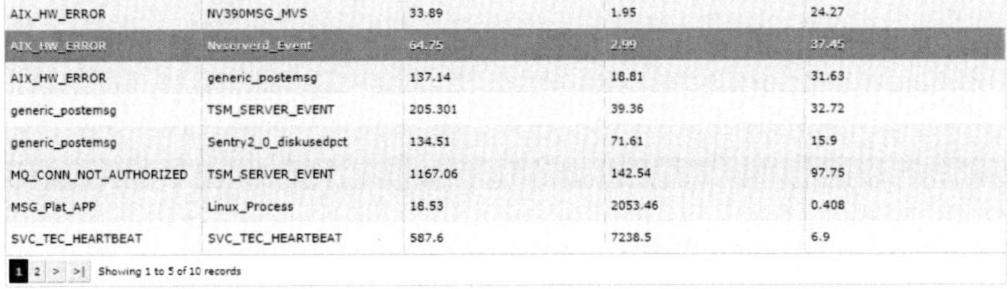

Mining Temporal Dependencies

Signal To Noise (SNR) Greater Than: 10.0   Query

Temporal Dependencies

Antecedent	Consequent	Mean of Lag	Standard Variance of Lag	Signal To Noise
TEC_ERROR	Ticket_Retry	0.34059	0.107178	1.04
AIX_HW_ERROR	AIX_HW_ERROR	10.92	0.98	11.03
AIX_HW_ERROR	NV390MSG_MVS	33.89	1.95	24.27
AIX_HW_ERROR	Recovered_Event	64.75	2.99	37.45
AIX_HW_ERROR	generic_postmsg	137.14	18.81	31.63
generic_postmsg	TSM_SERVER_EVENT	205.301	39.36	32.72
generic_postmsg	Sentry2_0_diskusedpct	134.51	71.61	15.9
MQ_CONN_NOT_AUTHORIZED	TSM_SERVER_EVENT	1167.06	142.54	97.75
MSG_Plat_APP	Linux_Process	18.53	2053.46	0.408
SVC_TEC_HEARTBEAT	SVC_TEC_HEARTBEAT	587.6	7238.5	6.9

1 2 > >| Showing 1 to 5 of 10 records

FIGURE 5.11: Temporal dependencies are discovered by setting the SNR threshold and are displayed in a table. The number of temporal dependencies depends on the SNR setting. (See color insert.)

of SNR is provided in the text box, which is able to measure the strength of the temporal dependency.

The temporal dependency graph is constructed according to the dependency rules in Figure 5.10. In the temporal dependency graph, the nodes represent the events, and the edge between two events indicates a temporal dependency. The number of edges in the graph decreases as a larger threshold of SNR is provided. All the related events are provided in the table as well for convenient exploration.

5.5 Summary

Time lag is one of most important characteristics associated with temporal patterns. This chapter mainly focuses on time lag mining for temporal patterns, and both non-parametric and parametric methods are presented for discovering time lags between correlated events. In order to evaluate the proposed methods, a case study and an integrated system for time lag mining are presented.

However, some challenges in time lag discovery need to be addressed in the future. First, existing models need to be extended to discover temporal patterns with more complicated distributions of time lags, such as patterns with possibly multiple time lags or having complicated distribution laws. Moreover. it is still a difficult task to discover the dependencies among multiple events rather than pairwise dependencies.

5.6 Glossary

Dependent Pattern: Event pattern containing correlated events.

Event: Temporal data with discrete data item values.

Non-Parametric Method: The non-parametric method makes no assumptions about the probability distributions of the variables being assessed.

Parametric Method: The parametric method assumes that the data have come from a type of probability distribution and makes inferences about the parameters of the distribution.

Time Lag: The time interval between events, describing the temporal order of events.

Chapter 6

Log Event Summarization

Yexi Jiang and Tao Li

Florida International University
Nanjing University of Posts and Telecommunications

6.1 Introduction

Many systems, from computing systems, physical systems, business systems, to social systems, are only observable through the events they emit. It is well-known that event logs are reliable sources for people to understand the underlying dynamic system. To learn the behavior of a target dynamic system, one popular solution is to leverage the pattern mining technique to uncover the hidden temporal patterns from its logs.

In general, modern systems are instrumented to generate a huge number of events. These events describe the running status and activities of each component, including operational changes, security-related operations, and system failures, etc. As the size of event logs grow dramatically and the pattern mining technique tends to return all interesting patterns, the amount of mined patterns would be far beyond the processing capability of the human beings. Due to this fact, people gradually realized that it is wise to have a global overview of the observed system before conducting the detailed system analysis, instead of directly diving into the ocean of the patterns. To meet this need, some research efforts in the area of event mining have been shifted to event summarization in recent years.

This chapter focuses on the problem of event summarization. First, we introduce the background as well as some basic concepts about event summarization in Section 6.1. Then, we introduce two popular categories of summarization methods (i.e., frequency-based event summarization and temporal-dynamic-based event summarization) in Section 6.2 and Section 6.3, respectively. In both sections, we present the intuition, basic concepts, the concrete method, as well as the corresponding experimental evaluation of the summarization methods. In Section 6.4, we introduce a flexible and powerful event summarization framework to integrate different event summarization solutions and facilitate event analysis. Finally, we discuss the potential future research directions and conclude this chapter.

The size of event logs

As reported by Xu et al. [231] in 2009, a moderate distributed system (a 200-node Hadoop cluster) is able to generate more than 12 million log messages every day, and a large distributed system would generate 5 orders of magnitude more messages compared with the moderate one [230]. In terms of storage space, the daily storage costs can be up to terabytes (2^{40} bytes), even petabytes (2^{50} bytes). In addition, due to the complexity of the systems, pattern mining algorithms could easily generate hundreds of thousands of patterns based on the logs. In such cases, it is difficult for human analysts to discover useful information from such a large amount of patterns.

6.1.1 What is Event Summarization?

Event summarization, as its name suggests, is a process to summarize the characteristics (mainly including temporal dynamics) of the events within the given system logs. From a functionality perspective, event summarization is a complementary technique rather than a substitute for event pattern mining. Compared with the patterns mined from off-the-shelf pattern mining techniques, summarized results are easier to be understood by the event analysts. The results of event summarization allow system analysts to obtain an overview of the system running status at a quick glance. According to the description of Kiernan and Terzi [119], a typical event summarization technique should have the following properties:

- *Brevity and accuracy*: The generated summary should be concise compared with the mined patterns obtained from the same piece of log. Moreover, it should also be able to precisely describe the status of the target system.

- *Hierarchical description*: The generated summary should be able to reflect the high level structure of the events. Besides the high level description, it should also be able to reveal information about local patterns.

- *Parameter free*: The parameters of the event summarization algorithm should be as few as possible. An ideal case is that no extra tuning is needed when event analysts are using the summarization solution.

6.1.2   Event Summarization vs. Event Pattern Mining

An obvious distinction between event summarization and event pattern mining (introduced in Chapter 4) is that event summarization is able to generate concise and summarized results compared with event pattern mining. In fact, besides the aforementioned characteristic, these two types of techniques are different in several other perspectives. Table 6.1 briefly summarizes their differences.

TABLE 6.1: Distinction between event pattern mining and event summarization

	Event Pattern Mining	Event Summarization
Functionality	Detailed analysis	Exploration
Result Representation	Concrete patterns and rules	Concise representation
Result Granularity	High level	Low level

6.1.2.1   Functionality

From a functionality perspective, event summarization is mainly used for exploration and investigation, while event pattern mining is mainly suitable for detailed data analysis. In practice, the analysis goal is often unclear when the event log is obtained at first. Even experienced analysts don't know how to correctly analyze the events at the beginning. In this case, a global overview of the whole log is helpful and useful for analysts to quickly obtain the main idea of the system status. Event summarization is able to provide a global overview and make suggestions for further analysis. Based on the summarization results, analysts can have a good understanding of the overall status and can set up a good analysis plan. Moreover, as event pattern mining typically involves a lot of parameter tuning, the summarization results can also provide hints and guidance on how to set the parameters.

6.1.2.2   Result Representation

Generally, as shown in Table 4.7, the results of event mining are represented by various types of patterns or rules. For example, frequent episode mining techniques [158, 127, 234] are able to discover the event subsequences that frequently appear in an event sequence. Given an event sequence denoted by <

$(E_1, t_1), (E_2, t_2), \dots >$, where E_i takes value from a finite event type set $\mathcal{E}$ and t_i denotes the timestamp when E_i occurs, the episode mining technique discovers and exhaustively lists all the frequent patterns in the form of $E_i \to E_j \to E_k$. Due to the large number of events and event types in modern computing systems, this technique can easily generate a large number of patterns or rules. Different variations [63, 94, 106] of the basic episodes mining algorithm can generate different sets of patterns or rules, but the basic forms of their patterns or rules are the same.

Different from patterns or rules generated by the event mining techniques, the results generated by event summarization are more concise. Moreover, different event summarization techniques can generate different representations, such as segmentation models [119, 120, 177], hidden Markov models [175, 227], graphs [21], and event relationship networks [176, 112]. Analysts can freely choose different representations according to their concrete requirements.

Event Relationship Network

An event relationship network (ERN) is a kind of descriptive model proposed in [219]. It is a graphical representation of temporal relationships among events. This model is a useful model to bridge the knowledge discovery process with the system implementation process and has been widely used in IT system management and business services management. From the perspective of event summarization, ERN can provide a concise yet expressive representation for describing the temporal dynamics of the events.

6.1.2.3 Result Granularity

As mentioned in Section 6.1.2.1, event summarization acts as a complementary solution rather than a substitute for pattern mining. In terms of the result granularity, the results of event summarization are coarser than those provided by pattern mining algorithms. Event summarization algorithms generally only generate results that reflect the high level perspectives about the event relationships. For example, the summarized results often only tell which groups of events are correlated with each other and the change in temporal dynamics. On the other hand, the results of pattern mining usually contain more detail, including the list of patterns or rules, the detailed event relationships, and the concrete parameters describing the relationships.

6.1.3 Event Summarization vs. Frequent Itemset Summarization

6.1.3.1 Introduction

Frequent itemset summarization is an extension of frequent itemset (pattern) mining. It is proposed to address some of the limitations of frequent itemset mining, including redundancy and interpretability. Traditional frequent itemset mining can generate a large number of frequent patterns and many of the generated patterns can be redundant. Once the number of discovered patterns is greater than hundreds, manual investigation becomes infeasible. More advanced patterns, such as *closed frequent patterns* [17], *maximal frequent patterns* [37, 92], *top-k patterns* [100, 188, 226], and *condensed patterns* [172], have been proposed to make the mining results more compact. However, these approaches can only partially solve the redundancy problem since the number of generated patterns can still be very large.

To effectively address the redundancy problem, researchers have developed pattern summarization methods to summarize the frequent patterns with more condensed formats. In general, two kinds of models have been proposed to summarize the frequent patterns: the *pattern profile* [233] and the *Markov random field (MRF)* [223].

For *pattern-profile*-based summarization, the whole set of frequent patterns can be clustered into K groups of patterns and each group is described by a *pattern profile*. A *pattern profile* is essentially a generalization of a *closed frequent pattern*. It can be described as a triple $< \mathbf{p}, \phi, \rho >$, where $\mathbf{p}$ denotes the probability distribution vector learned from the dataset, ϕ denotes the master pattern used to represent a set of similar patterns in a group, and ρ denotes the support. To conduct the clustering, the *K-means* algorithm is used and the similarity between two frequent patterns (each frequent pattern is represented as a special kind of *pattern profile*) is measured based on the *Kullback-Leibler* divergence [125] between their distribution vectors.

Non-Derivable Frequent Itemset [51]

A frequent itemset I is non-derivable if its support cannot be exactly inferred from the support of its sub-itemsets based on the inclusion-exclusion principle.

MRF-based summarization mainly focuses on using *non-derivable* frequent itemsets to construct the MRF as the summary of the whole dataset. The summarization is conducted using a level-wise approach. Generally, all 1-itemsets are used to construct an MRF to infer the supports for all 2-itemsets. Then the 2-itemsets whose support cannot be inferred are used to update the MRF. The process continues until all the itemsets are checked. The resulting MRF is a concise summary of the original dataset.

6.1.3.2 Distinctions

According to the description of frequent itemset summarization, the distinctions between event summarization and frequent itemset summarization can be summarized as follows.

Summarization Data Objects: Although frequent itemset summarization and event summarization have similar tasks, they are working on different types of data objects. Frequent itemset summarization techniques focus on summarizing the transaction type data — the itemsets; while event summarization techniques focus on summarizing temporal datasets. Transaction type data usually do not have time information, or the time information is not critical or important.

Summarization Perspective: Frequent itemset summarization techniques pay more attention to presenting summaries that describe the frequent itemsets, while event summarization techniques pay more attention to generating summaries describing the temporal dynamics of the events. This is because the time information in an event log is a critical piece of information. Besides the pattern frequency, people who analyze the event log also pay close attention to the time information in the summary results.

6.1.4 Category of Event Summarization

Event summarization is a general type of solution to organize and represent the information extracted from the events. In recent years, several event summarization approaches have been proposed. Although each solution is distinct from the others, they can be categorized into two types: *summarizing with frequency change* and *summarizing with temporal dynamics*.

6.2 Summarizing with Frequency Change

One major direction of event summarization is *to provide a summary of the given event log from the perspective of frequency change.* Generally, these methods leverage the segmentation model to provide a high level overview of the sequence by identifying global intervals on the whole event sequence. In each segment, the events are summarized by a local model, in a way similar to clustering. The local model is able to group the event types into a number of clusters, where the event types in the same cluster have similar frequency and vice versa.

To better illustrate the idea of this approach, Example 6.1 gives an example of the event sequence. In general, the event sequence can be denoted as S that records the occurrences of events during the time range $[1, n]$. Moreover, each event occurrence can be represented in the form (E, t), where E denotes the event type coming from a set $\mathcal{E} = \{E_1, \cdots, E_m\}$, and t denotes the time of the occurrence.

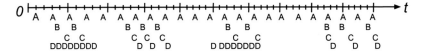

FIGURE 6.1: An example event sequence.

Example 6.1 *Figure 6.1 shows an example event sequence consisting of four event types, i.e., $\mathcal{E} = \{A, B, C, D\}$. The event sequence records the occurrences of all the event types from time 0 to time 40. It can be seen that some patterns might exist in this event sequence. For example, events B, C and D seem to appear sequentially.*

One perspective of event summarization is to find an appropriate summary that balances conciseness and accuracy. To find an appropriate summary in such a way, Kiernan and Terzi proposed a method [119] which reduces the event summarization problem to an optimization problem. In particular, the proposed method solved this problem from the information theory perspective: *the best summary of an event sequence is the one with shortest description length quantified by the number of bits.* The *minimum description length (MDL)* principle [30, 90, 89] is leveraged to conduct the model (summary) selection by finding a balance between summary coding length and description accuracy.

Concretely, event summarization in [119] is formulated as follows: Suppose there is an event sequence S with time range $[1, n]$, and let $\mathcal{E} = \{E_1, E_2, \cdots, E_m\}$. The goal of finding the best summary is to identify the best segmentation of the event sequence over $[1, n]$, as well as the best grouping of event types within each segment according to appearance frequency. Such a data description model is called the *segmental grouping* model.

Figure 6.2 illustrates how this method summarizes the event sequence given in Example 6.1. As shown in Figure 6.2, the whole sequence has been partitioned into four segments (using the encoding strategy we will discuss in Section 6.2.1). Moreover, as shown in Figure 6.3, the event types are grouped within each segment according to their local frequency.

6.2.1 Preliminaries of Event Encoding

To better understand how the best summary can be found using the techniques of information theory, some basic concepts need to be introduced first.

An event sequence S can be denoted as an $m \times n$ matrix, where $S(i, t) = 1$ denotes that an event with type E_i occurs at time t. In this matrix, multiple

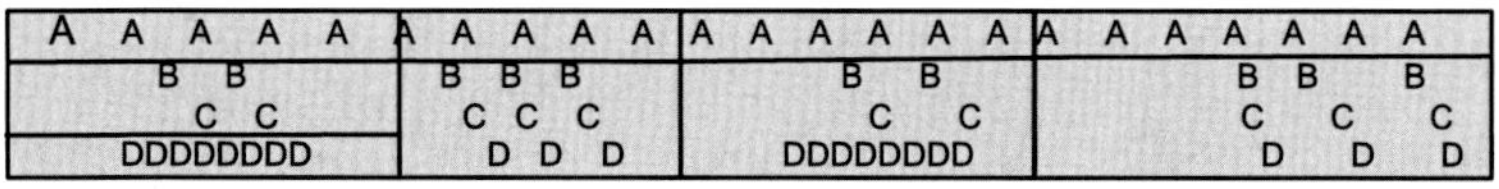

A A A A A	A A A A A	A A A A A A	A A A A A A
B B	B B B	B B	B B B
C C	C C C	C C	C C C
DDDDDDD	D D D	DDDDDDD	D D D

FIGURE 6.2: Event summarization result produced by the solution of [119].

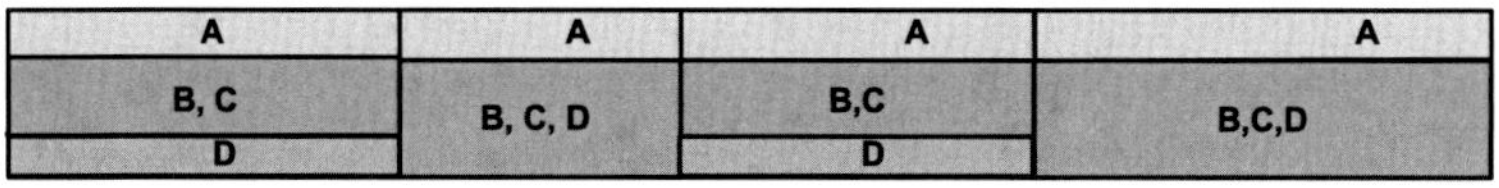

A	A	A	A
B, C	B, C, D	B,C	B,C,D
D		D	

FIGURE 6.3: A high level overview of summary.

'1's in column t represent multiple events occurring simultaneously at timestamp t. Figure 6.4 demonstrates the corresponding matrix to depict the event sequence given in Example 6.1. As shown in Figure 6.4, the example event sequence is denoted as a 4×40 matrix, where each row denotes the event occurrences of a particular type, and each column denotes the event occurrences of each timestamp.

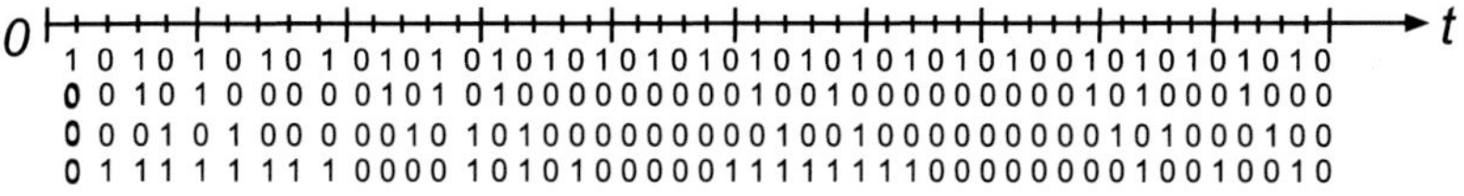

```
0 |++++|++++|++++|++++|++++|++++|++++|++++|++++|++++| ▶ t
  1 0 10 1 0 10 1 0101 010101010101010101010101001010101010
  0 0 10 1 0 00 0 0101 0100000000001001000000000001010001000
  0 0 01 0 1 00 0 0010 1010000000001001000000000001010000100
  0 1 11 1 1 11 1 0000 1010100000011111111000000000100100010
```

FIGURE 6.4: The corresponding matrix for the event sequence in Example 6.1.

Given an event sequence S, the interval (segment) $S_i \subseteq [1, n]$ is used to represent a subsequence of S, i.e., S_i is used to denote an $m \times |S_i|$ matrix of the original matrix of S. Furthermore, the number of occurrences of events with type E_j in interval (segment) S_i is denoted as $n(E_j, S_i)$. To make the notation uncluttered, we use interval and segment interchangeably in this section and use $n(E, S_i)$ instead of $n(E_j, S_i)$ if the event type is not specified in the context.

As mentioned earlier, the idea of summarizing the event sequence is to partition S into segments, i.e., $S = (S_1, S_2, \cdots, S_k)$. Since the summary should neither miss any important information nor contain any redundant information, these segments should be contiguous and non-overlapping. After segmentation, there are $k + 1$ positions, $\{b_1, b_2, \cdots, b_i, \cdots, b_{k+1} | 2 \le i \le k\}$, to represent the boundaries of these k segments. Taking Example 6.1 as an example, the event sequence is partitioned into four segments, as shown in Figure 6.2. Correspondingly, the boundaries of these segments are $\{1, 10, 21, 29\}$.

For a specific segment S_i, we aim to find a partition of event types $\Pi = \{X_1, \cdots, X_i, \cdots, X_l | X_i \subseteq \mathcal{E}\}$ such that the following properties are satisfied.

a) Each cluster X_i is a subset of the event type set, i.e., $X_i \subseteq \mathcal{E}$;

b) No cluster is overlapped with any other cluster, i.e., $\forall X_i, X_j$; we have $X_i \cap X_j = \emptyset$ if $i \neq j$;

c) The union of all the clusters covers the event set $\mathcal{E}$, i.e., $\cup_i X_i = \mathcal{E}$.

As shown in Figure 6.3, segment S_1 consists of three groups, $X_1 = \{E_A\}, X_2 = \{E_B, E_C\}, X_3 = \{E_D\}$. It is easy to validate that such a partition satisfies all the aforementioned properties.

For each group X_i, $p(X_i)$ is used to denote the probability of an event of type $E \in X_i$ within in segment S_i. Considering S_1 in Figure 6.2, we can obtain

$$p(X_1) = \frac{n(A, S_1)}{|S_1|} = \frac{3}{5},$$

$$p(X_2) = \frac{n(B, S_1) + n(C, S_1)}{2|S_1|} = \frac{3}{10},$$

$$p(X_3) = \frac{n(D, S_1)}{|S_1|} = \frac{4}{5}.$$

Based on the aforementioned preliminaries, the goal of segmentation-based summarization can be formulated as follows: given an event sequence S, identify the set of boundaries that partition S into k disjoint segments $(S_1, S_2, \cdots, S_k)$. Moreover, within each segment, identify the partition of event types that best describes the event occurrences in the segment regarding frequency. The partition scheme and the grouping in each segment constitute the summary of the given event sequence S.

Before diving into the details of the summarization algorithms, it is necessary to introduce how the summarization problem is formulated as the optimization problem and how to represent the problem from the information theory perspective.

6.2.2   The Encoding Scheme

As mentioned before, information theory techniques are used to quantify the candidate summaries in terms of the number of bits. The *minimum description length (MDL)* principle can be used as a guide to pick the best candidate as the result.

In general, *MDL* is used to pick the best hypothesis that describes the data. In the scenario of event summarization, *MDL* is used for model (summary) selection.

6.2.2.1 Encoding of Global Segmentation

A summary describes the segmentation of the event sequence $S = (S_1, S_2, \cdots, S_k)$. To encode a segment, based on MDL, only two pieces of information are needed: the boundary of the segment, and the information of the event types grouping in the segment $\text{LL}(S_i)$.

Minimum Description Length

The concept of *minimum description length* was first proposed around the 1980s by Jorma Rissanen [184, 185]. Its origin can be dated back to the concept of *Kolmogorov complexity* [197, 198], proposed by Ray Solomonoff and Andrey Kolmogorov in the 1960s. Basically, *Kolmogorov complexity* measures the complexity of a sequence as the length of the shortest program that outputs the sequence and then halts. Intuitively, it can be interpreted that the lower the complexity, the more regular the sequence is. However, two problems of *Kolmogorov complexity* make it impractical [89]: *uncomputability* and *large constants*.

To overcome these two limitations, the concept of *MDL* has been proposed as an approximate estimation of *Kolmogorov complexity*. *MDL* follows the insight of *viewing learning as data compression*. There are various ways of representing *MDL* and the simplest one is *two-part code MDL*. Given the data D and a list of candidate models (hypotheses) $\mathcal{H}$, *MDL* would pick the best models that minimize the encoding length of the data, i.e.,

$$L(D) = L(H) + L(D|H),$$

where $L(H)$ denotes the encoding length, in bits, of the model and $L(D|H)$ denotes the encoding length of describing the data using the model H. This equation intuitively shows that the best model is the one that well balances the model complexity (reflected as the encoding length of model $L(H)$) and the model error (reflected as the encoding length of the data given the model $L(D|H)$).

As the goal of event summarization is to find the best representative summary for a given piece of event log, *MDL* is an intuitive and natural choice by most event summarization solutions. For the application of event summarization, $L(H)$ quantifies the amount of information needed to describe the segmentation model of the summarization form, and $L(D|H)$ quantifies the amount of information needed for the summarization model to describe the concrete events.

As the length of the event sequence is n, $\log n$ bits are enough to describe any location in the sequence. Moreover, since two contiguous segments share the same boundary, on average, only one boundary is needed to describe one segment. Therefore, the total number of bits to describe the summary is

$$
\mathrm{TL}(S) = \sum_{i=1}^{k} \{\log n + \mathrm{LL}(S_i)\}
$$

$$
= k \log n + \sum_{i=1}^{k} \mathrm{LL}(S_i), \tag{6.1}
$$

where $\mathrm{LL}(S_i)$ denotes the encoding length of *local grouping* of the event types in each segment.

6.2.3   Summarization Algorithm

Having obtained the encoding scheme of the event sequence, the next step is to design the algorithms to find the optimal summary with the shortest encoding length. To solve this problem, a two-step polynomial time algorithm is proposed in [119] to respectively find the best local grouping and the segmentation solution. Technically, the proposed method leverages dynamic programming techniques to identify the optimal solution in polynomial time. Moreover, to further increase efficiency, alternative sub-optimal solutions using greedy strategy are also adopted. For the details of the algorithms, interested readers can refer to [119].

6.2.4   Performance Evaluation

To demonstrate the efficiency and effectiveness of the summarization solution, experimental evaluation is needed.

In terms of efficiency, two aspects of the solution are evaluated: the information compression ability and the time to perform the summarization. The information compression ability is quantified as the *compression ratio*, which indicates the ratio between the summarization results generated by the proposed algorithm A and the baseline solution, i.e.,

$$
CR(A) = \frac{\mathrm{TL}(S, M_A)}{\mathrm{TL}(S, M_{unit})},
$$

where M_{unit} indicates the naive description strategy that each event occurrence is described separately. That is, an event sequence with length n would have n segments and each segment would have $|\mathcal{E}|$ groups.

As shown in Table 6.2, four variations of the summarization algorithm, *DP-DP*, *DP-Greedy*, *Greedy-DP*, and *Greedy-Greedy*, are evaluated on three real *Windows event log* datasets. The *DP-DP* solves both the global segmentation and local grouping with *dynamic programming*; *DP-Greedy* solves the global segmentation with *dynamic programming* while solving local grouping with *greedy strategy*; *Greedy-DP* solves the global segmentation with *greedy strategy* while solving local grouping with *dynamic programming*; and *Greedy-Greedy* solves both the global segmentation and local grouping with *greedy strategy*.

It can be observed that the running time of different alternative algorithms varies vastly, from 1 second to almost 10 hours. This is largely due to the selected strategy and the characteristics of the datasets. In general, *dynamic programming* would cost more time than the *greedy strategy*. This is because *dynamic programming* is able to find the exact optimal solution, while *greedy strategy* cannot make such a guarantee.

In terms of compression ratio, the variation is large across different datasets but is stable among different alternative algorithms. It can be observed that the compression ratio is as little as 0.03 in one dataset. That is to say, compared with the original event sequence, the summary only requires as low as 3% of the information.

TABLE 6.2: Experiments with real *Windows event log* datasets (results are obtained from [119])

	application log	security log	system log
Number of events	2673	7548	6579
Number of event types	45	11	64
Running time (Seconds)			
DP-DP	3252	2185	34691
DP-Greedy	976	2373	8310
Greedy-DP	18	1	91
Greedy-Greedy	7	1	24
Compression Ratio			
DP-DP	0.04	0.32	0.03
DP-Greedy	0.04	0.32	0.03
Greedy-DP	0.04	0.34	0.03
Greedy-Greedy	0.04	0.33	0.03

6.2.5   Other Solutions

Besides the solution we introduced in the previous section, several other algorithms are also proposed to summarize data from the perspective of frequency change. The work of Wang et al. [227] extended the aforementioned work by adding more inter-segment information to reveal more detail about the system dynamics hidden in the event sequence.

To summarize the event sequence in this way, the following conjectures are made [227]:

1) a system should operate in different states;

2) in each state, the system exhibits stable behavior;

3) state transitions have certain regularity.

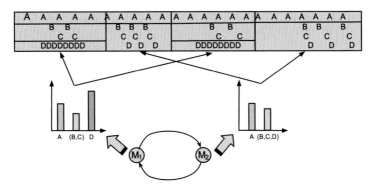

FIGURE 6.5: An example of summarizing events with HMM.

According to the conjectures, *hidden Markov model* is leveraged to model the state transitions of the system given its event sequence. Figure 6.5 illustrates how this work summarizes the event sequence in Example 6.1. Assume there are two states obtained from the example event sequence:

- State M_1, in which event D occurs the most frequently, events B and C occur the least frequently, and event A lies in the middle. The first and the third segments belong to this state.

- State M_2, in which event A occurs frequently while events B, C, and D occur less frequently. The second and the fourth segments belong to this state.

Clearly, this kind of summarization result is more understandable and more meaningful, as it reveals more interesting insights of the system. Similar to the previous work [119], the problem of finding the best summary that describes the state transition of the system is also formulated as an optimization problem, and the goal is to find the best segmentation as well as the *HMM* that describes the given event sequence with the least amount of information. In short, the amount of information to describe the event sequence is quantified as the number of bits used to describe the set of models $\mathcal{M}$ and the set of segments $\mathcal{I}$, i.e.,

$$Q^*(\mathcal{M}, \mathcal{I}) = C_d + C_s, \tag{6.2}$$

$$Q(\mathcal{M}^*, \mathcal{I}^*) = \operatorname*{argmin}_{\mathcal{M}, \mathcal{I}} Q(\mathcal{M}, \mathcal{I}). \tag{6.3}$$

In Eq.(6.2), each model in $\mathcal{M}$ is composed of a set of m probabilities ($M_i = (p_i(E_1), p_i(E_2), \cdots, p_i(E_m))$). Moreover, C_d denotes the number of bits required to describe the event occurrences within all segments, and C_s denotes the number of bits to describe the segments. For the details of the encoding and the corresponding optimization algorithm, the interested reader can refer to [227].

6.3   Summarizing with Temporal Dynamics

The state-of-the-art frequency-change-based event summarization solutions are able to reveal the temporal dynamics of the segments, but fail to provide information about the temporal dynamics among events. As the events are more natural components than the generated segments (by the summarization algorithms), it is more intuitive to provide an event-centric description in the summary results.

The frequency-change-based summarization approaches can produce a comprehensive summary from the input event sequence. However, this result as well as the frequency-change-based summarization algorithms have several limitations:

(1) The frequency-change-based approaches focus on generating summaries that only demonstrate the frequency changes of event types across adjacent segments. However, they ignore the temporal information among event types within each segment. As a result, they fail to capture the temporal dynamics of event patterns.

(2) These algorithms generate the same number of event patterns with the same boundaries for all event types. The unified pattern boundary requirement is impractical since different event types can have different underlying generating mechanisms. Consider, in a distributed system, that events may come from a large number of nodes that may be irrelevant to each other. Therefore, requiring a global segmentation would be inappropriate since many real patterns will be broken. Instead, having different boundaries for different event types could improve the event pattern identification and lead to better summaries.

(3) The above-generated summary is difficult for system administrators to understand and take appropriate action. This is because system administrators may not have enough mathematical background to extract useful information from advanced mathematical models.

To address the above limitations, a novel approach called *natural event summarization (NES)* has been proposed by Jiang et al. in [112]. This approach first uses inter-arrival histograms to capture the temporal relationships among same-type and different-type events, then it finds a set of disjoint histograms to summarize the input event sequence based on *MDL*. Finally, the resulting summary is represented as an *event relationship network*.

There are multiple advantages of this approach. First, using inter-arrival histograms allows for different boundaries for different event types. This allows the summary to be more flexible. Second, the inter-arrival histograms provide a conducive way to describe two main types of the event patterns: *periodic patterns* and *correlation patterns*. These two patterns are able to capture the majority of the temporal dynamics of event sequences and can be used to generate the summaries. Moreover, many action rules can be derived almost directly from the generated summaries.

To better describe how *NES* works, Example 6.2 presents an illustrative example.

Example 6.2 *Continuing Example 6.1, in which the event sequence contains four event types. Suppose the event types are A "an event created by an antivirus process," B "the firewall asks for the access privilege," C "a port was listed as an exception," and D "the firewall operation mode has been changed." The frequency-change-based event summarization approaches (e.g., [227]) segment the sequence into four segments (see Figure 6.5). Within each segment, this method groups the event types based on their occurrence frequency. Moreover, an HMM is leveraged to model the state transition between the segments.*

Figure 6.6 shows the output summary generated by the *NES* method according to the example event sequence in Example 6.1. In the example event sequence, events with type C always appear after B during the whole time period. We can also observe that during time period $[t_1, t_2]$ and $[t_3, t_6]$, events with type D also appear after B. Therefore, two correlation patterns, $B \rightarrow C$ and $B \rightarrow D$ (associated with the corresponding time periods), can be identified. From the example event sequence, we can also observe that the events with type A appear regularly throughout the whole time period. Therefore, all the instances of event type A can be summarized as only one pattern. Since event type A is the antivirus monitoring process event, its stable period indicates that this process works normally.

6.3.1 Approach Overview

The framework of *natural event summarization* is shown in Figure 6.7. As previously mentioned, this approach is designed based on summarizing the inter-arrival histograms which capture the distribution of time intervals between events. These histograms provide a concise way to describe *periodic patterns* of the same event type and the *correlation patterns* of different event types. The reason for focusing on the aspect of temporal patterns of the event sequence is that this kind of information tells most of the story of the status and behavior of the system.

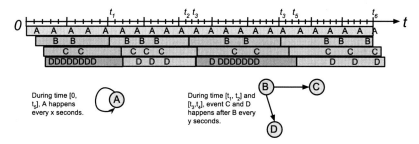

FIGURE 6.6: An example for *natural event summarization* [112].

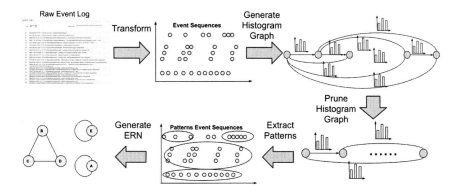

FIGURE 6.7: The *natural event summarization* framework proposed in [112].

In *natural event summarization*, the event summarization problem is for-mulated as finding a set of disjoint inter-arrival histograms. To achieve this goal, *MDL* is leveraged for model selection. It is known that the techniques of *MDL* have also been used by existing frequency-change-based event summa-rization algorithms. However, different from its usage in previous works, *MDL* is used here for encoding the inter-arrival histograms and for identifying the set of disjoint histograms. The problem of finding a set of disjoint histograms can be solved optimally by seeking the shortest path from the histogram graph that represents the temporal relations among histograms (introduced in detail later). To further improve the efficiency of event summarization, an alternative solution to obtain approximate summarization results is also proposed. This alternative solution leverages the multi-resolution property of wavelet trans-formation to reduce the size of the histogram graph to achieve faster processing speed. The final summarization results of *natural event summarization* can be described as an *event relationship network* where many actionable rules are readily available.

6.3.2   Interval Histograms

To better understand how *natural event summarization* solves this problem, the concept of inter-arrival histograms as well as the inter-arrival distribution of time interval between events are first introduced.

Suppose an event sequence S comprises of a series of event occurrences in the form of (e, t) ordered by the associated timestamp t. Given two event types x and y, let $S^{(xy)}$ be the subsequence of S that only contains events of types x and y. Suppose $S^{(xy)}$ is split into k disjoint segments $S^{(xy)} = (S_1, S_2, \cdots, S_k)$. An inter-arrival histogram (or interval histogram) $h_{xy}(S_i)$ is used to capture the distribution of time interval between events of type x and type y in S_i. Specifically, the bin $h_{xy}(S_i)[b]$ is the total number of intervals whose length is b. Let $next(t, y)$ denote the timestamp of the first occurrence of an event with type y that occurs after timestamp t in S_i.

Definition 6.1 *Inter-arrival histogram:*

$$h_{xy}(S_i)[b] = |\{i | e_i = x, next(t_i, y) - t_i = b\}|,$$

where t_i denotes the timestamp of e_i.

If $x \neq y$, then the inter-arrival histograms capture the time intervals for the events of different types; for the case of $x = y$, they capture the time intervals of events of the same type. Given an interval histogram, we can use a standard histogram to approximate it. The standard histogram is formally defined in Definition 6.2.

Definition 6.2 *Standard Histogram: A special kind of interval histogram with one or two non-empty bins and all these non-empty bins have the same value $\frac{\#intervals}{n_{non}}$, where $\#intervals$ indicates the number of intervals and n_{non} indicates the number of non-empty bins. $\bar{h}_{xy}(S_i)$ is used to denote the corresponding standard histogram of $h_{xy}(S_i)$.*

Note that the aforementioned two types of temporal patterns, *periodic patterns* and *correlation patterns*, can be easily described using standard histograms. The *periodic patterns* and *correlation patters* are formally defined in Definition 6.3.

Definition 6.3 *Periodic pattern and correlation pattern: A pattern is a 5-tuple (t_s, t_e, x, y, P), where 1) t_s and t_e denote the start position and end position of the event sequence described by the pattern, respectively; 2) x and y denote the types of events involved in the pattern; 3) P contains the periodic parameters. The pattern can contain 1 or 2 period parameters, which indicate the inter-arrival value between event x and y. Moreover, if $x = y$, this pattern is a periodic pattern, otherwise, it is a correlation pattern.*

To help understand the definitions, Example 6.3 gives a detailed showcase about how to utilize standard histogram and periodic/correlation patterns to summarize a given event sequence.

Example 6.3 *Given an event sequence S, the timestamps for two event types E_a and E_b and their occurrences are listed in Table 6.3. Suppose there is only one segment in S and there exists a periodic pattern for E_a and a correlation pattern between E_a and E_b. The segment is described by inter-arrival histograms $h_{aa}(S)$ and $h_{ab}(S)$ in Figure 6.8 and approximated by two standard histograms, shown in Figure 6.9.*

TABLE 6.3: Occurrences of event types E_a and E_b

Event type	Occurrence timestamp
E_a	5, 10, 16, 21, 25, 31, 35, 40, 46, 51, 56, 61, 66, 70, 76, 81, 86, 92, 97,102, 107
E_b	7, 12, 18, 22, 26, 33, 36, 42, 47, 52, 57, 62, 67, 72, 78, 83, 88, 94, 98, 103, 108
S for $h_{aa}(S)$	The same as the first row.
S for $h_{ab}(S)$	The union of the first two rows.

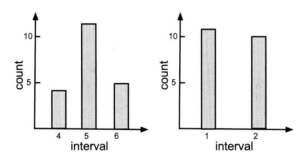

FIGURE 6.8: Inter-arrival histogram $h_{aa}(S)$ (left) and inter-arrival histogram $h_{ab}(S)$ (right).

It can be seen that the histograms of the example show clear patterns. However, the histograms can be vague and large for sequences with many events. The two histograms shown in Figure 6.8 and their corresponding standard histograms in Figure 6.9 are just two of many candidate histograms that can possibly depict the event relationships/patterns hidden in Example 6.3. It seems easy to find the most appropriate standard histograms for the example with only one segment, but the best standard histograms are not easily identified in a real-world scenario, as neither the best segments nor the best histograms are known. In fact, it is very challenging to accurately and efficiently find the most suitable combination of the standard histograms to describe the event sequence.

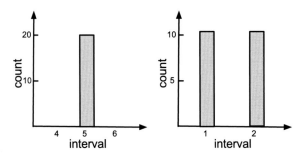

FIGURE 6.9: Standard histogram that best approximates $h_{aa}(S)$ (left) and $h_{ab}(S)$ (right).

6.3.3   Finding the Best Histograms with MDL

To find the best standard histograms, *NES* also leverages the *MDL* techniques, that is, encoding the histogram in bits, and finds the best combinations of standard histograms that require the minimum number of bits.

To show how to quantify the amount of information of the summaries, the encoding scheme of the histograms needs to be introduced first. In this section, how the standard histograms are encoded is first introduced. Then, given an inter-arrival histogram, how it can be approximated using a standard histogram will be described. Finally, the problem of using histograms to summarize the event sequence will be formulated.

6.3.3.1   Encoding Standard Histograms

Given an event subsequence $S^{(xy)}$ of event type x and y with disjoint segments $S^{(xy)} = (S_1, \cdots, S_k)$, to encode a standard histogram $\bar{h}_{xy}(S_i)$, the following components need to be included. These components are necessary and sufficient to describe a histogram.

1. **Event type depicted by the histogram.** Each histogram should be associated with one or two event types, depending on the type of relationship it depicts. Given the set of event types $\mathcal{E}$, it is enough to use $L(m) = \log |\mathcal{E}|$ bits to represent each event type.

2. **Boundaries of S_i.** The relationship depicted by an interval histogram has two boundaries indicating where the corresponding segment is. Each boundary requires $L(b) = \log |S^{(xy)}|$ bits to encode its information. As the subsequence is just a projection of the original event sequence on specific event types, the length of subsequences, including events with type x and y, is actually the same length of the whole event sequence, i.e., $|S^{(xy)}| = |S|$ for $\forall E_x, E_y \in \mathcal{E}$.

3. **Information of non-empty bins in the histogram.** This piece of information can be encoded using

$$L(bin) = \log \delta + \log i_{max} + \log |S| + \sum_{i=1}^{n_{non}} \log i_{max} + \sum_{i=1}^{n_{non}} \log |S_i|.$$

The coding length consists of five terms. The first term uses $\log \delta$ bits to encode the largest interval i_{max} in the segment S_i, where δ denotes the allowed largest interval (represented as the largest value in the x-axis of a histogram). In the framework of *NES*, it is set as the number of seconds in one day. The second term uses $\log i_m ax$ bits to encode the number of non-empty bins n_{non}. Since the largest interval is i_{max}, it is enough to use $\log(i_{max})$ bits to represent such information. The third term uses $\log |S|$ bits to encode the length of S_i. Since, in the extreme situation, the length of the longest segment equals the length of the whole sequence (there is only one segment), it is enough to use $\log |S|$ bits to represent such information. The fourth and fifth terms encode all the indices (n_{non} of them need to be encoded) and the number of elements contained in each of the n_{non} bins, respectively.

Putting them all together, the number of bits needed for encoding a standard histogram $\bar{h}_{xy}(S_i)$ is

$$L(\bar{h}_{xy}(S_i)) = L(m) + L(b) + L(bin).$$

6.3.3.2 Encoding Interval Histograms

Given an inter-arrival histogram $h_{xy}(S_i)$, we want to measure how well this histogram can be represented by an event pattern, or equivalently, how well it can be approximated by standard histograms.

Histogram distance. Histogram distance describes how much information is needed to depict the *necessary bin element movements* defined in [57] to transform $\bar{h}(S_i)$ into $h(S_i)$. To make notations uncluttered, we drop the subscripts xy and they should be clear from the context. The code length of the distance can be calculated as

$$L(h[S_i]|\bar{h}[S_i]) = \sum_{i \in Non} |be_i - bs_i| \log(i_{max}), \qquad (6.4)$$

where Non is the union of the indices sets of non-empty bins in both histograms, and be_i and bs_i denote the value (number of elements) of bin i in $h[S_i]$ and $\bar{h}[S_i]$, respectively. For each element at bin i, we can assign a new bin index to indicate where it should be moved. Eq.(6.4) measures the bits of information needed by summing up the elements in unmatched bins.

In summary, the amount of information required to describe an inter-arrival histogram $h(S_i)$ using an event pattern $\bar{h}(S_i)$ equals the summation of the code length for $\bar{h}(S_i)$ and the distance between $h(S_i)$ and $\bar{h}(S_i)$. Since there may be multiple standard histograms, we define the code length for an interval histogram $h(S_i)$ as

$$L(h(S_i)) = argmin_{\bar{h}(S_i) \in \bar{H}(S_i)} L(\bar{h}(S_i) + L(h(S_i)|\bar{h}(S_i)), \qquad (6.5)$$

where $\bar{H}(S_i)$ is the set of all possible standard histograms on S_i.

6.3.4 Problem Statement for Histogram-Based Event Summarization

Given an event sequence D, for each subsequence S containing event types x and y, the minimum coding length $L(S)$ for S is defined as

$$L(S) = \arg\min_{\{S_1, S_2, \ldots, S_k\}} \sum_i L(h(S_i)). \qquad (6.6)$$

Since the boundaries for different subsequences are independent, the minimum description length for the input event sequence D is quantified as

$$L(D) = \sum_{S \in D} L(S). \qquad (6.7)$$

Hence the event summarization problem is to *find the best set of segments* $\{S_1, S_2, ..., S_k\}$ *as well as the best approximated standard histograms to achieve the minimum description length.*

6.3.5 The NES Algorithm

Having introduced how the histograms are encoded and how the problem is formulated, now we can go into the details of the algorithm that finds the best solution. First, we introduce a heuristic algorithm that can find the best set of segments of $S^{(xy)}$ in polynomial time. Then we present the method of generating ERN using the event patterns.

6.3.5.1 Finding the Best Segmentation

The problem of finding the best set of segments can be easily reduced to the problem of finding a shortest path from the generated histogram graph G. The histogram graph G is generated as follows:

1. Given $S^{(xy)}$, let n_{xy} be the number of inter-arrivals between event x and y (x, y can be the same type) in $S^{(xy)}$, generate n_{xy} vertices and label them with the positions of each x (1 to n_{xy}).

2. Add $edge(a, b)$ from vertex $v[a]$ to vertex $v[b]$ for each vertex pair $v[a], v[b]$, where $1 \leq a < b \leq n_{xy}$. Assign the weight of each $edge(a, b)$

as $L(h(S_i))$, where S_i starts at position a and ends at b. Note that, to compute $L(h(S_i))$, we need to find the best standard histogram $\bar{h}(S_i)$ for $h(S_i)$ in the sense that $L(h(S_i))$ is minimized (as shown in Eq.(6.5)). This can be done using a greedy strategy. Given $h(S_i)$, we can sort the bins in decreasing order based on their values. Then we iteratively perform the following two steps: (1) generating $\bar{h}(S_i)$ using the top i bins, (2) computing $L(h(S_i))$, (3) increasing i by 1. The iteration continues until $L(h(S_i))$ begins to increase. The $\bar{h}(S_i)$ corresponding to the minimum description length $L(h(S_i))$ is often referred as the best standard histogram for $h(S_i)$.

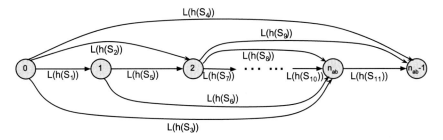

FIGURE 6.10: An example histogram graph.

After generating the histogram graph, the classical shortest path algorithm (e.g., *Dijkstra* algorithm) can be used to find the vertices on the shortest path from $v[1]$ to $v[n_{xy}]$. Figure 6.10 shows an example histogram graph and Algorithm 3 illustrates the *summarization* process of our natural event summarization framework (*NES* for short). In line 4, the algorithm generates a set of event subsequences from D; there are m subsequences for the same event type (i.e., $x = y$) and $m^2 - m$ subsequences for different event types (i.e., $x \neq y$). Line 6 generates the directed acyclic histogram graph for each subsequence S and uses the *Dijkstra* algorithm to find the shortest path $P = (v[i_1], v[i_2], ..., v[i_p])$. The best segmentation solution contains the segments $< v[i_1], v[i_2] >, < v[i_2], v[i_3] >, ..., < v[i_p - 1], v[i_p] >$. Lines 8 and 9 represent each segment using the best fitted event patterns (i.e., the best standard histograms), and put them into the set $\mathcal{R}$.

For each histogram graph G, the *Dijkstra* algorithm requires $O(|E| + |V| \log |V|) = O(|S|^2)$ time. Therefore, the total running time is $O((m+m(m-1))|S|^2) = O(|D|^2)$.

6.3.6 Generating Summarization Graph

Although the set of event patterns can be described in text, we show that they can be used to construct an easy-to-understand event relationship network (ERN) which produces a concise yet expressive representation of the

---

Algorithm 3 The NES Algorithm

---

1. **input:** event sequence D.
2. **output:** all relationships $\mathcal{R}$.
3. Identify m from S, relationship set $\mathcal{R} \leftarrow \emptyset$;
4. Separate D into a set of S;
5. **for all** S **do**
6.   Generate directed graph G;
7.   Use **Dijkstra**(G) to find shortest path P;
8.   Generate relationships R from P;
9. $\mathcal{R} \leftarrow \mathcal{R} \bigcup R$;
10. **end for**
11. **return** $\mathcal{R}$;

---

event summary. The procedure for building ERN is straightforward: it first generates the vertices for each event type involved in any event patterns, and then adds edges for event patterns and stores necessary information (e.g., segmentation, periods, and time intervals) onto the edges.

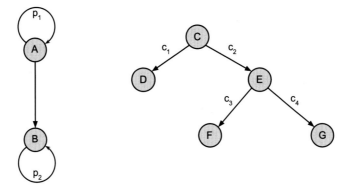

FIGURE 6.11: An example ERN graph.

Figure 6.11 shows an example ERN graph. It contains two periodic patterns, $A \xrightarrow{p_1} A$, $B \xrightarrow{p_2} B$, and five correlation patterns, $A \xrightarrow{c_1} B$, $C \xrightarrow{c_2} D$, $C \xrightarrow{c_3} E$, $E \xrightarrow{c_4} F$, $E \xrightarrow{c_5} G$. For simplicity, the ranges of segments are ignored.

6.3.7 Efficiency Improvement

The NES algorithm described in Section 6.3.5 finds the best segmentation by checking all positions in S, which is computation intensive. In fact, given an event subsequence S, boundaries should only be located at positions where inter-arrival times change rapidly, because segmentation at smooth places would waste encoding bits. Based on this observation, an effective pruning algorithm is proposed in [112]. This algorithm is able to prune a large part of boundaries that are unlikely to be the boundaries of segments. It greatly accelerates the summarization process by reducing the size of the histogram graph. By utilizing multi-resolution analysis (MRA) of wavelet transformation, the pruning can be done in linear time in the worst case.

6.3.7.1 Preprocessing

For ease of pruning, some preprocessing steps are needed. Given an event subsequence S, it is preprocessed as follows:

1. *Obtaining inter-arrival sequences*: given $S = (< e, t_1 >, \cdots, < e, t_{|S|} >)$, transform it into inter-arrival sequence $V = (t_2 - t_1, t_3 - t_2, \cdots, t_{|S|} - t_{|S|-1})$;

2. *Padding*: append 0's to the tail of the sequence until the length of an interval sequence equals a power of 2;

3. *Transforming*: use the *Haar* wavelet [95, 142, 205, 129] as the the wavelet function and apply fast wavelet transformation (FWT) on V to obtain the transformation result W.

The resulting W contains the wavelet coefficients of the inter-arrival sequence, which is the input of our pruning algorithm.

6.3.7.2 Pruning Unlikely Boundaries

Due to the multi-resolution analysis (MRA) property of wavelet transformation, the deviation of inter-arrivals in V can be viewed from W at different resolutions. Since wavelet transformation captures both the resolution and the location information, for each $W[i]$, the corresponding segment in V can be quickly located. For example, if $|V| = 1024$, the elements $W[1]$ and $W[2]$ contain the averaging information and the "difference" information of the highest resolution (in this example, resolution 1024) of original series, respectively. The elements $W[3]$ and $W[4]$ contain the information of V at resolution 512. Specifically, $W[3]$ corresponds to the first half of V and $W[4]$ corresponds to the second half of V.

By taking advantage of such a property, our pruning algorithm identifies the inter-arrival deviation in a top-down manner. The basic idea of the algorithm is as follows: it checks the element $W[i]$, starting from $i = 2$, which contains the deviation of inter-arrival for the whole sequence V. There are three possible cases:

Case I: If $W[i]$ is small, it means the corresponding subsequence in V for $W[i]$ is smooth enough and segmentation is not needed. In this case, the algorithm records the boundaries of the segment, and then stops.

Case II: If $W[i]$ is large, it means the deviation of inter-arrivals in the corresponding subsequence in V is too large. In this case, the subsequence needs to be split into two halves and the algorithm needs to perform recursively.

Case III: If $W[i]$ records the deviation of inter-arrivals at the lowest resolution, the algorithm just records the start and end boundaries and returns.

Algorithm 4 Algorithm of *BoundaryPruning*

---

1. **input:** $W, level, i$.
2. **output:** Boundary set B after pruning.
3. Set $B \leftarrow \emptyset$;
4. $threshold \leftarrow \frac{W[1]}{2^{\log |W| - level}}$;
5. $spectrum \leftarrow W[i]$;
6. **if** $spectrum < threshold$ or reaches to the lowest resolution **then**
7.   Add corresponding boundaries to B;
8. **else**
9. $i_1 = 2i - 1, i_2 = 2i$;
10. $B_1 \leftarrow$ BoundaryPruning$(W, level - 1, i_1)$;
11. $B_2 \leftarrow$ BoundaryPruning$(W, level - 1, i_2)$;
12. $B \leftarrow B \cup B_1 \cup B_2$
13. **end if**
14. **return** B;

Algorithm 4 provides the pseudocode for *BoundaryPruning*. The parameter *level* (initialized as $\log |W|$) denotes the current level of resolution that the algorithm checks, and i denotes the current position in transformed result W (i.e., $W[i]$) to be checked. The algorithm calculates the corresponding threshold as $\frac{W[1]}{2^{\log |W| - level}}$, which reflects the average deviation of inter-arrival at resolution 2^{level} and changes dynamically according to the *level*.

Example 6.4 uses a sample dataset to illustrate how the pruning algorithm works.

Example 6.4 *An input inter-arrival sequence V is shown in Figure 6.12. The algorithm starts from the highest resolution. It finds that $W[2] = 3$ is too large, so the whole inter-arrival sequence cannot be segmented with only one segment. At a lower resolution, the algorithm finds that $W[4]$ is small enough, so the corresponding subsequence $< 2, 1, 2, 1, 2, 1, 3, 1 >$ can be considered as one segment. For the element $W[3] = -2$ representing the first half of V, it is still too large and the corresponding subsequence $< 1, 1, 1, 1, 1, 3, 1, 1 >$ cannot be considered as only one segment. Hence the algorithm drills down to a lower resolution to do the same check task. Finally, the algorithm divides V into 5 segments, and 6 boundaries are recorded and the remaining 11 boundaries are pruned. Figure 6.13 shows the effect of BoundaryPruning in reducing the size of the histogram graph.*

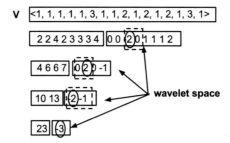

FIGURE 6.12: Segments information in a wavelet spectrum sequence.

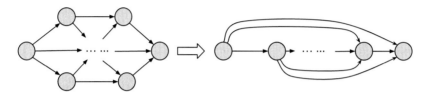

FIGURE 6.13: Before pruning, the histogram graph contains 17 vertices and 136 edges; after pruning, the histogram graph contains only 6 vertices and 14 edges.

The pruning algorithm only scans W once. In general cases, the algorithm does not need to check all the elements in W. If the inter-arrival sequence is smooth enough, the algorithm would stop checking at a high resolution. Only in the worst case, the algorithm has to check every element in W. Since $|W| = |V| = |S| - 1$, the algorithm runs in $o(|S|)$ for the average case and $O(|S|)$ in the worst case.

6.3.8 Performance Evaluation

The evaluation of *NES* is conducted in a similar way as described in Section 6.2.4, where the compression ratio and the efficiency are investigated.

Table 6.4 shows the experimental evaluation results by applying *NES* to the *Windows event log*s (the same kinds of logs used in Section 6.2.4). Besides an alternative angle of summarization, *NES* shows significant improvement over previous approaches in terms of processing time. The frequency-change-based summarization methods require more than a thousand seconds to find the optimal summarization solution while the *NES* methods only cost around 10% of the time. In terms of compression ratio, *NES* can generate the summaries with highly compressed information. It is shown that the compression ratio can be as low as 0.0216, which indicates that the summary is only 2% the size of the original event sequence.

Figure 6.14 shows an example summarization result for the security log.

TABLE 6.4: Experimental evaluation results

	application log	security log	system log
Number of events	5634	21850	3935
Event types	100	17	50
Running time (seconds)			
NES	173	3102	108
NES-Prune	22	56	4
Compression ratio			
NES	0.0597	0.0312	0.0454
NES-Prune	0.0531	0.0216	0.0464

The resulting *ERN*s are immediately useful for managing computer systems. A system administrator can devise automatic event handling for each pattern type. For example, in the context of security monitoring, periodic event patterns with a short period (e.g., the one formed by event type 861) is usually caused by a malicious or ill-configured program that attempts to exploit security holes. Once such a pattern is identified, a security response process should be triggered. A correlation pattern usually represents an episode of an evolving problem going through various phases. One can devise proactive event condition-action rules to prevent serious incidents from happening [112].

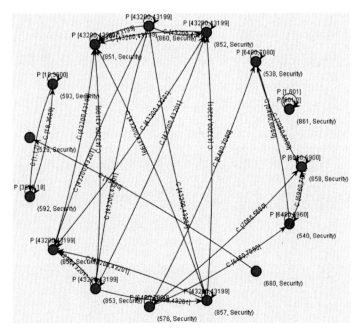

FIGURE 6.14: An example summarization result for the security log.

6.4 Facilitating the Summarization Tasks

Besides the researchers who are working on proposing concrete event summarization methods, a lot of other researchers have also been working on providing various other summarization methods [176, 191, 21, 216]. Each of these approaches defines its own way of summarizing event sequences. A brief summary of these methods is illustrated in Table 6.5.

TABLE 6.5: A brief summary of the event summarization methods

Paper	Category	Description
Peng, Perng & Li, 2007 [176]	Temporal Dynamics	Using a correlation graph ERN to summarize the correlation between events.
Kiernan & Terzi, 2008 [119]	Frequency Change	Using segmentation to summarize changes over time and using the event frequency group to summarize events within each time period.
Aharon et al., 2009 [21]	Other	Clustering the events and using the clusters as the summary.
Kiernan & Terzi, 2009 [120]	Frequency Change	Similar to [119], but allowing mismatch among segments.
Wang et al., 2010 [227]	Frequency Change	Extension of [119]. Using the Markov model to represent the transition between segments.
Schneider et al., 2010 [191]	Temporal Dynamics	Using a graph to represent the relations of *AlwaysFollowedBy*, *AlwaysPrecededBy*, and *NeverFollowedBy* among events.
Jiang, Perng & Li, 2011 [112]	Temporal Dynamics	A richer form of [176]. Summarizing the events from the perspective of periodic patterns and correlation patterns.
Tatti & Vreeken, 2012 [216]	Temporal Dynamics	Summarizing the events using a set of serial episodes under the guidance of MDL.

Apart from solving the summarization problem from the algorithmic perspective, some efforts [77] have also been made toward providing various event summarization representations. From all these explorations, it can be concluded that event summarization is not a problem that can be handled by a single model or algorithm. In fact, there are tons of ways to conduct event summarization for different users with different purposes. To obtain an event summary from different perspectives, an analyst has to re-preprocess the data and change the program time after time. This is a drain on analysts' productivity.

The predicament of event summarization is very similar to that of the time when every data-intensive task had to use a separate program for data manipulation. The data representation and query problems were eventually addressed by the *ER* model and *SQL*. Following the historical path of *DBMS* and query languages, it is clear that event summarization as well as event analysis should also be abstracted to an independent software system with a uniform data model and an expressive query language.

An event summarization system has to be flexible enough so that real-life scenarios can be adequately and efficiently handled and supported. The following are some typical scenarios that an event analyst would encounter.

Scenario 1 *An analyst obtains a system log of the whole year, but he only wants to view the summary of the events that are recorded in the latest 30 days. Also, he wants to see the summary without the trivial event "firewall scan." Moreover, he wants to see the summarization with the hourly granularity.*

Scenario 2 *After viewing summarization results, the analyst suspects that one particular time period of events behaves abnormally, so he wants to conduct anomaly detection just for that period to find out more details.*

Scenario 3 *The system has generated a new set of security logs for the current week. The analyst wants to merge the new log into the repository and also to summarize the merged log with the daily granularity.*

To handle the work in the first scenario using existing event summarization methods, we need to perform the following tasks: (1) write a program or use the existing program to extract the events that occurred during the specified time range; (2) write or leverage an existing program to remove the irrelevant event types; (3) write or leverage an existing program to aggregate the events by hour; and (4) feed the pre-processed events to existing event summarization methods to obtain the summary. Similarly, about the same amount of work is needed for the second and the third scenarios. To handle the task in the second scenario, three things need to be done: (1) identify the suspicious patterns from the summary, and then locate the root cause events from the original event logs. (2) write or leverage an existing program to extract the targeted portion of events from the original log. (3) feed the extracted events to a specified anomaly detection algorithm. For the third scenario, the analyst first needs to write or use an existing program to merge the events. This program should be able to handle the problems of granularity inconsistency, event type inconsistency, and time range discontinuity. After merging the two logs, the analyst has to do all the work he does for the first scenario. Note that, if parameter tuning is needed, a typical summarization task requires hundreds of such iterations in the aforementioned scenarios. Therefore, it is inefficient and tedious.

Similar to online analytical processing (OLAP) as an exploration process for transactional data, event summarization is also a trial-and-error process for temporal event data. As event summarization requires repetitive exploration of the events from different views, we believe *it is necessary to have an integrated framework to enable users to easily, interactively, and selectively extract, summarize, and analyze the temporal event data.* Event summarization should be the first step of any other mining tasks, and its goal is to enable analysts to quickly gain the general idea of the events.

To meet the above requirements, a flexible and extensible event summarization framework called *META* is proposed in [113] to facilitate multi-resolution summarization as well as its associated tasks. Instead of inventing new summarization algorithms, *META* focuses on filling the missing component of the event summarization task and making it a complete knowledge discovery process. Therefore, *META* is complementary and orthogonal to previous works that focus on proposing different event summarization algorithms.

META is designed with the following principles: 1) the framework should be flexible enough to accommodate many real-life scenarios, and 2) the framework should ease summarization task implementation as much as possible. Figure 6.15 shows the corresponding workflows of conducting the above scenarios with the *META* framework, including ad hoc summarization, event storing, recovering, updating, and merging. For each scenario, the analyst only needs to write and execute a short piece of script.

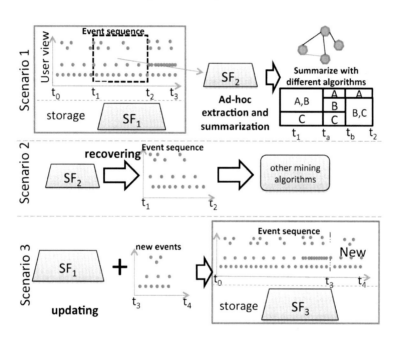

FIGURE 6.15: Summarization workflows of example scenarios.

In general, *META* transforms all the event sequences into a specifically designed multi-resolution model called *summarization forest*. This model can efficiently store the event sequences as well as the necessary meta-data. The *summarization forest* is designed to store and represent the event sequence in multi-resolution views with a specified precision. On top of the *summarization forest*, a set of basic operations is proposed to express summarization tasks. Each basic operation can be viewed as an atomic operation that directly operates the data. At a higher level, five commonly used event summarization tasks are presented by using the basic operations. These tasks include ad hoc summarization, event storing, recovering, updating, and merging. By using these event summarization tasks, analysts can quickly conduct event summarization with little extra effort, and their efficiency can be significantly increased.

6.4.1 The Multi-Resolution Data Model

In this section, we first describe how to use an *event vector*, an intermediate data structure, to represent the event sequence. Then we introduce the *summarization forest* (SF), a data model to store event sequences with multiple resolutions.

6.4.1.1 Vector Representation of Event Occurrences

Given an event sequence S with $|\mathcal{E}| = m$ event types and time range $[t_s, t_e]$, S is decomposed into m subsequences $S = (S_{e_1}, ..., S_{e_m})$; each contains the instances of one event type. Afterwards, each S_i is converted into an event vector V_i, where the indexes indicate the time and the values indicate the number of event occurrences. During conversion, the length of each vector is constrained to be $2^l, l \in \mathcal{Z}^+$, where l is the smallest value that satisfies $2^l \geq t_e - t_s$. In the vector, the first $t_e - t_s$ entries would record the actual occurrences of the event instances, and the remaining entries are filled with 0's. Example 6.5 provides a simple illustration of how we convert the event sequence.

Example 6.5 *The left figure in Figure 6.16 gives an event sequence containing three event types within time range $[t_1, t_{12}]$. The right figure shows the conversion result of the given event sequence. Note that the original event sequence is decomposed into three subsequences. Each subsequence representing one event type is converted to a vector with length 16. The numbers in bold indicate the actual occurrences of the events, and the remaining numbers are filled with 0's.*

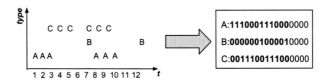

FIGURE 6.16: Converting the original event sequence to the vectors.

Vectors intuitively describe the occurrences of events, but this kind of representation is neither storage efficient (as it requires $O(|\mathcal{E}|n)$) nor analysis efficient (as it does not support multi-resolution analysis). To facilitate storage and analysis, the *summarization tree* is proposed to model the event occurrences of a single type. Furthermore, the *summarization forest* is proposed to model the event occurrences of the whole event log.

6.4.1.2 Summarization Tree

The summarization tree is used to store the event occurrences for a single event type. It is capable of providing both frequency and locality of occurrences simultaneously. Moreover, it satisfies the multi-resolution analysis (*MRA*) [155] requirements by representing the event occurrences with various subspaces. This property enables analysts to choose a proper subspace to view the data at a corresponding granularity. The summarization tree is formally defined below.

Definition 6.4 *A **summarization tree** (ST) is a balanced tree where all nodes store temporal information about the occurrences of events. The tree has the following properties:*

1. *Each summarization tree has two types of nodes: a summary node and description nodes.*

2. *The root is a summary node, and it has only one child. The root stores the total occurrences of the events throughout the event sequence.*

3. *All the other nodes are description nodes. They either have two children or no child. These nodes store the frequency difference between adjacent chunks (the frequency of the first chunk subtracted by that of its following chunk) of a sequence described by lower level nodes.*

4. *The height of the summarization tree is the number of levels of the description tree. The height of a node in a tree is counted from bottom to top, starting from 0. The nodes at height i store the frequency differences that can be used to obtain the temporal information of granularity i[1].*

Considering event type A in Example 6.5, Figure 6.17 shows its vector and the corresponding summarization tree. As illustrated in the figure, the summarization tree stores the sum of the occurrences frequency (six occurrences) at the root node, and the frequency differences (within the dashed box) in the description nodes at various granularities. Note that, at the same level of the tree, the description nodes store the differences between adjacent sequence chunks at the same granularity. The larger the depth, the more detailed differences they store. For example, at granularity 1, every two adjacent time slots in the original event sequence are grouped into one chunk, and the grouped event sequence is 21021000. Correspondingly, in the summarization

---

[1] According to the property of *MRA*, the time precision of nodes decreases exponentially as the index of their granularity increases. For example, if the precision of the original data is 1 second, the corresponding tree nodes at granularity i represent the data every 2^i seconds.

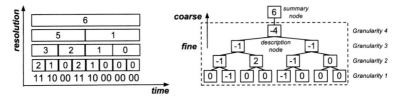

FIGURE 6.17: Relationship between vector and ST.

tree, the frequency differences of each adjacent time slot $(0, -1, 0, 0, -1, 0, 0, 0)$ are recorded at the leaf level. Similarly, the frequency differences at various granularities are recorded in the description nodes at the corresponding levels.

It is clear that the space complexity of the summarization tree is $O(|T|)$, where $|T| = n$ and n is the length of the vector. From the storage perspective, directly storing the tree has no benefit for space saving. Basically, there are two ways to reduce the space complexity of a summarization tree: *detail pruning* and *sparsity storage*.

6.4.1.3   Detail Pruning

In practice, analysts may only care about the high-level overview of the event occurrences. Consequently, there is no need to store all the details of the event sequences. As the summarization tree describes the event occurrences in a top-down manner (i.e., a coarse-to-fine strategy), the storage can be saved by removing the lower levels of the description nodes. The pruned tree still contains enough details for analysis, and an analyst who analyzes a long-term event log would not care about the event occurrences at the second precision. Due to the hierarchical structure of the tree, we can reduce the storage space exponentially. Lemma 6.1 shows how much space can be reduced through pruning. For example, the original tree has a height of 14 levels and 8192 (or 2^{13}) nodes. If the tree is pruned by removing the last 6 levels, the size of tree will become $\frac{1}{2^6}|T| = 128$, which is only about 1.5% of the original size. The pruned tree is still able to describe event occurrences at the 1-minute granularity.

Lemma 6.1 *Suppose the height of the summarization tree is H; if we only keep the nodes with a height larger than or equal to k, the size of the pruned tree is 2^{H-k}.*

Proof: According to Property 3 of the definition of the summarization tree, besides the summarization node, the summarization tree is a perfect binary tree. If only the nodes with height larger than or equal to k are kept, the number of remaining nodes in the perfect binary tree is $\sum_{i=k}^{H-1} 2^{H-1-i} = 2^{H-k} - 1$. Therefore, the total size of the summarization tree after pruning is 2^{H-k}.

6.4.1.4 Sparsity Storage

Another way to reduce the space is to only store the non-empty nodes of the tree. The majority of event types rarely appear in the event sequence. In this case, the corresponding vector will be dominated by 0s. Accordingly, the transformed summarization tree will also contain many 0s. For example, event type X only occurs twice throughout a 2-hour (7200-second) event sequence. The first occurrence is the first second, and the second occurrence is the last second. The number of nodes in the corresponding summarization tree is 8192, but there are only 28 non-zero nodes. Lemma 6.2 provides a lower bound on how many zero nodes exist in a summarization tree.

Lemma 6.2 *Suppose the occurrence proportion (the probability of occurrences at any time) of event type X is $r = \frac{\#X}{n}$, where n is the length of the vector that stores the event occurrences, and the proportion of zero nodes at height h is $p_h = \max(1 - 2^{h+1}r, 0)$ for the corresponding summarization tree.*

Proof: The number of zero nodes can be calculated from the bottom level to the top level. It is trivial to know that besides the root level, the number of nodes at height h is $n_h = \frac{|T|}{2^{h+1}}$. For each level, the number of zero nodes z_h equals the number of nodes n_h minus the number of non-zero nodes u_h.

Let's start with $h = 0$ (the leaf level). In the worst case, the event occurrences are uniformly distributed along the time-line. There are two cases according to r:

1. $0 \le r < \frac{1}{2}$. The event occurs in less than half of the time slots. In such a condition, $u_0 = \min(r|T|, n_0)$, and $z_0 = n_0 - u_0 = \frac{|T|}{2} - r|T|$. So, $p_0 = \frac{z_0}{n_0} = 1 - 2r$.

2. $\frac{1}{2} \le r \le 1$. The number of zero nodes at the leaf level can be 0. Since occurrences are uniformly distributed, it is possible that the event appears at least once in every two continuous time slots. In this case, $p_0 = 0$.

Therefore, the lower bound probability of the zero nodes at the leaf level is $p_0 = \max(1 - 2r, 0)$. When $h = 1$, in the worst case, the occurrences of non-zero nodes at the leaf level are still uniformly distributed, so $u_1 = \min(u_0, n_1)$. Therefore, $z_1 = n_1 - u_1 = \max(n_1 - u_0, 0)$ and $p_1 = \max(1 - 2^2r, 0)$. When $h > 1$, if the occurrences of non-zero nodes at a lower level are still uniformly distributed, the number of zero nodes $u_h = \min(u_{h-1}, n_h)$. Similar to the case of $h = 1$, $z_h = n_h - u_h$, and $p_h = \max(1 - 2^{h+1}r, 0)$.

Based on Lemma 6.1 and 6.2, we further show the space complexity of a summarization tree in Theorem 6.1.

Theorem 6.1 *The space complexity of a summarization tree with granularity k is $O(\frac{|T|}{2^k} - \sum_{i=k}^{H} max(\frac{|T|}{2^h} - 2^{h+1}r, 0))$, where $|T|$ is the length of the vector, H is the height of the summarization tree, and r is the occurrence proportion as described in Lemma 6.2.*

Proof: The proof is based on Lemma 6.1 and Lemma 6.2. The number of nodes with height (granularity) larger than or equal to k is $2^{H-k} = \frac{|T|}{2^k}$ according to Lemma 6.1. For each level $h \geq k$, the number of zero nodes is $n_h p = max(\frac{|T|}{2^h} - 2^{h+1}r, 0)$, and the sum of all nodes with height larger than or equal to k is $\sum_{i=k}^{H} \frac{|T|}{2^h} - 2^{h+1}r$. Therefore, the number of non-zero nodes in the summarization tree is $\frac{|T|}{2^k} - \sum_{i=k}^{H} max(\frac{|T|}{2^h} - 2^{h+1}r, 0)$.

It is true that the second term will become 0 when r is sufficiently large. However, based on the empirical study, most of the event types occur rarely, and therefore $0 < r \ll 1$.

6.4.1.5   Summarization Forest

A *summarization forest* is a data model which contains all the summarization trees. In one forest, there are $|\mathcal{E}|$ summarization trees. Each stores the events of one event type. Besides trees, the summarization forest also stores the necessary meta-data. The summarization forest is formally defined in Definition 6.5.

Definition 6.5 *A summarization forest (SF) is a 6-tuple $\mathcal{F} =< \mathcal{E}, \mathcal{T}, t_s, t_e, l, r >$, where:*

1. *$\mathcal{E}$ denotes the set of the event types in the event sequence.*

2. *$\mathcal{T}$ denotes the set of summarization trees.*

3. *t_s and t_e denote the start timestamp and end timestamp of the event sequence represented by $\mathcal{F}$, respectively.*

4. *l denotes the full size of each ST, including the zero and non-zero nodes. All the trees have the same full size.*

5. *r denotes the resolution of each ST. All the trees are in the same resolution.*

Note that, since the summarization trees are stored in the sparsity style, the actual number of nodes that are stored for each tree can be different and should be much less than the full size. Given a summarization forest, the original event sequences can be recovered.

6.4.2   Basic Operations

In this section, we propose a set of basic operators which are built on top of the data model we proposed. These operators form the summarization language, which is the foundation of the event summarization tasks presented in our framework. The motivation of proposing a summarization language is to make the event summarization flexible and allow advanced analysts to define the ad hoc summarization tasks to meet potential new needs.

The basic operators are categorized into two families: the *data transformation operators* and the *data query operators*. The operators of the first family focus on transforming data from one type to another, and they are not directly used for summarization work. The operators of the second family focus on retrieving/manipulating data in a read-only way, and they provide the flexibility of generating the summarization. To make the notations easy to follow, we list all the symbols of all these operations in Table 6.6. We will introduce their meanings later in this section.

6.4.2.1 Data Transformation Operators

The data transformation operators include *vectorize, unvectorize, encode, decode, prune,* and *concatenate*. Their functionalities are listed as follows:

Vectorize and **Unvectorize**: *Vectorize* is used to convert the single event type subsequence D_i into a vector V_i while *unvectorize* does the reverse. Both of them are unary, and represented by symbol $\circ$ and $\bullet$, respectively. Semantically, these two operators are complementary operators, i.e., $D_i = \bullet(\circ(D_i))$ and $V_i = \circ(\bullet(V_i))$.

Encode and **Decode**: *Encode* is used to convert the vector V_i into a summarization tree T_i while *decode* does the reverse. Similar to vectorize/unvectorize, *encode* and *decode* are complementary operators and both of them are unary. We use $\triangleleft$ and $\triangleright$ to denote them, respectively.

Prune: The operator *prune* is unary, and it operates on the summarization tree. It is used to remove the most detailed information of the events by pruning the leaves of a summarization tree. Note that this operator is unrecoverable. Once it is used, the target summarization tree will permanently lose the removed level. We use $\ominus$ to denote this operator.

Concatenate: The operator *concatenate* is a binary operator. It combines two SFs into a big one and also updates the meta-data. We use $\uplus$ to denote this operation. Note that only the SFs with the same resolution can be concatenated.

6.4.2.2 Data Query Operators

Data query operators include *select, project, zoom,* and *describe*. They all take the *summarization forest* $\mathcal{F}$ as the input. The data query operators are similar to the data manipulation language (DML) in SQL, which provide query flexibility to users.

Their functionalities are listed as follows:

Project: The operator *project* is similar to the "projection" in relational algebra. It is a unary operator written as $\Pi_{e_{(1)},e_{(2)},...,e_{(k)}}(\mathcal{F})$. The operation is defined as picking the summarization trees whose event types are in the subset of $\{e_{(1)},...,e_{(k)}\} \subseteq \mathcal{E}$.

Select: The operator *select* is similar to the "selection" in relational algebra.

TABLE 6.6: Notations of basic operations

Operation	Symbol	Description
Vectorize	$\circ(D_i)$	Vectorizes the subsequence D_i.
Unvectorize	$\bullet(V_i)$	Unvectorizes the vector V_i.
Encode	$\triangleleft(V_i)$	Encodes V_i into a summarization tree T_i.
Decode	$\triangleright(T_i)$	Decodes T_i back to vector V_i.
Prune	$\ominus(T_i)$	Prunes the most detailed information of T_i.
Concatenate	$\mathcal{F}_1 \uplus \mathcal{F}_2$	Concatenates two SFs $\mathcal{F}_1$ and $\mathcal{F}_2$.
Project	$\Pi_{e_{(1)},...}(\mathcal{F})$	Extracts events of types $c_{(1)}, ..., c_{(k)}$ from $\mathcal{F}$.
Select	$\sigma_{[t_1,t_2]}(\mathcal{F})$	Picks the events occurring between time $[t_1, t_2]$.
Zoom	$\tau_i(\mathcal{F})$	Aggregates the events with granularity u.
Describe	Υ_{name}	Uses algorithm *name* for event summarization.

It is a unary operator written as $\sigma_{[t_1,t_2]}(\mathcal{F})$.

Zoom: The operator *zoom* is used to control the resolution of the data. It is a unary operator written as $\tau_u(\mathcal{F})$, where u is the assigned resolution, the larger, the coarser.

Describe: The *describe* operator indicates which algorithm is used to summarize the events. Its implementation depends on the concrete algorithm and all the previous event summarization papers can be regarded as developing concrete describe operators. For example, *NES* [112] summarizes the events with periodic and inter-arrival relationships. The *describe* operation is written as $\Upsilon_{name}(\mathcal{F})$, where *name* is the name of summarization algorithm used for describing the events. If necessary, the analyst can implement her/his own *describe* algorithm that follows the specification of our framework.

In our implementation, the time complexity of all these operators is lower than $O(|\mathcal{E}||T|\log|T|) = O(|\mathcal{E}|n\log n)$.

6.4.3 Event Summarization Tasks

To fulfill the requirements of analysts discussed previously, we introduce five commonly used event summarization tasks: *summarization, storing, recovering, merging,* and *updating,* using the previously defined basic operators as the building blocks. The intention here is to demonstrate the expressive capability of the basic operators, instead of giving a thorough coverage of all the possible tasks.

6.4.3.1 Summarization Task

Summarization task is the core of event summarization, and all prior works about event summarization focus on this problem. Based on the defined basic operators, analysts can summarize the events in a flexible way. In our framework, any summarization task can be described by the expression

$$\Upsilon_{name}(\sigma^*_{[t_1,t_2]}\tau^*_u\Pi^*_{E\in\mathcal{P}(\mathcal{E})}(\mathcal{F})).$$

The symbol $*$ denotes conducting the operation 0+ times. With the combination of operators, analysts are able to summarize **any** subset of events in **any** resolution during **any** time range with **any** summarization algorithm.

One thing that should be noted is that the order of the operators can be changed, but the summarization results of different orders are not guaranteed to be the same. For example, a commonly used implementation of the *describe* operator is based on the minimum description length principle [112, 120]. Such implementation aims to find a model that describes the events with least information. Therefore, the results of $\Upsilon_{name}(\tau_u(\mathcal{F}))$ and $\tau_u(\Upsilon_{name}(\mathcal{F}))$ are possibly different.

6.4.3.2 Storing Task

Storing is an important task. Converting the raw event log time after time is time consuming with low management efficiency. This task enables analysts to convert the events into a uniform data mode only once and reuse it afterwards. The store task can be written as

$$\mathcal{F} = \bigcup_{e_i\in\mathcal{E}_I} \ominus^*(\triangleleft(\circ(D_i))),$$

where $\mathcal{E}_I$ denotes the set of event types that analysts are interested in, and $\bigcup$ denotes putting all the trees together to form the SF. Analysts are able to pick **any** time resolution and **any** subset of all the event types for storage.

6.4.3.3 Recovering Task

The recovering task is the link between the event summarization and other data mining tasks. After finding the interesting piece of event logs via the summarization results, analysts should be able to transform the selected portion of the SF back to its original events, so they can use other data mining techniques for further analysis. The recover task can be expressed as

$$\bullet(\triangleright(\sigma^*_{[t_1,t_2]}(\tau_u(\Pi^*_{E\in\mathcal{E}_I}(\mathcal{F}))))).$$

This expression shows that analysts can selectively recover the piece of events with **any** subset of event types, at **any** time range and **any** time resolution.

6.4.3.4 Merging and Updating Tasks

Both merging and updating tasks focus on the maintenance of stored SF, but their motivations are different.

The merging task is conducted when analysts obtain the SFs with disjoint

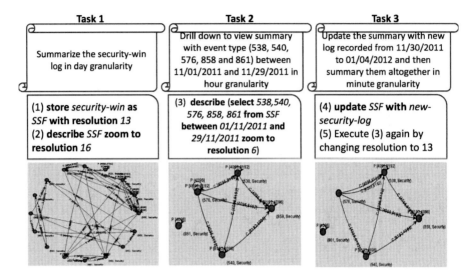

FIGURE 6.18: Summarizing with META.

time periods and want to archive them altogether. Suppose $\mathcal{F}_1$ and $\mathcal{F}_2$ denote two SFs, where $\mathcal{F}_2$ contains more details (contains lower resolution level). The merging task can be expressed as

$$\mathcal{F}_{new} = \mathcal{F}_1 \uplus \ominus^*(\mathcal{F}_2).$$

As shown in the above expression, when we merge two summarization trees with different resolutions, the SF with higher granularity would be pruned to meet the SF with lower granularity. Then these two SFs would be merged with the *concatenate* operation.

The updating task is conducted when analysts want to update the existing SF with a new piece of event log. It can be expressed by basic operators as

$$\mathcal{F}_{new} = \mathcal{F} \uplus (\bigcup_{e_i \in \mathcal{E}_I} \ominus^*(\triangleleft(\circ(D_i)))),$$

where the operand of $\bigcup$ is similar to the operand of $\bigcup$ in the storing task. First, the new set of subsequence D_i will be vectorized and then encoded into an SF $\mathcal{F}$. Then the new SF would be merged into the old SF in the same way as the *merge* task.

6.4.4   An Illustrative Case Study

To demonstrate how *META* facilitates summarization, we list three tasks (the 1st row) as well as the corresponding statement (the 2nd row) in Figure 6.18 to show how analysts work on a *security-win* dataset. We also attach corresponding summarization results (3rd row) by implementing the *describe* operator according to [112].

As shown in Figure 6.18, analysts only need to write one or two commands for each task. All the details are handled by the framework. Besides convenience, *META* also improves the reusability of data due to the SF's natural property. Once the security-win log is stored in the SF, it is directly available for all the three tasks, and there is no need to generate or maintain any intermediate data.

Without META, analysts need to write programs on their own to conduct the data transformation and extraction. Taking Task 2, for instance, analysts would write several programs to transform the events in hourly resolution, to pick out the records related to the event types 538, 540, 576, 858, 861, and to extract the records occurring between 11/01/2011 and 1/29/2011. Analysts would do similar tedious work when facing the other two tasks.

6.5 Summary

In this chapter, we have introduced event summarization, a novel perspective on presenting the regularity of the running status of systems. Different from the traditional pattern-mining-based representation, the results generated via event summarization are more concise. These kinds of results can help system analysts quickly gain the main idea of how the systems are running. If the summarization results indicate any kind of interest, system analysts can pay close attention to that particular part of the logs and can leverage advanced pattern mining algorithms to help find useful information.

In general, event analysis is a trial-and-error process for temporal event data. It requires repetitive rounds of analysis in order to find useful information. For the tasks of event analysis, event summarization should be the first step before any other procedures, as it gives system analysts an overview of the system and lets them use less effort before locating the key problem of the systems.

Event summarization is still in its rudimentary stage; there is still a lot of future work to do. For example, current efforts about event summarization mainly focus on how to present a more intuitive summarization; little attention has been paid to the problem of making good use of the summarization results. It is conceivable that the event summarization results have potential usage in areas such as event prediction and anomaly detection. Therefore, it is believed that more research about the application of event summarization will be seen in the near future.

6.6 Glossary

Event Occurrence: An instance of an event with a certain type E_i and a timestamp indicating when E_i happens.

Event Summarization: A data mining technique used to present a high-level overview of a given piece of event sequence from the perspective of temporal dynamics.

Information Theory: A branch of electronic engineering and computer science that works on the quantification of information into the unit of bits.

Minimum Description Length(MDL): A formalization of Occam's razor in the area of information theory. Its basic idea is that the best hypothesis for a given set of data is the one that leads to the best compression of the data. MDL is usually used for model selection.

Part III

Applications

Chapter 7

Data-Driven Applications in System Management

Wubai Zhou, Chunqiu Zeng, Liang Tang, and Tao Li

Florida International University
Nanjing University of Posts and Telecommunications

Performing a detailed diagnosis for a system issue mainly includes problem identification (i.e., identifying and detecting the problems), determination (i.e., fault diagnosis and root cause analysis), and resolution (i.e., providing resolutions). System diagnosis requires a deep understanding about the target system. In real-world IT infrastructures, many system issues are repeated and the associated resolutions can be found in the relevant events and tickets resolved in the past. In this chapter, we present several data-driven applications for system diagnosis.

7.1 System Diagnosis

7.1.1 Introduction

Figure 7.1 illustrates the typical workflow of problem detection, determination, and resolution for the IT service provider prescribed by the ITIL specification [7]. Incident management, one of the most critical processes in IT service management [8], aims at resolving the incident and quickly restoring the provision of services while relying on monitoring or human intervention to detect the malfunction of a component. In the case of problem detection, the monitoring runs on the servers, which computes metrics for the hardware and software performance at regular intervals. Those metrics are then compared to acceptable thresholds, known as *monitoring situations*, and any violation would result in an alert. If the alert persists beyond a predefined delay, the monitoring emits an event. Events coming from an IT environment are consolidated in an enterprise console, which analyzes the monitoring events and creates incident tickets in a ticketing system [215]. The information accumulated in the tickets is used by the system administrators (sysAdmins) for problem determination and resolution. The efficiency of these resources is critical for the provisioning of the services [114]. Table 7.1 shows the definitions of all types of *alert*, *event*, and *ticket*. According to their definitions, the monitoring should minimize the number of generated *false positive alerts* since they will bring extra manpower costs in resolving *false positive tickets* created from those alerts [46, 71]. Moreover, missed *false negative alerts* might bring severe system crashes so we should optimize the monitoring configuration to decline those alerts. In particular, Chapter 3 presents several techniques for optimizing monitoring configuration by eliminating false positive alerts and false negative alerts.

Many IT service providers usually rely on partial automation for incident diagnosis and resolution, with an intertwined operation of the sysAdmins and an automation script. Often the sysAdmins' role is limited to executing a known remediation script, while in some scenarios the sysAdmin performs a complex root cause analysis [241, 78]. Removing the sysAdmin from the process completely if it is feasible would reduce human error and speed up restoration of service. The move from partially to fully automated problem remediation would elevate service delivery to a new qualitative level where automation is a complete and independent process, and where it is not fragmented due to the need for adapting to human-driven processes. In this chapter, we mainly focus on mining valuable knowledge from these historical events and tickets to efficiently improve the performance of system diagnosis using data mining techniques.

7.1.2 Review of Related Literature

Ticket classification: Since incidents and problems can occur at different levels of the software and hardware stack, one major activity to facilitate system diagnosis is to create leading indicators (a.k.a., signature or failure

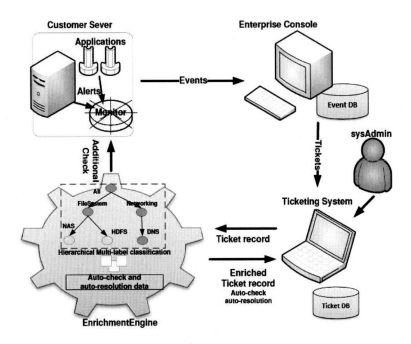

FIGURE 7.1: Problem detection, determination, and resolution. (See color insert.)

codes), which are used to classify incidents into groups for root cause analysis and failure trend monitoring [73]. Some example incident categories include application not available, disk usage threshold exceeded, system down, printer not printing, and password reset. The incident categories are usually determined through analyzing the incident records (a.k.a., incident tickets), which store incident details such as client name, platform, failure descriptions, severity code, resolution approaches, and various timestamps. Many studies have been conducted in classifying IT management tickets. For example, Zeng et al. [240] proposed a hierarchical approach to classify maintenance request tickets for automated dispatch to the appropriate service delivery personnel. Diao et al. [70] proposed a rule-based crowdsourcing approach by combining classification rules with crowdsourcing (i.e., socialize and execute rules using social networking) for ticket classification.

Predicting system behaviors: Incident tickets have been used in many predictive and classification tasks in system diagnosis [93, 67, 115, 45, 28]. For example, the decision of when to modernize which elements of the server HW/SW (hardware/software) stack is often done manually based on simple business rules. Bogojeska et al. [42, 43], however, alleviated this problem by supporting the decision process with an automated approach based on incident tickets and server attributes. As a first step, the proposed approach identifies

TABLE 7.1: Definitions for alert, event, and ticket

False Positive Alert	An alert for which the system administrator does not need to take any action.
False Negative Alert	A missed alert that is not captured due to inappropriate monitoring configuration.
False Alert	False positive alert.
Real Alert	An alert that requires the system administrator to fix the corresponding problem on the server.
Alert Duration	The length of time from an alert creation to its clearing.
Transient Alert	An alert that is automatically cleared before the technician opens its corresponding ticket.
Event	The notification of an alert to the Enterprise Console.
False Positive Ticket	A ticket created from a false positive alert.
False Negative Ticket	A ticket created manually identifying a condition that should have been captured by automatic monitoring.
False Ticket	A ticket created from a false alert.
Real Ticket	A ticket created from a real alert.

and ranks servers with problematic behaviors as candidates for modernization. Second, a random forest classifier is used to evaluate the impact of different modernization actions and suggest the most effective ones. Formally, let S denote the p-dimensional space where the p features are extracted from incident ticket data (such as tickets volumes and ticket severities) and server configuration information (such as server family, age, OS family and so on). Each server is then represented by a vector $x \in S$ which is used as an input for a predictive model M. Once trained on the available set of servers, for each x, M associates it with a probability of being a problematic server, i.e., $M(x) \in [0,1]$. $M(x)$ can then be used to rank all servers and identify the problematic ones (e.g., those with $M(x) > 0.5$). Moreover, the predictive model can evaluate the impact of different server modernization actions and suggest the most effective ones. Let $a : S \times P_a \mapsto S$ denote an arbitrary parameterized improvement action. The action is represented as a function which associates an input vector x of a server and an action parameter $p \in P_a$ with a vector of the modified server features $\tilde{x} = a(x,p)$. Note that $\tilde{x}$ is obtained after such an improvement action has been performed. This means that $\tilde{x}$ represents x with new features according to the action's effect. Thus it is feasible to measure the improvement of a parameterized action (a, p_a) by the difference between the prediction for the server before and after the modification, i.e., $I(a, p_a) = M(x) - M(\tilde{x})$. This enables us to choose actions that yield high improvements. Many other problems can also be addressed using historical incident tickets. Branch et al. [47] utilized ticket properties to predict service delivery efforts. Giurgiu et al. [85] presented a comprehensive analysis of labor efforts and their impact factors to solve incident tickets in data centers according to ticket attribute value such as ticket severity and ticket failure code (a.k.a ticket class label).

Ticket recommendation: Automatic techniques of recommending relevant historical tickets with resolutions can significantly improve the efficiency of root cause analysis and incident ticket resolving. Based on the relevant tickets, IT staff can correlate related system problems that happened before and perform a deeper system diagnosis. The solutions described in relevant historical tickets also provide best practices for solving similar issues. Recommendation technique has also been widely studied in e-commerce and online advertising areas. Existing recommendation algorithms can be categorized into two types. The first type is learning-based recommendation, in which the algorithm aims to maximize the rate of user response, such as the user click or conversation. The recommendation problem is then naturally formulated as a prediction problem. It utilizes a prediction algorithm to compute the probability of the user response on each item. Then, it recommends the one having the largest probability. Most prediction algorithms can be utilized in the recommendation, such as naive Bayes, linear regression, logistic regression, and matrix factorization [159, 39]. The second type of recommendation algorithm focuses on the relevance of items or users, rather than the user response. Lots of algorithms proposed for promoting products to online users [32, 72, 123, 147] belong to this type. They can be categorized as item-based [190, 116, 167] and user-based algorithms [217, 123, 32, 72]. Tang et al. [214] proposed item-based recommendation algorithms (where every incident ticket is regarded an item) to assist system administrators in resolving the incoming incident tickets that are generated by monitoring systems.

7.1.3   Content of the Chapter

In this rest of chapter, we present three different data-driven applications in system management. Particularly, an efficient algorithm is first introduced to search similar sequential textual event segments from large server event datasets for problem diagnosis [209]. For ticket classification, we present a hierarchical multi-label classification method, based on contextual loss, to correctly classify incident tickets to automate the enrichment engine shown in Figure 7.1. For problem resolution, a recommendation methodology and its several extensions are reviewed in service management.

7.2 Searching Similar Sequential Textual Event Segments

Sequential data is prevalent in many real-world applications such as bioinformatics, system security, and networking. Similarity search is one of the most fundamental techniques in sequential data management. A lot of efficient approaches are designed for searching over symbolic sequences or time series data, such as DNA sequences, stock prices, network packets, and video streams. A textual event sequence is a sequence of events, where each event is a plain text or message. For example, in system management, most system logs are textual event sequences which describe the corresponding system behaviors, such as the starting and stopping of services, detection of network connections, software configuration modifications, and execution errors [210, 168, 154, 208, 232]. System administrators utilize event logs to understand system behaviors. Similar system events reveal potential similar system behaviors in history which help administrators to diagnose system problems. For example, four log messages collected from a supercomputer [14] at Sandia National Laboratories are listed below:

```
- 1131564688 2005.11.09 en257 Nov 9 11:31:28 en257/en257
ntpd[1978]: ntpd exiting on signal 15
- 1131564689 2005.11.09 en257 Nov 9 11:31:29 en257/en257
ntpd: failed
- 1131564689 2005.11.09 en257 Nov 9 11:31:29 en257/en257
ntpd: ntpd shutdown failed
- 1131564689 2005.11.09 en257 Nov 9 11:31:29 en257/en257
ntpd: ntpd startup failed
```

The four log messages describe a failure in restarting of the ntpd (Network Time Protocol daemon). The system administrators need to first know the reason the ntpd could not restart and then come up with a solution to resolve this problem. A typical approach is to compare the current four log messages with the historical ntpd restarting logs and see their difference. Then the administrators can find out which steps or parameters might cause this failure. To retrieve the relevant historical log messages, the four log messages can be used as a query to search over the historical event logs. However, the size of the entire historical logs is usually very large, so it is not efficient to go through all event messages. For example, IBM Tivoli Monitoring 6.x [5] usually generates over 100G bytes system events for just one month from 600 Windows servers. Searching over such a large scale event sequence is challenging and the searching index is necessary for speeding up this process. Current system management tools and software packages can only search a single event by keywords or relational query conditions [5, 13, 10]. However, a system behavior is usually described by several continuous event messages, not just a single event, as shown in the above `ntpd` example. In addition, the number of event messages for a system behavior is not a fixed number, so it is hard to decide what is the appropriate segment length for building the index.

Existing search indexing methods for textual data and sequential data can be summarized into two different categories: textual data based and sequential data based. In our problem, however, each of them has its own limitations. For the textual data, locality-sensitive hashing (LSH) [84] with the Min-Hash [48] function is a common scheme. But these LSH-based methods only focus on unordered data [84, 31, 203]. In a textual event sequence, the order information cannot be ignored since different orders indicate different execution flows of the system. For sequential data, the segment search problem is a sub-string matching problem. Most existing methods are hash index based, suffix tree based, suffix arrays based or BOWTIE based [88, 156, 122, 23, 126, 36]. These methods can keep the order information of elements, but their sequence elements are single values rather than texts. Their search targets are matched substrings. In our problem, similar segments not need to be matched substrings.

7.2.1 Problem Formulation

Let $S = e_1 e_2 ... e_n$ be a sequence of n event messages, where e_i denotes the i-th event, $i = 1, 2, ..., n$. $|S|$ denotes the length of sequence S, which is the number of events in S. $\mathcal{E}$ denotes the universe of events. $sim(e_i, e_j)$ is a similarity function which measures the similarity between event e_i and event e_j, $e_i \in \mathcal{E}$, and $e_j \in \mathcal{E}$. The Jaccard coefficient [207] with 2-shingling [49] is utilized as the similarity function $sim(\cdot, \cdot)$ because each event is a textual message.

Definition 7.1 (Segment) *Given a sequence of events $S = e_1 ... e_n$, a segment of S is a sequence $L = e_{m+1} e_{m+2} ... e_{m+l}$, where l is the length of L, $l \leq n$, and $0 \leq m \leq n - l$.*

The problem is formally stated as follows.

Problem 7.1 (Problem Statement) *Given an event sequence S and a query event sequence Q, find all segments with length $|Q|$ in S which are similar to Q.*

Similar segments are defined based on event similarity. Given two segments $L_1 = e_{11} e_{12} ... e_{1l}$, $L_2 = e_{21} e_{22} ... e_{2l}$, we consider the number of dissimilar events in L_1 and L_2. If the number of dissimilar event pairs is at most k, then L_1 and L_2 are similar. This definition is also called k-dissimilar:

$$N_{dissim}(L_1, L_2, \delta) = \sum_{i=1}^{l} z_i \leq k,$$

where

$$z_i = \begin{cases} 1, & sim(e_{1i}, e_{2i}) < \delta \\ 0, & \text{otherwise} \end{cases},$$

and δ is a user-defined threshold for event similarity. The k-dissimilar corresponds to the well-known k-mismatch or k-error in the subsequence matching problem [140].

7.2.1.1 Potential Solutions by LSH

The locality-sensitive hashing (LSH) [84] with the Min-Hash [48] function is a common scheme for the similarity search over texts and documents. LSH is a straightforward solution for our problem. We can consider each segment as a small "document" by concatenating its event messages. Figure 7.2 shows a textual event sequence $S = e_1 e_2 ... e_{i+1} e_{i+2} ...$, where e_i is a textual event. In this sequence, every four adjacent event messages are seen as a "document," such as L_{i+1}, L_{i+2} and so on. The traditional LSH with the Min-Hash function can be utilized on these small "documents" to speed up a similar search. This solution is called LSH-DOC as a baseline method. However, this solution ignores the order information of events, because the similarity score obtained by the Min-Hash does not consider the order of elements in each "document."

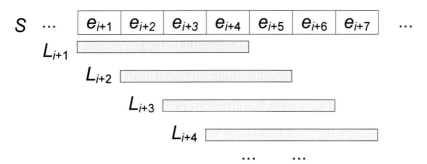

FIGURE 7.2: An example of LSH-DOC.

To preserve the order information, we can distribute the hash functions to individual regions of segments. For example, the length of the indexed segment is 4, and we have 40 hash functions. We assign every 10 hash functions to every event in the segment. Then, each hash function can only be used to index the events from one region of the segment. Figure 7.3 shows a sequence S with several segments $L_{i+1}, ..., L_{i+4}$, where $p_1, ..., p_4$ are four regions of each segment and each region contains one event. Every p_j has 10 hash functions to compute the hash values of the contained event, $j = 1, ..., 4$. If the hash signatures of two segments are identical, it is probable that every region's events are similar. Thus, the order information is preserved. This solution is called LSH-SEP as another baseline method.

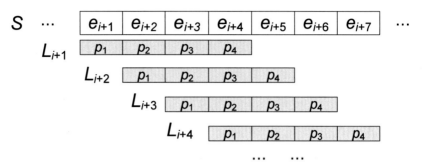

FIGURE 7.3: An example of LSH-SEP.

k-dissimilar segments are two segments which contain at most k dissimilar events inside. To search the k-dissimilar segments, a common approach is to split the query sequence Q into $k + 1$ non-overlapping segments. If a segment L has at most k dissimilar events to Q, then there must be one segment of Q which has no dissimilar event with its corresponding region of L. Then, we can use any search method for exact similar segments to search the k-dissimilar segments. This idea is applied in many biological sequence matching algorithms [23]. But there is a drawback to the two previous potential solutions: *they all assume that the length of indexed segments l is equal to the length of query sequence $|Q|$.* The query sequence Q is given by the user at runtime, so $|Q|$ is not fixed. However, if we do not know the length of the query sequence Q in advance, we cannot determine the appropriate segment length l for building the index. If $l > |Q|$, none of the similar segments could be retrieved correctly. If $l < |Q|$, we have to split Q into shorter subsegments of length l, and then query those shorter subsegments instead of Q. Although all correct similar segments can be retrieved, the search cost would be large, because the subsegments of Q are shorter than Q and the number of retrieved candidates is thus larger [140]. Figure 7.4 shows an example for the case $l < |Q|$. Since

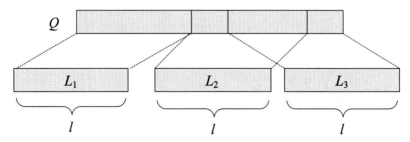

FIGURE 7.4: An example of $l < |Q|$.

the length of indexed segments is l and less than $|Q|$, LSH-DOC and LSH-SEP have to split Q into subsegments L_1, L_2 and L_3, $|L_i| = l$, $i = 1, .., 3$. Then, LSH-DOC and LSH-SEP use three subsegments to query the segment candidates. If a segment candidate is similar to Q, its corresponding region must be similar to a subsegment L_i, but not vice versa. Therefore, the acquired candidates for L_i must be more than those for Q. Note that scanning a large number of candidates is time consuming. Therefore, the optimal case is $l = |Q|$. But $|Q|$ is not fixed at runtime.

7.2.2 Suffix Matrix Indexing

Let h be a hash function from the LSH family. h maps an event to an integer, $h : \mathcal{E} \to \mathcal{Z}_h$, where $\mathcal{E}$ is the universe of textual events, and $\mathcal{Z}_h$ is the universe of hash values. In the suffix matrix, Min-Hash [48] is the hash function. By taking a Min-Hash function h, a textual event sequence $S = e_1...e_n$ is mapped into a sequence of hash values $h(S) = h(e_1)...h(e_n)$. Suppose we have m independent hash functions, we can have m distinct hash value sequences. Then, we create m suffix arrays from the m hash value sequences, respectively. The suffix matrix of S is constructed by the m suffix arrays, where each row is a suffix array.

Definition 7.2 (Suffix Matrix) *Given a sequence of events $S = e_1...e_n$ and a set of independent hash functions $H = \{h_1, ..., h_m\}$, let $h_i(S)$ be the sequence of hash values, i.e., $h_i(S) = h_i(e_1)...h_i(e_n)$. The suffix matrix of S is $\mathbf{M}_{S,m} = [A_1^T, ..., A_m^T]^T$, where A_i^T is the suffix array of $h_i(S)$ and $i = 1, ..., m$.*

We illustrate the suffix matrix by an example as follows:

Example 7.1 *Let S be a sequence of events, $S = e_1e_2e_3e_4$. H is a set of independent hash functions for events, $H = \{h_1, h_2, h_3\}$. For each event and hash function, the computed hash value is shown in Table 7.2.*

TABLE 7.2: An example of a hash value table

Event	e_1	e_2	e_3	e_4
h_1	0	2	1	0
h_2	3	0	3	1
h_3	1	2	2	0

Let $h_i(S)$ denote the i-th row of Table 7.2. By sorting the suffixes in each row of Table 7.2, we could get the suffix matrix $\mathbf{M}_{S,m}$ below.

$$\mathbf{M}_{S,m} = \begin{bmatrix} 3 & 0 & 2 & 1 \\ 1 & 3 & 0 & 2 \\ 3 & 0 & 2 & 1 \end{bmatrix}.$$

For instance, the first row of $\mathbf{M}_{S,m}$: 3021 is the suffix array of $h_1(S) = 0210$.

There are a lot of efficient algorithms for constructing suffix arrays [88, 156, 122]. The simplest algorithm sorts all suffixes of the sequence with a time complexity $O(n \log n)$. Thus, the time complexity of constructing the suffix matrix $\mathbf{M}_{S,m}$ is $O(mn \log n)$, where n is the length of the historical sequence and m is the number of hash functions.

7.2.2.1 Searching over the Suffix Matrix

Similar to the traditional LSH, the search algorithm based on a suffix matrix consists of two steps. The first step is to acquire the candidate segments. These candidates are potentially similar segments to the query sequence. The second step is to filter the candidates by computing their exact similarity scores. Since the second step is straightforward and is the same as the traditional LSH, we only present the first step of the search algorithm.

Given a set of independent hash functions $H = \{h_1, ..., h_m\}$ and a query sequence $Q = e_{q1}e_{q2}...e_{qn}$, let $\mathbf{Q}_H = [h_i(e_{qj})]_{m \times n}$, $\mathbf{M}_{S,m}(i)$ and $\mathbf{Q}_H(i)$ denote the i-th rows of $\mathbf{M}_{S,m}$ and $\mathbf{Q}_H$, respectively, $i = 1, ..., m$, $j = 1, ..., n$. Since $\mathbf{M}_{S,m}(i)$ is a suffix array, we obtain those entries that matched $\mathbf{Q}_H(i)$ by a binary search. $\mathbf{M}_{S,m}$ has m rows; we can apply m binary searches to retrieve m entry sets. If one segment appears at least r times in the m sets, then this segment is considered to be a candidate. Parameters r and m will be discussed later in this section.

Algorithm 5 states the candidates search algorithm. $h(i)$ is the i-th hash function in H. Q_{h_i} is the hash-value sequence of Q mapped by h_i. SA_i is the i-th row of the suffix matrix $\mathbf{M}_{S,m}$, and $SA_i[l]$ is the suffix at position l in SA_i. $CompareAt(Q_{h_i}, SA_i[l])$ is a subroutine to compare the order of two suffixes Q_{h_i} and $SA_i[l]$ for the binary search. If Q_{h_i} is greater than $SA_i[l]$, it returns 1; if Q_{h_i} is smaller than $SA_i[l]$, it returns -1; otherwise, it returns 0. $Extract(Q_{h_i}, SA_i, pos)$ is a subroutine to extract the segments candidates from the position pos. Since H has m hash functions, $C[L]$ records the number of times that the segment L is extracted in m iterations. The final candidates are only those segments which are extracted at least r times.

If a segment L of S is returned by Algorithm 5, we say that L is **reached** by this algorithm. We illustrate how the binary search works for one hash function $h_i \in H$ in the following example.

Example 7.2 *Given an event sequence S with a hash function $h_i \in H$, we compute the hash value sequence $h_i(S)$, shown in Table 7.3. Let the query sequence be Q, and $h_i(Q) = 31$, where each digit represents a hash value. The*

TABLE 7.3: Hash value sequence $h_i(S)$

$h_i(S)$	5	3	1	4	3	1	0
Position	0	1	2	3	4	5	6

sorted suffixes of $h_i(S)$ are shown in Table 7.4. We use $h_i(Q) = 31$ to search all matched suffixes in Table 7.4. In Algorithm 5, by using the binary search, we could find the matched suffix: 310. Then, the extract subroutine probes the

---

Algorithm 5 SearchCandidates (Q, δ)

Parameter: Q : query sequence, δ: threshold of event similarity;
Result: $\mathcal{C}$: segment candidates.
1: Create a counting map $\mathcal{C}$
2: **for** $i = 1$ **to** $|H|$ **do**
3:     $Q_{h_i} \leftarrow h_i(Q)$
4:     $SA_i \leftarrow \mathbf{M}_{S,m}(i)$
5:     $left \leftarrow 0, right \leftarrow |SA_i| - 1$
6:     **if** $CompareAt(Q_{h_i}, SA_i[left]) < 0$ **then**
7:        **continue**
8:     **end if**
9:     **if** $CompareAt(Q_{h_i}, SA_i[right]) > 0$ **then**
10:      **continue**
11:    **end if**
12:    $pos \leftarrow -1$
13:    *// Binary search*
14:    **while** $right - left > 1$ **do**
15:      $mid \leftarrow \lfloor (left + right)/2 \rfloor$
16:      $ret \leftarrow CompareAt(Q_{h_i}, SA_i[mid])$
17:      **if** $ret < 0$ **then**
18:        $right \leftarrow mid$
19:      **else if** $ret > 0$ **then**
20:        $left \leftarrow mid$
21:      **else**
22:        $pos \leftarrow mid$
23:        **break**
24:      **end if**
25:    **end while**
26:    **if** $pos = -1$ **then**
27:      $pos \leftarrow right$
28:    **end if**
29:    *// Extract segment candidates*
30:    **for** $L \in Extract(Q_{h_i}, SA_i, pos)$ **do**
31:      $\mathcal{C}[L] \leftarrow \mathcal{C}[L] + 1$
32:    **end for**
33: **end for**
34: **for** $L \in \mathcal{C}$ **do**
35:    **if** $\mathcal{C}[L] < r$ **then**
36:      del $\mathcal{C}[L]$
37:    **end if**
38: **end for**

---

neighborhood of suffix 310, to find all matched suffixes with $h_i(Q)$. Finally, the two segments at positions 4 and 1 are extracted. If the two segments are

TABLE 7.4: Sorted suffixes of $h_i(S)$

Index	Position	Hashed Suffix
0	6	0
1	5	10
2	2	14310
3	4	310
4	1	314310
5	3	4319
6	0	5314310

extracted for at least r independent hash functions, then the two segments are the final candidates returned by Algorithm 5.

Lemma 7.1 *Given an event sequence S and a query event sequence Q, L is a segment of S, $|L| = |Q|$, δ_1 and δ_2 are two thresholds for similar events, $0 \le \delta_2 < \delta_1 \le 1$, then:*

- *if $N_{dissim}(L, Q, \delta_1) = 0$, then the probability that L is reached by Algorithm 5 is at least $F(m - r; m, 1 - \delta_1^{|Q|})$;*

- *if $N_{dissim}(L, Q, \delta_2) \ge k$, $1 \le k \le |Q|$, then the probability that L is reached by Algorithm 5 is at most $F(m - r; m, 1 - \delta_2^k)$,*

where $F(\cdot; n, p)$ is the cumulative distribution function of binomial distribution $B(n, p)$, and r is a parameter for Algorithm 5.

Proof: Let's first consider the case $N_{dissim}(L, Q, \delta_1) = 0$, which indicates all corresponding events in L and Q are similar and the similarity is at least δ_1. The hash function h_i belongs to the LSH family, so we have $Pr(h_i(e_1) = h_i(e_2)) = sim(e_1, e_2) \ge \delta_1$. Both L and Q have $|Q|$ events, so for one hash function, the probability that hash values of all those events are identical is at least $\delta_1^{|Q|}$. Once those hash values are identical, L must be found by a binary search over one suffix array in $\mathbf{M}_{S,m}$. Hence, for one suffix array, the probability of L being found is $\delta_1^{|Q|}$. $\mathbf{M}_{S,m}$ has m suffix arrays. The number of those suffix arrays that L is found follows the binomial distribution $B(m, \delta_1^{|Q|})$. Then, the probability that there are at least r suffix arrays that L is reached is $1 - F(r; m, \delta_1^{|Q|}) = F(m - r; m, 1 - \delta_1^{|Q|})$. The second case that $N_{dissim}(L, Q, \delta_2) \ge k$ indicates there are at least dissimilar k events and their similarities are less than δ_2. The probability that hash values of all those events in L and Q are identical is at most δ_2^k. The proof is analogous to that of the first case.

Lemma 7.1 ensures that, if a segment L is similar to the query sequence Q, then it is very likely to be reached by our algorithm; if L is dissimilar to the query sequence Q, then it is very unlikely to be reached. The probabilities shown in this lemma are the false negative probability and the false positive probability. The choice of r controls the tradeoff between the probabilities. The F-measure is a combined measurement for the two factors [189]. The optimal r is the one that maximizes the F-measure score. Since r can only be an integer, we can enumerate all possible values of r from 1 to m to find the optimal r.

However, this algorithm cannot handle the case that there are two dissimilar events inside L and Q. The algorithm narrows down the search space step by step according to each element of Q. A dissimilar event between Q and Q's similar segments in L would lead the algorithm to incorrect following steps.

7.2.3 Randomly Masked Suffix Matrix

Figure 7.5 shows an example of a query sequence Q and a segment L. There is only one dissimilar event pair between Q "1133" and L "1933," which is the second one, 9 in L with 1 in Q. Clearly, the traditional binary search cannot find "1933" by using "1133" as the query. To overcome this problem,

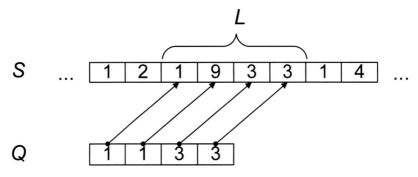

FIGURE 7.5: Dissimilar events in segments.

a straightforward idea is to skip the dissimilar event between Q and L. However, the dissimilar event can be any event inside L. We do not know which event is the dissimilar event to skip before knowing Q. If two similar segments are allowed to have at most k dissimilar events, the search problem is called the k-dissimilar search. Our proposed method is summarized as follows:

Offline Step:

1. Apply f min-hash functions on the given textual sequence to convert it into f hash-valued sequences.

2. Generate f random sequence masks and apply them to the f hash-valued sequences (one to one).

3. Sort the f masked sequences to f suffix arrays and store them with the random sequence masks to disk files.

Online Step:

1. Apply f min-hash functions on the given query sequence to convert it into f hash-valued sequences.

2. Load the f random sequence masks and apply them to the f hash-valued query sequences.

3. Invoke f binary searches by using the f masked query sequences over the f suffix arrays and find segment candidates that have been extracted at least r times.

7.2.3.1 Random Sequence Mask

A sequence mask is a sequence of bits. If these bits are randomly and independently generated, this sequence mask is a random sequence mask.

Definition 7.3 *A random sequence mask is a sequence of random bits in which each bit follows Bernoulli distribution with parameter θ: $P(bit = 1) = \theta$, $P(bit = 0) = 1 - \theta$, where $0.5 \leq \theta < 1$.*

Figure 7.6 shows a hash-value sequence $h(S)$ and two random sequence masks: M_1 and M_2. $M_i(h(S))$ is the masked sequence by the *AND* operator: $h(S)$ *AND* M_i, where $i = 1, 2$. White cells indicate the events that are kept in $M_i(h(S))$, and dark cells indicate those events to skip. The optimal mask

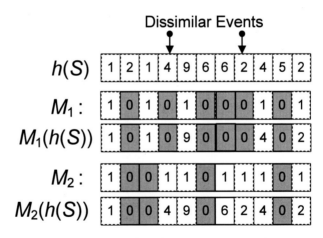

FIGURE 7.6: Random sequence mask.

is the one such that all dissimilar events are located in the dark cells. In other words, the optimal mask is able to skip all dissimilar events. We call this kind of random sequence masks the *perfect* sequence masks. In Figure 7.6, there are two dissimilar events in S: the fourth event and the eighth event. M_1 skips the fourth event and the eighth event in their masked sequences, so M_1 is a *perfect* sequence mask. Once we have a *perfect* sequence mask, previous search algorithms can be applied on these masked hash value sequences without considering dissimilar events.

Lemma 7.2 *Given an event sequence S, a query sequence Q, and f independent random sequence masks with parameter θ, let L be a segment of S, $|Q| = |L|$. If the number of dissimilar event pairs of L and Q is k, then the probability that there are at least m perfect sequence masks is at least $F(f - m; f, 1 - (1 - \theta)^k)$, where F is the cumulative probability function of binomial distribution.*

Proof: Since each bit in each mask follows the Bernoulli distribution with parameter θ, the probability that the corresponding bit of one dissimilar event is 0 is $1 - \theta$ in one mask. Then, the probability that all corresponding bits of k dissimilar events are 0 is $(1 - \theta)^k$ in one mask. Hence, the probability that one random sequence mask is a *perfect* sequence mask is $(1 - \theta)^k$. Then, $F(f - m; f, 1 - (1 - \theta)^k)$ is the probability that this case happens m times in f independent random sequence masks.

7.2.3.2 Randomly Masked Suffix Matrix

A randomly masked suffix matrix is a suffix matrix where each suffix array is masked by a random sequence mask. We use $\mathbf{M}_{S,f,\theta}$ to denote a randomly masked suffix matrix, where S is the event sequence to index, f is the number of independent LSH hash functions, and θ is the parameter for each random sequence mask. Note that $\mathbf{M}_{S,f,\theta}$ still consists of f rows by $n = |S|$ columns.

Lemma 7.3 *Given an event sequence S, a randomly masked suffix matrix $\mathbf{M}_{S,f,\theta}$ of S and a query sequence Q, L is a segment of S, $|L| = |Q|$. If the number of dissimilar events between L and Q is at most k, then the probability that L is reached by Algorithm 5 is at least*

$$Pr_{reach} \geq \sum_{m=r}^{f} F(f - m; f, 1 - (1 - \theta)^k) \cdot F(m - r; m, 1 - \delta^{|Q| \cdot \theta}),$$

where δ and r are parameters of Algorithm 5.

This probability combines the two probabilities in Lemma 7.1 and Lemma 7.2. m becomes a hidden variable, which is the number of *perfect* sequence masks. By considering all possible m, this lemma is proved. Here the expected number of kept events in every $|Q|$ events by one random sequence mask is $|Q| \cdot \theta$.

7.2.4 Analytical Search Cost

Given an event sequence S and its randomly masked suffix matrix $\mathbf{M}_{S,f,\theta}$, $n = |S|$, the cost of acquiring candidates mainly depends on the number of binary searches on suffixes. Recall that $\mathbf{M}_{S,f,\theta}$ is f by n and each row of it is a suffix array. So f binary searches must be executed and the cost of each binary search is $\log n$. The total cost of acquiring candidates is $f \log n$.

The cost of filtering candidates mainly depends on the number of candidates acquired. Let $\mathcal{Z}_h$ denote the universe of hash values. Given an event sequence S and a set of hash functions H, $\mathcal{Z}_{H,S}$ denotes the set of hash values output by each hash function in H with each event in S. $\mathcal{Z}_{H,S} \subseteq \mathcal{Z}_h$, because some hash value may not appear in the sequence S. On average, each event in S has $Z = |\mathcal{Z}_{H,S}|$ distinct hash values. Let Q be the query sequence. For each suffix array in $\mathbf{M}_{S,f,\theta}$, the average number of acquired candidates is

$$N_{Candidates} = \frac{n}{Z^{|Q| \cdot \theta}}.$$

The total number of acquired candidates is at most $f \cdot N_{Candidate}$. A hash table is used to merge the f sets of candidates into one set. Its cost is $f \cdot N_{Candidate}$. To sum up the two parts, given an interleaved suffix matrix $\mathbf{M}_{S,f,\theta}$ and a query sequence Q, the total search cost is

$$Cost_{search} = f \cdot (\log n + \frac{n}{Z^{|Q| \cdot \theta}}).$$

7.2.4.1   Why Potential Solutions Are Not Efficient?

For potential solutions (i.e., LSH-DOC and LSH-SEP) and the suffix matrix, the second part of the cost is the major cost of the search. Here we only consider the number of acquired candidates to compare the analytical search cost. The average number of acquired candidates by LSH-DOC and LSH-SEP is at least

$$N'_{Candidates} = \frac{n}{Z^{|Q|/(k+1)}}.$$

When $|Q| \cdot \theta \geq \log_Z f + |Q|/(k+1)$, $f \cdot N_{Candidate} \leq N'_{Candidates}$. Z depends on the number of 2-shinglings, which is approximated to the square of the vocabulary size of log messages. Hence, Z is a huge number, and $\log_Z f$ can be ignored. Since $\theta \geq 0.5$, $k \geq 1$, we always have $|Q| \cdot \theta \geq |Q|/(k+1)$. Therefore, the acquired candidates of the suffix matrix are less than or equal to those of LSH-DOC and LSH-SEP.

7.2.5   Offline Parameter Choice

The parameters f and θ balance the search costs and search result accuracy. These two parameters are decided in the offline step before building the suffix matrix. Let $Cost_{max}$ be the search cost budget; the parameter choosing problem is to maximize Pr_{reach} subject to $Cost_{search} \leq Cost_{max}$. A practical issue is that the suffix matrix is constructed in the offline phase, but $|Q|$ and δ can only be known in the online phase. A simple approach to find the optimal f and θ is using the historical queries to estimate $|Q|$ and δ. This procedure can be seen as a *training* procedure. Once the two offline parameters are obtained, other parameters are found by solving the maximization problem. The objective function Pr_{reach} is not convex, but it can be solved by the enumeration method since all tuning parameters are small integers.

The next question is how to determine $Cost_{max}$. We can choose $Cost_{max}$ according to the average search cost curve. Figure 7.7 shows a curve about the analytical search cost and the probability Pr_{reach}, where $m = \lfloor Cost_{search}/(\log n + \frac{n}{|\mathcal{Z}_{H,S}||Q|^\theta}) \rfloor$. According to this curve, we suggest users choose $Cost_{max}$ between 100 and 200, because larger search costs would not significantly improve accuracy.

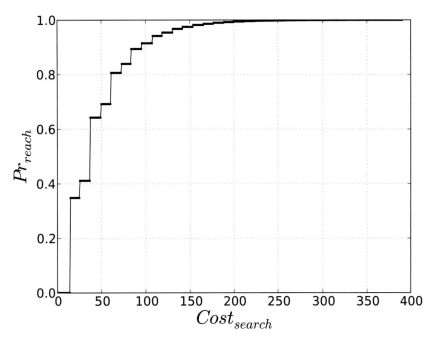

FIGURE 7.7: Average search cost curve ($n = 100K, |\mathcal{Z}_{H,S}| = 16, \theta = 0.5, |Q| = 10, \delta = 0.8, k = 2$).

7.2.6 Evaluation

In this section, experiments are conducted on real system event logs to evaluate the SuffixMatrix method.

7.2.6.1 Experimental Platform

LSH-DOC, LSH-SEP, and SuffixMatrix are implemented in Java 1.6. Table 7.5 summarizes the experimental machine.

TABLE 7.5: Experimental machine

OS	CPU	JRE	JVM Heap Size
Linux 2.6.18	Intel Xeon(R) @ 2.5GHz, 8 core, 64bits	J2SE 1.6	2G

7.2.6.2 Data Collection

The experimental system logs are collected from two different real systems. Apache HTTP error logs are collected from the server machines in the computer lab of a research center and have about 236,055 log messages. Logs of ThunderBird [14] are collected from a supercomputer at Sandia National Lab. The first 350,000 log messages from the ThunderBird system logs are used for this evaluation.

Testing Queries: Each query sequence is a segment randomly picked from the event sequence. Table 7.6 lists detailed information about six groups, where $|Q|$ indicates the length of the query sequences. The true results for each query are obtained by the *brute-force* method, which scans through every segment of the sequence one by one to find all true results.

TABLE 7.6: Testing query groups

Group	Num. of Queries	$|Q|$	k	δ
TG1	100	6	1	0.8
TG2	100	12	3	0.65
TG3	100	18	5	0.6
TG4	100	24	7	0.5
TG5	100	30	9	0.5
TG6	100	36	11	0.5

7.2.6.3 Baseline Methods

The SuffixMatrix method is compared with two baseline methods, LSH-DOC and LSH-SEP. The two baseline methods are both LSH-based methods for sequential data. In order to handle k-dissimilar approximation queries, the indexed segment length l for LSH-DOC and LSH-SEP can be at most $|Q|/(k+1) = 3$, so we set $l = 3$.

7.2.6.4 Online Search

Suffix-matrix- and LSH-based methods all consist of two steps. The first step is to search segment candidates from its index. The second step is filtering acquired candidates by computing their exact similarities. Because of the second step, the precision of the search results is always 1.0. Thus, the quality of results only depends on the recall. By using appropriate parameter settings, all the methods can achieve high recalls, but we also consider the associated time cost. For a certain recall, if the search time is smaller, the performance is better. An extreme case is that the *brute-force* method always has 100% recall, but it has to visit all segments of the sequence, so the time cost is huge. We define the recall ratio as a normalized metric for evaluating the goodness of the search results:

$$RecallRatio = \begin{cases} \frac{Recall}{SearchTime}, & Recall \geq recall_{min} \\ 0, & \text{otherwise} \end{cases},$$

where $recall_{min}$ is a user-specified threshold for the minimum acceptable recall. If the recall is less than $recall_{min}$, the search results are then not acceptable to users. In our evaluation, $recall_{min} = 0.5$, which means any method should capture at least half of the true results. The unit of the search time is milliseconds. *RecallRatio* is expressed as the portion of true results obtained per millisecond. Clearly, the higher the *RecallRatio*, the better the performance.

LSH-DOC, LSH-SEP, and suffix matrix have different parameters. We vary the value of each parameter in each method, and then select the best performance of each method for comparison. LSH-DOC and LSH-SEP have two parameters to set, which are the length of hash vectors b and the number of hash tables t. Note that b varies from 5 to 35 and t varies from 2 to 25. We also consider the different number of buckets for LSH-DOC and LSH-SEP. Due to the Java heap size limitation, the number of hash buckets is fixed at 8000. For suffix matrix, r is chosen according to the method mentioned before. In the experiments, f and m vary from 2 to 30 and θ varies from 0.5 to 1.

Figures 7.8 and Figure 7.9 show the *RecallRatios* for each testing group. Overall, suffix matrix achieves the best performance on the two datasets. However, LSH-based methods outperform suffix matrix on short queries (TG1). Moreover, in Apache Logs with TG4, LSH-SEP is also better than suffix matrix.

To find out why, in TG1, suffix matrix performs worse than LSH-DOC or LSH-SEP, we record the number of acquired candidates for each method and the number of true results. Figures 7.10 and 7.11 show the actual acquired candidates for each testing group with each method. Table 7.7 shows the numbers of true results for each testing group. From the two figures, we observe that suffix matrix acquired many more candidates than other methods in TG1. In other words, suffix matrix has a higher collision probability of dissimilar segments in its hashing scheme.

TABLE 7.7: Number of true results

Dataset	TG1	TG2	TG3	TG4	TG5	TG6
ThunderBird Logs	4.12	2.81	27.46	53.24	57.35	7.21
Apache Logs	378.82	669.58	435.94	1139.15	1337.23	990.63

To overcome this problem, a common trick in LSH is to make the hash

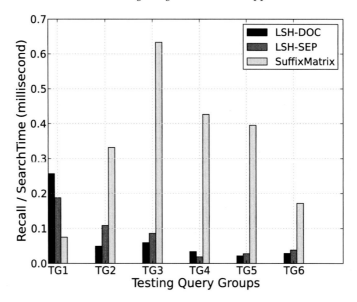

FIGURE 7.8: RecallRatio comparison for ThunderBird log.

functions be "stricter." For example, there are $d + 1$ independent hash functions in the LSH family, $h_1,...,h_d$ and h. We can construct a "stricter" hash function $h' = h(h_1(x), h_2(x), ..., h_d(x))$. If two events e_1 and e_2 are not similar, i.e., $sim(e_1, e_2) < \delta$, the collision probability of h_i is $Pr[h_i(e_1) = h_i(e_2)] = sim(e_1, e_2) < \delta$, which can be large if δ is large, $i = 1, ..., d$. But the collision probability of h' is

$$Pr[h'(e_1) = h'(e_2)] = \prod_{i=1}^{n} Pr[h_i(e_1) = h_i(e_2))]$$
$$= [sim(e_1, e_2)]^d < sim(e_1, e_2).$$

Figure 7.12 shows the performance of the suffix matrix by using "stricter" hash functions (denoted as "SuffixMatrix(Strict)") in TG1. Each "stricter" hash function is constructed by 20 independent Min-Hash functions. The testing result shows "SuffixMatrix(Strict)" outperforms all other methods for both Thunderbird logs and Apache logs in TG1. Table 7.8 presents the parameters and other performance measures of "SuffixMatrix(Strict)." By using "stricter" hash functions, the suffix matrix reduces 90% to 95% of previous candidates. As a result, the search time becomes much smaller than before. The choice of the number of hash functions for a "stricter" hash function, d, is a tuning parameter and determined by the data distribution. Note that the parame-

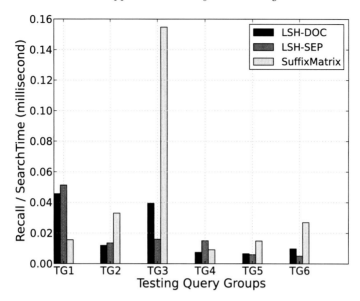

FIGURE 7.9: RecallRatio comparison for Apache log.

ters of LSH-DOC and LSH-SEP in this test are already tuned by varying the values of b and t.

TABLE 7.8: "SuffixMatrix(Strict)" for TG1

Dataset	Parameters	$Recall$	$SearchTime$	Num. Probed
ThunderBird Logs	$m = 2, \theta = 0.9$	0.9776	1.23 ms	5.04
Apache Logs	$m = 2, \theta = 0.8$	0.7279	2.24ms	152.75

To verify Lemma 7.3, we vary each parameter of suffix matrix and test the recall of search results. We randomly sample 100,000 log messages from the ThunderBird logs and randomly pick 100 event segments as the query sequences. The length of each query sequence is 16. Other querying criteria are $k = 5$ and $\delta = 0.5$. Figure 7.13 shows that the increase of m will improve the recall. Figure 7.14 verifies that if r becomes larger, the recall will decrease. Since the random sequence masks are randomly generated, the trends of the recall are not stable and a few jumps are in the curves. But generally, the recall curves drop down when we enlarge θ for the random sequence mask. To sum up, the results shown in these figures can partially verify Lemma 7.3.

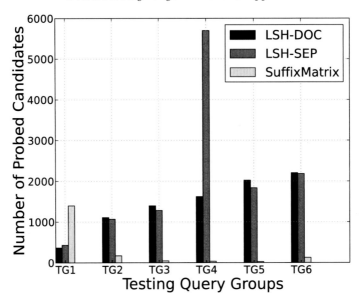

FIGURE 7.10: Number of probed candidates for ThunderBird log.

7.2.6.5 Offline Indexing

Space cost is an important factor for evaluating these methods [36, 88, 82, 140]. If the space cost is too large, the index cannot be loaded into the main memory. To exclude the disk I/O cost for online searching, we load all event messages and index data into the main memory. The total space cost can be directly measured by the allocated heap memory size in JVM. Note that the allocated memory does not only contain the index, it also includes the original log event messages, 2-shinglings of each event message, and the corresponding Java object information maintained by JVM. We use Java object serialization to compute the exact size of the allocated memory. Figure 7.15 and Figure 7.16 show the total memory size used for each testing group. The parameters of each method are the same as in Figure 7.8 and Figure 7.9. The total space costs for LSH-SEP and suffix matrix are almost the same because they both build the hash index for each event message only once. But LSH-DOC builds the hash indices for each event l times since each event is contained by l continuous segments, where l is the length of the indexed segment and $l = 3$.

Indexing time is the time cost for building the index. Figure 7.17 and Figure 7.18 show the indexing time for each method. The time complexities of LSH-DOC and LSH-SEP are $O(nlbt \cdot c_h)$ and $O(nbt \cdot c_h)$, where n is the number of event messages, l is the indexed segment length, b is the length of the hash vector, t is the number of hash tables, and c_h is the cost of the Min-Hash function for one event message. Although for each testing group, the

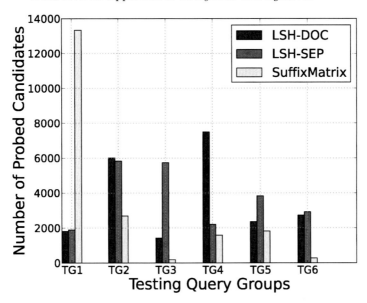

FIGURE 7.11: Number of probed candidates for Apache log.

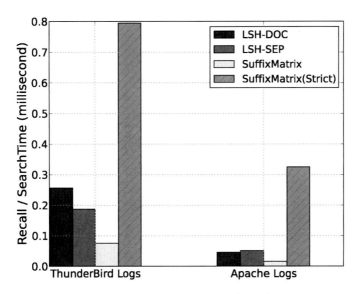

FIGURE 7.12: RecallRatio for TG1.

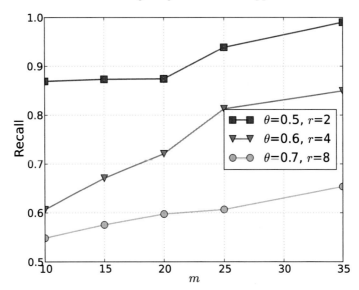

FIGURE 7.13: Varying m.

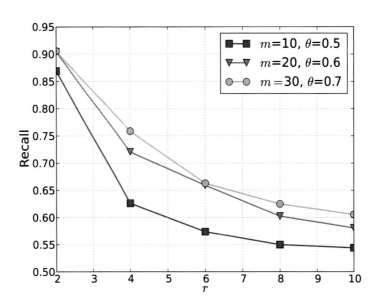

FIGURE 7.14: Varying r.

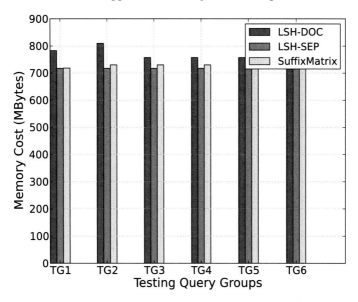

FIGURE 7.15: Peak memory cost for ThunderBird log.

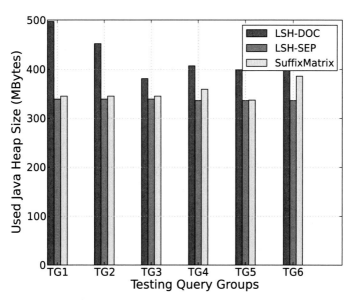

FIGURE 7.16: Peak memory cost for Apache log.

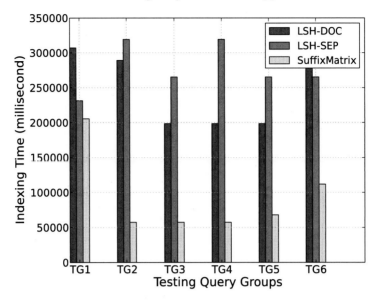

FIGURE 7.17: Indexing time for ThunderBird log.

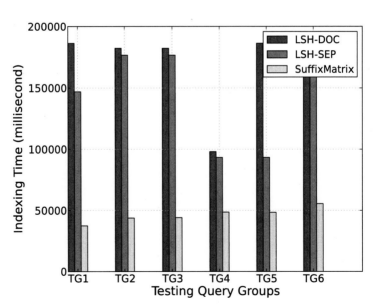

FIGURE 7.18: Indexing time for Apache log.

selected LSH-DOC and LSH-SEP may have different b and t, in general LSH-SEP is more efficient than LSH-DOC. The time complexity of suffix matrix for building the index is $O(mn \log n + mn \cdot c_h)$, where m is the number of rows of the suffix matrix. It seems that the time complexity of suffix matrix is bigger than LSH-based methods if we only consider n as a variable. However, as shown in Figure 7.17 and Figure 7.18, suffix matrix is actually the most efficient method in building an index. The main reason is $m \ll b \cdot t$. In addition, the time cost of the Min-Hash function, c_h, is not small since it has to randomly permute the 2-shinglings of an event message.

7.3 Hierarchical Multi-Label Ticket Classification

Maximal automation of routine IT maintenance procedures is an ultimate goal of IT service management [69]. System monitoring, an effective and reliable means for IT problem detection, generates monitoring tickets to be processed by system administrators. IT problems are naturally organized in a hierarchy by specialization. The problem hierarchy is used to help triage tickets to the processing team for problem resolving.

In the infrastructure overview for ticket enrichment and auto-remediation represented by Figure 7.1, the enrichment engine allows classification of monitoring tickets by applying hierarchical multi-label classification, then finding the most effective classification, and finally invoking an automated action: auto-resolution script or auto-check script for enriching or resolving the ticket. In the case where auto-resolution seems unfeasible, the enriched ticket is assigned to a sysAdmin for a review. Ticket classification can reduce human error and speed up restoration of service. In this section, we introduce an effective method and a system to address the uncertainty of classification.

7.3.1 Hierarchical Multi-Label Classification

The hierarchical classification problem has been extensively investigated in the past ([54, 74, 65, 64, 87, 104, 187, 204]). As a more general case, hierarchical multi-label classification, where an instance can be labeled with nodes belonging to more than one path or a path without ending on a leaf in the hierarchy, has received much attention.

The recent literature considers several approaches to address the hierarchical multi-label classification problem. The first approach employs existing classification algorithms to build a classifier for each class label independently without any consideration of the hierarchical dependencies of labels. This approach leads to difficult interpretation of the classification result due to the hierarchical inconsistency when an instance is labeled as positive on the child label but labeled as negative on the parent label. A second approach is to adapt existing single-label classification algorithms, such as decision trees [41, 221]. A third approach is based on the first approach but applies some post-process to automatically guarantee the hierarchical consistency [55, 56, 35, 228]. We will focus on the third approach in this section.

For hierarchy information, hierarchical loss (H-loss) has been proposed in [55]. The main idea is that any mistake occurring in a subtree does not matter if the subtree is rooted with a mistake as well. As illustrated in (f) of Figure 7.19, the H-loss only counts once for the label Database even though a mistake also takes place in label DB2 and Down (i.e., db2 is down). This idea is consistent with the scenario of problem diagnosis, since there is no need for further diagnosis in the successive children labels if the reason for the problem has already been excluded in the parent label. However, H-loss could be misleading. For example, (f) in Figure 7.19, after the solution related to database is wrongly recommended, it is bad to refer the solutions belonging to the successive categories, such as DB2 and DOWN.

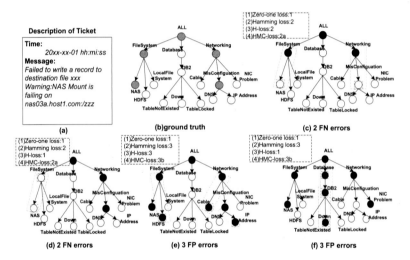

FIGURE 7.19: A hierarchical multi-label classification problem in the IT environment. A ticket instance is shown in (a). (b) The ground truth for the ticket with multiple class labels. (c), (d), (e), and (f) Four cases with misclassification. Assuming the cost of each wrong class label is 1, Zero-one loss, Hamming loss, H-loss, HMC-loss are given for misclassification. Notably, to calculate the HMC-loss, the cost weights for FN and FP are a and b respectively. The misclassified nodes are marked with a red square. The contextual misclassification information is indicated by the green rectangle.

The HMC-loss [228] function proposes weighting the misclassification with the hierarchy information while avoiding the deficiencies of the H-loss. It also differentiates the misclassification between the false negative (i.e., FN) and the false positive (i.e., FP) with different penalty costs. In Figure 7.19, assuming *a* and *b* are the misclassification penalties for FN and FP, respectively, (c) and (d) have two FN misclassification errors, so both of them incur $2a$ HMC-loss. Moreover, (e) and (f) suffer $3b$ HMC-loss since they get three FP misclassification errors. However, HMC-loss fails to show the distinction between (c) and (d). In the scenario of the resolution recommendation, based on (c), more diverse solutions are recommended since the ticket is related to both FileSystem and Networking, while only the solutions related to Networking are considered as solution candidates in (d). However, HMC-loss cannot differentiate predictions in (e) and (f). In the scenario of problem diagnosis, intuitively, we prefer (e) to (f) because the minor mistakes in multiple branches are not worse than the major mistakes in a single branch. Based on the discussion above, the main problem of HMC-loss is that it does not hierarchically consider the contextual information for each misclassification label (the contextual misclassification information is indicated with a green rectangle in Figure 7.19). The concept of the contextual information for each misclassified label is given in Section 7.3.1.2.

7.3.1.1 Problem Description

Let $\mathbf{x} = (x_0, x_1, ..., x_{d-1})$ be an instance from the d-dimensional input feature space χ, and $\mathbf{y} = (y_0, y_1, ..., y_{N-1})$ be the N-dimensional output class label vector where $y_i \in \{0, 1\}$. A multi-label classification assigns a multi-label vector $\mathbf{y}$ to a given instance $\mathbf{x}$, where $y_i = 1$ if $\mathbf{x}$ belongs to the ith class, and $y_i = 0$ otherwise. We denote the logical complement of y_i by $\widetilde{y}_i = 1 - y_i$.

The hierarchical multi-label classification is a special type of multi-label classification when a hierarchical relation H is predefined on all class labels. The hierarchy H can be a tree or an arbitrary DAG (directed acyclic graph). For simplicity, we focus on H being the tree structure, leaving the case of the DAG to future work.

In the label hierarchy H, each node i has a label $y_i \in \mathbf{y}$. Without loss of generality, we denote the root node by 0 and its label by y_0. For each node i, let $pa(i)$ and $ch(i)$ be the parent and children nodes, respectively, of the node i. An indicator function I_e of a boolean expression e is defined as

$$I_e = \begin{cases} 1, & e \ is \ true; \\ 0, & e \ is \ false. \end{cases} \tag{7.1}$$

A hierarchical multi-label classification assigns an instance $\mathbf{x}$ an appropriate multi-label vector $\hat{\mathbf{y}} \in \{0, 1\}^N$ satisfying the Hierarchy Constraint below.

Definition 7.1 (Hierarchy Constraint) *Any node i in the hierarchy H is labeled positive (i.e., 1) if either the root node or its parent is labeled positive. In other words,*

$$y_i = 1 \Rightarrow \{i = 0 \vee y_{pa(i)} = 1\}. \tag{7.2}$$

7.3.1.2 Hierarchical Loss Function

Note that $\hat{\mathbf{y}}$ denotes the prediction vector and $\mathbf{y}$ denotes the ground truth. To take into account Hierarchy Constraint in Definition 7.1 while finding the optimal prediction, the following definition is given:

Definition 7.2 *(Contextual Misclassification Information) Given a node i in hierarchy H, the contextual misclassification information depends on whether the parent node of i is misclassified when a misclassification error occurs in node i.*

There are four cases of misclassification of node i using contextual misclassification information, as shown in Figure 7.20.

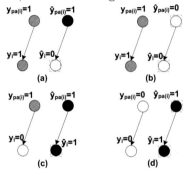

FIGURE 7.20: Four cases of contextual misclassification are shown in (a–d) for node i. Here the left pair is the ground truth; the right pair is the prediction. The misclassified nodes are marked with a red square.

The following four cases of contextual misclassification information are incorporated into the loss function to solve the optimization problem, i.e., the best predicted value compatible with the hierarchy H.

- case (a): False negative error occurs in node i, while the parent node $pa(i)$ is correctly predicted.

- case (b): False negative error occurs in both node i and $pa(i)$.

- case (c): False positive error occurs in node i, while the parent node $pa(i)$ is correctly labeled positive.

- case (d): Both node i and $pa(i)$ are labeled false positive.

Referring to [228, 56], a misclassification cost C_i is given according to the position information of node i in the hierarchy H. And $\{w_i | 1 \leq i \leq 4\}$ are the different penalty costs for the above four cases, respectively. Accordingly, a new flexible loss function named CH-loss (<u>C</u>ontextual <u>H</u>ierarchical loss) is defined as follows

$$\ell(\hat{\mathbf{y}}, \mathbf{y}) = w_1 \sum_{i>0}^{N-1} y_i y_{pa(i)} \widetilde{\hat{y}}_i \hat{y}_{pa(i)} C_i + w_2 \sum_{i>0}^{N-1} y_i y_{pa(i)} \widetilde{\hat{y}}_i \widetilde{\hat{y}}_{pa(i)} C_i$$
$$+ w_3 \sum_{i>0}^{N-1} \widetilde{y}_i y_{pa(i)} \hat{y}_i \hat{y}_{pa(i)} C_i + w_4 \sum_{i>0}^{N-1} \widetilde{y}_i \widetilde{y}_{pa(i)} \hat{y}_i \hat{y}_{pa(i)} C_i. \tag{7.3}$$

Next we show that the popular loss functions, such as HMC-loss, Hamming-loss, and H-loss, are special cases of the CH-loss function.

By setting α and β to be the penalty costs for false negative (FN) and false positive (FP) respectively, and noting that the root node is always correctly labeled, the HMC-loss function defined in [228] may be expressed as

$$\ell_{HMC}(\hat{\mathbf{y}}, \mathbf{y}) = \alpha \sum_{i>0}^{N-1} y_i \widetilde{\hat{y}}_i C_i + \beta \sum_{i>0}^{N-1} \widetilde{y}_i \hat{y}_i C_i. \tag{7.4}$$

Proposition 7.3 *The HMC-loss function is a special case of the CH-loss function when $w_1 = w_2 = \alpha$ and $w_3 = w_4 = \beta$.*

Proposition 7.4 *The Hamming-loss function is a special case of the CH-loss function when $w_1 = w_2 = w_3 = w_4 = 1$ and $C_i = 1$.*

It is established in [228] that the Hamming-loss function is a special case of HMC-loss when $\alpha = \beta = 1$ and $C_i = 1$. Combining the result with Proposition 7.3, Proposition 7.4 is straightforward.

The H-loss function (see [228]) cannot be reduced to the HMC-loss function, while H-loss is a special case of the CH-loss function. Remember that the H-loss function is defined in [55] as follows

$$\ell_H(\hat{\mathbf{y}}, \mathbf{y}) = \sum_{i>0}^{N-1} I_{\hat{y}_i \neq y_i} I_{\hat{y}_{pa(i)} \neq y_{pa(i)}} C_i. \tag{7.5}$$

Proposition 7.5 *The H-loss function is a special case of the CH-loss function when $w_1 = 1$, $w_2 = 0$, $w_3 = 1$, and $w_4 = 0$.*

Summarization of special cases of CH-loss is shown in Table 7.9.

7.3.2 Expected Loss Minimization

In this section the previously defined CH-loss function is used to predict $\hat{\mathbf{y}}$ given instance $\mathbf{x}$ by minimizing the expected CH-loss. Let $\mathbf{y}$ be the true multi-label vector of $\mathbf{x}$, and $P(\mathbf{y}|\mathbf{x})$ be the conditional probability that $\mathbf{y}$ holds given $\mathbf{x}$. The expected loss of labeling $\mathbf{x}$ with $\hat{\mathbf{y}}$ is defined by

$$LE(\hat{\mathbf{y}}, \mathbf{x}) = \sum_{\mathbf{y} \in \{0,1\}^N} \ell(\hat{\mathbf{y}}, \mathbf{y}) P(\mathbf{y}|\mathbf{x}). \tag{7.6}$$

TABLE 7.9: Special cases of CH-loss

Goal	CH-loss parameter settings
Minimize Hamming loss	$w_1 = w_2 = w_3 = w_4 = 1$, $C_i = 1$
Minimize HMC-loss	$w_1 = w_2 = \alpha$, $w_3 = w_4 = \beta$, C_i is defined by user
Minimize H-loss	$w_1 = w_3 = 1$, $w_2 = w_4 = 0$, $C_i = 1$
Increase recall	w_1 and w_2 are larger than w_3 and w_4
Increase precision	w_3 and w_4 are larger than w_1 and w_2
Minimize misclassification errors occur in both parent and children nodes	$w_2 > w_1$ and $w_4 > w_3$

Let $\hat{\mathbf{y}}^*$ be (one of) the optimal multi-label vector(s) that minimizes the expected CH-loss. Based on Bayesian decision theory, the problem is described as

$$\hat{\mathbf{y}}^* = \arg \min_{\hat{\mathbf{y}} \in \{0,1\}^N} LE(\hat{\mathbf{y}}, \mathbf{x}) \tag{7.7}$$

s.t. $\hat{\mathbf{y}}$ satisfies the Hierarchy Constraint in Definition 7.1.

The key step in solving Problem (7.7) is how to estimate $P(\mathbf{y}|\mathbf{x})$ in Eq.(7.6) from the training data. In order to simplify the problem, an assumption that all the labels in the hierarchy are conditionally independent from each other given the labels of their parents is given in [55, 56, 228]. Since all the data instances are labeled positive at root node 0, therefore $P(y_0 = 1|\mathbf{x}) = 1$ and $P(y_0 = 0|\mathbf{x}) = 0$. Due to the independency assumption:

$$P(\mathbf{y}|\mathbf{x}) = \prod_{i=1}^{N-1} P(y_i|y_{pa(i)}, \mathbf{x}). \tag{7.8}$$

Thus, to estimate $P(\mathbf{y}|\mathbf{x})$, the first step is to estimate $P(y_i|y_{pa(i)})$ for each node i. The nodewise estimation may be done by utilizing binary classification algorithms, such as logistic regression or support vector machine. To deal with a significant computational load of the nodewise estimation, the calculation can be parallelized.

The hierarchy constraint implies that $P(y_i = 1|y_{pa(i)} = 0) = 0$ and $P(y_i = 1|\mathbf{x}) = P(y_i = 1, y_{pa(i)} = 1|\mathbf{x})$. In order to simplify the notation, we denote

$$p_i = P(y_i = 1|\mathbf{x}) = P(y_i = 1, y_{pa(i)} = 1|\mathbf{x}). \tag{7.9}$$

Then p_i can be computed based on $P(y_i = 1|y_{pa(i)} = 1, \mathbf{x})$ as

$$p_i = P(y_i = 1|\mathbf{x}) = P(y_i = 1|y_{pa(i)} = 1, \mathbf{x})p_{pa(i)}. \tag{7.10}$$

By combining the definition of CH-loss with Eq.(7.6) and Eq.(7.9), the computation of loss expectation $LE(\hat{\mathbf{y}}, \mathbf{x})$ can be rewritten using p_i notation as

Proposition 7.6 (Expected Loss)

$$LE(\hat{\mathbf{y}}, \mathbf{x}) = w_1 \sum_{i>0}^{N-1} \widetilde{\hat{y}}_i \hat{y}_{pa(i)} C_i p_i + w_2 \sum_{i>0}^{N-1} \widetilde{\hat{y}}_i \widetilde{\hat{y}}_{pa(i)} C_i p_i +$$

$$w_3 \sum_{i>0}^{N-1} \hat{y}_i \widetilde{\hat{y}}_{pa(i)} C_i (p_{pa(i)} - p_i) + w_4 \sum_{i>0}^{N-1} \hat{y}_i \hat{y}_{pa(i)} C_i (1 - p_{pa(i)}). \tag{7.11}$$

Based on the expected loss described in Eq.(7.11), Problem (7.7) is reformulated as follows:

Proposition 7.7 *The minimization problem (7.7) is equivalent to the maximization problem below.*

$$\hat{\mathbf{y}}^* = \arg \max_{\hat{y} \in \{0,1\}^N} LE_\delta(\hat{\mathbf{y}}, \mathbf{x})$$
$$s.t.\ \hat{\mathbf{y}}\ satisfies\ the\ hierarchy\ constraint \tag{7.12}$$

where

$$LE_\delta(\hat{\mathbf{y}}, \mathbf{x}) = \sum_{i>0}^{N-1} \hat{y}_{pa(i)}(w_2 - w_1)C_i p_i +$$

$$\sum_{i>0}^{N-1} \hat{y}_i [w_1 C_i p_i - w_3 C_i (p_{pa(i)} - p_i) - w_4 C_i (1 - p_{pa(i)})].$$

Problem (7.12) is still challenging since it contains two free variables y_i and $y_{pa(i)}$ under the hierarchy constraint.

To simplify the problem further, we introduce notations $\sigma_1(i)$ and $\sigma_2(i)$ as follows:

$$\sigma_1(i) = \sum_{j \in child(i)} (w_2 - w_1)C_j p_j. \tag{7.13}$$

Particularly, if $ch(i) = \varnothing$, $\sigma_1(i) = 0$, and

$$\sigma_2(i) = w_1 C_i p_i - w_3 C_i (p_{pa(i)} - p_i) - w_4 C_i (1 - p_{pa(i)}). \tag{7.14}$$

Let $\sigma(i)$ be a function of node i defined as

$$\sigma(i) = \begin{cases} \sigma_1(i), & i = 0; \\ \sigma_1(i) + \sigma_2(i), & i > 0. \end{cases} \tag{7.15}$$

Eq.(7.15) implies:

Proposition 7.8

$$LE_\delta(\hat{\boldsymbol{y}}, \boldsymbol{x}) = \sum_i \hat{y}_i \sigma(i). \tag{7.16}$$

Based on Eq.(7.16), the solution to Problem (7.12) is equivalent to the one of problem (7.17).

$$\hat{\mathbf{y}}^* = \arg \max_{\hat{y} \in \{0,1\}^N} \sum_i y_i \sigma(i) \tag{7.17}$$

s.t. $\hat{\mathbf{y}}$ satisfies the hierarchy constraint.

The solution of Problem (7.17) by a greedy algorithm is described in the next section.

7.3.3   Algorithms and Solutions

As discussed in previous sections, there are three key steps to obtain the hierarchical multi-labeling of the instances having minimal CH-loss.

1. Estimate the probability of p_i for each node i based on the training data.

2. Use p_is to compute the $\sigma(i)$ defined by Eq.(7.15).

3. Obtain the optimal predictor $\hat{\mathbf{y}}^*$ as a solution of Problem (7.17).

Estimating p_i

According to Eq.(7.10), p_i can be computed by estimating the probability $P(y_i = 1|y_{pa(i)} = 1, \mathbf{x})$. For each node i with a positively labeled parent node, a binary classifier is built based on existing methods, such as logistic regression or support vector machine. Given an instance $\mathbf{x}$, we apply thresholding described in [178] to convert the real output of the classifier to estimate $P(y_i = 1|y_{pa(i)} = 1, \mathbf{x})$.

The task of building classifiers for all the nodes is a significant load. Since the building process of the classifier on each node only relies on the related training data and all the classifiers are mutually independent, we parallelize the task to improve performance [238].

Then, the values of p_i are computed by applying Eq.(7.9) while traversing the nodes in the hierarchy. The time complexity of p_i computation is $O(N)$, where N is the number of nodes in the hierarchy.

Computing $\sigma(i)$

With p_i available, σ can be computed based on Eq.(7.15) by recursively traversing each node of the hierarchy. Since each node in the hierarchy needs to be accessed twice, once for computing σ_1 and the other for computing σ_2, the time complexity of the $\sigma(i)$ evaluation is also $O(N)$.

Obtaining $\hat{\mathbf{y}}^*$

The value $\hat{\mathbf{y}}^*$ is obtained by solving the maximization problem (7.17). Bi and Kwok [35] proposed the greedy algorithm CSSA, based on the work in [29] that allows for solving Problem (7.17) efficiently. However, CSSA only works under an assumption that the number of labels to be associated with a predicted instance is known. That assumption rarely holds in practice. In [228], the HIROM algorithm is proposed to avoid the deficiency of CSSA by giving the maximum number of labels related to a predicting instance. During the process of finding the maximum number of labels, HIROM gets the optimal $\hat{\mathbf{y}}^*$ by comparing all possible $\hat{\mathbf{y}}$s with different numbers of labels related to a predicting instance.

A greedy labeling algorithm GLabel (**Algorithm 6**) is suggested to solve Problem (7.17). This algorithm finds the optimal $\hat{\mathbf{y}}^*$ without knowing the maximum number of labels for the predicting instance. It labels the node (or super node) i with maximum $\sigma(i)$ to be positive by searching in the hierarchy. If the parent node of i is negative, then i and its parent are merged into a super node whose σ value is the average σ value of all the nodes contained in the super node (Figure 7.21). The labeling procedure stops when the maximum σ value is negative or all nodes are labeled positive.

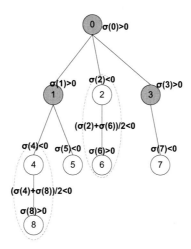

FIGURE 7.21: Figure illustrates a hierarchy with nine nodes and the steps of algorithm 6. Nodes labeled positive are green. A dotted ellipse marks a super node composed of the nodes in it.

Since the labeling procedure for each node may involve a merging procedure, the time complexity is no worse than $O(N log(N))$, the same as HIROM. However, as shown in the experimentation section below, GLabel performs more efficiently than HIROM while not requiring knowledge of the maximum number of labels.

Algorithm 6 $GLabel(\mathbf{H})$, $\mathbf{H}$ is the label hierarchy, with σ available

---

 1: define L as a set, and initialize $L = \{0\}$
 2: define U as a set, and initialize $U = \mathbf{H}\backslash\{0\}$
 3: **while** TRUE **do**
 4:     **if** all the nodes in $\mathbf{H}$ are labeled **then**
 5:         **return** L
 6:     **end if**
 7:     find the node i with maximum $\sigma(i)$
 8:     **if** $\sigma(i) < 0$ **then**
 9:         **return** L
10:     **end if**
11:     **if** all the parents of i are labeled **then**
12:         put i into L, and remove it from U
13:     **else**
14:         merge i with its parent as a super node i^*
15:         $\sigma(i^*) =$ average σ values of the two nodes
16:         put the i^* into U
17:     **end if**
18: **end while**

7.3.4   Experimentation

7.3.4.1   Setup

The experiments are performed over the ticket dataset generated by monitoring the IT environments of a large IT service provider. The number of tickets in the experiment amounts to about 23,000 in total. From the whole ticket dataset, 3000 tickets are sampled randomly to build the testing dataset, while the rest of the tickets are used to build the training dataset. The class labels come from the predefined catalog information for problems occurring during maintenance procedures. The whole catalog information of problems is organized in a hierarchy, where each node refers to a class label. The catalog contains 98 class labels; hence there are 98 nodes in the hierarchy. In addition, the tickets are associated with three labels on average and the height of the hierarchy is three as well.

The features for each ticket are built from the short text message describing the symptoms of the problem. First, natural language processing techniques are applied to remove the stop words and build Part-Of-Speech tags for the words in the text. The nouns, adjectives, and verbs in the text are extracted for each ticket. Second, we compute the TF-IDF scores of all words extracted from the text of tickets. The words with the top 900 TF-IDF scores are kept as the features for the tickets. Third, the feature vector of each ticket has 900 components, where the value of each feature is the frequency of the feature word occurring in the text of the ticket.

Based on the features and labels of the tickets, a binary classifier is built

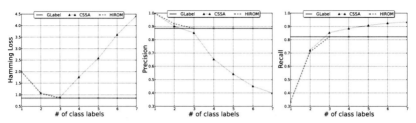

(a) The lowest Hamming loss: CSSA gets 0.8876 at # 3; HIROM gets 0.8534 at # 4; GLabel gets 0.8534.

(b) Varying precision during minimizing the Hamming loss

(c) Varying recall during minimizing the Hamming loss

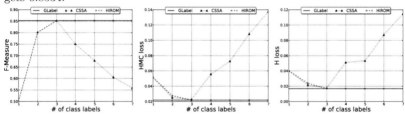

(d) Varying FMeasure score during minimizing the Hamming loss

(e) The lowest HMC-Loss: CSSA gets 0.0227 at # 3; HIROM gets 0.0219 at # 4; GLabel gets 0.0219.

(f) The lowest H-Loss: CSSA gets 0.0176 at # 3; HIROM gets 0.0168 at # 3; GLabel gets 0.0167.

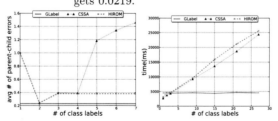

(g) The lowest AVG. parent-child error: CSSA gets 0.237 at # 2; HIROM gets 0.2440 at #2; Glabel gets 0.2304.

(h) Time complexity with respect to the number of classes related to each predicting ticket

FIGURE 7.22: Experiments involving tickets.

for each node in the hierarchy with the SVM algorithm using library libSVM [9]. The training data for each node i are the tickets with a positive parent label. To speed up evaluation of the 98 SVM classifiers, the process of training classifiers is parallelized, using the fact that all the classifiers are independent.

The experiments are mainly conducted by comparing the proposed GLabel algorithm with state-of-the-art algorithms such as CSSA and HIROM. Note that, in the end, benefits of hierarchical classification are also shown in comparison to the "Flat" classification.

7.3.4.2 Hamming Loss

The GLabel algorithm can obtain optimal $\hat{\mathbf{y}}^*$ with minimum Hamming loss by setting the parameters for Hamming loss, since Hamming loss is a special case of CH-loss. Given $w_1 = w_2 = w_3 = w_4 = 1$ for GLabel, $\alpha = \beta = 1$ for HIROM, and $C_i = 1$ for both of them, empirical results are displayed in (a)–(d) of Figure 7.22. (a) shows that the GLabel algorithm can automatically find the optimal $\hat{\mathbf{y}}^*$ with minimum Hamming loss, while both CSSA and HIROM require the number of class labels and the maximum number of class labels, respectively, to get the optimal $\hat{\mathbf{y}}^*$. With the increasing number of class labels, HIROM gets lower Hamming loss until it reaches the optimal $\hat{\mathbf{y}}^*$ with minimum Hamming loss by choosing a large enough number of class labels. However, CSSA may get larger Hamming loss as the number of class labels increases. (b)–(d) show that, in comparison to Hamming loss, the Glabel algorithm shows good performance in Precision, Recall, and F-Measure scores.

7.3.4.3 HMC-Loss

The HMC-loss considers loss with respect to the node position in the hierarchy. Following [228], the C_i is defined as

$$C_i = \begin{cases} 1, & i = 0; \\ \dfrac{C_{pa(i)}}{\text{\# of } i\text{'s siblings}}, & i > 0. \end{cases} \tag{7.18}$$

To simplify, $w_1 = w_2 = w_3 = w_4 = 1$ is set for Glabel and $\alpha = \beta = 1$ for HIROM as well. Figure 7.22e shows that the Glabel algorithm obtains the same lowest HMC-loss as the HIROM algorithm does. Note that HIROM is tuned for minimizing the HMC-loss.

7.3.4.4 H-Loss

In order to get the minimum H-loss, we set $w_1 = w_3 = 1$, $w_2 = w_4 = 0$ for GLabel, $\alpha = \beta = 1$ for HIROM, and $C_i = 1$ for all three algorithms. Figure 7.22f shows that GLabel gets the lowest H-loss in comparison to HIROM and CSSA minimums. The HIROM and CSSA algorithms cannot get the optimal $\hat{\mathbf{y}}^*$ with minimal H-loss.

7.3.4.5 Misclassifications Occur in Both Parent and Child Labels

The worst error from the loss point of view is the misclassification of both parent and child nodes. Such misclassification is denoted as a parent-child error. In terms of CH-loss, GLabel can minimize the number of such cases by setting $w_1 = w_3 = 1$, $w_2 = w_4 = 10$ with more penalties in parent-child errors. For comparison, we set in CSSA and HIROM $\alpha = \beta = 1$, and C_i according to Eq.(7.18). In Figure 7.22g, GLabel reaches the minimum average number of parent-child errors, while the CSSA and HIROM algorithms do not minimize the parent-child errors since they do not consider the contextual misclassification information in their loss function.

7.3.4.6 Time Complexity

In order to evaluate the time complexity, the same parameters are fixed but the number of classes labels is increased, as shown in Figure 7.22h. Three algorithms are run for 40 rounds and get the average time consumed. The Figure 7.22h shows that the running time of GLabel is independent of the number of labels, while the other algorithms require more running time as the number of labels increases. Hence, the GLabel algorithm is more efficient than the other two algorithms, especially in the cases with large numbers of class labels.

7.3.4.7 Comparison Study with "Flat" Classifier

To set up a "Flat" classification, a classifier is built for each label independently without considering the hierarchy constraint. The SVM algorithm is one of the best performing algorithms used to classify the ticket data with each binary class label. In order to decrease the parent-child error, we set $w_1 = w_3 = 1$, $w_2 = w_4 = 10$, and C_i as Eq.(7.18). In addition, the hierarchy error is defined as the average number of violated hierarchy constraints.

TABLE 7.10: Comparison with the "Flat" classification

Metric	SVM	GLabel
CH-loss	4.2601	2.6889
Parent-child error	0.3788	0.1729
Hierarchy error	0.0102	0.0

Table 7.10 shows that the GLabel algorithm has better performance in terms of CH-loss and parent-child error. Furthermore, the "Flat" SVM classification suffers on average 0.0102 hierarchy errors with each ticket, while GLabel complies with the hierarchy constraint and does not have hierarchy errors.

7.4   Ticket Resolution Recommendation

Monitoring software systems are designed to actively capture events and automatically generate incident tickets or event tickets. Repeating events generate similar event tickets, which in turn have a vast number of repeated problem resolutions likely to be found in earlier tickets. This section presents an analysis of the historical event tickets from a large service provider and introduces several resolution-recommendation algorithms for event tickets utilizing historical tickets.

7.4.1   Background

In Section 7.1.1, we introduced integrated infrastructure of problem detection, determination, and Resolution in service management, shown in Figure 7.1. Each event is stored as a database record which consists of several related attributes with values describing the system status at the time this event was generated. For example, a CPU-related event usually contains the CPU utilization and paging utilization information. A capacity-related event usually contains the disk name and the size of disk used/free space. Typically, different types of events have different sets of related attributes. The problem resolution of every ticket is stored as a textual description of the steps taken by the system administrator to resolve this problem.

7.4.1.1   Repeated Resolutions of Event Tickets

We analyzed the ticket data from three different accounts managed by IBM Global Services. One observation is that many ticket resolutions repeatedly appear in the ticket database. For example, for a low disk capacity ticket, common resolutions include deletion of temporal files, backup data, addition of a new disk, and so on. Unusual resolutions are very rare.

TABLE 7.11: Data summary

Dataset	Num. of Servers	Num. of Tickets	Time Frame
account1	1,145	50,377	55 days
account2	614	6,121	29 days
account2	391	4,066	48 days

The collected ticket sets from the three accounts are denoted by account1, account2 and account3, respectively. Table 7.11 summarizes the three datasets. Figure 7.23 shows the numbers of tickets and distinct resolutions, and Figure

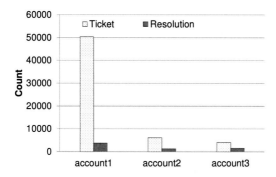

FIGURE 7.23: Numbers of tickets and distinct resolutions.

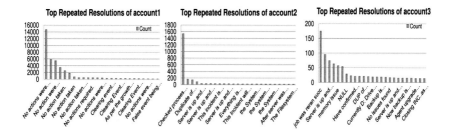

FIGURE 7.24: Top repeated resolutions for event tickets.

7.24 shows the top repeated resolutions in each dataset. It is seen that the number of distinct resolutions is much smaller than the number of tickets, in other words, multiple tickets share the same resolutions. For example, in Figure 7.24, the most common resolution, "No actions were...", appears more than 14,000 times in account1.

7.4.2 Basic KNN-Based Recommendation

Given an incoming event ticket, the objective of the resolution recommendation is to find k resolutions as close as possible to the the true one for some user-specified parameter k. The recommendation problem is often related to that of predicting the top k possible resolutions. A straightforward approach is to apply the KNN algorithm, which searches the K nearest neighbors of the given ticket (K is a predefined parameter) and recommends the top $k \leq K$ representative resolutions among them [190, 207]. The nearest neighbors are indicated by similarities of the associated events of the tickets.

Table 7.12 lists the notations used in this section. Let $D = \{t_1, ..., t_n\}$ be the set of historical event tickets and t_i be the i-th ticket in D, $i = 1, ..., n$. Let $r(t_i)$ denote the resolution description of t_i; $e(t_i)$ is the associated event of t_i. Given an event ticket t, the nearest neighbor of t is the ticket t_i which maximizes $sim(e(t), e(t_i))$, $t_i \in D$, where $sim(\cdot, \cdot)$ is a similarity function for events. Each event consists of event attributes with values. Let $A(e)$ denote

TABLE 7.12: Notations

Notation	Description
D	Set of historical tickets
$|\cdot|$	Size of set
t_i	i-th event ticket
$r(t_i)$	Resolution description of t_i
$e(t_i)$	Associate event of t_i
$c(t_i)$	Type of ticket t_i, $c(t_i) = 1$ indicates t_i is a real ticket, $c(t_i) = 0$ indicates t_i is a false ticket.
$A(e)$	Set of attributes of event e
$sim(e_1, e_2)$	Similarity of events e_1 and e_2
$sim_a(e_1, e_2)$	Similarity of a values of events e_1 and e_2
K	Number of nearest neighbors in the KNN algorithm
k	Number of recommended resolutions for a ticket, $k \leq K$

the set of attributes of event e. The similarity of events is computed as the summation of the similarities for all attributes. There are three types of event attributes: categorical, numeric, and textual (shown in Table 7.13). Given an

TABLE 7.13: Event attribute types

Type	Example
Categorical	host name, process name, ...
Numeric	CPU utilization, disk free space percentage, ...
Textual	event message,...

attribute a and two events e_1 and e_2, $a \in A(e_1)$ and $a \in A(e_2)$, the values of a in e_1 and e_2 are denoted by $a(e_1)$ and $a(e_2)$. The similarity of e_1 and e_2 with respect to a is

$$
sim_a(e_1, e_2) = \begin{cases} I[a(e_1) = a(e_2)], & \text{if } a \text{ is categorical,} \\ \frac{|a(e_1) - a(e_2)|}{max|a(e_i) - a(e_j)|}, & \text{if } a \text{ is numeric,} \\ Jaccard(a(e_1), a(e_2)), & \text{if } a \text{ is textual,} \end{cases}
$$

where $I(\cdot)$ is the indicator function returning 1 if the input condition holds, and 0 otherwise. Let $max|a(e_i) - a(e_j)|$ be the size of the value range of a. $Jaccard(\cdot, \cdot)$ is the Jaccard index for the *bag-of-words model* [189], frequently used to compute the similarity of two texts. Its value is the proportion of common words in the two texts. Note that, for any type of attribute, inequality $0 \le sim_a(e_1, e_2) \le 1$ holds. Then, the similarity for two events e_1 and e_2 is computed as

$$
sim(e_1, e_2) = \frac{\sum_{a \in A(e_1) \cap A(e_2)} sim_a(e_1, e_2)}{|A(e_1) \cup A(e_2)|}. \tag{7.19}
$$

Clearly, $0 \le sim(e_1, e_2) \le 1$. To identify the type of attribute a, we only need to scan all appearing values of a. If all values are composed of digits and a dot, a is numeric. If some value of a contains a sentence or phrase, then a is textual. Otherwise, a is categorical.

7.4.3   The Division Method

Traditional recommendation algorithms focus on the accuracy of the recommended results. However, in automated service management, false alarms are unavoidable in both the historical and incoming tickets [211]. The resolutions of false tickets are short comments such as "this is a false alarm," "everything is fine," and "no problem found." If we recommend a false ticket's resolution for a real ticket, it would cause the system administrator to overlook the real system problem, and none of the information in this resolution is helpful. Note that, in a large enterprise IT environment, overlooking a real system problem may have serious consequences, such as system crashes. Therefore, we consider incorporation of penalties in the recommendation results. There are two cases meriting a penalty: recommendation of a false ticket's resolution for a real ticket, and recommendation of a real ticket's resolution for a false ticket. The penalty in the first case should be larger since the real ticket is more important. The two cases are analogous to the *false negative* and *false positive* in prediction problems [207], but note that our recommendation target is the ticket resolution, not its type. A false ticket's event may also have a high similarity with that of a real one. The objective of the recommendation algorithm is now maximized accuracy under minimized penalty.

A straightforward solution consists in dividing all historical tickets into two sets comprising the real and false tickets, respectively. Then, it builds a KNN-based recommender for each set. Another ticket type predictor is created, establishing whether an incoming ticket is real or false, with the appropriate recommender used accordingly. The division method works as follows: it first uses a type predictor to predict whether the incoming ticket is real or false. If it is real, then it recommends the tickets from the real historic tickets; if it is false, it recommends the tickets from the false historic tickets. The historic tickets are already processed by the system administrator, so their types are known and we do not have to predict them.

The division method is simple, but relies heavily on the precision of the ticket type predictor, which cannot be perfect. If the ticket type prediction is correct, there will be no penalty for any recommendation result. If the ticket type prediction is wrong, every recommended resolution will incur a penalty. For example, if the incoming ticket is real, but the predictor says it is a false ticket, this method only recommends false tickets. As a result, all the recommendations would incur penalties.

7.4.4   The Probabilistic Fusion Method

To overcome the limitation of the division method, we develop a probabilistic fusion method. The framework of the basic KNN-based recommendation is retained, with difference that the penalty and probability distribution of the ticket type are incorporated in the similarity function.

Let λ be the penalty for recommending a false ticket's resolution for a real ticket, and $1 - \lambda$ that for recommending a real ticket's resolution for a false one. λ can be specified by the system administrator based on the actual cost of missing a real alert, $0 \leq \lambda \leq 1$. Larger λ indicates a greater importance of real tickets. The penalty function is

$$\lambda_t(t_i) = \begin{cases} \lambda, & t \text{ is a real ticket, } t_i \text{ is a false ticket} \\ 1 - \lambda, & t \text{ is a false ticket, } t_i \text{ is a real ticket} \\ 0, & \text{otherwise,} \end{cases}$$

where t is the incoming ticket and t_i is the historical one whose resolution is recommended for t. Conversely, an award function can be defined as $f_t(t_i) = 1 - \lambda_t(t_i)$. Since $0 \leq \lambda_t(t_i) \leq 1$, $0 \leq f_t(t_i) \leq 1$.

Let $c(\cdot)$ denote the ticket type. $c(t_i) = 1$ indicates t_i is a real ticket; $c(t_i) = 0$ indicates t_i is a false ticket. Since t is an incoming ticket, the value of $c(t)$ is not known. Using a ticket type predictor, we can estimate the distribution of $P[c(t)]$. The idea of this method is to incorporate the expected award in the similarity function. The new similarity function $sim'(\cdot, \cdot)$ is defined as

$$sim'(e(t), e(t_i)) = E[f_t(t_i)] \cdot sim(e(t), e(t_i)), \tag{7.20}$$

where $sim(\cdot, \cdot)$ is the original similarity function defined by Eq. (7.19), and $E[f_t(t_i)]$ is the expected award, $E[f_t(t_i)] = 1 - E[\lambda_t(t_i)]$. If t_i and t have the same ticket type, then $E[f_t(t_i)] = 1$ and $sim'(e(t), e(t_i)) = sim(e(t), e(t_i))$, otherwise $sim'(e(t), e(t_i)) < sim(e(t), e(t_i))$. Generally, the expected award is computed as

$$
\begin{aligned}
E[f_t(t_i)] &= E[1 - \lambda_t(t_i)] = 1 - E[\lambda_t(t_i)] \\
&= 1 - \sum_{c(t), c(t_i) \in 0,1} P[c(t), c(t_i)] \lambda_t(t_i).
\end{aligned}
$$

We can assume that a new ticket t and historical ticket t_i are independent, i.e., $P[c(t), c(t_i)] = P[c(t)] \cdot P[c(t_i)]$. Then, the expected penalty is

$$
E[\lambda_t(t_i)] = \sum_{c(t), c(t_i) \in 0,1} P[c(t)] \cdot P[c(t_i)] \cdot \lambda_t(t_i).
$$

Since $c(t_i)$ is already fixed, substituting $\lambda_t(t_i)$, we obtain

$$
E[\lambda_t(t_i)] = \begin{cases} P[c(t) = 0] \cdot (1 - \lambda), & t_i \text{ is a real ticket} \\ P[c(t) = 1] \cdot \lambda, & t_i \text{ is a false ticket.} \end{cases}
$$

Note that all factors in the new similarity function are of the same scale, i.e., $[0, 1]$, thus $0 \leq sim'(\cdot, \cdot) \leq 1$.

Prediction of Ticket Type

Given an incoming ticket t, the probabilistic fusion method needs to estimate the distribution of $P[c(t)]$. The division method also has to predict whether t is a real ticket or a false ticket. There are many binary classification algorithms for estimating $P[c(t)]$. In our implementation, we utilize another KNN classifier. The features are the event attributes and the classification label is the ticket type. The KNN classifier first finds the K nearest tickets in D, denoted as $D_K = \{t_{j_1}, ..., t_{j_k}\}$. Then, $P[c(t) = 1]$ is the proportion of real tickets in D_K and $P[c(t) = 0]$ is the proportion of false tickets in D_K. Formally,

$$
\begin{aligned}
P[c(t) = 1] &= |\{t_j | t_j \in D_K, c(t_j) = 1\}| / K \\
P[c(t) = 0] &= 1 - P[c(t) = 1].
\end{aligned}
$$

7.4.5 Metric Learning Method

7.4.5.1 Representation of Monitoring Tickets

Attribute level features are used in the traditional KNN algorithm for recommendation. However, attribute-level feature representation is not interpretable and often contains a lot of noise.

Further observation indicates that each monitoring ticket describes the existing problems (e.g., low capacity, high CPU, utilization) in service, and the associated ticket resolution should be highly relevant to the problems. For example, Table 7.14 presents some sample monitoring tickets for "low free space" and their corresponding resolutions. The problems in these tickets are described by the "SUMMARY" attribute and they all share the similar semantic meaning "low free space." Therefore, it is better to use features semantically capturing these problems, instead of attribute-level features, to represent monitoring tickets. Therefore, Latent Dirichlet Allocation [40](LDA) is proposed to perform feature extraction, which can first extract hidden topics and then encode monitoring tickets using topic level features.

The steps for using LDA for feature extraction are

- Represent each monitoring ticket as a document by concatenating each attribute after stop words removal and tokenization.

- Use historical tickets to train an LDA model.

- Inference feature vectors using the trained LDA model for both incoming events and historical monitoring tickets.

After those steps, monitoring tickets can be encoded as feature vectors and the cosine similarity can then be applied to measure their similarities.

7.4.5.2 Incorporating the Resolution Information

In previous KNN-based recommendation approaches, resolutions are ranked according to the similarity measurement using the event information only. However, the resolutions often reveal their prevalence in historical tickets and contain important information about the events, which can be used to improve the recommendation performance. There are two practical motivations for incorporating the resolution information:

1. In a K nearest neighbor search, historical tickets with resolutions that are highly relevant to an incoming event should be ranked higher than those tickets having similar event descriptions, but with fewer related resolutions.

2. In a K nearest neighbor search, those tickets with resolutions that are more prevalent should be ranked higher than those with less prevalent resolution, even if their event descriptions are similar.

Table 7.14 presents four tickets having similar event descriptions (shown in the "SUMMARY" attribute) from account1. All four tickets describe a "low free space" problem. In practice, however, the resolution from Ticket 1 should have a higher rank than the one from Ticket 4 since the resolution from Ticket 1 is more informative. Similarly, resolutions from Ticket 1 and Ticket 2 should have higher ranks than the one from Ticket 3 because of their higher prevalence.

In Section 7.4.2, $sim(e, e(t_i))$ is computed to find the K nearest neighbors of an incoming event e, in which $e(t_i)$ is the event information associated with the i-th ticket. To incorporate the resolution information, $sim(e, t_i)$ (i.e., similarity between an incoming event and the i-th ticket), rather than $sim(e, e(t_i))$,

TABLE 7.14: Tickets for explaining motivation of incorporating resolution information

ticketID	SUMMARY	RESOLUTION
1	The logical disk has a low amount of free space. Percent available: 2 Threshold: 5	After deleting old uninstall files, the logical disk has now over 10% of free disk space.
2	The percentage of used space in the logic disk is 90 percent. Threshold: 90 percent	After deleting old uninstall files, the logical disk has now over 15% of free disk space.
3	File system is low. The percentage of available space in the file system is 10 percent. Threshold: 90 percent	After delprof run, the server now has more than 4gb of free space.
4	The logical disk has a low amount of free space. Percent available: 3 Threshold: 5	No trouble was found, situation no longer persists.

is used in the algorithm. $sim(e, t_i)$ can be easily computed since e and t_i can be vectorized with the same dimensions after using topic-level features.

7.4.5.3 Metric Learning

In previous sections, we improve the recommendation algorithm by using topic-level features and incorporating resolution information into a K nearest neighbor search. However, we still treat each feature equally in computing the similarity measure. According to our observation, topics extracted from the LDA model should have different contributions to the similarity measurement since some topics contain the major descriptive words about events while the others may consist of less meaningful words. For example, Table 7.15 lists two topics for illustration. Apparently Topic 30 contains more descriptive words than Topic 14 and thus we should assign a larger weight to Topic 30 in the similarity measurement. We adopt metric learning [124] to achieve this goal.

TABLE 7.15: First six words are extracted to represent topics trained from LDA

topicID	SUMMARY
14	server wsfpp1 lppza0 lppzi0 nalac application
30	server hung condition responding application apps

The metric learning problem aims at learning a distance function tuned to a particular task, and has been shown to be useful when used in conjunction with nearest-neighbor methods and other techniques that rely on distances or similarities [79]. Mahalanobis distance is commonly used for vectorized inputs, which can avoid one feature dominating the computation of the Euclidean distance. In the metric learning literature, the term "Mahalanobis distance" is often used to denote any distance function of the form

$$d_A(x, y) = (x - y)^T A(x - y), \tag{7.21}$$

where A is some positive semi-definite (PSD) matrix, and x, y are the feature vectors. To facilitate the learning process, in metric learning, a slightly modified form of distance function is commonly used, as described below [124]:

$$d_A(x, y) = x^T A y. \tag{7.22}$$

Suppose we have n historical tickets $t_1, t_2, \ldots, t_n$ and n corresponding resolutions $r(t_1), r(t_2), \ldots, r(t_n)$. The resolution categories are considered as supervision for metric learning since intuitively similar resolutions solve similar issues. We pre-calculate matrix $R \in R^{n*n}$ in which $R_{i,j} = sim(r(t_i), r(t_j))$. The objective is to learn a similarity function $S_A(\vec{t_i}, \vec{t_j})$ by solving the optimization problem

$$
\begin{aligned}
f(A) &= min \sum_{i=1}^{n} \sum_{j=1}^{n} ||R_{i,j} - S_A(\vec{t_i}, \vec{t_j})||^2 \\
&= min||R - SAS^T||^2,
\end{aligned}
\tag{7.23}
$$

in which $S_A(\vec{t_i}, \vec{t_j}) = \vec{t_i}^T * A * \vec{t_j}$ ($\vec{t_i}$ and $\vec{t_j}$ are feature vectors for ticket t_i and t_j) are used instead of $S_A(e(\vec{t_i}), e(\vec{t_j}))$ as a way of keeping the benefits of incorporating the resolution information into the K nearest neighbor search. Since matrix A is constrained to be a PSD matrix, the projected gradient descent algorithm can be directly applied to solve the optimization problem in Eq.(7.23). In each iteration of gradient descent, the new updated matrix A will be projected into a PSD matrix as the initial value for the next iteration. Singular value thresholding [50] has been applied to project A into a PSD matrix by setting all A's negative eigenvalues to be zero.

The following is the gradient for Eq.(7.23):

$$
\begin{aligned}
\frac{\delta f(A)}{\delta A} &= \frac{\delta((R - SAS^T)^T (R - SAS^T))}{\delta A} \\
&= 2S^T SAS^T S - 2S^T AS
\end{aligned}
\tag{7.24}
$$

The resolution categories are usually provided by system administrators. With the available category information, the similarity between two resolutions is computed as

$$
sim(r(t_i), r(t_j)) = \begin{cases} 1, & \text{if } r(t_i), r(t_j) \text{ are in same category,} \\ 0, & \text{otherwise.} \end{cases}
$$

7.4.6   Evaluation for Probabilistic Fusion Method

Four algorithms are implemented: KNN, weighted KNN, the division method, and the probabilistic fusion method, which are denoted by KNN, WeightedKNN, Divide, and Fusion, respectively. Two algorithms, Divide and Fusion, are based on the weighted KNN algorithm framework. The KNN-based algorithm is chosen as the baseline because it is the most widely used Top-N item-based recommendation algorithm. Certainly, SVM can be used to predict the ticket type to be false or real. But here the core idea is not about classification, but to combine the penalty for the misleading resolution into the recommendation algorithm.

7.4.6.1   Experimental Data

Experimental event tickets are collected from three accounts managed by IBM Global Services: account1, account2, and account3. The monitoring events are captured by IBM Tivoli Monitoring [5]. The ticket sets are summarized in Table 7.11.

7.4.6.2   Accuracy

For each ticket set, the first 90% of tickets are used as the historic tickets and the remaining 10% of tickets are used for testing. The hit rate is a widely used metric for evaluating the accuracy in item-based recommendation algorithms [66, 116, 167].

$$\text{Accuracy} = \text{Hit-Rate} = |Hit(C)|/|C|,$$

where C is the testing set, and $Hit(C)$ is the set for which one of the recommended resolutions is *hit* by the true resolution. If the recommendation resolution is truly relevant to the ticket, we say that the recommended resolution is *hit* by the true resolution.

Since real tickets are more important than false ones, we define another accuracy measure, weighted accuracy, which assigns weights to real and false tickets. The weighted accuracy is computed as

$$\text{Weighted Accuracy} = \frac{\lambda \cdot |Hit(C_{real})| + (1 - \lambda) \cdot |Hit(C_{false})|}{\lambda \cdot |C_{real}| + (1 - \lambda) \cdot |C_{false}|},$$

where C_{real} is the set of real testing tickets, C_{false} is the set of false testing tickets, $C_{real} \cup C_{false} = C$, λ is the importance weight of the real tickets, $0 \le \lambda \le 1$; it is also the penalty mentioned in Section 7.4.4. In this evaluation, $\lambda = 0.9$, since the real tickets are much more important than the false tickets in reality. We also test other large λ values, such as 0.8 and 0.99. The accuracy comparison results have no significant change.

K and k are varied from 1 to 20 to obtain different parameter settings. Figures 7.25 and 7.26 are the testing results for $K = 10, k = 3$ and $K = 20, k = 5$. The comparison results for other parameter settings are similar to the two

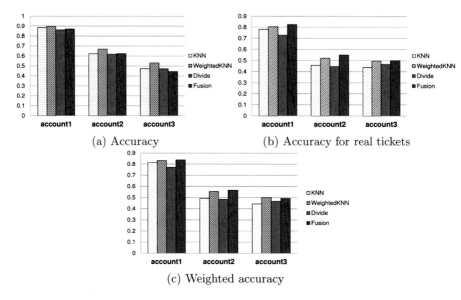

(a) Accuracy

(b) Accuracy for real tickets

(c) Weighted accuracy

FIGURE 7.25: Test results for $K = 10$, $k = 3$.

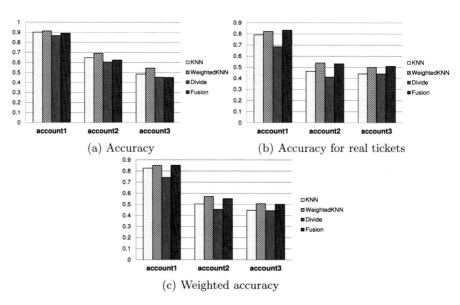

(a) Accuracy

(b) Accuracy for real tickets

(c) Weighted accuracy

FIGURE 7.26: Test results for $K = 20$, $k = 5$.

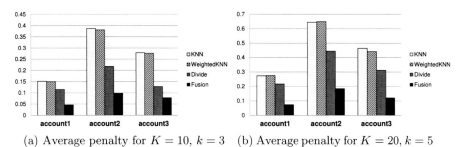

(a) Average penalty for $K = 10$, $k = 3$ (b) Average penalty for $K = 20$, $k = 5$

FIGURE 7.27: Average penalty for varying K and k.

figures. It is seen that the weighted KNN algorithm always achieves the highest accuracy in the three datasets. But for real tickets, our proposed probabilistic fusion method outperforms other algorithms (Figure 7.25b and Figure 7.26b). As for the weighted accuracy in Figure 7.25c and Figure 7.26c, the weighted KNN and the probabilistic fusion are still the two best algorithms, and neither of them outperforms the other in all datasets. Overall, the performances of all four algorithms are very close. For each comparison, the accuracy gap between the highest one and the lowest one is about 10%.

7.4.6.3 Penalty

Figure 7.27a and Figure 7.27b show the average penalty for each testing ticket. A higher importance is assigned to the real tickets, $\lambda = 0.9$. As shown by these figures, The division method and the probabilistic fusion method have smaller penalties than the traditional KNN-based recommendation algorithms. The probabilistic fusion method outperforms the division method, which relies heavily on the ticket type predictor. Overall, the probabilistic fusion method only has about 1/3 of the penalties of the traditional KNN-based algorithms.

7.4.6.4 Overall Performance

An overall quantity metric is used for evaluating the recommendation algorithms, covering both the accuracy and the average penalty. It is defined as overall score = weighted accuracy / average penalty. If the weighted accuracy is higher or the average penalty is lower, then the overall score becomes higher and the overall performance is better. Figure 7.31a and Figure 7.31b show the overall scores of all algorithms for two parameter settings. It is seen that our proposed algorithms are always better than the KNN-based algorithms in each dataset.

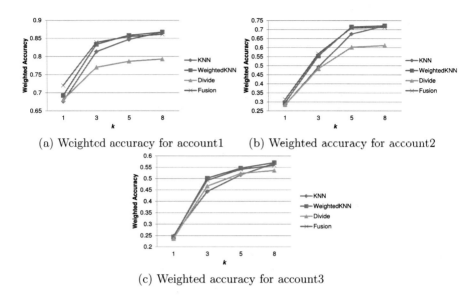

(a) Weighted accuracy for account1   (b) Weighted accuracy for account2

(c) Weighted accuracy for account3

FIGURE 7.28: Weighted accuracy by varying k, $K = 10$.

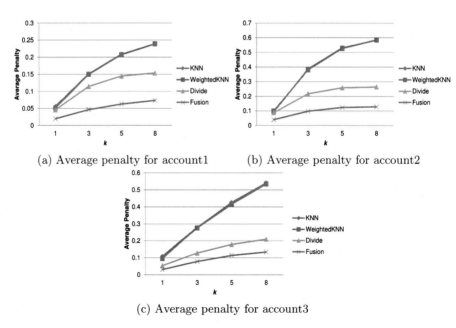

(a) Average penalty for account1   (b) Average penalty for account2

(c) Average penalty for account3

FIGURE 7.29: Average penalty by varying k, $K = 10$.

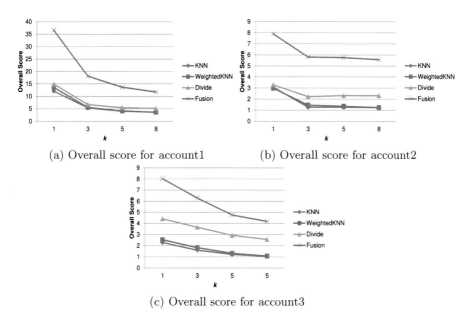

(a) Overall score for account1

(b) Overall score for account2

(c) Overall score for account3

FIGURE 7.30: Overall score by varying k, $K = 10$.

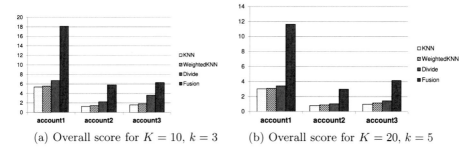

(a) Overall score for $K = 10$, $k = 3$

(b) Overall score for $K = 20$, $k = 5$

FIGURE 7.31: Overall score for varying K and k.

7.4.6.5   Variation of Parameters

To compare the results of each algorithm, the number of each recommendation resolution, k, is varied. Figures 7.28, 7.29, and 7.30 show the weighted accuracies, average penalties, and overall scores by varying k from 1 to 8, with $K = 10$. For other values of K, the comparison results are similar to the three figures. As shown by Figure 7.28, when increasing the value of k, the size of the recommendation results becomes larger. Then the probability of one recommended resolution being *hit* by the true resolution also increases. Therefore, the weighted accuracy becomes higher. Except the division method, all algorithms have similar weighted accuracies for each k. However, as k is increased and there are more recommended resolutions, there are more potential penalties in the recommended resolutions. Hence, the average penalty also becomes higher (Figure 7.29). Finally, Figure 7.30 compares the overall performance by varying k. Clearly, the probabilistic fusion method outperforms other algorithms for every k.

7.4.7   Evaluation for Metric Learning Method

The evaluation between the probabilistic fusion method and the metric learning method is differentiated since the latter one is an extension of the previous one. The dataset used here is totally different.

Another four algorithms are implemented here: weighted KNN using the attribute level features, the weighted KNN method using the topic level features, the method incorporating historical resolution information, and the methods using an improved similarity metric after applying metric learning, which are denoted by WKNN, LDABaselineKNN, CombinedLDAKNN, and MLCombinedLDAKNN, respectively. We show experimental results between WKNN and LDABaselineKNN since they prove that topic level features do not cause information loss compared to attribute level features. The LDABaselineKNN algorithm is the baseline for CombinedLDAKNN, which itself is the baseline for MLCombinedLDAKNN.

7.4.7.1   Experimental Data

Experimental monitoring tickets are collected from three different accounts managed by IBM Global Services: account4, account5, and account6. The monitoring events are captured by IBM Tivoli Monitoring [5]. The ticket sets are summarized in Table 7.11. To evaluate metric learning, 1000 labeled tickets with resolution categories are obtained from account4. Table 7.16 shows three sample categories of resolutions [42].

7.4.7.2   Evaluation Metric

In general, several resolutions can be recommended for a single testing instance. To consider the relativeness of all recommended resolutions, the

TABLE 7.16: Three resolution types with the event description they resolved

resolution class	resolved event key words
Server unavailable	Server unavailable due to unexpected shutdown, reboot, defect hardware, system hanging
Disk/FS capacity shortage	Disk or file system capacity problems and disk failure
Performance inefficiency	Performance and capacity problems of CPU or memory

average similarity (avgSim) is used as one evaluation metric and is given by

$$\text{avgSim} = \frac{1}{N} \sum_{i=1}^{N} \sum_{j=1}^{n_i} sim(r_{io}, r_j)/n_i,$$

in which N is the number of testing instances, and n_i is the number of recommended resolutions for testing instance i and r_{io} is its original resolution, and r_j is its jth recommended resolution. The Jaccard similarity is used to calculate $sim(r_{io}, r_j)$.

Mean Average Precision (MAP) [242] is widely used for recommendation evaluation. It considers not only the relativeness of all recommended results, but also the ranks of the recommended results.

$$\text{MAP@n} = \sum_{i=1}^{N} ap@n_i/N,$$

N is the number of a testing instance, $ap@n$ is given by

$$\text{ap@n} = \sum_{k=1}^{n} p(k)\delta r(k),$$

where k is the rank in the sequence of retrieved resolutions, n is the number of retrieved resolutions, $p(k)$ is the precision at cut-off k in the list, and $\delta r(k)$ is the change in recall from items $k-1$ to k.

7.4.7.3 Choosing the Number of Topics

Figure 7.32 shows the experimental results of choosing the proper number of topics for training the LDA model using dataset account4. The results show that $numTopics = 300$ is a proper setup for the number of topics. Thus, $numTopics = 300$ is chosen for all the following experiments.

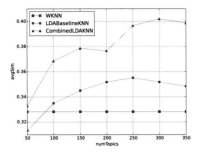

FIGURE 7.32: Accuracy varies for different *numTopics* for dataset account4.

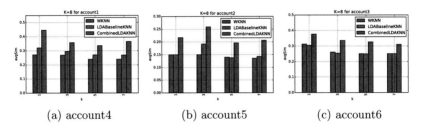

(a) account4   (b) account5   (c) account6

FIGURE 7.33: Test results for three accounts by varying k for $K = 8$.

7.4.7.4   Overall Performance

The *average similarity* is used for comparing the performance among WKNN, LDABaselineKNN, and CombinedLDAKNN. When resolution categories are available, *MAP@n* is used for comparing the performance between CombinedLDAKNN and MLCombinedLDAKNN since it explicitly considers the relativeness of the recommended results.

To compare the results of each algorithm, we vary the number of recommended resolutions, k. Figures 7.33 and 7.34 show the *average similarity* scores by setting $k = 1, 3, 5, 7$, respectively, with $K = 8$ and $K = 16$. As shown in Figure 7.33 and Figure 7.34, topic level features are better than attribute level features for account4 and account5 and slightly worse for account6 by comparing algorithm WKNN and LDABaselineKNN. CombinedLDAKNN always outperforms LDABaselineKNN, which proves the effectiveness of incorporating the resolution information into K nearest neighbor search.

Figure 7.35, Figure 7.36, and Figure 7.37 illustrate the usefulness of metric learning. In these figures, the X-axis and the Y-axis are the event id's ordered by the resolution categories, and the color indicates the similarity score. As shown in Figure 7.35 and Figure 7.36, similarity scores between monitoring tickets with resolutions from the same category are enhanced while similarity scores between monitoring tickets with resolutions from different categories are reduced. Therefore, for example, for a testing instance whose original

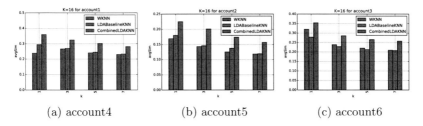

(a) account4   (b) account5   (c) account6

FIGURE 7.34: Test results for three accounts by varying k for $K = 16$.

resolution belongs to category i, more resolutions from category i will be retrieved first after applying metric learning.

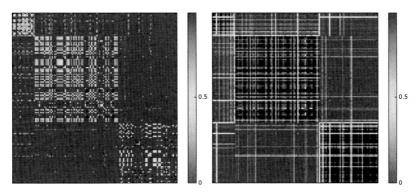

FIGURE 7.35: Similarity measure before and after metric learning for a training set. (See color insert.)

Figure 7.37 uses *MAP* to evaluate the performance of CombinedLDAKNN and MLCombinedLDAKNN. As shown in Figure 7.37, overall MAP scores of MLCombinedLDAKNN are higher and more stable than CombinedLDAKNN when K increases. It indicates that MLCombinedLDAKNN can retrieve more related resolutions first and thus is more robust to noisy resolutions compared to CombinedLDAKNN, which proves the effectiveness of metric learning.

7.5 Summary

In this chapter, we introduced several data-driven applications in system management aiming to improve the efficiency of large IT service management and thus increase the competitiveness of IT service providers. Today's competitive business climate, as well as the complexity of service environments,

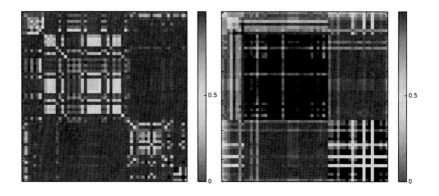

FIGURE 7.36: Similarity measure before and after metric learning for a testing set. (See color insert.)

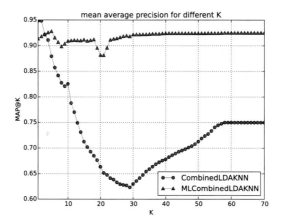

FIGURE 7.37: Mean average precision (MAP) varying parameter K of the underlying KNN algorithm.

demands efficient and cost-effective service delivery and support in system management.

First, we studied the search problem of locating similar system behaviors over large-scale textual log sequences. System administrators utilize the event logs to understand system behaviors and efficient search approaches will greatly help administrators to diagnose system problems. Several indexing techniques are described in this chapter for facilitating the similarity search. Extensive experiments on real system events, logs, and tickets demonstrate the effectiveness and efficiency of the proposed approaches.

Second, we proposed an efficient approach to address the hierarchical multi-label ticket classification problem in system management. The tickets' labels are used to distribute tickets to the specific processing team for problem resolving. Particulary, the contextual hierarchical loss (CH-loss) function has been defined which not only includes several traditional loss definitions as special cases, but also better represents the misclassification error of hierarchical multi-label problems. A greedy algorithm *Glabel* was proposed to solve the optimization problem involved with the CH-loss function. Extensive experiments on a real industrial ticket dataset illustrated the flexibility and superiority of the proposed approach.

Last but not the least, we studied the problem of resolution recommendation for monitoring tickets in an automated service management, which has great potential to reduce human labor in service management. A basic KNN-based recommendation approach was first proposed based on our analysis of historical tickets. Then different penalties were incorporated into the underlying KNN algorithm considering different risks of recommending resolutions from false tickets or positive tickets. Moreover, metric learning methods are used to automatically learn a better distance measurement for resolution recommendation.

7.6   Glossary

DAG: Directed acyclic graph, which is a graph having directed edges; no cycle exists in the graph.

KNN: K-nearest neighbor.

LDA: Latent Dirichlet Allocation topic model.

LSH: Locality-sensitive hashing.

Monitoring Situations: Configured acceptable thresholds of hardware and software performance metrics in system management, violation of which will result in an alert.

sysAdmin: System administrator who is responsible for the upkeep, configuration, and reliable operation of computer systems, especially computer servers.

Chapter 8

Social Media Event Summarization Using Twitter Streams

Chao Shen and Tao Li

Florida International University
Nanjing University of Posts and Telecommunications

8.1   Introduction

8.1.1   Social Media Events and Twitter

Social media sites (e.g., Facebook, Twitter, and YouTube) have emerged as new information channels for users to receive and to exchange information. In this chapter, we focus on social media event summarization, a method to provide meaningful summaries by analyzing a large number of posts of the social media. Different from log event summarization in Chapter 6 that aims to summarize the temporal patterns from the event log sequence, social media event summarization mainly focuses on presenting a high-level overview of the progress of an occurring event in a narrative way. In a typical social media event summarization,[1] multiple aspects of an event will be reported, including the time, the location, the participants, and the progress of the event. Leveraging the summary, people can quickly gain the main idea of the event without reading a large number of posts/tweets.

In this chapter, we would like to introduce the methodology of social media event summarization using Twitter as the example. Twitter is a popular microblog service with millions of active users and nearly 170 million daily posts. It is considered a useful platform for people to get information about the things happening around the world. Compared with conventional information channels like news web sites and blogs, Twitter has several unique advantages. First, it has a real-time nature. With brevity guaranteed by a 140-character limit, integration with mobiles' short message service, and the popularity of Twitter's mobile applications, Twitter messages (a.k.a. tweets) are typically designed for answering "what I am doing" or "what's happening," and can typically reflect events as they happen. For example, we could detect a tweet related to a shooting crime 10 minutes after the shots are fired, while the first news report would appear approximately 3 hours later. Meanwhile, tweets have broad coverage over all types of real-world events, due to Twitter's large number of users, including verified accounts such as news agents, organizations, and public figures. Every user can report whatever is happening around him or her, important or trivial. Thus, tweets cover nearly every aspect of daily life, from national breaking news (e.g., earthquakes), local events (e.g., car accidents), to personal feelings.

Besides being a communication tool for people to share and exchange information in their social network, Twitter is becoming one of the large information providers on a wide variety of real-world events. These events range from unplanned events like the Iran election protests and earthquakes to planned events like sports games and Apple developers conferences. For this reason, the content of such social media sites is particularly useful for keeping people

---

[1] For the rest of this chapter, the term *event summarization* refers to *social media event summarization*.

informed and updated on the events happening in real time with their user-contributed messages. Although a large volume of tweets provides enough information about events, they impose challenges for people to access and extract the real information from a stream of tweets about the event along with a lot of noise.

8.1.2   Social Media Event Summarization

Social media event summarization aims to provide a textual description of the events of interest. Given a data stream consisting of chronologically ordered text pieces related to an event, the event summarization system aims to generate an informative textual description that can capture all the important moments. Ideally, the summary should be produced in a progressive manner as the event unfolds. The resulting summaries and related analysis tools can serve as a complementary means to traditional journalistic practice.

Event summarization using social media data streams is a challenging task that has not been fully studied in the past. Existing studies [169, 163, 224, 145] on automatic text summarization often focus on the news articles, as driven by the annual evaluation of DUC (Document Understanding Conference)[2] and TAC (Text Analysis Conference).[3] However, news articles represent a text genre that is drastically different from social media text. The news is often produced by the professional writers with well-polished sentences and grammatical structures. When the sentences are extracted from the documents and concatenated to form a summary, the summarization results are often of good quality since the sentences are mostly self-explanatory. On the other hand, tweets are produced by users with diverse backgrounds. Tweets are short and notoriously noisy, containing a wide variety of non-standard spellings (e.g., abbreviations, acronyms, spelling errors, etc.) [146]. When individual tweets are taken out of the conversational thread to form an event summary, the meaning of the generated summary can be difficult for people to understand and interpret. While many of the literature studies employ the extractive approach for summary tweet selection [146, 225, 143], we discuss a pattern-based summarization approach in this chapter which allows the creation of informative event descriptions using automatically mined patterns.

Event summarization using tweets is also related to the recent event detection on Twitter, which is one of the most important research tasks on Twitter data. The task can be traced back to event detection on news stories, which was extensively researched as part of the Topic Detection and Tracking (TDT) project [22], which mainly deals with the event-based organization of newswire stories. Event detection in tweets is conceptually similar to the clustering task (commonly referred to as detection) from the TDT project. In both tasks, a system is presented with a continuous stream of time-ordered documents, and

---

[2]http://duc.nist.gov/
[3]http://www.nist.gov/tac/

it needs to place each of the documents into the most appropriate event-based cluster.

Detecting events on microblog streams is more challenging than event detection on news articles due to the different types and volumes of documents. In nature, event tweets are closely associated with the timeline and are drastically different from a collection of news articles. Most existing techniques proposed for news documents cannot be adapted to tweets. First, the volume of documents is several orders of magnitude larger in microblogs, which means that event detection systems must be extremely efficient to run in real time. Second, the assumption that every news story somehow belongs to undiscovered event topics cannot be held for tweets. Furthermore, microblog posts tend to be very noisy, of very limited length (tweets are restricted to 140 characters), and frequently contain spelling or grammar errors. These differences imply that approaches developed for the TDT project tend to be slow for real-time applications and extremely vulnerable to the noise found in microblog streams.

8.1.3   Content of the Chapter

Note that, given a Twitter stream about a particular event, social event summarization aims to provide a text description on the progress of the event. In this chapter, we propose a general framework for social event summarization which includes three important components: tweet context analysis, sub-event detection, and tweet summarization. Tweet context analysis aims to extract important semantic units (e.g., segments, participants, and topics) about an event from a Twitter stream, sub-event detection identifies important moments (e.g., a surge of interest from users) about the extracted semantic units of an event, and tweet summarization generates the text description to describe the progress of the event.

The rest of this chapter is organized as follows: Section 8.2 formulates the problem of social event summarization with tweets, and introduces the general framework along with its three important components. Sections 8.3, 8.4, and 8.5 describe the three components: tweet context analysis, sub-event detection, and tweet summarization, respectively. Section 8.6 presents the empirical evaluation of event summarization. Finally, we conclude the chapter and list future research directions in Section 8.7.

8.2   Problem Formulation

The Topic Detection and Tracking (TDT) project [22] defines an event as something that happens at some specific time and place. It is similar to events we are interested in in social event summarization using tweets, but there are two major differences. We are more interested in the events which (1) last for at least a certain amount of time, and (2) are composed of various activities.

For those events which happened within a very short time period and are composed of only a single activity, like traffic accidents and crimes, conventional multi-document summarization methods can be directly used to generate an event summary by treating tweets as documents. For those events which last for a long enough period and are composed of different activities, generating the summary is quite challenging and imperative.

Although a lot of tweets discuss views and opinions and express personal feelings about some events, due the length limit, it is difficult to analyze them for sentiment and opinion analysis. So here we are more interested in the factoid information carried by tweets about the activities in an event, instead of how people think after the event. In addition, while the location information of an event is helpful to distinguish different events, it is not essential to summarizing the progress of an event.

Definition 8.1 *In the task of social event summarization using tweets, an event is something that occurs in a certain place for a period of time involving different activities.*

Examples of social events include sports games, TV programs, natural disasters, etc.

Definition 8.2 *Given a stream of tweets, social event summarization using tweets means generating a short textual description presenting the important activities and progress of an event.*

Social event summarization using tweets is quite challenging, since the inputs can be very large and may contain a lot of noise. Given a Twitter stream about a particular event, event summarization using tweets can be conducted by addressing the following three questions:

- How to extract important and easily interpreted semantic units (e.g., segments, participants, and topics) about an event. The semantic units themselves can provide a global overview of the event. In addition, with the semantic units, we can "zoom-in" to the semantic unit level and further analysis can be conducted for each semantic unit. By organizing the overall event stream into different semantic units, we might obtain more coherent tweet data with less noise.

- How to identify important moments during of an event. These important moments are referred to as sub-events, when something significant occurs at a certain time. These sub-events are of critical importance, as they often represent a surge of interest from the Twitter audience. Therefore, sub-events can be good representatives of events, and the key information corresponding to the sub-events should be reflected in the event summary.

- How to summarize multiple tweets about a sub-event. Basically, tweet summarization extracts the representative tweets and forms a comprehensive and informative coverage of the event progress. Although multi-document summarization has been widely studied for decades, it cannot be directly applied to tweet summarization since tweets are quite different from documents.

In this chapter, to address the aforementioned questions, a general framework for social event summarization is presented which includes three important components: tweet context analysis, sub-event detection, and tweet summarization. In particular, tweet text analysis extracts important semantic units (e.g., segments, participants, and topics), sub-event detection identifies important moments, and tweet summarization generates the text description. In the next three sections, we will discuss technical approaches for the three components.

8.3   Tweet Context Analysis

In this section, we discuss technical approaches to extract important semantic units (e.g., segments, participants, and topics) about an event from a Twitter stream.

8.3.1   Word Segment Detection

One simple way to detect semantic units is to consider the frequency change of unigrams. However, a single unigram can be very ambiguous and contain many noises. Instead of using unigrams, Li et al. [130] proposed an approach to detect segments. A segment is one or more consecutive words (or phrase) in a tweet message, which can be a named entity like "LeBron James" or some other semantically meaningful unit like "OKC vs Miami." Apparently, compared with a unigram, a segment is more interpretable and contains more specific information than a unigram.

Given a tweet $d \in \mathcal{D}$, the problem of tweet segmentation is to split d into m non-overlapping and consecutive segments, $d = s_1 s_2 \ldots s_m$, where a segment s_i is either a word (or unigram) or a phrase (or multi-gram). The tweet segmentation problem is formulated as an optimization problem with the following objective function in [130]:

$$\arg \max_{s_1,\ldots,s_m} \mathcal{C}(d) = \sum_{i=1}^{m} \mathcal{C}(si), \qquad (8.1)$$

where $\mathcal{C}$ is the function that measures the stickiness of a segment or a tweet.

A high stickiness score of a segment $s = <w_1, \ldots, w_n>$ indicates that the segment should not be further split. The stickiness measure is defined in [130] as

$$C(s) = \mathcal{L}(s) \cdot e^{\mathcal{Q}(s)} \cdot \mathcal{S}(SCP(s)), \qquad (8.2)$$

which is composed of three terms. The function $\mathcal{L}$ is defined as

$$\mathcal{L}(s) = \begin{cases} \frac{|s|-1}{|s|} & \text{for } |s| > 1 \\ 1 & \text{for } |s| > 1 \end{cases} \qquad (8.3)$$

where $|s|$ is the segment length. $\mathcal{Q}(s)$ is the probability that s appears as the anchor text in the Wikipedia articles containing s. SCP is defined to measure the "cohesiveness" of a segment s by considering all possible binary segmentations, as shown in Eq.(8.4):

$$SCP(s) = \log \frac{Pr(s)^2}{\frac{1}{n-1} \sum_{i=1}^{n-1} Pr(w_1, \ldots, w_i) Pr(w_{i+1} \ldots w_n)}, \qquad (8.4)$$

where $Pr()$ can be estimated by a language model [179] using a very large corpus or using Microsoft Web N-Gram service, and the logarithm value is used to avoid underflow. Note that SCP is used in the sigmoid function (S).

Once a tweet is decomposed into segments, sub-event detection can be conducted based on segments (rather than on unigrams) to get bursty segments in a time window t. If there may be several bursty segments in the same time window, segment clustering can be performed by comparing sets of tweets associated to segments.

8.3.2 Participant Detection

Instead of identifying all meaningful phrases by conducting segmentation on the large corpus of tweet text data, Shen et al. [195] proposed an approach to detect "participants" based on named entities. In [195], participants are defined as the entities that play a significant role in shaping the event progress. A "participant" can denote an event-participating person, organization, product line, or other named entity. For example, the NBA player "*LeBron Raymone James*" can be represented by {*LeBron James, LeBron, LBJ, King James, L. James*}, where each proper noun represents a unique mention of the participant.

In the proposed approach for participant detection, named entities are first identified as proper noun phrases from tweet streams using the CMU TweetNLP tool [83], and the infrequent ones are dropped from further processing using a threshold ψ. Then a hierarchical agglomerative clustering is used to cluster them into individual candidate event participants. Two entity names are considered similar if they share (1) lexical resemblance, and (2) contextual similarity. For example, in the following two tweets "*Gotta respect Anthony Davis, still rocking the unibrow*," "*Anthony gotta do something about that unibrow*," the two names *Anthony Davis* and *Anthony* are referring to the same participant and they share both character ("anthony") and context words ("unibrow," "gotta"). We use $sim(c_i, c_j)$ to represent the similarity between two names c_i and c_j. It is defined as

$$sim(c_i, c_j) = lex\_sim(c_i, c_j) \times cont\_sim(c_i, c_j),$$

where the lexical similarity ($lex\_sim(\cdot)$) is defined as a binary function representing whether a mention c_i is an abbreviation, acronym, or part of another mention c_j, or if the character edit distance between the two mentions is less than a threshold. The context similarity ($cont\_sim(\cdot)$) of two mentions is the cosine similarity between their context vectors $\vec{v}_i$ and $\vec{v}_j$. The bottom-up agglomerative clustering is performed on the filtered named entities until a stopping threshold δ has been reached. The clustering approach naturally groups the frequent proper nouns into participants. The **participant streams** are then formed by gathering the tweets that contain one or more mentions in the participant cluster.

Once the participants are detected from a stream, the stream can be divided into several sub-streams (with overlapping), and sub-event detection can be conducted on every sub-stream. If a sub-event is detected on one sub-stream, its corresponding candidate participant is output as a participant. However, some sub-events, which involve several participants, may be detected multiple times from different participant streams, so that post-processing is needed to combine these redundant sub-events into a single one. In [195], two heuristics are used for post-processing, if two detected sub-events are

- located closely in the timeline, with peak times within a small time window (e.g., 2 minutes), and

- share similar word distributions: among the top words with highest probabilities in the word distributions, there are sufficient common words.

8.3.3   Topic Modeling

Topic modeling is a powerful tool to discover underlying topics from a document set [40]. In topic modeling, each topic can be represented by a probability distribution (e.g., multi-nomial) of words or phrases. So topic modeling is more expressive than the clustering of words where each cluster consists of a set of words, and it also addresses the word ambiguity problem since a word can appear in different topics with different meanings. Topic modeling was first applied to well-written document sets (e.g., news articles). For summarizing events using tweets, we are more interested in bursty topics, which attract more attention from Twitter users. In [68] a topic model is proposed to capture such bursty topics.

In [68], the tweet stream is assumed to be generated by a mixture of $C + 1$ topics. In particular, C latent topics are bursty, where each topic c

has a word distribution ϕ^c, and the other topic is the background with a word distribution ϕ^B that captures common words. In the standard Latent Dirichlet Allocation (LDA) model, a document contains a mixture of topics (each represented by a topic distribution), and each word has a hidden topic label. While this is a reasonable assumption for long documents, for short text of tweets, a single tweet is most likely to be about a single topic. Therefore, a single hidden variable is associated with each post to indicate its topic. To model the observation that tweets published around the same time are more likely about the same topic than some random tweets, we assume that there is a global topic distribution θ^t for each time point t. On the tweet stream, besides tweets about events, which are time sensitive, there are even more tweets about users' personal encounters and interests. Therefore a time-independent topic distribution θ^u for each user is introduced to capture her/his long-term topical interests.

Diao et al. [68] assume the following generation process for all the tweets in the stream. When user u publishes a tweet at time point t, she/he first decides whether to write about an event topic or a personal topic. If she/he chooses the former, she/he then selects a topic according to θ^t. Otherwise, she/he selects a topic according to her/his own topic distribution θ^u. With the chosen topic, words in the post are generated from the word distribution for that topic or from the background word distribution that captures the white noise.

8.4   Sub-Event Detection Methods

In this section, we discuss techniques to detect sub-events on a stream of an event. Sub-events are important moments about an event and they often represent a surge of interest from the Twitter audience. It should be pointed out, there are similarities between sub-event detection within an event and general event detection on the whole coarse-level tweet stream.

8.4.1   Bursty Segment Detection

Burst segmentation detection is to identify those important segments of moments during the time period of the stream. To calculate the tweet frequency, we assume the document stream $\mathcal{D}$ is divided into T epochs. The length of an epoch depends on different applications and can be one day for long-term events or a minute for short-term events. Increasing epoch length may smooth out small spikes in longer events and can sometimes help in finding larger trends. Then the stream can be referred to as $\{D_t = d_{t1}, d_{t2}, \ldots, d_{ti}, \ldots, d_{t|D_t|}\}$, where $t \in \{1, 2, \ldots, T\}$ is the index of an epoch, and each epoch contains a sequence of tweets ordered by their timestamps. Let $m_t = |D_t|$ denote the tweet frequency in time window t.

8.4.1.1 Anomaly Detection

Bursty segments can be simply taken as those moments at which tweet frequencies are anomalies. Under the assumption that tweet frequency in an epoch should be a Gaussian distribution, $m_t \sim N(\mu, \delta^2)$, anomaly detection can be conducted by comparing the tweet frequency m_t with the expected frequency plus α times the standard deviation. Then a bursty segment can be identified as those continuous epochs satisfying

$$m_t > \mu + \alpha\delta. \tag{8.5}$$

Based on this simple idea, some variations have been developed. For example, in [130], instead of using Eq. (8.5) directly, a bursty probability function is defined as

$$P_b(t) = S(10 \times \frac{m_t - (\mu - \delta)}{\delta}), \tag{8.6}$$

where $S(\cdot)$ is a sigmoid function, so that top bursty epochs can be selected. Moreover, different ways are applied to estimate μ and δ in practice. Marcus et. al [160] estimate the initial μ and δ using the first k epoches, $m_1, \ldots, m_k$, and then update them online as

$$\mu_t = \lambda\mu_{t-1} + (1 - \lambda)m_t, \tag{8.7}$$

$$\delta_t = \lambda\delta_{t-1} + (1 - \lambda)|m_t - \mu_{t-1}|. \tag{8.8}$$

In [130, 91], retrospective detection is conducted using a global tweet stream $D_1^G, \ldots, D_T^G$. Let $N_t = |D_t^G|$ denote the total number of tweets published within epoch t, the probability of observing frequency m_t of event-related tweets in t can be modeled by a binomial distribution,

$$P_f(m_t) = \binom{N_t}{m_t} p^{m_t}(1 - p)^{N_t - m_t}, \tag{8.9}$$

where p is the expected probability of event tweets in a random epoch. When N_t is large as in a Twitter stream, $P_f(m_t)$ can be approximated with a Gaussian distribution,

$$P_f(m_t) \sim \mathcal{N}(N_t p, N_t p(1 - p)). \tag{8.10}$$

Thus, for epoch t, $\mu = N_t p$ and $\delta = \sqrt{N_t p(1 - p)}$.

8.4.1.2 Hidden Markov Model

In [121, 110], $m_1, \ldots, m_T$ are assumed to be generated by two Poisson distributions corresponding to a bursty state and a normal state, respectively. Let μ_0 and μ_1 denote the expected counts for the normal state and the bursty state, respectively. Let ν_t denote the state for the epoch t, where $\nu_t = 0$ indicates the normal state and $\nu_t = 1$ indicates the bursty state. The probability of observing a count of m_t is

$$p(m_t|\nu_t = l) = \frac{e^{n u_l} \nu_l^{m_t}}{m_t!}, \qquad (8.11)$$

where l is either 0 or 1. The state sequence $(\mu_0, \ldots, \mu_t)$ is a Markov chain with the following transition probabilities: $p(\nu_t = l|\nu_{t-1} = l) = \delta_l$. Dynamic programming can then be used to uncover the underlying state sequence for a series of counts.

8.4.2 Combining Burstiness and Content Information

In some cases, sub-event detection purely based on burst volume can be misleading. For instance, if two sub-events occur close together in time (e.g., an interception followed shortly by a touchdown in a football event) and both of them generate significant tweets, then their respective tweets might get smeared into one seemingly continuous burst in tweet volume. However, a careful examination of the word distribution of the tweets in this burst would reveal the presence of the two different sub-events. Thus, a good segmentation should consider changes in the language model along with changes in tweet volume.

8.4.2.1 Hidden Markov Model

In the aforementioned hidden Markov model (HMM) in Section 8.4.1.2, a hidden state is either 1 or 0, indicating whether or not the current time is a bursty state. Chakrabarti and Punera [58] proposed a variation of HMM, which can be seen as an extended HMM that incorporates the content information by categorizing a bursty state into several topics.

In the extended model, three sets of word distributions are used to generate words: (1) $\theta_{s=1\ldots|S|}^S$, which is specific to a type of sub-event s but is the same for all events, captures those common words used across different events for the same type of sub-events. For example, "good shot" can be generated by θ_{SCORE} for all basketball names. (2) $\theta_{s=1\ldots|S|,g\in G}^{SG}$, which is specific to a particular type of sub-event s for a particular event g, captures those words that only occur in some of the events, like proper names. (3) θ^B is a background distribution of words over all states and events.

Assume that an event g is composed of a sequence of hidden states $Z = \{z_1, z_2, \ldots\}$, where $z_i \in S$, and S is the set of states corresponding to $|S|$ different types of sub-events. As in the standard HMM, A_{jk} is the probability of transitioning from state j to state k. Instead of using direct emission distributions to model how the observation symbols are generated from hidden states, each word in a time slice may be generated from state i according to

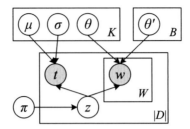

FIGURE 8.1: Plate notation of the mixture model.

one of the three aforementioned distributions with probability $\phi_i^{(s)}$, $\phi_i^{(sg)}$, and $\phi_i^{(bg)}$.

Besides the content change between sub-events, the model also tries to capture the burstiness of tweet volume. This is achieved by treating the fraction of tweet words in the current time slice as part of the observable variable, which is generated by state i using a geometric distribution with parameter κ_i.

On a large tweet corpus, which includes several events of the some types, parameters $\{A, \kappa_i, \theta_s^S, \theta_{s,g}^{SG}, \theta^B, \phi_i^{(s)}, \phi_i^{(sg)}, \phi_i^{(bg)}\}$ can be trained using the Expectation-Maximization (EM) algorithm. When applying the trained parameters to a new event, the optimal sequence of hidden states can be obtained, and the consecutive time slices with the same state can be extracted as a sub-event.

8.4.2.2 Temporal-Content Mixture Model

The temporal-content mixture model is proposed in [195], where a sub-event is modeled to correspond to a topic that emerges from the data stream, is intensively discussed during a short period, and then gradually fades away. The tweets corresponding to a sub-event thus demand not only "temporal burstiness" but also a certain degree of "lexical cohesiveness." To incorporate both the time and content aspects of the sub-events, a mixture model approach for sub-event detection is developed in [195]. Figure 8.1 shows the plate notation.

In the proposed model, with the assumption that there are K sub-event topics, each tweet d in the data stream D is generated from a topic $z = 1 \ldots K$, weighted by π_z. Each topic is characterized by both its content and time aspects. The content aspect is captured by a multinomial distribution over the words, parameterized by θ, while the time aspect is characterized by a Gaussian distribution, parameterized by μ and σ, where μ represents the average time point that the sub-event emerges and σ determines the duration of the sub-event. In addition, there is often a background or "global" topic $z = B$ that is being constantly discussed over the entire event process and does not present the desired "burstiness" property. A uniform distribution $U(t_b, t_e)$ is used to model the time aspect of these "background" topics, with t_b and t_e being the event beginning and end time points. The content aspect of a background topic is modeled by a similar multinomial distribution θ_B, estimated based on the frequency of a word in the stream as

$$\theta_B(w) \propto \sum_{i=1}^{\text{current}} S_i \frac{\sum_{d \in S_i} n(w,d)}{|S_i|}, \tag{8.12}$$

where $n(w,d)$ is the number of word w in tweet d, and the number of tweet in the segment $|S_i|$ is used to penalize the segments with more tweets, where sub-events may occur. We use the maximum likelihood estimation for other parameters. The data likelihood can be represented as

$$\mathcal{L}(D) = \prod_{d \in D} \sum_{z \in 1...K,B} \{\pi_z p_z(t_d) \prod_{w \in d} p_z(w)\} \tag{8.13}$$

where $p_z(t_d)$ models the timestamp of tweet d under the topic z, which is defined as

$$p_z(t_d) = \begin{cases} N(t_d; \mu_z, \sigma_z) & \text{if } z \text{ is a sub-event topic} \\ U(t_b, t_e) & \text{if } z \text{ is background topic} \end{cases} \tag{8.14}$$

and $p_z(w)$ corresponds to the word distribution in topic z, that is, $p_z(w) = p(w; \theta_z)$.

The EM algorithm is used to find the parameters as listed below:

E-step:

$$p(z_d = j) \propto \tag{8.15}$$

$$\begin{cases} \pi_j N(d; \mu_j, \sigma_j) \prod_{w \in d} p(w; \theta_j) & \text{if } j <= K \\ \pi_j U(t_b, t_e) \prod_{w \in d} p(w; \theta_j') & \text{else} \end{cases} \tag{8.16}$$

M-step:

$$\pi_j \propto \sum_d p(z_d = j) \tag{8.17}$$

$$p(w; \theta_j) \propto \sum_d p(z_d = j) \times c(w,d) \tag{8.18}$$

$$p(w; \theta_j') \propto \sum_d p(z_d = j) \times c(w,d) \tag{8.19}$$

$$\mu_j = \frac{\sum_d p(z_d = j) \times t_d}{\sum_{j=1}^{K} \sum_d p(z_d = j)} \tag{8.20}$$

$$\sigma_j^2 = \frac{\sum_d p(z_d = j) \times (t_d - \mu_j)^2}{\sum_{j=1}^{K} \sum_d p(z_d = j)} \tag{8.21}$$

EM Post-processing: A topic re-adjustment was performed after the EM process. We merge two sub-events in a data stream if they (1) locate closely in the timeline, with peaks times within a 2-minute window, where peak time of a sub-event is defined as the slice that has the most tweets associated with this sub-event; and (2) share similar word distributions if their symmetrized KL divergence is less than a threshold ($thresh_{sim} = 5$). We then re-run the EM process to obtain the updated parameters. The topic re-adjustment process continues until the number of sub-events and background topics does not change further.

8.5   Multi-Tweet Summarization

In this section, we discuss extractive tweet summarization methods for generating the text description to describe the progress of an event. An extractive multi-tweet summarization problem can be formalized as: given a set of tweets T, we want to extract a subset $S \subset T$, such that the number of posts in S is less than pre-defined threshold k (i.e., $|S| \leq k$), and S can well represent T.

8.5.1   Hybrid TF-IDF: An Extractive Summarization Method

Sharifi et al. [193] find that, due to the unstructured, unconnected, and short characteristics of Twitter posts, simple frequency-based summarizers, like hybrid TF-IDF as they proposed, achieve better performance than more complex cluttering or graph-based summarizers. Hybrid TF-IDF weights are calculated in Eq.(8.22):

$$W(s) = \frac{\sum_{i=0}^{\#WordsInPost} W(w_i)}{nf(s)}$$
$$W(w_i) = tf(w_i)\ln(idf(w_i))$$
$$tf(w_i) = \frac{\#OccurrencesOfWordInAllPosts}{\#WordsInAllPosts} \quad (8.22)$$
$$idf(w_i) = \frac{\#Posts}{\#PostsInWhichWordOccurs}$$
$$nf(s) = max[MinimumThreshold, \#WordsInPost]$$

where $W(\cdot)$ is a weight function of a tweet of a word, nf is a normalization factor, w_i is the i-th word, and s is a post. Different from standard TF-IDF weight, Hybrid TF-IDF weight takes each tweet as a document in $idf(w_i)$ calculation while it takes whole tweets as a single psuedo-document in $tf(w_i)$. As a result, repeating words will have higher weights, since the number of their occurrences is large, and the number of tweets containing them is less. The summarizer extracts the tweets with the largest hybrid TF-IDF weights iteratively. Note that, at each iteration, the summarizer first filters out those tweets whose similarities to the tweets in the extracted set are larger than a threshold.

8.5.2 Phrase Reinforcement Algorithm: An Abstractive Summarization Method

The Phrase Reinforcement algorithm (PR) [194] begins with a starting query phrase. For either side of the starting phrase, before and after, the algorithm builds a graph representing the common sequence of words.

After the graph is constructed, the PR algorithm assigns a weight to every node in order to prevent longer phrases from dominating the output. In particular, stop words are given a weight of zero. The remaining words are given weights which are determined by their counts and how far away they are from the root node, as shown in Eq.(8.23):

$$Weigth(node) = Count(node) - RootDistance(node) * \log_b Count(node).$$
$$(8.23)$$

Finally, once the graph is constructed and weighted, the PR algorithm is ready to generate a partial summary. To do so, the PR algorithm searches for the path with the largest total weight by comparing all paths that begin with the root node and end with a non-root node. This path is denoted as the best partial path since it only represents one half of the summary (i.e., the most common phrase occurring either before or after the topic phrase). In order to generate the remaining half of the summary, the PR algorithm is essentially repeated by initializing the root node with the partial summary and rebuilding the graph. The most heavily weighted path from this new graph is the final summary produced by the PR algorithm.

8.6 Experiments

This section provides empirical evaluation for different components of twitter event summarization. For context analysis, we focus on the participant detection method to show its performance and effectiveness as an basis of sub-event detection and event summarization. For sub-event detection, which is the most important module in Twitter event summarization, we compare various aforementioned methods of sub-event detection in terms of the sub-event detected and the final event summarization results, using hybrid TF-IDF as the multi-tweet summarization method.

8.6.1　Data Corpus of Events

We collected related tweets for six real-world events, including five NBA basketball games and the keynote speech in Apple's Worldwide Developers Conference 2012 (WWDC 2012)[4].

The tweet streams corresponding to these events are collected using the Twitter streaming API[5] with pre-defined keyword sets. For NBA games, we use the team names, first names and last names of players and head coaches as keywords for retrieving the event tweets; for the WWDC conference, the keyword set contains 20 terms related to the Apple event, such as wwdc, apple, mac, etc. We collect the tweets for the period of time when these scheduled events are taking place; nevertheless, certain non-event tweets could also be included due to the broad coverage of the keywords used. During pre-processing, we filter out the tweets containing URLs, non-English tweets , and retweets since they are less likely to contain new information regarding the event progress. Table 8.1 shows statistics of the event tweets after the filtering process.

TABLE 8.1: Statistics of the datasets, including five NBA basketball games and the WWDC 2012 conference event

Name		Event Description and Date	Duration	#Tweets
celticsvs76ers		Celtics vs. 76ers on 05/23/2012	3h30m	245,734
celticsvsheat	N	Celtics vs. Heat on 05/30/2012	3h30m	345,335
heatvsokc	B	Heat vs. Thunder on 06/21/2012	3h30m	332,223
lakersvsokc	A	Lakers vs. Thunder on 05/19/2012	3h10m	218,313
spursvsokc		Spurs vs. Thunder on 05/31/2012	3h	254,670
wwdc		Keynote speech in WWDC'12 on 06/11/2012	3h30m	163,775

8.6.2　Data Labeling and Evaluation Metrics

8.6.2.1　Participant Detection

Table 8.2 shows participant examples of the event *spursvsokc and* wwdc. We note that many of the examples have different mentions/phrases/representations, e.g., *gregg popovich, greg popovich,* and *popovich* are referring to the head coach of the team Spurs; *macbook, macbook pro, mbp* refer to a line of products from Apple.

In order to evaluate the participant detection results, we manually cluster the phrases and only keep those clusters referring to some real participants of the events as the gold standard data (or the ground truth data). We conduct the evaluation on both the participant and phrase levels. On the participant

---

[4]https://developer.apple.com/wwdc/
[5]https://dev.twitter.com/docs/streaming-apis

TABLE 8.2: Example participants for the NBA game Spurs vs Okc (2012-5-31) and the WWDC'12 conference

Example Participants – NBA game
westbrook, russell westbrook
james, james harden, harden
gregg popovich, greg popovich, popovich
kevin durant, kd, durant
oklahoma city thunder, oklahoma, thunder, okc, okc thunder

Example Participants – WWDC Conference
macbook, mbp, macbook pro, pro
mba, macbook air
google maps, google
wwdc, apple wwdc
os, mountain, os x mountain, os x
iphone 4s, iphone 3gs, iphone

level, our goal is to calculate how many participants have been correctly detected; on the mention level, we try to decide, for a reference participant, how many phrases referring to it have been correctly detected.

Denote the system-detected and the gold standard participant clusters as T_s and T_g, respectively. We define a **correct participant** as a system-detected participant with more than half of its associated mentions included in a gold standard participant (referred to as the **hit participant**). As a result, we can define the participant-level precision and recall as below:

$$participant\text{-}prec = \#correct\text{-}participants/|T_s|;$$
$$participant\text{-}recall = \#hit\text{-}participants/|T_g|.$$

Note that a correct participant may include incorrect mentions, and that more than one correct participant may correspond to the same hit participant, both of which are undesirable. In the latter case, we use **representative participant** to refer to the correct participant which contains the most mentions in the hit participant. In this way, we build a 1-to-1 mapping from the detected participants to the ground truth participants. Next, we define **correct mentions** as the union of the overlapping mentions between all pairs of representatives and hit participants. Then we calculate the mention-level precision and recall as the number of correct mentions divided by the total mentions in the system or the gold standard participant clusters.

TABLE 8.3: An example clip of the play-by-play of an NBA game (*heatvsokc*)

Time	Action (Sub-event)	Score
9:22	Chris Bosh misses 10-foot 2-point shot	7-2
9:22	Serge Ibaka defensive rebound	7-2
9:11	Kevin Durant makes 15-foot 2-point shot	9-2
8:55	Serge Ibaka shooting foul (Shane Battier draws the foul)	9-2
8:55	Shane Battier misses free throw 1 of 2	9-2
8:55	Miami offensive team rebound	9-2
8:55	Shane Battier makes free throw 2 of 2	9-3

8.6.2.2 Sub-Event Detection

For evaluation of sub-event detection and the final event summarization, we construct the gold standard sub-events manually based on the play-by-play data from ESPN[6] for NBA game events and live updates from MacRumors[7] web sites for WWDC 2012, which provide detailed descriptions of the NBA and WWDC events as they unfold. Table 8.3 and Table 8.4 show example clips of the play-by-play of an NBA game and live updates of WWDC, respectively. In the tables, the column "Time" corresponds to the minutes left in the current quarter of the game and "Score" shows the score between the two teams.

Ideally, each item in the live coverage descriptions may correspond to a sub-event in the tweet stream, but in reality, not all actions would attract enough attention from the Twitter audience. In addition, the play-by-play events of NBA game are generated from templates for games so that those sub-events out of the court (e.g., commercials during the break and interviews after the game) are ignored. So a human annotator manually filters out the actions that do not lead to any burst in the corresponding participant stream. For each sub-event identified by the annotator, the following extra information is added manually:

1. the actual time for play-by-play of NBA games since "Time" as the first column in Table 8.3 is according to a "game clock." For the *wwdc* event, the first column in Table 8.4 is used directly as the actual time,

2. participants involved in the sub-event,

3. extracted tweets with a total length limit of 140 bytes as an extractive summary.

---

[6]http://espn.go.com/nba/scoreboard
[7]http://www.macrumorslive.com/archive/wwdc12/

TABLE 8.4: An example clip of the live updates of WWDC 2012

Time	Description
10:00 am	Keynote starting! Siri is introducing things
10:01 am	Telling... Absolutely terrible jokes.
	"I am excited about the new Samsung,
	not the phone, the refrigerator."
10:16 am	New notebooks coming!!!
	Along with OSX and iOS updates.
	Phil is coming on stage to show off notebook lineup.
	...

Note that there is no well-defined boundary concerning whether a sub-event should be included in the gold standard set or not, which is very subjective. Instead of allowing sub-event detection methods to return an arbitrary number of sub-events, k sub-events with the largest probability are required to be returned for evaluation, where k is equal to the number of sub-events in the golden sets. A system-detected sub-event is considered to match the gold standard sub-event if its peak time is within a 2-minute window of the gold standard. Then accuracy is calculated as the number of matched sub-events over k as the evaluation measure.

8.6.2.3 Event Summarization

To evaluate the final summaries of an event, we following the work in [206] to evaluate summarization for a document stream using a modified version of ROUGE score [144], which is widely used as an automatic evaluation for document summarization tasks. ROUGE measures the quality of a summary by counting the unit overlaps between the candidate summary and a set of reference summaries. Several automatic evaluation methods are implemented in ROUGE, such as ROUGE-N, ROUGE-L, ROUGE-W, and ROUGE-SU. ROUGE-N is an n-gram recall computed as follows.

$$\text{ROUGE-N} = \frac{\sum_{S \in \text{ref}} \sum_{\text{gram}_n \in S} \text{Count}_{\text{match}}(\text{gram}_n)}{\sum_{S \in \text{ref}} \sum_{\text{gram}_n \in S} \text{Count}(\text{gram}_n)} \quad (8.24)$$

where n is the length of the n-gram, and ref stands for the reference summaries. $\text{Count}_{\text{match}}(\text{gram}_n)$ is the number of co-occurring n-grams in a candidate summary and the reference summaries, and $\text{Count}(\text{gram}_n)$ is the number of n-grams in the reference summaries. ROUGE-L uses the longest common subsequence (LCS) statistics, while ROUGE-W is based on weighted LCS

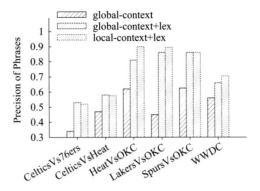

FIGURE 8.2: Precision of participant detection performance on phrase level.

and ROUGE-SU is based on skip-bigram plus unigram. Each of these evaluation methods in ROUGE can generate three scores (recall, precision, and F-measure). However, ROUGE scores cannot be applied directly to the summarization of a tweet stream. In our case, given a tweet stream about an event, since the same n-grams that appear at distant time points describe different sub-events, they should be regarded as different n-grams. In our manually labeled and system-generated summaries, each n-gram is associated with a timestamp (which is that of the sub-event that the n-gram describes). Making use of such temporal information, we modify ROUGE-N to ROUGE^T-N. The new measure is calculated as

$$\text{ROUGE}^T\text{-N} = \frac{\sum_{S \in \text{ref}} \sum_{\text{gram}_n^t \in S} \text{Count}_{\text{match}^T}(\text{gram}_n^t)}{\sum_{S \in \text{ref}} \sum_{\text{gram}_n^t \in S} \text{Count}(\text{gram}_n^t)}, \quad (8.25)$$

where gram_n^t is a unique n-gram with a timestamp, and $\text{Count}_{\text{match}^T}(\text{gram}_n^t)$ returns the minimum of occurrence of n-gram with timestamp t in S and the number of matched n-grams in a candidate summary. The distance between the timestamp of a matched n-gram and t needs to be within a constant and it is set to 1 min in our experiments.

8.6.3   Experimental Results

8.6.3.1   Participant Detection

Figure 8.2, Figure 8.3, Figure 8.4, and Figure 8.5 show the phrase- and participant-level precision and recall scores. We experimented with different similarity measures for the agglomerative clustering approach. The "global context" means that the context vectors are created from the entire data stream; this may not perform well since different participants can share similar global context. For example, the terms "shot," "dunk," "rebound" can appear in the context of any NBA players and are not discriminative enough.

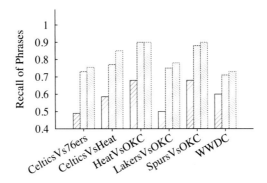

FIGURE 8.3: Recall of participant detection performance on phrase level.

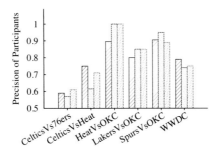

FIGURE 8.4: Precision of participant detection performance on participant level.

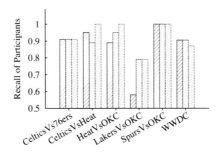

FIGURE 8.5: Recall of participant detection performance on participant level.

We found that adding the lexical similarity measure greatly boosted the clustering performance, especially on the mention level. In addition, combining the lexical similarity with the local context is even more helpful for some events. We notice that two events (celtics vs 76ers and celtics vs heat) yield relatively low precision on both participant and mention levels. Taking a close look at the data, we found that these two events accidentally co-occurred with other

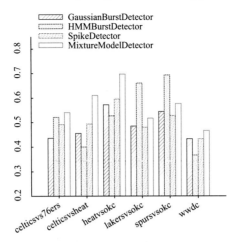

FIGURE 8.6: Sub-event detection performance of different methods without participant detection.

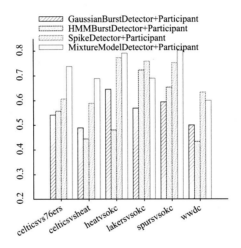

FIGURE 8.7: Sub-event detection performance of different methods with participant detection.

popular events, namely, the TV program "American Idol" finale and the NBA draft. The keyword-based data crawler thus includes many noisy tweets in the event streams, leading to some false participants being detected.

Table 8.5 lists comparative sub-event detection methods discussed in Section 8.4. For each of them, we also implement their participant-based version, which detects participants first, then detects sub-events on the participant streams instead of the whole stream, and finally combines the detected sub-events. The experimental results are presented in Figure 8.6 and Figure 8.7. It can be observed from the figures that, GaussianBurstDetector and Sp-

TABLE 8.5: Summary of comparative algorithms

Algorithm	Description
GaussianBurstDetector	The anomaly detection method assuming tweets volume of an epoch subject to Gaussian distribution
HMMBurstDetector	Hidden Markov model in which the bursty and non-bursty epochs are modeled by two hidden states.
SpikeDetector	Online version of GaussianBursyDetector, estimating mean and derivation online.
MixtureModel	Temporal and content mixture model.

kieDetector have similar performance, since both of them conduct anomaly detection assuming the volume of stream is subject to the Gaussian distribution. Their essential difference is that GaussianBurstDetector uses the mean and derivation of the stream volume over time as an static input, while SpikeDetector estimates the mean and derivation dynamically. Because of the difference, SpikeDetector outperforms GaussianBurstDetector when conducting detection based on participants, in which local spikes are more obvious. HMMBurstDetector achieves the best performance on heatvsokc and spursvsokc, but performs poorly on some other datasets. One possible reason is that HMMBurstDetector assumes the same generative model for different events. However, heights of volume spikes of sub-events may vary a lot across different events, even within a single event. That's also why participant detection does not boost the method, since when the whole stream is divided into participant streams, their variation can also be very large. Compared with other methods, MixtureModel provides a competitive and robust sub-event detection performance over different datasets.

We further applied the event-detection methods on participant streams, and Figure 8.8 shows the micro average of sub-event detection accuracy on participant streams for each event. We can observe that: 1) The accuracy of sub-event detection on participant streams is typically higher than that on event streams. 2) MixtureModel outperforms GaussianBurstDetector, HMMBurstDetector, and SpikeDetector. All these methods work well for participants with few sub-events, while MixtureModel is able to detect more correct sub-events for those popular participants.

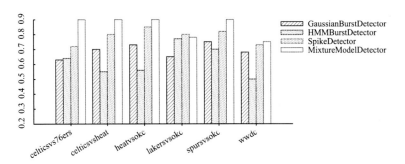

FIGURE 8.8: Participant detection performance on phrase level.

8.6.3.2 Event Summarization

TABLE 8.6: F-1 score of ROUGE-2 of event summarization using different sub-event detection methods

Methods	celticsvs76ers	celticsvsheat	heatvsokc	lakersvsokc	spursvsokc	wwdc
GaussianBurstDetector	0.0762	0.0818	0.0725	0.0632	0.0630	0.0990
+Participant	0.0906	0.0903	0.0952	0.1030	0.0779	0.1270
HMMBurstDetector	0.1082	0.0613	0.0744	0.0900	0.0864	0.0896
+Participant	0.0948	0.0865	0.0761	0.1073	0.0830	0.1086
SpikeDetector	0.0795	0.0912	0.0794	0.0606	0.0734	0.0936
+Participant	0.1076	0.1147	0.1100	0.1118	0.0872	0.1462
MixtureModelDetector	0.0909	0.1059	0.0858	0.0754	0.0774	0.1133
+Participant	0.1236	0.1289	0.1215	0.1102	0.0891	0.1477

We implemented hybrid TF-IDF as the multi-tweet summarization method and applied it to the results of different sub-event detection methods. Table 8.6 shows the F-1 score of ROUGE-2, which is a widely used metric for multi-document summarization. Compared with the results of sub-event detection, we can see that the results of final event summarization generally reflect the results of sub-event detection, which is a vital step in event summarization.

8.7 Conclusion and Future Work

In this chapter, we study the problem of social event summarization using Twitter data. Given a Twitter stream about a particular event, social event summarization aims to provide a text description of the progress of the event. We propose a general framework for social event summarization which includes three important components: tweet context analysis, sub-event detection, and tweet summarization. For each component, we discuss various solutions. Finally, empirical evaluation is conducted using real Twitter datasets to compare various solutions.

Event summarization using social media data is a relative new problem emerging with social media. Social media increases the explosion of information and results in huge amounts of noisy, unstructured, temporal document data on the Internet. There are many research topics that have not been fully explored. Some of these topics are 1) How can a summary of an event be better evaluated? Especially when an event is large and complex, it is difficult for a person to manually create the summary. 2) How can we use other information from social media, like social network and geotags, to improve summarization? 3) How can we integrate topic modeling and sentiment analysis in the analysis?

8.8 Glossary

Event: Generally an event is something that happens at some specific time and place. In this chapter, an event is something that occurs in a certain place for a period of time involving different activities.

Participants: Participants are the entities that play a significant role in shaping the event progress.

Social Event Summarization: Given a Twitter stream about a particular event, social event summarization aims to provide a text description of the progress of the event.

Sub-events: Sub-events are important moments about an event and they often represent a surge of interest from the Twitter audience.

Tweets: Tweets are Twitter messages.

Bibliography

[1] Apache HTTP Server: An Open-Source HTTP Web Server. http://httpd.apache.org/.

[2] FileZilla: An open-source and free FTP/SFTP solution. http://filezilla-project.org.

[3] Hadoop: An Open-Source MapReduce computing platform. http://hadoop.apache.org/.

[4] HP OpenView: Network and Systems Management Products. http://www8.hp.com/us/en/software/enterprise-software.html.

[5] IBM Tivoli: Integrated Service Management software. http://www-01.ibm.com/software/tivoli/.

[6] IBM Tivoli Monitoring. http://www-01.ibm.com/software/tivoli/products/monitor/.

[7] ITIL. http://www.itil-officialsite.com.

[8] ITIL. http://www.itil-officialsite.com/home/home.aspx.

[9] libSVM. http://www.csie.ntu.edu.tw/~cjlin/libsvm.

[10] LogLogic: A real-time log analysis and report generation system. http://www.splunk.com/.

[11] MySQL: The world's most popular open source database. http://www.mysql.com.

[12] PVFS2: The state-of-the-art parallel I/O and high performance virtual file system. http://pvfs.org.

[13] Splunk: A commercial machine data managment engine. http://www.splunk.com/.

[14] ThunderBird: A supercomputer in Sandia National Laboratories. http://www.cs.sandia.gov/~jrstear/logs/.

[15] Avinash Achar, A Ibrahim, and PS Sastry. Pattern-growth based frequent serial episode discovery. *Data & Knowledge Engineering*, 87:91–108, 2013.

[16] Avinash Achar, Srivatsan Laxman, and PS Sastry. A unified view of the apriori-based algorithms for frequent episode discovery. *Knowledge and Information Systems*, 31(2):223–250, 2012.

[17] Charu C Aggarwal and Jiawei Han. *Frequent Pattern Mining*. Springer, 2014.

[18] Rakesh Agrawal, Tomasz Imieliński, and Arun Swami. Mining association rules between sets of items in large databases. In *ACM SIGMOD Record*, volume 22, pages 207–216. ACM, 1993.

[19] Rakesh Agrawal and Ramakrishnan Srikant. Mining sequential patterns. In *Data Engineering, 1995. Proceedings of the Eleventh International Conference on*, pages 3–14. IEEE, 1995.

[20] Shipra Agrawal, Supratim Deb, K.V.M. Naidu, and Rajeev Rastogi. Efficient detection of distributed constraint violations. In *Proceedings of ICDE*, pages 1320–1324, Istanbul, Turkey, 2007.

[21] Michal Aharon, Gilad Barash, Ira Cohen, and Eli Mordechai. One graph is worth a thousand logs: Uncovering hidden structures in massive system event logs. In *Proceedings of the European Conference on Machine Learning and Knowledge Discovery in Databases: Part I*, ECML PKDD '09, pages 227–243, Berlin, Heidelberg, 2009. Springer-Verlag.

[22] James Allan. *Topic Detection and Tracking: Event-Based Information Organization*. Kluwer Academic Publishers, Norwell, MA, USA, 2002.

[23] Stephen Altschul, Warren Gish, Webb Miller, Eugene Myers, and David J. Lipman. Basic local alignment search tool. *Journal of Molecular Biology*, 215(3):403–410, 1990.

[24] Kai Keng Ang, Zheng Yang Chin, Haihong Zhang, and Cuntai Guan. Mutual information-based selection of optimal spatial–temporal patterns for single-trial EEG-based BCIs. *Pattern Recognition*, 45(6):2137–2144, 2012.

[25] Luc Anselin. Local indicators of spatial associationlisa. *Geographical Analysis*, 27(2):93–115, 1995.

[26] Algirdas Avizienis, Jean-Claude Laprie, and Brian Randell. *Fundamental Concepts of Dependability*. University of Newcastle upon Tyne, Computing Science, 2001.

[27] Jay Ayres, Jason Flannick, Johannes Gehrke, and Tomi Yiu. Sequential pattern mining using a bitmap representation. In *Proceedings of the eighth ACM SIGKDD International Conference on Knowledge Discovery and Data Mining*, pages 429–435. ACM, 2002.

[28] Moonish Badaloo. An examination of server consolidation: Trends that can drive efficiencies and help businesses gain a competitive edge. *White paper on IBM Global Services*, 2006.

[29] Richard G Baraniuk and Douglas L Jones. A signal-dependent time-frequency representation: Fast algorithm for optimal kernel design. *Signal Processing, IEEE Transactions on*, 42(1):134–146, 1994.

[30] Andrew Barron, Jorma Rissanen, and Bin Yu. The minimum description length principle in coding and modeling. *Information Theory, IEEE Transactions on*, 44(6):2743–2760, 1998.

[31] Mayank Bawa, Tyson Condie, and Prasanna Ganesan. Lsh forest: self-tuning indexes for similarity search. In *International World Wide Web Conference (WWW)*, pages 651–660, 2005.

[32] Robert M. Bell and Yehuda Koren. Scalable collaborative filtering with jointly derived neighborhood interpolation weights. In *Proceedings of IEEE International Conference on Data Mining (ICDM)*, pages 43–52, 2007.

[33] Sergey Bereg, Marcin Kubica, Tomasz Walen, and Binhai Zhu. RNA multiple structural alignment with longest common subsequences. *Journal of Combinatorial Optimization*, 13(2):179–188, 2007.

[34] Philip A. Bernstein and Laura M. Haas. Information integration in the enterprise. *Commun. ACM*, 51(9):72–79, 2008.

[35] Wei Bi and James T. Kwok. Multi-label classification on tree-and dag-structured hierarchies. In *Proceedings of the 28th International Conference on Machine Learning (ICML-11)*, pages 17–24, 2011.

[36] Paul Bieganski, John Riedl, John V. Carlis, and Ernest F. Retzel. Generalized suffix trees for biological sequence data: Applications and implementation. In *Proceedings of HICSS*, pages 35–44, Dallas, Texas, USA, May 1994.

[37] Albert Bifet and Ricard Gavaldà. Mining frequent closed trees in evolving data streams. *Intelligent Data Analysis*, 15(1):29–48, 2011.

[38] Mikhail Bilenko, Sugato Basu, and Raymond J. Mooney. Integrating constraints and metric learning in semi-supervised clustering. In *Proceedings of International Conference on Machine Learning (ICML)*, Alberta, Canada, July 2004.

[39] Christopher M Bishop et al. *Pattern Recognition and Machine Learning*, volume 1. Springer New York, 2006.

[40] David M Blei, Andrew Y Ng, and Michael I Jordan. Latent Dirichlet Allocation. *Journal of Machine Learning Research*, 3:993–1022, 2003.

[41] Hendrik Blockeel, Leander Schietgat, Jan Struyf, Sašo Džeroski, and Amanda Clare. *Decision trees for hierarchical multilabel classification: A case study in functional genomics*. Springer, 2006.

[42] Jasmina Bogojeska, Ioana Giurgiu, David Lanyi, George Stark, and Dorothea Wiesmann. Impact of hw and os type and currency on server availability derived from problem ticket analysis. In *2014 IEEE Network Operations and Management Symposium (NOMS 2014)*, pages 1–9. IEEE, 2014.

[43] Jasmina Bogojeska, David Lanyi, Ioana Giurgiu, George Stark, and Dorothea Wiesmann. Classifying server behavior and predicting impact of modernization actions. In *2013 International Conference on Network and Service Management (CNSM 2013)*, pages 59–66, 2013.

[44] Khellaf Bouandas and Aomar Osmani. Mining association rules in temporal sequences. In *Computational Intelligence and Data Mining, 2007. CIDM 2007. IEEE Symposium on*, pages 610–615. IEEE, 2007.

[45] Jean S Bozman and Katherine Broderick. Server refresh: Meeting the changing needs of enterprise IT with hardware/software optimization. *IDC Whitepaper*, 2010.

[46] Joel W Branch, Yixin Diao, Emi K Olsson, Larisa Shwartz, and Li Zhang. Predicting service delivery costs under business changes, August 30 2013. US Patent App. 14/015,293.

[47] Joel W. Branch, Yixin Diao, and Larisa Shwartz. A framework for predicting service delivery efforts using IT infrastructure-to-incident correlation. In *Network Operations and Management Symposium (NOMS)*. IEEE, 2014.

[48] Andrei Z. Broder, Moses Charikar, Alan M. Frieze, and Michael Mitzenmacher. Min-wise independent permutations. In *Proceedings of ACM Symposium on the Theory of Computing (STOC)*, pages 327–336, Dallas, Texas, USA, May 1998.

[49] Andrei Z. Broder, Steven C. Glassman, Mark S. Manasse, and Geoffrey Zweig. Syntactic clustering of the web. *Computer Networks (CN)*, 29(8-13):1157–1166, March 1997.

[50] Jian-Feng Cai, Emmanuel J Candès, and Zuowei Shen. A singular value thresholding algorithm for matrix completion. *SIAM Journal on Optimization*, 20(4):1956–1982, 2010.

[51] Toon Calders and Bart Goethals. Mining all non-derivable frequent itemsets. In *Principles of Data Mining and Knowledge Discovery*, pages 74–86. Springer, 2002.

[52] Lius A. Castillo, Paul D. Mahaffey, and Jeff P. Bascle. Apparatus and method for monitoring objects in a network and automatically validating events relating to the objects. U.S. Patent, December 2008. US 7,469,287 B1.

[53] Mete Celik, Shashi Shekhar, James P Rogers, James A Shine, and Jin Soung Yoo. Mixed-drove spatio-temporal co-occurence pattern mining: A summary of results. In *In Proceedings of IEEE International Conference on Data Mining (ICDM)*, volume 6, pages 119–128, 2006.

[54] Nicolò Cesa-Bianchi, Claudio Gentile, and Luca Zaniboni. Hierarchical classification: combining bayes with svm. In *Proceedings of the 23rd International Conference on Machine Learning*, pages 177–184. ACM, 2006.

[55] Nicolò Cesa-Bianchi, Claudio Gentile, and Luca Zaniboni. Incremental algorithms for hierarchical classification. *Journal of Machine Learning Research*, 7:31–54, 2006.

[56] Nicolo Cesa-Bianchi and Giorgio Valentini. Hierarchical cost-sensitive algorithms for genome-wide gene function prediction. *JMLR Workshop and Conference Proceedings*, 8:14–29, 2010.

[57] Sung-Hyuk Cha and Sargur N Srihari. On measuring the distance between histograms. *Pattern Recognition*, 35(6):1355–1370, 2002.

[58] Deepayan Chakrabarti and Kunal Punera. Event summarization using tweets. In *Proceedings of the Fifth International AAAI Conference on Weblogs and Social Media (ICWSM)*, pages 66–73, 2011.

[59] Joong Hyuk Chang. Mining weighted sequential patterns in a sequence database with a time-interval weight. *Knowledge-Based Systems*, 24(1):1–9, 2011.

[60] Nitesh V Chawla, Kevin W Bowyer, Lawrence O Hall, and W Philip Kegelmeyer. Smote: Synthetic minority over-sampling technique. *Journal of Artificial Intelligence Research*, 16:321–357, 2002.

[61] Hewlett-Packard Development Company. Hp openview management solutions for your adaptive enterprise. http://www.managementsoftware.hp.com/.

[62] Aron Culotta and Jeffrey S. Sorensen. Dependency tree kernels for relation extraction. In *Proceedings of Annual Meeting of the Association for Computational Linguistics(ACL)*, pages 423–429, Barcelona, Spain, July 2004.

[63] Gautam Das, King-Ip Lin, Heikki Mannila, Gopal Renganathan, and Padhraic Smyth. Rule discovery from time series. In *KDD*, volume 98, pages 16–22, 1998.

[64] Ofer Dekel, Joseph Keshet, and Yoram Singer. Large margin hierarchical classification. In *Proceedings of the Twenty-First International Conference on Machine Learning*, page 27. ACM, 2004.

[65] Ofer Dekel, Joseph Keshet, and Yoram Singer. An online algorithm for hierarchical phoneme classification. In *Machine Learning for Multimodal Interaction*, pages 146–158. Springer, 2005.

[66] Mukund Deshpande and George Karypis. Item-based top-n recommendation algorithms. *ACM Transactions on Information Systems*, 22(1):143–177, January 2004.

[67] Giuseppe A Di Lucca, Massimiliano Di Penta, and Sara Gradara. An approach to classify software maintenance requests. In *Proceedings of International Conference on Software Maintenance*, pages 93–102. IEEE, 2002.

[68] Qiming Diao, Jing Jiang, Feida Zhu, and Ee-Peng Lim. Finding bursty topics from microblogs. In *Proceedings of the 50th Annual Meeting of the Association for Computational Linguistics (ACL)*, pages 536–544, 2012.

[69] Yixin Diao, Aliza Heching, David Northcutt, and George Stark. Modeling a complex global service delivery system. In *Proceedings of the 2011 Winter Simulation Conference (WSC)*, pages 690–702. IEEE, 2011.

[70] Yixin Diao, Hani Jamjoom, and David Loewenstern. Rule-based problem classification in IT service management. In *Cloud Computing, 2009. CLOUD'09. IEEE International Conference on*, pages 221–228. IEEE, 2009.

[71] Yixin Diao, Linh Lam, Larisa Shwartz, and David Northcutt. Predicting service delivery cost for non-standard service level agreements. In *Network Operations and Management Symposium (NOMS), 2014 IEEE*, pages 1–9. IEEE, 2014.

[72] Yi Ding and Xue Li. Time weight collaborative filtering. In *ACM CIKM*, pages 485–492, 2005.

[73] Ricardo Luis dos Santos, Juliano Araujo Wickboldt, Roben Castagna Lunardi, Bruno Lopes Dalmazo, Lisandro Zambenedetti Granville, Luciano Paschoal Gaspary, Claudio Bartolini, and Marianne Hickey. A solution for identifying the root cause of problems in IT change management. In *Integrated Network Management (IM), 2011 IFIP/IEEE International Symposium on*, pages 586–593. IEEE, 2011.

[74] Susan Dumais and Hao Chen. Hierarchical classification of web content. In *Proceedings of the 23rd Annual International ACM SIGIR Conference on Research and Development in Information Retrieval*, pages 256–263. ACM, 2000.

[75] Rick Durrett. *Probability: Theory and Examples*. Cambridge University Press, 2010.

[76] Cristian Estan, Stefan Savage, and George Varghese. Automatically inferring patterns of resource consumption in network traffic. In *Proceedings of ACM SIGCOMM Conference*, pages 137–148, 2003.

[77] Common Event Expression. Common event expression. http://cee.mitre.org.

[78] Noam A Fraenkel, Guy Goldstein, Ido Sarig, and Refael Haddad. Root cause analysis of server system performance degradations, May 18 2004. US Patent 6,738,933.

[79] Andrea Frome, Yoram Singer, Fei Sha, and Jitendra Malik. Learning globally-consistent local distance functions for shape-based image retrieval and classification. In *Computer Vision, 2007. ICCV 2007. IEEE 11th International Conference on*, pages 1–8. IEEE, 2007.

[80] Jing Gao, Guofei Jiang, Haifeng Chen, and Jiawei Han. Modeling probabilistic measurement correlations for problem determination in large-scale distributed systems. In *Proceedings of International Conference on Distributed Computing Systems (ICDCS)*, pages 623–630, 2009.

[81] Minos N Garofalakis, Rajeev Rastogi, and Kyuseok Shim. Spirit: Sequential pattern mining with regular expression constraints. In *VLDB*, volume 99, pages 7–10, 1999.

[82] Mohammadreza Ghodsi and Mihai Pop. Inexact local alignment search over suffix arrays. In *Proceedings of IEEE International Conference on Bioinformatics and Biomedicine (BIBM)*, pages 83–87, Washington, DC, USA, September 2009.

[83] Kevin Gimpel, Nathan Schneider, Brendan O'Connor, Dipanjan Das, Daniel Mills, Jacob Eisenstein, Michael Heilman, Dani Yogatama, Jeffrey Flanigan, and Noah A. Smith. Part-of-speech tagging for twitter: Annotation, features, and experiments. In *Proceedings of the 49th Annual Meeting of the Association for Computational Linguistics: Human Language Technologies (ACL-HLT)*, pages 42–47, 2011.

[84] Aristides Gionis, Piotr Indyk, and Rajeev Motwani. Similarity search in high dimensions via hashing. In *Proceedings of VLDB*, pages 518–529, Edinburgh, Scotland, UK, September 1999.

[85] Ioana Giurgiu, Jasmina Bogojeska, Sergii Nikolaiev, George Stark, and Dorothea Wiesmann. Analysis of labor efforts and their impact factors to solve server incidents in datacenters. In *Cluster, Cloud and Grid Computing (CCGrid), 2014 14th IEEE/ACM International Symposium on*, pages 424–433. IEEE, 2014.

[86] Genady Grabarnik, Abdi Salahshour, Balan Subramanian, and Sheng Ma. Generic adapter logging toolkit. In *Proceedings of First IEEE International Conference on Autonomic Computing(ICAC-04)*, pages 308–309, 2004.

[87] Michael Granitzer. Hierarchical text classification using methods from machine learning. *Master's Thesis, Graz University of Technology*, 2003.

[88] Roberto Grossi and Jeffrey Scott Vitter. Compressed suffix arrays and suffix trees with applications to text indexing and string matching. *SIAM J. Comput.*, 35(2):378–407, 2005.

[89] Peter D Grünwald. *The Minimum Description Length Principle*. The MIT Press, 2007.

[90] Peter D Grünwald, In Jae Myung, and Mark A Pitt. *Advances in Minimum Description Length: Theory and Applications*. MIT press, 2005.

[91] Adrien Guille and Cecile Favre. Mention-anomaly-based event detection and tracking in twitter. In *Proceedings of 2014 IEEE/ACM International Conference on Advances in Social Networks Analysis and Mining (ASONAM)*, pages 375–382, 2014.

[92] Tias Guns, Siegfried Nijssen, and Luc De Raedt. k-pattern set mining under constraints. *Knowledge and Data Engineering, IEEE Transactions on*, 25(2):402–418, 2013.

[93] Rajeev Gupta, K Hima Prasad, Laura Luan, Daniela Rosu, and Christopher Ward. Multi-dimensional knowledge integration for efficient incident management in a services cloud. In *Services Computing, 2009. SCC'09. IEEE International Conference on*, pages 57–64. IEEE, 2009.

[94] Valery Guralnik and Jaideep Srivastava. Event detection from time series data. In *Proceedings of the Fifth ACM SIGKDD International Conference on Knowledge Discovery and Data Mining*, KDD '99, pages 33–42, New York, NY, USA, 1999. ACM.

[95] Alfred Haar. Zur theorie der orthogonalen funktionensysteme. *Mathematische Annalen*, 69(3):331–371, 1910.

[96] Alon Y. Halevy, Naveen Ashish, Dina Bitton, Michael Carey, Denise Draper, Jeff Pollock, Arnon Rosenthal, and Vishal Sikka. Enterprise information integration: Successes, challenges and controversies. In *SIGMOD '05: Proceedings of the 2005 ACM SIGMOD International Conference on Management of Data*, pages 778–787, New York, NY, USA, 2005. ACM.

[97] Greg Hamerly and Charles Elkan. Learning the k in k-means. In *Proceedings of NIPS*, Vancouver, British Columbia, Canada, December 2003.

[98] Jiawei Han, Micheline Kamber, and Jian Pei. *Data Mining: Concepts and Techniques*. Morgan Kaufmann Publishers, third edition, 2011.

[99] Jiawei Han, Jian Pei, Behzad Mortazavi-Asl, Qiming Chen, Umeshwar Dayal, and Mei-Chun Hsu. Freespan: frequent pattern-projected sequential pattern mining. In *Proceedings of the Sixth ACM SIGKDD International Conference on Knowledge Discovery and Data Mining*, pages 355–359. ACM, 2000.

[100] Jiawei Han, Jianyong Wang, Ying Lu, and Petre Tzvetkov. Mining top-k frequent closed patterns without minimum support. In *Proceedings. 2002 IEEE International Conference on Data Mining*, pages 211–218. IEEE, 2002.

[101] Joseph L. Hellerstein, Sheng Ma, and C-S Perng. Discovering actionable patterns in event data. *IBM Systems Journal*, 41(3):475–493, 2002.

[102] Joseph L. Hellerstein, Sheng Ma, and Chang-Shing Perng. Discovering actionable patterns in event data. *IBM Systems Journal*, 43(3):475–493, 2002.

[103] Antonio Hernandez-Barrera. Finding an $o(n^2 \log n)$ algorithm is sometimes hard. In *Proceedings of the 8th Canadian Conference on Computational Geometry*, pages 289–294, August 1996.

[104] Thomas Hofmann, Lijuan Cai, and Massimiliano Ciaramita. Learning with taxonomies: Classifying documents and words. In *NIPS Workshop on Syntax, Semantics, and Statistics*, 2003.

[105] Evan Hoke, Jimeng Sun, and Christos Faloutsos. InteMon: Intelligent system monitoring on large clusters. In *Proceedings of International Conference on Very Large Database (VLDB)*, pages 1239–1242, 2006.

[106] Frank Höppner. Discovery of temporal patterns. In *Principles of Data Mining and Knowledge Discovery*, pages 192–203. Springer, 2001.

[107] Paul Horn. Automatic computing: IBM's prospective on the state of information technology. http://www.research.ibm.com/autonomic, 2001. IBM Corporation.

[108] K Houck, S Calo, and A Finkel. Towards a practical alarm correlation system. In *Integrated Network Management IV*, pages 226–237. Springer, 1995.

[109] International Business Machines Corp (IBM). IBM Tivoli. http://www-306.ibm.com/software/tivoli/.

[110] Alexander Ihler, Jon Hutchins, and Padhraic Smyth. Adaptive event detection with time-varying poisson processes. In *Proceedings of the 12th ACM SIGKDD International Conference on Knowledge Discovery and Data Mining*, pages 207–216. ACM, 2006.

[111] Khan Irfan and Jain Anoop. A comprehensive survey on sequential pattern mining. *International Journal of Engineering Research and Technology*, 2012.

[112] Yexi Jiang, Chang-Shing Perng, and Tao Li. Natural event summarization. In *Proceedings of the 20th ACM International Conference on Information and Knowledge Management*, CIKM '11, pages 765–774, Glasgow, Scotland, 2011. ACM.

[113] Yexi Jiang, Chang-Shing Perng, and Tao Li. Meta: Multi-resolution framework for event summarization. In *SIAM International Conference on Data Mining*, 2014.

[114] Yexi Jiang, Chang-Shing Perng, Tao Li, and Rong Chang. Intelligent cloud capacity management. In *Network Operations and Management Symposium (NOMS), 2012 IEEE*, pages 502–505. IEEE, 2012.

[115] Cristina Kadar, Dorothea Wiesmann, Jose Iria, Dirk Husemann, and Mario Lucic. Automatic classification of change requests for improved it service quality. In *SRII Global Conference (SRII), 2011 Annual*, pages 430–439. IEEE, 2011.

[116] George Karypis. Evaluation of item-based top-n recommendation algorithms. In *Proceedings of ACM International Conference on Information and Knowledge Management*, pages 247–254, 2001.

[117] Srinivas R. Kashyap, Jeyashankher Ramamirtham, Rajeev Rastogi, and Pushpraj Shukla. Efficient constraint monitoring using adaptive thresholds. In *Proceedings of International Conference on Data Engineering (ICDE)*, pages 526–535, Cancun, Mexico, 2008.

[118] Jeffrey O. Kephart and David M. Chess. The vision of autonomic computing. *Computer*, pages 41–50, 2003.

[119] Jerry Kiernan and Evimaria Terzi. Constructing comprehensive summaries of large event sequences. In *Proceedings of the 14th ACM SIGKDD International Conference on Knowledge Discovery and Data Mining*, KDD '08, pages 417–425, New York, NY, USA, 2008. ACM.

[120] Jerry Kiernan and Evimaria Terzi. Constructing comprehensive summaries of large event sequences. *ACM Trans. Knowl. Discov. Data*, 3(4):21:1–21:31, December 2009.

[121] Jon Kleinberg. Bursty and hierarchical structure in streams. *Data Mining and Knowledge Discovery*, 7(4):373–397, 2003.

[122] Pang Ko and Srinivas Aluru. Space efficient linear time construction of suffix arrays. *J. Discrete Algorithms*, 3(2-4):143–156, 2005.

[123] Yehuda Koren. Collaborative filtering with temporal dynamics. In *KDD*, pages 447–456, 2009.

[124] Brian Kulis. Metric learning: A survey. *Foundations & Trends in Machine Learning*, 5(4):287–364, 2012.

[125] Solomon Kullback and Richard A Leibler. On information and sufficiency. *The Annals of Mathematical Statistics*, pages 79–86, 1951.

[126] Ben Langmead, Cole Trapnell, Mihai Pop, and Steven L Salzberg. Ultrafast and memory-efficient alignment of short DNA sequences to the human genome. *Genome Biology*, 10, 2009.

[127] Srivatsan Laxman, P Shanti Sastry, and KP Unnikrishnan. Fast algorithms for frequent episode discovery in event sequences. In *Proc. 3rd Workshop on Mining Temporal and Sequential Data*, 2004.

[128] Srivatsan Laxman, PS Sastry, and KP Unnikrishnan. A fast algorithm for finding frequent episodes in event streams. In *Proceedings of the 13th ACM SIGKDD International Conference on Knowledge Discovery and Data Mining*, pages 410–419. ACM, 2007.

[129] Ülo Lepik and Helle Hein. *Haar Wavelets*. Springer, 2014.

[130] Chenliang Li, Aixin Sun, and Anwitaman Datta. Twevent: Segment-based event detection from tweets. In *Proceedings of the 21st ACM International Conference on Information and Knowledge Management*, pages 155–164. ACM, 2012.

[131] Hongfei Li, Catherine A Calder, and Noel Cressie. Beyond Moran's I: Testing for spatial dependence based on the spatial autoregressive model. *Geographical Analysis*, 39(4):357–375, 2007.

[132] Jiuyong Li. Robust rule-based prediction. *IEEE Trans. Knowl. Data Eng. (TKDE)*, 18(8):1043–1054, August 2006.

[133] Tao Li, Feng Liang, Sheng Ma, and Wei Peng. An integrated framework on mining logs files for computing system management. In *Proceedings of the Eleventh ACM SIGKDD International Conference on Knowledge Discovery in Data Mining*, pages 776–781. ACM, 2005.

[134] Tao Li and Sheng Ma. Mining temporal patterns without predefined time windows. In *Data Mining, 2004. ICDM'04. Fourth IEEE International Conference on*, pages 451–454. IEEE, 2004.

[135] Tao Li and Wei Peng. A clustering model based on matrix approximation with applications to cluster system log files. In *Proceedings of the 16th European Conference on Machine Learning*, pages 625–632, 2005.

[136] Tao Li and Wei Peng. Mining logs files for computing system management. In *Proceedings of 2015 International Conference on Autonomic Computing (ICAC 2005)*, pages 319–340, 2005.

[137] Tao Li, Wei Peng, Charles Perng, Sheng Ma, and Haixun Wang. An integrated data-driven framework for computing system management. *IEEE Transactions on Systems, Man and Cybernetics, Part A: Systems and Humans*, 40(1):90–99, Jan. 2010.

[138] Tao Li and Chang-Shing Perng. Kdd-2006 workshop report: Theory and practice of temporal data mining. *SIGKDD Explorations*, 8(2):96–97, 2006.

[139] Tao Li, Chang-Shing Perng, and Sheng Ma. Guest editorial: Special issue on temporal data mining: Theory, algorithms and applications. *Data Mining and Knowledge Discovery*, 16(1):1–3, 2008.

[140] Yinan Li, Allison Terrell, and Jignesh M. Patel. Wham: A high-throughput sequence alignment method. In *Proceedings of ACM International Conference on Management of Data (SIGMOD)*, 2011.

[141] Feng Liang, Sheng Ma, and Joseph L Hellerstein. Discovering fully dependent patterns. In *Proceedings of SIAM International Conference on Data Mining (SDM)*, pages 511–527. SIAM, 2002.

[142] Shu-Hsien Liao, Pei-Hui Chu, and Pei-Yuan Hsiao. Data mining techniques and applications–A decade review from 2000 to 2011. *Expert Systems with Applications*, 39(12):11303–11311, 2012.

[143] Chen Lin, Chun Lin, Jingxuan Li, Dingding Wang, Yang Chen, and Tao Li. Generating event storylines from microblogs. In *Proceedings of the 21st ACM International Conference on Information and Knowledge Management*, CIKM '12, pages 175–184, New York, NY, USA, 2012. ACM.

[144] Chin-Yew Lin. ROUGE: A package for automatic evaluation of summaries. In *Workshop on Text Summarization Branches Out*, 2004.

[145] Hui Lin and Jeff Bilmes. A class of submodular functions for document summarization. In *Proceedings of the 49th Annual Meeting of the Association for Computational Linguistics: Human Language Technologies-Volume 1*, pages 510–520. Association for Computational Linguistics, 2011.

[146] Fei Liu, Fuliang Weng, and Xiao Jiang. A broad-coverage normalization system for social media language. In *Proceedings of the 50th Annual Meeting of the Association for Computational Linguistics (ACL)*, pages 1035–1044, 2012.

[147] Liwei Liu, Nikolay Mehandjiev, and Dong-Ling Xu. Multi-criteria service recommendation based on user criteria preferences. In *Proceedings of the Fifth ACM Conference on Recommender Systems*, pages 77–84, 2011.

[148] Huma Lodhi, Craig Saunders, John Shawe-Taylor, Nello Cristianini, and Chris Watkins. Text classification using string kernels. *The Journal of Machine Learning Research*, 2:419–444, March 2002.

[149] Yun Lu, Mingjin Zhang, Tao Li, Yudong Guang, and Naphtali Rishe. Online spatial data analysis and visualization system. In *Proceedings of the ACM SIGKDD Workshop on Interactive Data Exploration and Analytics*, pages 71–78. ACM, 2013.

[150] Chen Luo, Jian-Guang Lou, Qingwei Lin, Qiang Fu, Rui Ding, Dongmei Zhang, and Zhe Wang. Correlating events with time series for incident diagnosis. In *Proceedings of the 20th ACM SIGKDD International Conference on Knowledge Discovery and Data Mining*, pages 1583–1592. ACM, 2014.

[151] Sheng Ma and Joseph L Hellerstein. Mining mutually dependent patterns. In *Proceedings IEEE International Conference on Data Mining(ICDM)*, pages 409–416. IEEE, 2001.

[152] Sheng Ma and Joseph L Hellerstein. Mining partially periodic event patterns with unknown periods. In *Data Engineering, 2001. Proceedings. 17th International Conference on*, pages 205–214. IEEE, 2001.

[153] David Maier. The complexity of some problems on subsequences and supersequences. *Journal of the ACM*, 25:322–336, April 1978.

[154] Adetokunbo Makanju, A. Nur Zincir-Heywood, and Evangelos E. Milios. Clustering event logs using iterative partitioning. In *Proceedings of ACM KDD*, pages 1255–1264, Paris, France, June 2009.

[155] Stephane G Mallat. A theory for multiresolution signal decomposition: the wavelet representation. *IEEE Transactions on Pattern Analysis and Machine Intelligence*, 11(7):674–693, 1989.

[156] Udi Manber and Eugene W. Myers. Suffix arrays: A new method for on-line string searches. *SIAM J. Comput.*, 22(5):935–948, 1993.

[157] Heikki Mannila, Hannu Toivonen, and A Inkeri Verkamo. Discovering frequent episodes in sequences extended abstract. In *1st Conference on Knowledge Discovery and Data Mining, Montreal, CA*, 1995.

[158] Heikki Mannila, Hannu Toivonen, and A Inkeri Verkamo. Discovery of frequent episodes in event sequences. *Data Mining and Knowledge Discovery*, 1(3):259–289, 1997.

[159] Christopher D. Manning and Hinrich Schuetze. *Foundations of Statistical Natural Language Processing*. MIT Press, 1999.

[160] Adam Marcus, Micha'el S. Bernstein, Osama Badar, David R. Karger, Samuel Madden, and Robert C. Miller. Twitinfo: Aggregating and visualizing microblogs for event exploration. In *Proceedings of the SIGCHI Conference on Human Factors in Computing Systems*, pages 227–236, 2011.

[161] Steven Mccanne and Van Jacobson. The bsd packet filter: A new architecture for user-level packet capture. In *USENIX Technical Conference*, pages 259–270, 1993.

[162] Carl H Mooney and John F Roddick. Sequential pattern mining–approaches and algorithms. *ACM Computing Surveys (CSUR)*, 45(2):19, 2013.

[163] Ani Nenkova and Kathleen McKeown. A survey of text summarization techniques. In *Mining Text Data*, pages 43–76. Springer, 2012.

[164] Thin Nguyen, Dinh Phung, Brett Adams, and Svetha Venkatesh. Event extraction using behaviors of sentiment signals and burst structure in social media. *Knowledge and Information Systems*, 37(2):279–304, 2013.

[165] Juan Carlos Niebles, Hongcheng Wang, and Li Fei-Fei. Unsupervised learning of human action categories using spatial-temporal words. *International Journal of Computer Vision*, 79(3):299–318, 2008.

[166] Kang Ning, Hoong Kee Ng, and Hon Wai Leong. Finding patterns in biological sequences by longest common subsequences and shortest common supersequences. In *Proceedings of IEEE International Conference on Bioinformatics and Bioengineering (BIBE)*, pages 53–60, Arlington, Virginia, USA, 2006.

[167] Xia Ning and George Karypis. SLIM: Sparse linear methods for top-n recommender systems. In *ICDM*, pages 497–506, 2011.

[168] Adam J. Oliner, Alex Aiken, and Jon Stearley. Alert detection in system logs. In *Proceedings of IEEE International Conference on Data Mining(ICDM)*, pages 959–964, 2008.

[169] You Ouyang, Wenjie Li, Sujian Li, and Qin Lu. Applying regression models to query-focused multi-document summarization. *Information Processing & Management*, 47(2):227–237, 2011.

[170] Debprakash Patnaik, Srivatsan Laxman, Badrish Chandramouli, and Naren Ramakrishnan. Efficient episode mining of dynamic event streams. In *Proceedings of IEEE International Conference on Data Mining (ICDM)*, pages 605–614, 2012.

[171] Michael J. Pazzani, Christopher J. Merz, Patrick M. Murphy, Kamal Ali, Timothy Hume, and Clifford Brunk. Reducing misclassification costs. In *Proceedings of International Conference on Machine Learning (ICML)*, pages 217–225, New Brunswick, NJ, USA, July 1994.

[172] Jian Pei, Guozhu Dong, Wei Zou, and Jiawei Han. On computing condensed frequent pattern bases. In *Proceedings of 2002 IEEE International Conference on Data Mining*, pages 378–385. IEEE, 2002.

[173] Jian Pei, Jiawei Han, Behzad Mortazavi-Asl, Helen Pinto, Qiming Chen, Umeshwar Dayal, and Mei-Chun Hsu. Prefixspan: Mining sequential patterns efficiently by prefix-projected pattern growth. In *2013 IEEE 29th International Conference on Data Engineering (ICDE)*, pages 0215–0215. IEEE Computer Society, 2001.

[174] Jian Pei, Jiawei Han, Behzad Mortazavi-Asl, and Hua Zhu. Mining access patterns efficiently from web logs. In *Knowledge Discovery and Data Mining: Current Issues and New Applications*, pages 396–407. Springer, 2000.

[175] Wei Peng, Tao Li, and Sheng Ma. Mining logs files for data-driven system management. *SIGKDD Explor. Newsl.*, 7(1):44–51, June 2005.

[176] Wei Peng, Charles Perng, Tao Li, and Haixun Wang. Event summarization for system management. In *Proceedings of the 13th ACM SIGKDD International Conference on Knowledge Discovery and Data Mining*, KDD, pages 1028–1032, New York, NY, USA, 2007. ACM.

[177] Quang-Khai Pham, Guillaume Raschia, Noureddine Mouaddib, Regis Saint-Paul, and Boualem Benatallah. Time sequence summarization to scale up chronology-dependent applications. In *Proceedings of the 18th ACM Conference on Information and Knowledge Management*, CIKM '09, pages 1137–1146, New York, NY, USA, 2009. ACM.

[178] John Platt et al. Probabilistic outputs for support vector machines and comparisons to regularized likelihood methods. *Advances in Large Margin Classifiers*, 10(3):61–74, 1999.

[179] Jay M Ponte and W Bruce Croft. A language modeling approach to information retrieval. In *Proceedings of the 21st Annual International ACM SIGIR Conference on Research and Revelopment in Information Retrieval*, pages 275–281. ACM, 1998.

[180] Marcus J. Ranum, Kent Landfield, Michael T. Stolarchuk, Mark Sienkiewicz, Andrew Lambeth, and Eric Wall. Implementing a generalized tool for network monitoring. In *USENIX Systems Administration Conference*, pages 1–8, 1997.

[181] V. Chandra Shekhar Rao and P. Sammulal. Survey on sequential pattern mining algorithms. *International Journal of Computer Applications*, 76(12):24–31, August 2013. Full text available.

[182] Robbert Van Renesse, Kenneth P. Birman, and Werner Vogels. Astrolabe: A robust and scalable technology for distributed system monitoring, management, and data mining. *ACM Transactions on Computer Systems*, 21:164–206, 2003.

[183] IBM Market Research. Autonomic computing core technology study, 2003.

[184] Jorma Rissanen. Modeling by shortest data description. *Automatica*, 14(5):465–471, 1978.

[185] Jorma Rissanen. A universal prior for integers and estimation by minimum description length. *The Annals of Statistics*, pages 416–431, 1983.

[186] Sheldon M Ross. *Stochastic Processes*, volume 2. John Wiley & Sons New York, 1996.

[187] Miguel E Ruiz and Padmini Srinivasan. Hierarchical text categorization using neural networks. *Information Retrieval*, 5(1):87–118, 2002.

[188] Abdus Salam and M Sikandar Hayat Khayal. Mining top-k frequent patterns without minimum support threshold. *Knowledge and Information Systems*, 30(1):57–86, 2012.

[189] Gerard Salton and Michael McGill. *Introduction to Modern Information Retrieval*. McGraw-Hill, 1984.

[190] Badrul M. Sarwar, George Karypis, Joseph A. Konstan, and John T. Riedl. Application of dimensionality reduction in recommender system – a case study. In *ACM WebKDD Workshop*, 2000.

[191] Sigurd Schneider, Ivan Beschastnikh, Slava Chernyak, Michael D Ernst, and Yuriy Brun. Synoptic: summarizing system logs with refinement. *Workshop Proceedings on Managing Large-Scale Systems via the Analysis of System Logs and the Application of Machine Learning Techniques (SLAML)*, 2010.

[192] D. J. Schroeder. *Astronomical Optics*. Academic Press, 1999.

[193] Beaux Sharifi, Mark-Anthony Hutton, and Jugal K. Kalita. Experiments in microblog summarization. In *Proceedings of the 2010 IEEE Second International Conference on Social Computing*, pages 49–56, 2010.

[194] Beaux Sharifi, Mark-Anthony Hutton, and Jugal K. Kalita. Summarizing microblogs automatically. In *Proceedings of the 2010 Annual Conference of the North American Chapter of the Association for Computational Linguistics (NAACL)*, pages 685–688, 2010.

[195] Chao Shen, Fei Liu, Fuliang Weng, and Tao Li. A participant-based approach for event summarization using twitter streams. In *Proceedings of the 2013 Conference of the North American Chapter of the Association for Computational Linguistics: Human Language Technologies (NAACL-HLT 2013)*, pages 1152–1162, 2013.

[196] Vikas Sindhwani and Prem Melville. Document-word co-regularization for semi-supervised sentiment analysis. In *Proceedings of IEEE International Conference on Data Mining (ICDM)*, pages 1025–1030, 2008.

[197] Ray J Solomonoff. A preliminary report on a general theory of inductive inference. In *Technic Report, Zator Company*, 1960.

[198] Ray J Solomonoff. A formal theory of inductive inference: Part I. *Information and Control*, 7(1):1–22, 1964.

[199] Ramakrishnan Srikant and Rakesh Agrawal. Mining quantitative association rules in large relational tables. In *Proceedings of ACM SIGMOD*, pages 1–12, 1996.

[200] Ramakrishnan Srikant and Rakesh Agrawal. Mining quantitative association rules in large relational tables. *ACM SIGMOD Record*, 25(2):1–12, 1996.

[201] Seshan Srirangarajan, Michael Allen, Ami Preis, Mudasser Iqbal, Hock Beng Lim, and Andrew J Whittle. Wavelet-based burst event detection and localization in water distribution systems. *Journal of Signal Processing Systems*, 72(1):1–16, 2013.

[202] John Stearley. Towards informatic analysis of syslogs. In *Proceedings of IEEE International Conference on Cluster Computing*, pages 309–318, San Diego, California, USA, September 2004.

[203] Benno Stein. Principles of hash-based text retrieval. In *SIGIR*, pages 527–534, 2007.

[204] Aixin Sun and Ee-Peng Lim. Hierarchical text classification and evaluation. In *Proceedings IEEE International Conference on Data Mining*, pages 521–528. IEEE, 2001.

[205] Edward W Sun and Thomas Meinl. A new wavelet-based denoising algorithm for high-frequency financial data mining. *European Journal of Operational Research*, 217(3):589–599, 2012.

[206] Hiroya Takamura, Hikaru Yokono, and Manabu Okumura. Summarizing a document stream. In *Proceedings of the 33rd European Conference on Advances in Information Retrieval (ECIR)*, pages 177–188, 2011.

[207] Pang-Ning Tan, Michael Steinbach, and Vipin Kumar. *Introduction to Data Mining*. Addison Wesley, 2005.

[208] Liang Tang and Tao Li. LogTree: A framework for generating system events from raw textual logs. In *Proceedings of IEEE International Conference on Data Mining (ICDM)*, pages 491–500, December 2010.

[209] Liang Tang, Tao Li, Shu-Ching Chen, and Shunzhi Zhu. Searching similar segments over textual event sequences. In *Proceedings of the 22nd ACM International Conference on Information and Knowledge Management*, CIKM '13, pages 329–338, New York, NY, USA, 2013. ACM.

[210] Liang Tang, Tao Li, and Chang-Shing Perng. LogSig: Generating system events from raw textual logs. In *Proceedings of ACM International Conference on Information and Knowledge Management*, pages 785–794, 2011.

[211] Liang Tang, Tao Li, Florian Pinel, Larisa Shwartz, and Genady Grabarnik. Optimizing system monitoring configurations for non-actionable alerts. In *Proceedings of IEEE/IFIP Network Operations and Management Symposium*, pages 34–42, 2012.

[212] Liang Tang, Tao Li, and Larisa Shwartz. Discovering lag intervals for temporal dependencies. In *Proceedings of the 18th ACM SIGKDD International Conference on Knowledge Discovery and Data Mining*, pages 633–641. ACM, 2012.

[213] Liang Tang, Tao Li, Larisa Shwartz, and Genady Grabarnik. Identifying missed monitoring alerts based on unstructured incident tickets. In *Proceedings of International Conference on Network and Service Management (CNSM)*, pages 143–146, 2013.

[214] Liang Tang, Tao Li, Larisa Shwartz, and Genady Grabarnik. Recommending resolutions for problems identified by monitoring. In *Proceedings of IEEE/IFIP International Symposium on Integrated Network Management*, pages 134–142, 2013.

[215] Liang Tang, Tao Li, Larisa Shwartz, Florian Pinel, and Genady Ya Grabarnik. An integrated framework for optimizing automatic monitoring systems in large IT infrastructures. In *Proceedings of the 19th ACM SIGKDD International Conference on Knowledge Discovery and Data Mining*, pages 1249–1257. ACM, 2013.

[216] Nikolaj Tatti and Jilles Vreeken. The long and the short of it: summarising event sequences with serial episodes. In *Proceedings of the 18th ACM SIGKDD International Conference on Knowledge Discovery and Data Mining*, pages 462–470. ACM, 2012.

[217] Loren Terveen and Will Hill. Beyond recommender systems: Helping people help each other. In *HCI in the New Millennium*, pages 487–509, 2001.

[218] Sergios Theodoridis and Konstantinos Koutroumbas. *Pattern Recognition*. Academic Press, 2006.

[219] David Thoenen, Jim Riosa, and Joseph L Hellerstein. Event relationship networks: A framework for action oriented analysis in event management. In *Integrated Network Management Proceedings, 2001 IEEE/IFIP International Symposium on*, pages 593–606. IEEE, 2001.

[220] Brad Topol, David Ogle, Donna Pierson, Jim Thoensen, John Sweitzer, Marie Chow, Mary Ann Hoffmann, Pamela Durham, Ric Telford, Sulabha Sheth, and Thomas Studwell. Automating problem determination: A first step toward self-healing computing systems. IBM White Paper, October 2003. http://www-106.ibm.com/developerworks/autonomic/library/ac-summary/ac-prob.html.

[221] Celine Vens, Jan Struyf, Leander Schietgat, Sašo Džeroski, and Hendrik Blockeel. Decision trees for hierarchical multi-label classification. *Machine Learning*, 73(2):185–214, 2008.

[222] Ricardo Vilalta and Sheng Ma. Predicting rare events in temporal domains. In *Data Mining, 2002. ICDM 2003. Proceedings. 2002 IEEE International Conference on*, pages 474–481. IEEE, 2002.

[223] Chao Wang and Srinivasan Parthasarathy. Summarizing itemset patterns using probabilistic models. In *Proceedings of the 12th ACM SIGKDD International Conference on Knowledge Discovery and Data Mining*, pages 730–735. ACM, 2006.

[224] Dingding Wang, Tao Li, Shenghuo Zhu, and Chris Ding. Multi-document summarization via sentence-level semantic analysis and symmetric matrix factorization. In *Proceedings of the 31st Annual International ACM SIGIR Conference on Research and Development in Information Retrieval*, pages 307–314. ACM, 2008.

[225] Dingding Wang, Mitsunori Ogihara, and Tao Li. Summarizing the differences from microblogs. In *Proceedings of the 35th International ACM SIGIR Conference on Research and Development in Information Retrieval*, SIGIR '12, pages 1147–1148, New York, NY, USA, 2012. ACM.

[226] Peilong Wang, Xuan Yang, Yuanyuan Zhang, and Jiadong Ren. An algorithm based on temporary table for mining top-k closed frequent patterns in data streams. *International Journal of Digital Content Technology & its Applications*, 6(20), 2012.

[227] Peng Wang, Haixun Wang, Majin Liu, and Wei Wang. An algorithmic approach to event summarization. In *Proceedings of the 2010 ACM SIGMOD International Conference on Management of Data*, SIGMOD '10, pages 183–194, New York, NY, USA, 2010. ACM.

[228] Bi Wei and T. Kwok James. Hierarchical multilabel classification with minimum Bayes risk. In *Proceedings of the 12th International Conference on Data Mining*. IEEE, 2012.

[229] Kuai Xu, Zhi-Li Zhang, and Supratik Bhattacharyya. Profiling internet backbone traffic: Behavior models and applications. In *ACM SIGCOMM Conference*, pages 169–180, 2005.

[230] Wei Xu, Ling Huang, Armando Fox, David Patterson, and Michael Jordan. Experience mining Google production console logs. In *Workshop Proceedings on Managing Large-Scale Systems via the Analysis of System Logs and the Application of Machine Learning Techniques (SLAML)*, 2010.

[231] Wei Xu, Ling Huang, Armando Fox, David Patterson, and Michael I. Jordan. Detecting large-scale system problems by mining console logs. In *Proceedings of the ACM SIGOPS 22nd Symposium on Operating Systems Principles*, SOSP '09, pages 117–132, New York, NY, USA, 2009. ACM.

[232] Wei Xu, Ling Huang, Armando Fox, David A. Patterson, and Michael I. Jordan. Mining console logs for large-scale system problem detection. In *SysML*, December 2008.

[233] Xifeng Yan, Hong Cheng, Jiawei Han, and Dong Xin. Summarizing itemset patterns: a profile-based approach. In *Proceedings of the Eleventh ACM SIGKDD International Conference on Knowledge Discovery in Data Mining*, pages 314–323. ACM, 2005.

[234] Jiong Yang, Wei Wang, and Philip S. Yu. Mining asynchronous periodic patterns in time series data. *IEEE Trans. on Knowl. and Data Eng.*, 15(3):613–628, March 2003.

[235] Junjie Yao, Bin Cui, Yuxin Huang, and Xin Jin. Temporal and social context based burst detection from folksonomies. In *Proceedings of the Twenty-Fourth AAAI Conference on Artificial Intelligence (AAAI)*, pages 21–27, 2010.

[236] Xiaoxin Yin and Jiawei Han. CPAR: Classification based on predictive association rules. In *Proceedings of SIAM International Conference on Data Mining (SDM)*, 2003.

[237] Mohammed J Zaki. Spade: An efficient algorithm for mining frequent sequences. *Machine learning*, 42(1-2):31–60, 2001.

[238] Chunqiu Zeng, Yexi Jiang, Li Zheng, Jingxuan Li, Lei Li, Hongtai Li, Chao Shen, Wubai Zhou, Tao Li, Bing Duan, Ming Lei, and Pengnian Wang. FIU-Miner: A Fast, Integrated, and User-Friendly System for

Data Mining in Distributed Environment. In *Proceedings of the Nineteenth ACM SIGKDD International Conference on Knowledge Discovery and Data Mining*, pages 1506–1509, 2013.

[239] Chunqiu Zeng, Hongtai Li, Huibo Wang, Yudong Guang, Chang Liu, Tao Li, Mingjin Zhang, Shu-Ching Chen, and Naphtali Rishe. Optimizing online spatial data analysis with sequential query patterns. In *Proceedings of the 15th IEEE International Conference on Information Integration and Reuse*, pages 253–260. IEEE, 2014.

[240] Chunqiu Zeng, Tao Li, Larisa Shwartz, and Genady Ya Grabarnik. Hierarchical multi-label classification over ticket data using contextual loss. In *Proceedings of 2004 IEEE Network Operations and Management Symposium (NOMS)*, pages 1–8, 2014.

[241] Chunqiu Zeng, Liang Tang, Tao Li, Larisa Shwartz, and Genady Ya. Grabarnik. Mining temporal lag from fluctuating events for correlation and root cause analysis. In *Proceedings of the 10th International Conference on Network and Service Management (CNSM)*. IEEE, 2014.

[242] Mu Zhu. Recall, precision and average precision. *Department of Statistics and Actuarial Science, University of Waterloo, Waterloo*, 2004.

Index

For Product Safety Concerns and Information please contact our EU
representative GPSR@taylorandfrancis.com Taylor & Francis Verlag GmbH,
Kaufingerstraße 24, 80331 München, Germany

Printed and bound by CPI Group (UK) Ltd, Croydon, CR0 4YY

08/05/2025

01864552-0002